ECONOMICS AND THE
COMPETITIVE PROCESS

STUDIES IN GAME THEORY
AND MATHEMATICAL ECONOMICS

General Editor: Andrew Schotter (New York University)

Advisory Editorial Board:

William J. Baumol (New York University)
Dermot Gately (New York University)
Wassily Leontief (New York University)
William F. Lucas (Cornell University)
Martin Shubik (Yale University)
Gerald L. Thompson (Carnegie-Mellon University)

Volumes in this Series:

DIFFERENTIAL GAMES AND OTHER GAME-THEORETIC
TOPICS IN SOVIET LITERATURE,
by Alfred Zauberman

BIDDING AND AUCTIONING FOR PROCUREMENT
AND ALLOCATION,
edited by Yakov Amihud

GAME THEORY AND POLITICAL SCIENCE,
edited by Peter C. Ordeshook

ECONOMICS AND THE COMPETITIVE PROCESS
by James H. Case

ECONOMICS AND THE COMPETITIVE PROCESS

by

JAMES H. CASE

NEW YORK UNIVERSITY PRESS

NEW YORK · 1979

The medallion on the cover of this series was designed by the French contemporary artist Georges Mathieu as one of a set of medals struck in Paris by the Musée de la Monnaie in 1971. Eighteen medals were created by Mathieu to "commemorate 18 stages in the development of western consciousness." The Edict of Milan in 313 was the first, Game Theory, 1944, was number seventeen.

Contents

Chapter 2—Some Basic Games in Economics

Chapter 3—Auctions

Chapter 4—Inventory Decisions

Chapter 5—Investment Games and Customer Behavior

Chapter 6—Ad Games and a Cab Game

Part II—Differential Games

Chapter 7—Information and Its Uses

Chapter 8—Solving Differential Games

Preface

The title of this work is suggested by F. A. Hayek's short essay [4] on "The Meaning of Competition." In it he discusses briefly "the process of competition" and asserts that *exactly none* of its constituent elements such as advertising, undercutting, and product development are even possible under the conditions of "perfect competition." Yet perfect competition is the *only* kind of competition treated by conventional economic theory. It is a state of affairs for which he finds little justification.

To their credit, other members of the economic establishment seem no more anxious than Hayek to justify the status quo of their theory. Indeed, it has become almost fashionable for leaders in the field to chide their colleagues about it. Professor Leontief, for instance, chose in his presidential address to the American Economic Association (1970) to quote F. H. Hahn [3] to the effect that ". . . the achievements of economic theory in the last two decades are both impressive and in many ways beautiful. But it cannot be denied that there is something scandalous in the spectacle of so many people refining the analysis of economic states which they give no reason to suppose will ever, or have ever, come about. . . . It is an unsatisfactory and slightly dishonest state of affairs." Morgenstern [5] and Galbraith [2] have advanced similar views, charging that modern markets are typically the province of a few large and powerful corporations, whose principal activities are among those which Hayek showed to be impossible within the compass of existing economic theory. Most of the important industries in today's world are oligopolies, and oligopolists take part regularly in (among other things) the competitive process. This is a book about the constituent elements of that process; the competitors in it *can* and *do* compete.

Two notable attempts have been made in the past to bring competition within the purview of economic theory. The first was by A. Cournot [1] in 1838; the best known, by J. von Neumann and O. Morgenstern in their now classic work, *Theory of Games and Economic Behavior* [6] in 1944. Since its appearance both theories of competition have come to be subsumed under the title of *game theory*, and both have been marvelously extended in many ways. Each is designed expressly to remedy the ills the above-cited critics deplore. But neither one, not Cournot's (nowadays called the noncooperative theory) nor von Neumann and Morgenstern's (the cooperative theory), has ever come really to be *believed*! Indeed, since even the newer theory was twenty-five years old when

Leontief delivered his presidential address, and since the views he expressed are seriously challenged by no one, Cournot's original opinion would seem to be about as valid today as it was when he first expressed it. In 1838 he wrote, "Everyone has a vague idea of the effects of competition. Theory should have attempted to render this idea more precise; and yet . . . economic writers have not in the least improved on popular notions in this respect."

The reasons for the two theories' failure to attract believers are examined in Chapter I, wherein certain fundamental aspects of the competitive process are explored. It is argued that the cooperative theory is rightly disbelieved; propositions are deduced from it that are clearly preposterous. Cournot's theory, on the other hand, only benefits from the unusual scrutiny to which it is there subjected.

The rest of the book is devoted to my own development of noncooperative game theory. It is still the same theory that Cournot proposed, but with a new emphasis. The optimality he sought is subjugated to a property I call "robustness."

The games in the first six chapters, which together constitute Part I of the book, are among the simplest I am able to devise. This is to enable the reader to *decide for himself* whether or not to believe what is being said. But despite the simplicity of the games considered, there is no lack of economic insight to be realized from their study. In particular, I commend to the reader's attention the theory of auctions presented in Chapter III.

Part II is about differential games, wherein information is received and acted upon continually as the game progresses. Such games are more difficult than those of Part I, but certain elements of the competitive process seemingly cannot be modeled in any other way.

The book was not written as a textbook, but it can serve the purpose, especially as a number of problems are to be found in all but the last two chapters. Some of these are simple exercises; others are just questions whose answers I do not know. I once used some of the material from the first four chapters in a one-semester course on game theory (attended by sophomores, juniors, seniors, and graduate students) with generally encouraging results.

Of the many teachers to whom I owe thanks, I mention only three. Bob Thrall, my "doctor-father," challenged me to examine questions of the sort treated here at a time when I was concerned more with technique than with substance. Rufus Isaacs knows more that is worth knowing than any man alive. It was a pleasure and a privilege to occupy the office next to his for six years. Finally, Oskar Morgenstern encouraged me ceaselessly to write this book and saw finally to its publication, though he could not agree with many of its conclusions. It was a very generous act on the part of a man I shall always admire.

Finally, let me say that I have had, as I have written, the feeling that very basic matters were at issue and that fundamental facts concerning them were continually coming to light. I hope the reader will share my wonder at the simplicity of the discoveries reported here.

James H. Case

REFERENCES

1. Cournot, A., *Researches into the Mathematical Principles of the Theory of Wealth*, N. T. Bacon, trans., 2d ed. (New York: Kelley, 1971), xxiv + 213 pp.
2. Galbraith, J. K., *Economics and the Public Purpose* (Boston: Houghton Mifflin, 1973), xi + 321 pp.
3. Hahn, F., "Theoretical Assumptions and Non-observed Facts," *American Economic Review*, vol. 61, no. 1 (March 1971), p. 2.
4. Hayek, F. A., *Individualism and Economic Order* (Chicago: Univ. of Chicago Press, 1948), vii + 272 pp.
5. Morgenstern, O., "Thirteen Critical Points in Contemporary Economic Theory: An Interpretation," *Journal of Econ. Literature*, vol. X, no. 4 (1972).
6. von Neumann, J., and Morgenstern, O., *Theory of Games and Economic Behavior* (Princeton, N.J.: Princeton University Press, 1944), xvii + 625 pp.

Part I

Ordinary Games

Chapter 1

Games and Theories about Them

A game is a contest wherein several players choose, according to a specified set of rules from among a number of permitted alternative actions, in an effort to win certain rewards. Typically each player's reward depends not only on his own action or actions but on his opponents' as well. Chess, contract bridge, tennis, automobile racing, and some less frivolous pursuits all answer to the above rather imprecise description. So does baseball, which will serve as a first example.

1. BASEBALL

In baseball, the primal conflict is that between pitcher and batter. For simplicity, we assume that a three-ball-two-strike count has already been reached and that the pitcher has sufficient control to hit either the low outside (LO) or the high inside (HI) corner of the strike zone with his fastball at will. Or he can throw down the middle (M). He might, in practice, consider other options (curves, sliders, and the low inside corner, for example), but it suits our present illustrative purposes to limit him to the above three.

The basic reward structure is indicated in Figure 1.1A. The batter is good at hitting balls thrown down the middle, as indicated by the .400 average shown in the M portion of the strike zone. It is to be interpreted as an assertion that the batter will hit safely with probability .4 if the pitcher chooses M. He is also fairly good against HI pitches, since his average there is .300, and relatively poor (only .200) against LO ones. These probabilities are in rough accord with those suggested for himself by Ted Williams [1].

The batter's alternatives are guesses at where the pitch will be thrown. If he guesses LO, he can bend over and become a .400 hitter against LO pitches. But he does so at the expense of becoming only a .300 hitter against M pitches, and a .000 hitter against HI ones, even if he is not hit by them. Or he can guess HI, in which case the rewards indicated in Figure 1.1A must be shifted upward and to the right. The entire reward structure is therefore reflected in the following "payoff matrix." In it the pitcher's actions are listed across the top row, while

FIGURE 1.1A

PITCHER

(1.1.1)

		HI	M	LO
B A T T E R	HI	.4	.2	0
	M	.3	.4	.2
	LO	0	.3	.4

the batter's appear in the leftmost column. For example, the entry .3, which appears to the right of the batter's action *LO* and beneath the pitcher's action *M*, represents the batter's reward (i.e., the probability of his hitting safely) in the event that those are the alternatives chosen. There is no need to record the pitcher's reward in that event, as it is simply the probability (.7 in this case) that the batter will fail to hit safely when those are the actions taken.

From the matrix (1.1.1), it is clear that the pitcher should never choose *M*. For he can toss a die before each pitch and throw *HI* when it comes up one or two and *LO* on three or more. Such a procedure is called a "mixed (or random-ized) strategy," and may be denoted 1/3 *HI* + 2/3 *LO*. The pitcher's expected loss (pitcher's loss = 1 − batter's reward) from 1/3 *HI* + 2/3 *LO* is

(1.1.2)

4/30 when the batter chooses *HI*,
7/30 " " " " *M*, and
8/30 " " " " *LO*;

less in every case than the corresponding entry from the *M* column of (1.1.1). So we say that the pitcher's mixed strategy 1/3 *HI* + 2/3 *LO* "dominates" *M* because it earns him a higher expected reward than M regardless of what action the batter takes.

2. SADDLE POINTS

It was von Neumann [2] who first saw that such *matrix games* could always be solved in terms of mixed strategies. In the game at hand, for instance, the mixture $2/5\ HI + 3/5\ LO$ is optimal for the pitcher, and $4/5\ M + 1/5\ LO$ is optimal for the batter. The method by which these two strategies were computed is irrelevant to the present discussion.

To see that they are indeed optimal, one need only append an additional

(1.2.1)

P B	HI	M	LO	2/5 HI + 3/5 LO
HI	.4	.2	0	.16
M	.3	.4	.2	.24
LO	0	.3	.4	.24
4/5 M + 1/5 LO	.24	.38	.24	.24

row and column to (1.1.1) as in (1.2.1). Then the reward .24 in the lower-right-hand corner of (1.2.1) is both the largest in its column and the smallest in its row. Therefore, the pitcher can guarantee himself the reward .24 by playing the mixture $2/5\ HI + 3/5\ LO$, and he cannot guarantee himself a better one. Likewise, the batter can guarantee himself .24 by playing $4/5\ M + 1/5\ LO$ but cannot be certain of more.

The lower-right-hand corner of (1.2.1) is customarily called a "saddle point" of that matrix, and the pair $(2/5\ HI + 3/5\ LO,\ 4/5\ M + 1/5\ LO)$ is called the "saddle-point solution" of the associated matrix game. Von Neumann proved [2] that every matrix game has at least one saddle-point solution in mixed strategies and also pointed out that such solutions are easy to find if the reward matrix is not too large.

(1-1) *Exercise* Verify that $1/2\ A + 1/3\ B + 1/6\ C$ is an optimal strategy for both players in the game whose matrix is

	A	B	C
A	3	4	1
B	2	3	6
C	5	0	3

Since then, the theory of matrix games has been extensively explored, and a number of significant applications of that theory have been discovered. But those developments are amply explained elsewhere [3], [4] and will not be further dwelt on here. The games to be considered hereinafter typically are *not* matrix games. The latter have been introduced primarily to permit comment on the nature of their solutions.

3. CRITIQUE

The most remarkable feature of the saddle-point-solution concept is the extraordinary predictive burden of which it relieves the players. No longer must the batter reason "most of his pitches are *LO*, so I should guess *LO*, but knowing that I know this the pitcher will doubtless throw *HI*, so I shall . . . ," a cycle from which there is no escape. Since von Neumann, the argument [5] goes, the batter need only observe that an "optimal" mix of pitches exists and therefore his (rational) opponent will surely throw it. Hence nothing can be lost by using his own "optimal" mixture $4/5 \ M + 1/5 \ LO$, and perhaps something will be gained should the pitcher (inexplicably) interject a few *M*'s into his mixture. The pitcher, too, may of course engage in such reasoning.

Playing in this fashion, each "rational" player is guaranteed a reward no worse than .24 (which number is therefore called the "value" of the game) and may receive a better one if his opponent makes certain mistakes. But on the field, the argument loses some of its force. For the entries in the matrix (1.1.1), not being known a priori, have to be inferred from a record of past encounters. And the pitcher and batter may draw quite different inferences. So the batter's assumption that the pitcher will throw what he (the batter) takes to be an optimal mixture is just a guess like any other, and may even prove a bad one.

If, for instance, the pitcher persistently includes *M*'s in his mixture, it is probably because he doesn't believe the .400 shown in the middle of (1.1.1). And in that case the batter should doubtless eliminate *LO* from his own repertory until either the *M*'s disappear from the pitcher's mixture or he himself is forced to revise his opinion about the .400. For it is foolish to behave as though the pitcher were using the strategy $2/5 \ HI + 3/5 \ LO$ in the face of continued evidence to the contrary.

In short, the remarkable feature of the saddle-point solution discussed earlier is largely illusory here! The players are *not* relieved of the need to observe their opponent's behavior and to predict his future actions from the record of his past. This is due to the lack of information available concerning the game's reward structure and also to the fact that it is played not once but many times.

4. FOOTBALL

Football may be analyzed in a similar fashion. The decisive conflict in it occurs on third-down and long-yardage situations. Then the quarterback, or his coach, must choose one of several available offensive plays while the defensive captain must select an appropriate defense. For simplicity, let us assume that the QB has only two plays available, "run (R)" and "pass (P)," and the defensive captain decides whether to "blitz (B)" or "not blitz (NB)."* In reality the range of alternative actions is far broader.

If we take the probability of gaining the required yardage to be the QB's reward, the game matrix could be that shown in (1.4.1). Then the saddle-point

(1.4.1)

DC

	DC		
QB		B	NB
R		.8	.1
P		.2	.7

QB

solution of this game is $(5/12\,R + 7/12\,P, 1/2\,B + 1/2\,NB)$, as is easily shown by appending the appropriate row and column to (1.4.1), and the QB may expect to gain the needed yardage with probability .45.

Here, too, the matrix entries are not known and must be inferred independently by the players from a record of past encounters. Indeed, the entire discussion of the saddle-point strategies for "baseball" applies here too. In particular, the assumption that one's opponent will adopt a saddle-point strategy is only that—an assumption—which may prove either good or bad. The central point is that some assumption must be made, and the theory of matrix games provides a reasonable candidate.

(1-2) *Exercise* Suppose that a new matrix game is obtained from an old one by replacing each entry m in the original matrix with $cm + k$, c being a positive constant and k being any constant at all. Show that the optimal strategies for both players are the same in the two games.

(1-3) *Exercise* If one player in a matrix game has only two actions (or only two undominated ones), say A and B, his mixed strategies are all of the form $xA + (1 - x)B$, where x is the probability with which he takes action A. So if he chooses x while his opponent takes action i, the *expected payoff* in the game is $y = x\pi(A, i) + (1 - x)\pi(B, i)$. One may therefore graph expected payoff y against strategy x in an xy-coordinate plane; the graph is a straight-line segment. If i is one of $1, 2, \ldots, n$, there will be n such segments. When all of them are drawn, it is possible to read the optimal strategy for each player *and* the value

---

*A "blitz" is a somewhat risky maneuver wherein a defensive player, usually a linebacker, abandons his usual assignment in a headlong attempt to tackle the quarterback before he can rid himself of the ball.

of the game from the resulting picture. Do this for the game whose matrix is

maximizer

		1	2	3	4	5
	A	2	4	6	8	10
minimizer						
	B	7	5	1	3	9

5. GAMES WITH PURE-STRATEGY SOLUTIONS

Not all games require the introduction of mixed strategies for their solution.

$$(1.5.1) \qquad \begin{pmatrix} 50 & \boxed{90} & \boxed{\textcircled{18}} & 25 \\ 27 & \textcircled{5} & 9 & \boxed{95} \\ \boxed{64} & 30 & \textcircled{12} & 20 \end{pmatrix}$$

The matrix in (1.5.1), for instance, has a saddle point in its first row and third column. So 18 is the value of the game, and the maximizer can guarantee himself as much by always choosing the first row. And the minimizer can avoid any greater loss by choosing the third column.

When a game does have a saddle point in pure (unmixed) strategies, a very simple procedure will reveal the fact. For if one should circle the smallest element (or elements) in each row of the matrix and enclose in a square the largest element in each column, as has been done for the matrix (1.5.1), each saddle point of the matrix will be enclosed by both a circle and a square.

One should always begin the investigation of an unfamiliar matrix game with the circling-and-squaring procedure. For even if it fails to reveal a saddle point in the matrix, it can yield other useful information. A row, for instance, in which a square appears cannot be dominated by any other row or mixture of rows. And a column containing a circle is likewise *indomitable*. Thus, the procedure, when applied to the baseball matrix (1.1.1), reveals that the second column thereof is the *only* domitable row or column in it!

The circling-and-squaring procedure may also be used to demonstrate certain basic facts about matrix games. For instance, no circled element in the matrix, say $\textcircled{a_{pq}}$, can exceed any squared one $\boxed{a_{st}}$ since $\textcircled{a_{pq}} \leqslant a_{pt} \leqslant \boxed{a_{st}}$. In particular, the largest circled element does not exceed the smallest squared one. This fact is usually written

$$(1.5.2) \qquad \max_i \min_j a_{ij} \leqslant \min_j \max_i a_{ij}.$$

If the two quantities are equal, their common value is the value of the game. If not, the latter exceeds the former and the value lies in the interval between them. Finally, if the two elements a_{pq} and a_{st} are both circled and squared then $a_{pq} = a_{st}$ since neither can exceed the other. Then a_{pt} and a_{sq} are circled and squared as well. The above remarks remain valid, of course, when the given matrix is augmented by additional rows and columns corresponding to mixed strategies. Thus is established the important equivalence principle.

Equivalence Principle: If s_1 and s_2 are strategies available to player 1, while σ_1 and σ_2 are others available to 2, and if (s_1, σ_1), (s_2, σ_2) are saddle points in either pure or mixed strategies for a matrix game between 1 and 2, then (s_1, σ_2) and (s_2, σ_1) are saddle points as well.

This principle plays a decisive role in many developments of the theory of matrix games.

Some quite interesting games of frequent occurrence and substantial commercial import may be solved by means of the circling-and-squaring technique. The following game is played regularly among dealers in certain international markets.

(1-4) *Exercise* Use the circling and squaring technique to solve the game whose matrix is

	1	2	3	4
A	4	1	3	2
B	3	2	5	4
C	2	1	0	3

(1-5) *Exercise* Using the circling and squaring technique together with the method of problem (1-3), solve "baseball" (1.1.1) anew. Change the batting averages to taste and try it again.

(1-6) *Exercise* A matrix is called *skew-symmetric* if $a_{ij} + a_{ji} = 0$ for each row number i and column number j. Show that if a game has a skew-symmetric matrix, its value is zero and both players have the same optimal strategies.

6. AN IMPORT-EXPORT GAME

A shipment of some commodity is ordered from a foreign shipper by a domestic importer. But the price is not specified in the contract between them. Only the dependence of the price on the *quality* of the commodity is set forth therein. For simplicity, we shall assume quality to be measured on a scale from 0 to 20, fractional values not being allowed.

Typically, both the shipper and the importer will measure the quality of the shipment. But their measurements are subject to sampling error, so they may not agree. Therefore (and because neither really trusts the other to perform an honest measurement), a third opinion is commonly sought. Independent trade laboratories exist for the purpose and, for a fee, will submit an estimate of the quality of the goods. Thus, three independent reported estimates of that quality are available. The standard procedure is to average the two which most nearly agree and to discard the third. If one *is* the average of the other two, then it is the number chosen.

The independent laboratory (#2) is not a player in this game, because (unless bribed) its fee does not depend upon the price finally paid for the shipment. But both the shipper (#1) and the importer (#3) are players, since the latter must pay that price to the former. Their strategies are the amounts by which they *falsify* their estimates of the quality of the shipment. The payoff is the amount by which the accepted quality $\hat{Q}$ of the shipment, arrived at by the procedure described above, exceeds its true quality Q. Clearly the shipper would like to maximize that amount, and the importer to minimize it.

If x is the amount by which #1 falsifies his estimate E_1 of Q, while #3 falsifies his estimate E_3 thereof by y, it is clear that $\pi = \hat{Q} - Q$ is a function of the variables x and y. It remains to evaluate the function. To that end it may be observed that the value of the function $f(\cdot, \cdot, \cdot)$ of three variables R, S, T defined by

$$
\begin{aligned}
f(R, S, T) &= R && \text{if} \quad 2R - S - T = 0 \\
&= S && \text{if} \quad 2S - R - T = 0 \\
&= T && \text{if} \quad 2T - R - S = 0 \\
&= (R + S)/2 && \text{if} \quad (2R - S - T)(2S - R - T) > 0 \\
&= (R + T)/2 && \text{if} \quad (2R - S - T)(2T - R - S) > 0 \\
&= (S + T)/2 && \text{if} \quad (2S - R - T)(2T - R - S) > 0
\end{aligned}
$$

(1.6.1)

is the average of the two which most nearly agree, unless one of them is the average of the other two, in which case $f(R, S, T)$ is the one in the middle. Thus, when #1 *claims* his estimate of Q is R, #3 *claims* his is T, and the lab (#2) submits an estimate of S, one has $\hat{Q} = f(R, S, T)$.

Next let us assume that each agent $i = 1, 2, 3$ uses roughly the same sampling procedure, so that i's best estimate E_i of Q is of the form

(1.6.2) $E_i = Q + e_i$

e_i being an error term such that

(1.6.3)   prob. $\{e_i = k\}$ = prob. $\{e_i = -k\} = p_k$, $k = 0, 1, \ldots, n$, independent of i. Also assume that the lab invariably submits its best estimate $S = E_2$ while #1 and #3 submit the *biased* estimates $R = E_1 + x$ and $T = E_3 + y$. Then, writing $r = R - Q, s = S - Q$, and $t = T - Q$, we observe that

$$\text{prob. } \{E_1 + x = Q + x + e_1 = R\}$$
$$= \text{prob. } \{e_1 + x = R - Q = r\}$$
$$= \text{prob. } \{e_1 = r - x\} = p_{r-x}$$

and similarly that

(1.6.4)   prob. $\{E_2 = S\} = p_s$ and   prob. $\{E_3 + y = T\} = p_{t-y}$.

Moreover, since $f(R, S, T) = Q + f(r, s, t)$, one has

$$\hat{Q}(x,y) = \sum_{R=Q+x-n}^{Q+x+n} \sum_{S=Q-n}^{Q+n} \sum_{T=Q+y-n}^{Q+y+n} f(R, S, T)$$

(1.6.5) $\cdot$ prob. $\{E_1 + x = R$ and $E_2 = S$ and $E_3 + y = T\}$

$$= \sum_{r=y-n}^{x+n} \sum_{s=-n}^{n} \sum_{t=y-n}^{n} [Q + f(r, s, t)] p_{r-x} p_s p_{t-y}$$

so that finally

(1.6.6) $\pi(x,y) = \displaystyle\sum_{r=x-n}^{x+n} \sum_{s=-n}^{n} \sum_{t=y-n}^{y+n} f(r, s, t) \cdot p_{r-x} p_s p_{t-y}.$

Observe that as one might expect, $\pi(-x, y) = -\pi(x, -y)$ so that the *matrix* $\{\pi(x, -y)\}_{-m \le x, -y \le m}$ is skew-symmetric in the sense that it is the negative of its own transpose. Thus, [5] the *value* of the matrix game is zero* and the two player's optimal strategies are the same.

For the case $0 \le x \le 4, 0 \ge y \ge -4, n = 1$, and $p_0 = p_1 = p_{-1} = 1/3$, the matrix is shown in (1.6.7). And by circling and squaring, one quickly discovers

(1.6.7)

x \ y	0	-1	-2	-3	-4
0	0	-.30	(-.37)	-.22	-.07
1	.30	0	(-.02)	.13	.32
2	[.37]	[.02]	[0]	[.17]	[.44]
3	.22	-.13	(-.17)	0	.33
4	.07	-.32	(-.44)	-.33	0

that $x^* = 2 = -y^*$ is a saddle point. This is about as far as one would care to go by hand. But with the aid of a very simple computer program, more complicated and realistic cases may be considered.

*See *exercise* (1-6).

To describe the results, which are qualitatively the same for every case examined, it is necessary to indicate only the location of the circled and squared entries in the matrix. Thus, the previous game is well summarized (schematically, for $-10 \leqslant x, y \leqslant 10$) in Figure 1.6A. And the one which differs from it only in that $p_0 = 1/2$ and $p_1 = 1/4 = p_{-1}$ (i.e., in which sampling errors follow the binomial distribution) has a similar solution at $x^* = 1 = -y^*$, as indicated in Figure 1.6B. So, too, have the games for which sampling errors are more widely dispersed ($n = 3$ or $n = 6$), following either the binomial or uniform distributions. Those solutions appear in Figures 1.6C–1.6F. Only the matrix entries in the fourth quadrant of the xy-plane were computed for $n = 6$, to save expense, so the circles and squares in quadrants one and three are not shown.

In each case, the circles and squares appear to lie along smooth curves in the xy-plane, either of which may be obtained from the other by a reflection about the line $y = -x$, and the saddle point occurs at their intersection. Moreover, the optimal strategies seem always to involve *lying enough* so that there is little chance in the binomial cases and *none* in the uniform that the commodity is either as good as the shipper claims it to be or as bad as the importer does.

It should be observed that our results are as valid on a scale of zero to ten or zero to a hundred as they are for zero to twenty, as long as the probabilities $p_0, p_1, \ldots, p_n$ are appropriately chosen. But the computational effort of evaluating $\pi(x, y)$ increases as the cube of n, so more refined scales are expensive to

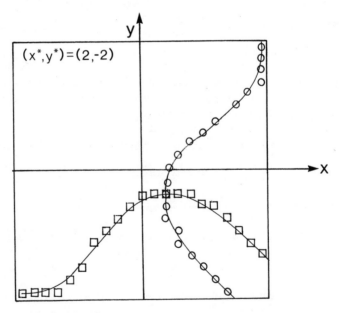

Width = 1 uniform

FIGURE 1.6A

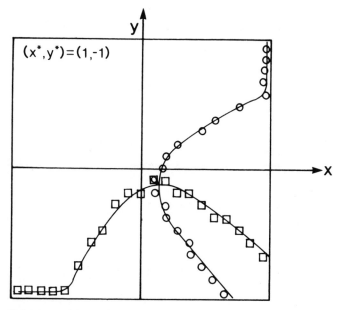

Width = 1 binomial

FIGURE 1.6B

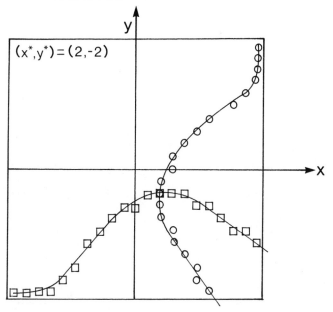

Width = 3 binomial

FIGURE 1.6C

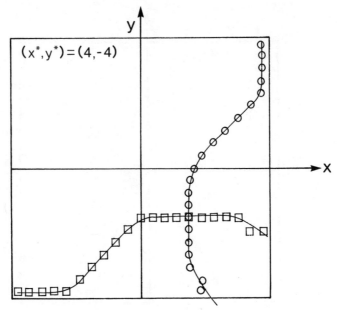

Width = 3 uniform

FIGURE 1.6D

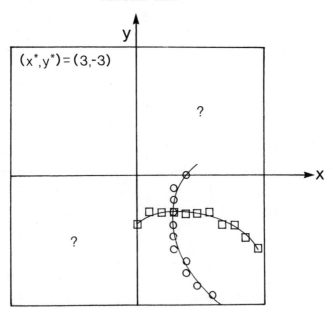

Width = 6 binomial

FIGURE 1.6E

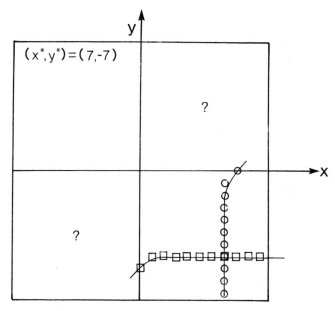

Width = 6 uniform

FIGURE 1.6F

work with. Doubtless a continuous scale $0 \leqslant Q \leqslant 1$ would provide the best model of all, but the integrations then required are complex. The above results are *not* valid when the true value of Q is close either to zero or to its upper limit. For then end effects come into play and the probabilities p_k and p_{-k} are no longer equal. And since the skew-symmetry of the matrix $\pi(x, y)$ is a consequence the symmetry of the probability distribution $\{p_k\}_{k=-n}^{n}$, the value of the game need no longer be zero. In practice, however, it seems likely that the relevant distributions are usually roughly symmetric, so neither player has an advantage.

The particular shape of the curves whereon the circles and squares lie constitutes a *structure*, which the six versions of the import-export game have in common, but which the matrix game (1.5.1) certainly does not exhibit. Because of that structure, the strategy $x^* = 3$ suggested by Figure 1.6E is a good one for the game depicted there, even if von Neumann's assumption concerning the rationality of the opponent is violated. For it is optimal not only when $y = y^* = -3$, but when $y = -1, -2, -4, -5$, or -6 as well. And it is nearly optimal against $y = 0, -7$, or -8. So unless it is expected that one's opponent will lie grossly ($y \leqslant -9$), or in the direction contrary to his own interest ($y > 0$), there is little doubt that $x = 3$ or $x = 4$ is the shipper's best choice. Indeed, there is little practically to choose between them, since $\pi(3, y)$ and $\pi(4, y)$ do not differ greatly when $-8 \leqslant y \leqslant 0$.

Moreover, the possibility that $y \leqslant -9$ is remote, since #3's quotation T could not then exceed R and would almost certainly be the value discarded. The possibility that $y \geqslant 0$ also seems remote. Thus, it would appear that a shipper who assumes $-8 \leqslant y \leqslant 0$ and predicates his choice of $x = 3$ or $x = 4$ on that assumption is behaving quite sensibly. His reward will be a good one even if his opponent makes an "irrational" choice $y \neq -3$. Indeed, so obvious is that fact in this particular game that one would expect shippers the world over to discover it, with or without the aid of von Neumann's theory and the circling-and-squaring technique.

Statisticians have a term for conclusions which do not depend precipitously upon the hypotheses from which they were deduced but which tend to persist in the face of perturbations on those hypotheses. They call such conclusions *robust*. We shall borrow their term here and apply it to strategies and actions. Thus, we shall call the action $x = 3$ robust because it is optimal (or nearly so) under a wide variety of competing assumptions concerning the likely behavior y of one's opponent; $x = 4$ probably deserves to be called robust as well.

Most of this book will be concerned with robust strategies and with the special structure of the games wherein they are found. But, like the statisticians who first used the term, we shall not endeavor to define robustness precisely. Hopefully its meaning will be clear in the contexts wherein it is discussed.

7. GAMES AND ENTERTAINMENT

The import-export game is a particularly fortuitous example, as it illustrates a number of points which must be borne in mind by any who would understand the nature of competitive commercial enterprise. Not the least of these is the unknown character of the opponents one may expect to encounter. Established commercial procedures, like the rules of the import-export game, have always taken cognizance of it. The decisive importance of "character" for game theory will become apparent presently.

Another point to bear in mind is that games which were invented for different reasons may be expected to have different kinds of solutions. Athletic contests with saddle points in pure strategies, and especially those with robust ones, make poor entertainment. If a contestant has a single action which is optimal (or nearly so) on every occasion, he must be expected to repeat it over and over again, thereby boring the spectators and eventually himself. Thus, our most popular recreational games, which were invented to divert the players and later modified* to amuse spectators as well, tend to have unstruc-

---

*Perhaps a few examples of such modification are in order. The first that springs to mind is from baseball, which outlawed the spitball (and other pitches requiring that the ball be doctored) and increased the resilience of the ball in 1920 to promote the hitting of home runs, after Babe Ruth's performance (29

tured matrices and mixed-strategy solutions. Such games provide considerable variety and are often fun both to play and to watch. But the games of commerce are *not* designed to entertain, and variety is *not* an asset to them. Indeed it is a liability. For their players seek, not diversion, but a steady and dependable living wage. Hence one should *expect* the games of commerce to have highly structured matrices and robust pure-strategy solutions, as does the import-export game.

Such expectations are repeatedly realized for the games discussed in this book. For both in matrix games (where structure appears as an interesting side-light) and in many-player ones (where it is an essential ingredient of the analysis), robust strategies abound. In short, "the playing fields of Eton" is an analogy which, like any other, can be pursued too far. There are substantial differences between the games of commerce and those of childhood. And if it is one's intent to comprehend the former, it is a mistake to overlook those differences.

8. BIDDING GAMES

The import-export game is in fact a bidding game, for the figures the players quote may be interpreted as bids (or candidate prices) that they would like to pay for the good in question. Many familiar games involve bidding for objects of unknown value, and so may be termed *bidding games*. The common acution, at which objects as diverse as cattle, used furniture, baseball players, and objects of art quite regularly change hands, is doubtless the most familiar.

The auction environment may be simulated (in the classroom, for instance) in a simple and instructive manner suggested by E. Capen and R. V. Clapp [16]. One takes, as an object of unknown value, an irregularly shaped glass vessel partially filled with nickels. The audience is allowed to examine the vessel, to shake it, and to compare it with a standard roll of (forty) nickels. Then they are allowed to bid their own money for the "object." If one intends to study the sealed-bid auction process, one may solicit sealed bids. Otherwise, audible bids may be entertained. If the role of the auctioneer is of interest, the jar of nickels may be *given* to a member of the audience with the understanding that he then try to auction it off to the others present. This is a particularly interesting way to play the game, for not only must the bidders decide how much they

---

home runs in 1919) indicated that attendance could be dramatically increased in that way. But ever stricter balk rules have kept the contrasting art of stealing bases in the game as well. And professional football, as it strove to escape the small towns of its origin (Canton, Ohio, Rockford, Illinois, etc.) for the bigger cities, reduced the girth of the ball by an inch and a half to promote the exciting forward pass. But the running and kicking parts of the game have never been allowed to disappear from it, for the fans appreciate variety and (arguably at least) mixed strategies.

are willing to pay for the object but the owner-auctioneer must determine the least offer he will accept.

To determine the magnitude of the doubt surrounding the value of the jar of nickels, an experiment has been performed. At a party attended by members of the Baltimore City League of Women Voters, such a jar was offered to the person who most nearly guessed its value. Thirty-six estimates were received, the best being an overestimate by a single nickel. All the guesses are displayed below in Table 1.8A; the jar actually contained three hundred and forty-one nickels. Clearly the estimates varied substantially. From them one can infer the likely outcomes of various possible experiments. If, for instance, the nickels had been given to the person who guessed 173, and the one who guessed 632 were designated the prospective buyer, it is nearly certain that they could have closed a deal. But had their roles been reversed, it would have been most unlikely. Or had the person who guessed 350 been given the pot and allowed to auction it off to the rest of the group, it seems likely she could have found a buyer.

Capen and Clapp [16] report having performed such experiments several times, before different audiences. However, being little interested in the behavior of the auctioneer, they always reserve that role to themselves. They also limit themselves to sealed-bid auctions, those being their primary interest. Only once, they assert, have they been unable to auction their jar of nickels for more than its true value. The reason is apparent from the data presented above; there are always bidders present who substantially overestimate the value of the property at auction. And even though they bid somewhat less than their estimates of its worth, the largest of their bids exceed its actual worth! In particular, the winner of a property bought at auction must expect disappointment, that is, that it will be less valuable than he had anticipated. Capen, Clapp, and Campbell [17] have called this phenomenon the "winner's curse"; the properties you buy tend to be the ones you most overestimate. The ones you guess right on go to someone else. The reality of this phenomenon is well documented empirically and has lately [19] been deduced on a priori grounds as well.

The above-named authors were originally prompted to investigate the auction

TABLE 1.8A
Estimates Received

900	600	500	356	256	200
859	550	480	350	250	173
691	525	480	342	250	150
655	523	415	310	240	145
650	505	400	300	200	99
632	500	381	284	200	42

process by their employer, the Atlantic-Richfield Oil Company. Industrywide studies indicated in the early 1960s that the oil companies en masse were, if not actually losing money on their offshore drilling operations in the Gulf of Mexico, at least earning less than any intended. And as their offshore drilling rights had all been acquired at auctions conducted by the U.S. Bureau of Land Management, it was natural to suppose that overly liberal bidding practices were at fault. In short, the industry had fallen prey to the winner's curse. What was needed was a quantitative method for determining appropriately conservative bidding strategies.

A somewhat modified version of the model of the auction process proposed by Capen, Clapp, and Campbell will be presented in Chapter III. It consists of a *simply directed many-player game*, as defined in Chapter II, which is *approximately solvable* in a sense there specified. At present, since we have no tools at our disposal for "solving" many-player games, we are content merely to describe this important class of them. In particular, we emphasize that bidding games are: (i) played in the real world with bids as large as $200 million for a single plot of offshore oil land; (ii) playable in the classroom or lecture hall using jars of nickels as properties for auction; and (iii) amenable to the concise mathematical analysis to be presented in Chapter III. Predictions of the analytic theory are experimentally verifiable by means of the device (ii) and appear to be borne out in the field (of actual oil-lease auctions) as well. In short, if it can be said that any quantitative theory in the managerial or social sciences *has applications*, and important ones at that, it can be said of the theory of bidding games. Yet that theory is only now assuming final form and being disseminated to the general scientific public.

9. ZERO AND NONZERO-SUM GAMES

Matrices are generally inadequate for representing the reward structures of many-player games. Rather, if the players be named $1, 2, 3, \ldots, N$, it is necessary to specify their rewards or payoffs as functions

$$
\begin{aligned}
&\pi_1(A_1, A_2, \ldots, A_N) \\
&\pi_2(A_1, A_2, \ldots, A_N) \\
&\qquad\vdots \\
&\pi_N(A_1, A_2, \ldots, A_N)
\end{aligned}
$$

(1.9.1)

of the actions $A_1, A_2, \ldots, A_N$ taken by the individual players. If, in particular, the sum

$$(1.9.2) \quad \pi_1(A_1, \ldots, A_N) + \pi_2(A_1, \ldots, A_N) + \cdots + \pi_N(A_1, \ldots, A_N)$$

is equal to a constant c, which is independent of the actions $A_1, A_2, \ldots, A_N$, the game is said to be a *constant-sum* game. In such games there is a "pot" of fixed size, and the players' actions affect only the size of their individual shares. But in nonconstant-sum games, or general-sum games, as they are more commonly called, the size of the pot may also depend upon the actions taken.

If $N = 2$ and both players have only a finite number of actions to choose from, the values of $\pi_1(A_1, A_2)$ may be recorded as the entries in a matrix, the rows corresponding to 1's alternatives and the columns to 2's. And if the game is also constant-sum, there is no need to record the values of $\pi_2(\cdot, \cdot)$, since $\pi_2(A_1, A_2) = c - \pi_1(A_1, A_2)$ always. Thus, the reward structures of our baseball and football examples, which are unit-sum games, are completely specified by the matrices (1.1.1) and (1.4.1). And that of the import-export game, which is zero-sum, is specified by (1.6.7). Clearly, if a game is constant sum, the particular value of the constant c is irrelevant to the players' strategic decisions. So one ordinarily speaks only of zero-sum games; all other constant-sum ones may be reduced to these in a trivial (and obvious) fashion.

As remarked earlier, von Neumann's theory appears adequate to answer conceptual questions about matrix games, though of course computational questions (for large matrices) remain. And sometimes the special internal structure of a particular game can add to or strengthen substantially the conclusions of that theory, as was the case for the import-export game. Moreover, von Neumann's theory can be extended to two-player zero-sum games with infinitely many alternative actions in a number of ways [3], [18]. But nonzero-sum games, especially those involving more than two players, are not yet understood, even in principle.

Indeed, there are at present several different theories of many-player games, each with its own definition of solution. Generally speaking, the theories are of two types. Those called *cooperative* continue the celebrated work of von Neumann and Morgenstern [5] and proceed on a very abstract plane. Basically, they seek to determine what distributions of reward among the several players can result from rational behavior on their parts, without ever specifying precisely what constitutes rational behavior. The *noncooperative* theories, on the other hand, have their origins in the last century and *seem* rather more concrete. To illustrate the points on which the two kinds of theory differ, we return to our discussion of the import-export game.

10. A THREE-PLAYER GAME

If the international laboratory's fee for testing a shipment is not fixed by convention but is negotiable, the import-export game is a three-player game. The treatment proposed by von Neumann and Morgenstern [5] for such games, and followed (to a point) by subsequent writers on the cooperative theory, proceeds as follows. First, a numerical *value* is assigned to each possible coalition of the set {1, 2, 3} of players. This number represents the amount that coalition can win in the game regardless of the behavior of the excluded players.

In this game, the value $v(1)$ of the coalition {1} consisting of the shipper alone is an undetermined sum s of money, namely the price the shipment would bring at its port of origin. The values $v(2)$ of {2} and $v(3)$ of {3} are both zero, since without the cooperation of the shipper the others can realize nothing from the sale of the shipment. Similarly the value $v(23)$ of the coalition {2, 3} is nil. But the value $v(12) = v(1) = s$, since the coalition {1, 2} has the ability to sell the shipment at its origin, and $v(13) = S > s$, since the shipment will bring more at its destination than at its origin and the coalition {1, 3} can sell it there if they can agree how to divide the proceeds. Finally $v(123) = S$, too, since the larger coalition cannot expect to sell the shipment for more than {1, 3} can.

Next the cooperative theories define an *imputation* to be a triple

$$(x_1, x_2, x_3)$$

of numbers such that

(1.10.1)
$$x_1 \geqslant v(1) = s, \quad x_2 \geqslant v(2) = 0, \quad x_3 \geqslant v(3) = 0,$$
$$\text{and} \quad x_1 + x_2 + x_3 = v(123) = S.$$

Here x_i is to be interpreted as a possible payment to player i, the inequalities providing assurance that none will have to accept less than he could get by refusing to cooperate and the last condition asserting that no potential profit will go unrealized.

Next an imputation (x_1, x_2, x_3) is said to dominate (y_1, y_2, y_3) through the coalition $\{i, j\}$ if

(1.10.2)
$$x_i > y_i, \quad x_j > y_j,$$
$$x_i + x_j \leqslant v(ij),$$

so that both members of $\{i, j\}$ prefer (x_1, x_2, x_3) to (y_1, y_2, y_3) and their joint winnings under the preferred arrangement do not exceed their earning capability. It will be observed that domination can occur only through the coalition {1, 3} in this game, since the inequality

(1.10.3)
$$v(i) + v(j) < v(ij)$$

holds in it only if $\{i, j\} = \{1, 3\}$. Finally, if (x_1, x_2, x_3) be any imputation such that $x_2 > 0$, then $(x_1 + x_2/2, 0, x_3 + x_2/2)$ is another which dominates it. So the undominated imputations in this game are those for which $x_2 = 0$.

The set of all undominated imputations *is* the most popular notion of a solution for such a game and is called the *core* of the game. In this particular game, it happens to be identical with the so-called *stable set*, the name now given to what von Neumann and Morgenstern originally called the *solution*.

The reason for the newer terminology is, of course, to distinguish the stable set from the host of other "solution concepts" such as core, Shapely value, and nucleolus, that have been proposed since. Indeed, all the above notions of solution (and doubtless others as well) lead to the same conclusion here, namely that $x_2 = 0$. In other words, the international laboratory* cannot hope to be paid for its services!

This startling conclusion is, in fact, a consequence of the most primitive assumptions of the cooperative theory. The members of the coalition $\{1, 3\}$ can share the amount S if they can decide how to divide it and must share a lesser amount if they cannot. Therefore, being rational men, they *will not fail* to agree on a division.

In other words, the service performed by the laboratory in limiting the players' avarice and disarming their dishonesty is no service at all to rational men. Such a conclusion, in which incidentally the noncooperative theory does not concur, could follow only from a rather singular view of rationality—one not shared by most who have written on the subject. Its consequences for an even more familiar game will be explored in the next section.

11. COLD WAR

In recent memory, world affairs have been dominated by the two military superpowers, whose armed might has continually increased through the gross expenditure of public funds. Each is willing to forgo the extra butter production which those funds could generate in favor of the additional safety from attack which guns provide. Let us try to construct a model of this "game."

We may call the nations 1 and 2, and let x and y be their respective defense budgets, measured in dollars (\$). We assume for simplicity that 1 can successfully answer any attack by 2 with probability

$$(1.11.1) \qquad \frac{x}{x+y}.$$

In addition to its simplicity, (1.11.1) has the properties that it (i) vanishes when x is zero and y positive; (ii) is unity when y is zero and x positive; and (iii) depends (monotonically) on the ratio y/x alone. And though (1.11.1) is undefined when $x = 0 = y$, it should have value 1 at the origin, for there there is no possibility that an attack will go unanswered.

We likewise assume that 2 can successfully respond to any attack by 1 with

---

*Players, who like the laboratory, add nothing to the power of any coalition they may join, are called dummies in cooperative game theory. They go unrewarded in virtually every version of that theory.

probability

(1.11.2)
$$\frac{y}{x+y}.$$

Each government is rewarded (with votes or other evidence of approbation from the governed) for a large safety factor (1.11.1) or (1.11.2). But it is also rewarded for butter production, and each dollar spent for guns is one not spent for butter. So we shall assume that the total rewards or "payoff functions" to the two governments are the weighted sums

(1.11.3)
$$\pi_1(x,y) = \frac{x}{x+y} - mx$$

$$\pi_2(x,y) = \frac{y}{x+y} - \mu y$$

m and μ being positive real numbers. Undeniably this assigns (through the choice of m and μ) dollar values to a unit of safety, and many will find such assignment repugnant. But as the need to consider trade-offs between butter and safety cannot be avoided here, we choose to do it in the simplest possible way.

A pair of actions (x,y) in this game (or in any other two-player game, for that matter) is called *Pareto optimal** if there does not exist another pair (x',y') of actions which rewards each player as well as (x, y), and at least one of them better. Similarly, in an N-player game, an N-tuple $(x_1, \ldots, x_N)$ of actions is called *Pareto optimal* if there exists no $(x'_1, \ldots, x'_N)$ rewarding each player as well as, and some player better than $(x_1, \ldots, x_N)$. It is an axiom of cooperative game theory that rational players will never settle on a vector of actions which is not *Pareto optimal*.

It requires no further knowledge of the theory to see that the game of Cold War has a single "cooperative solution," namely the allocations $x = 0 = y$. For if (x, y) is any other pair, $(x/2, y/2)$ is a third which affords each nation equal safety and more butter than does (x, y). So the only Pareto optimal pair of allocations is the null pair $(0, 0)$. Moreover, the same argument leads to the same conclusion if the number of nations is greater than two; the only Pareto optimal vector of allocations is the null vector $(0, \ldots, 0)$. And here the several cooperative theories of games [5], [6], [7] are in full agreement; rational players would never maintain armies because to do so they must direct resources from other more peaceful pursuits. Swords should be beaten into plowshares.

The noncooperative theory, on the other hand, concludes that it is entirely

---

*After Vilfredo Pareto (1848–1923), a leading Italian industrialist, economist, and sociologist of his time.

rational for nations to maintain armies, as will presently be shown. So the theories are in direct disagreement over the answer to the following question:

(Q)   Is it possible for the players of Cold War, through the exercise of reason alone, to reach an agreement whereby military expenditures will cease?

Clearly the answer to such a question must involve the limitations of pure reason. And those limitations have historically been the subject of numerous philosophical inquiries, Kant's *Critique of Pure Reason* being perhaps the best known. But those limitations have heretofore been ignored in the game-theoretic literature. Any discussion of them becomes unavoidably philosophical in tone.

12. RATIONAL BEHAVIOR

Von Neumann and Morgenstern [5] recognized that there exist diverse notions of reason and of rational behavior. So they based their arguments on certain properties of such behavior, which they took to be common to all its various forms. Those properties are described in their axioms,* which are largely the axioms of subsequent cooperative theories as well. And from the axioms follows an affirmative answer for Q.

If, on the other hand, we adopt some of the standard models of rational behavior that have historically been proposed, we can deduce a negative answer. We demonstrate this for one such model, namely the Stoic model.

This particular choice is motivated by a number of considerations: Stoicism has a notably concise and authentic summary in Epictetus' *Manual* [8], it speaks almost directly to the question at hand, and its views are not out of date even today. Thinkers as recent as A. E. Housman and Albert Schweitzer have [9, p. x] reiterated its creed, and it is the original source of much of modern democratic theory. Indeed, as the classicist Ludwig Edelstein [10,

*To those already acquainted with cooperative game theory, it should be pointed out that the decisive assumption of that theory is not to be found among its stated axioms. Rather it is a sort of "pre-axiom" used to motivate the basic definitions of the theory. Best stated on page 37 of [5], it is an assertion that *a coalition _____ of rational players, unilaterally able to earn a reward _____, will never settle for any lesser reward.* Thus if the first blank be filled in with "the coalition of all players" and the second with "the value of that coalition," the assumption justifies the "Pareto optimality" property $(x_1 + \cdots + x_n = v(N))$ of imputations. Or if the first blank contains some smaller coalition S and the second the inequality $\Sigma_{i \in S} x_i \geq v(S)$, the so-called "joint rationality" axiom emerges.

Because of this primitive assumption, the cooperative theory regards any incentive at all to cooperate as a *sufficient condition* for cooperation. In fact it is anything but sufficient, since there are quite common situations in which perfectly rational people *ignore* extraordinary incentives to cooperate. Subsequent examples will illustrate this (apparently not obvious) fact.

p. 96] has said, "their [the Stoics'] political theory still is, I believe, the political theory most dear to the hearts of all freedom-loving men." Thus, the Stoics' notion of rational man, which lies of course at the heart of their political theory, is implicit in many of the views which are today most widely held and universally admired. It would be difficult indeed to argue that the Stoics, rather than the axioms of cooperative game theory, mistake the nature of rational behavior.

The first line of the *Manual* reads "Some things are under our control, while others are not under our control." Later (in §19) we are told to ". . . despise the things that are not under our control," the most famous of all Stoic dicta. Its meaning is clarified in §14, where we read, "If you make it your will that your children and your wife and your friends should live forever, you are silly; for you are making it your will that things not under your control should be under your control, and that what is not your own should be your own. In the same way, too, if you make it your will that your slave-boy be free from faults, you are a fool; for you are making it your will that vice be not vice, but something else." In other words, a wise man should be careful in the choice of his objectives, and not be put in the position of desiring that which, because it is under the control of another, is beyond his own power to achieve. Farther on in §14 we find, "each man's master is the person who has the authority over what the man wishes or does not wish, so as to secure it, or take it away. Whoever, therefore, wants to be free, let him neither wish for anything, nor avoid anything, that is under the control of others; or else he is necessarily a slave."

To apply the precept to the game of Cold War, we have only to read "nation" for "man" in the latter passage. Thus, "each nation's master is the one which has authority over what that nation wishes or does not wish (in this case limited safety from attack), so as to secure it or take it away. . . ." Therefore, a wise nation will not simultaneously desire safety and be without a defense budget. For while $x = 0$, 2 may secure 1's safety by the action $y = 0$ or take it away by $y = \epsilon > 0$. While $x = 0$, 1 is slave to 2, according to the Stoic view.

This is an important point and merits closer scrutiny. For much depends on the *degree* to which the players control x and y. We assume for simplicity that either nation can change its defense budget by an arbitrary amount, but that an implementation period of one month is required for doing so. In other words, the decision to change must precede the actual change by a month. Moreover, implementation periods cannot overlap, so that no two changes may take place less than a month apart.

In these circumstances, the danger of the action $x = 0$ is readily apparent, for the arrangement $x = 0 = y$ is by its very nature a long term one. If, after fifteen months of disarmament, 1 suddenly discovers $y > 0$, there is nothing it can do to prevent a takeover by 2. Moreover, the same conclusion may be reached from a variety of other (more realistic) dynamic assumptions on the degree to which the players control x and y.

In short, it does not appear that the dangerous character of the action $x = 0$ is the result of an oversimplified model. It is not. It is a feature which the model and the real-world it seeks to mimic have in common. Real superpowers do not disarm because they, like Epictetus, are afraid of awakening one morning to find a rearmed enemy arrayed against them.

The meaning here seems remarkably clear. The action $x = 0$ is not, since 1 wishes safety, Stoic behavior. So if Stoic behavior is rational behavior, then Q has a negative answer and the axioms of cooperative game theory do not accurately describe *all* the forms of behavior which have traditionally been thought to be rational.

13. BEYOND REASON

A rational player, as described in the axioms of cooperative game theory, is a player who prefers large rewards to small ones. Stoic players do that too. But they refuse to equate certain rewards with those which can either be given or taken away by the other players.

To further elucidate the difference between the two notions of "rational player," let us ask what two Stoic players would require in addition to reason to achieve disarmament in the game of Cold War. Let us ask, that is, what kinds of conditions must prevail in order that two Stoics may agree to become slaves to one another. For Stoics conceivably could, under appropriate conditions, reach such an agreement.

Matrimony, for instance, is a familiar estate wherein each partner invests in the other extraordinary power over his or her own happiness, well-being, and peace of mind, becoming in the process (according to the Stoic view) a slave to the other. But it is one thing to assert that there *exist* pairs of rational beings who can achieve wedded bliss by such investment, it is quite another to claim that any two rational beings may so achieve it! Indeed, conventional wisdom would have it that the latter claim is untrue.

This is the nature of an important distinction whose existence the axioms of cooperative game theory deny. It is the distinction between arrangements that any pair of rational beings will find workable, and arrangements that demand a degree of "compatibility" for success. Nebulous though that distinction is, it seems a mistake to deny its existence.

14. THE PRISONER'S DILEMMA

A game that has been much discussed [4], [11] in the past is known as Prisoner's Dilemma. It concerns the choice two criminals face, who have together performed a theft and been apprehended while still in possession of the stolen goods.

Each will be interrogated separately by the authorities in an attempt to obtain a confession. If neither talks, they will both be convicted for possession of stolen goods, and each will serve a year in jail. If one talks and the other does not, the one who talks will receive a minimal sentence of five years for armed robbery, which will then be suspended by the judge so that no time need actually be served, and the book will be thrown at the silent offender who may then expect to serve twelve of the maximum fifteen years prescribed by law for the offense. And if both talk they will both receive minimal five-year sentences, which will then *not* be suspended by the judge. Thus, each player has a choice of two alternative actions, namely to talk (T) or to remain silent (S). And their "rewards" from the various pairs of actions may be displayed in the two matrices

(1.14.1)

A \ B	S	T
S	1	12
T	0	5

A \ B	S	T
S	1	0
T	12	5

in (1.14.1), wherein prisoner A's rewards are displayed in the first (the one on the left) and B's in the second. Such games are called "bimatrix games."

It will be observed that T dominates S for both players, since the sentences in the bottom row of the first matrix are shorter than those on the top, and the ones in the right column of the second matrix are shorter than those on the left. So one need not be surprised if both players choose T and serve five years.

On the other hand, it has often been asserted that any two rational thieves should choose S, for then they serve only one year each.

A Stoic thief analyzes the situation in advance, for he is told (in §4), "When you are on the point of putting your hand to some undertaking, remind yourself what the nature of that undertaking is." He reflects then that pulling the job in question requires an accomplice and that, if apprehended, he will want the accomplice to spend a year in jail for him. Thus, extraordinary power over his own well-being (or at least his physical whereabouts) is to be vested in that accomplice. Each will be, in the Stoic's sense, slave to the other. Therefore, the Stoic thief will select for the job not only a rational man but one with whom he enjoys excellent rapport as well. For he knows that Stoic reason alone does not suffice to achieve the outcome (S, S). Viewed in this manner, Prisoner's Dilemma loses much of its supposed air of paradox.

The pair (S, S) plays much the same role in prisoner's dilemma that $(0, 0)$ does in Cold War, for they are both unique Pareto optima. And there is in each game the incentive to agree in advance to those solutions, then double-cross the other player. For a successful double-cross yields the best of all possible rewards.

The effective difference between the two games lies in the fact that thieves choose their accomplices, but the superpowers do not determine which other nations will be superpowers.

15. UTOPIA

So far, the consequences of cooperative game theory that we have discussed actually follow from a single one of its axioms, namely the axiom of Pareto optimality. But there is another (tacit) assumption in the theory which also deserves mention.

Let us suppose that the entire world could be described in a single mathematical model. That model would be game-theoretic in nature, with every man a player. The rules would be natural law, and the rewards would be all the joys that life has to offer. And let us suppose that the cooperative solutions of this giant game were known, and (as sometimes happens) they were one and the same. That single solution would constitute a very detailed description of utopia, for it would allocate to every man his natural share of life's joys!

But it would not reveal how the utopian condition is to be achieved. For solutions in cooperative game theory are simply sets of imputations (allocations of reward) which the several players may expect to receive. They describe only the condition to be achieved, and *not* the procedure for achieving it.

There is an assumption implicit in the mere act of calling such a description a "solution"! Rational man, having been shown the nature of utopia, will not fail to achieve it. And such an assumption seems to equate reason with what is more often called "virtue," both in philosophical discussions and in ordinary conversation.

The two have, of course, been confused before. Indeed the early Stoics were themselves guilty of that confusion. And the foregoing discussion of Cold War demonstrates that of all such views the Stoic view of reason is *not* identical with the more common notions of virtue. To beat the swords into plowshares seems clearly the virtuous thing to do in that game, but most writers on ethical matters have maintained that reason and virtue are separate and distinct qualities. Schopenhauer, for instance, asserts [14] that reason is but a tool of the will and can serve an evil will as easily as a virtuous one; and Machiavelli [14] would deny that nations, while obviously capable of rational behavior, can ever be said to have virtue.

16. WHY TWO THEORIES?

The purpose of the foregoing discussion has been to exhibit the nature of the conclusions that can be drawn from the cooperative theory of games. They often constitute assertions that difficult humanitarian objectives can be achieved: the swords can be beaten into plowshares in Cold War; honor can be maintained among thieves in the Prisoner's Dilemma; and the utopian condition can persist in this world.

Each of these propositions has been argued historically, and capable individuals have worked diligently to achieve the objectives in question. But the objectives have always proved elusive, and from time to time arguments have been advanced as to why this must be so. Barriers of human nature lie in the path of these achievements and must be surmounted before the objectives can be realized. One such barrier consists of a Stoic's refusal to accept another's promise of reward as equivalent to the reward itself.

Yet when one asks *how* cooperative game theory proposes to surmount the various barriers, no answer is forthcoming; it is simply axiomatic that the barriers do not exist among rational players. Thus, in effect, the theory has begged a number of the timeless questions concerning human nature and capacity (taking always the most optimistic view on each) in order hopefully to give answers to more timely questions of current concern!

Because of the nature of the questions it is designed to answer, game theory is more than a branch of pure mathematics. It is also an effort at social thought. Indeed, as the preceding examples are designed to demonstrate, the cooperative theory belongs to a specific tradition in social thought. Cooperative game theory is a form of Utopian Socialism. Accordingly, it can amplify and refine the doctrines of that tradition, as mathematics often does. But it can never generate insight of a new or different kind. Small wonder then that cooperative game theory has *never found application.*

17. COURNOT'S THEORY

A very different kind of theory was proposed in 1838 by A. Cournot [12]. His procedure for games of the present sort begins with the determination of two functions $x^*(y)$ and $y^*(x)$ such that

(1.17.1)
$$\pi_1(x^*(y), y) > \pi_1(x, y) \quad \text{if} \quad x \neq x^*(y)$$
$$\pi_2(x, y^*(x)) > \pi_2(x, y) \quad \text{if} \quad y \neq y^*(x).$$

For the game of Cold War, for instance, these are

(1.17.2)
$$x^*(y) = \max \{0, \sqrt{y/m} - y\}$$
$$y^*(x) = \max \{0, \sqrt{x/\mu} - x\}.$$

Their graphs are as indicated in Figure 1.17A. In particular, they cross at $(0, 0)$, again at $(x^*, y^*) = (\mu/(m+\mu)^2), (m/(m+\mu)^2)$, and are tangent to the coordinate axes at the origin. Cournot suggested that player 1 might begin the game by observing 2's current allocation y and switching his own from x to $x^*(y)$. Then 2 would (presumably) switch from y to $y^*(x^*(y))$, and 1 would be forced to reply with the switch $x^*(y) \rightarrow x^*(y^*(x^*(y)))$, and so on. The result of this succession

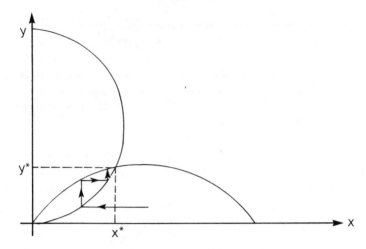

FIGURE 1.17A

of switches is a sequence of pairs (x_i, y_i) of defense budgets in the xy-plane, which converge to (x^*, y^*) as shown in Figure 1.17A. The pair (x^*, y^*) has the properties

(1.17.3)
$$\pi_1(x^*, y^*) > \pi_1(x, y^*)$$
$$\pi_2(x^*, y^*) > \pi_2(x^*, y),$$

which fact, together with the convergence to it of the process described above, led Cournot to call it a point of equilibrium and to regard it as the solution of the game. In 1950, J. Nash rediscovered the conditions (1.17.3) and proved that points satisfying them exist in each of a large class of games. So such points are now known almost universally as Nash equilibrium points, though occasionally Cournot's name still is mentioned.

The process Cournot suggested is the mode of play whereby each player guesses at every stage that his opponent's future action will be the same as his present one, then chooses for himself the action which will be optimal if his guess proves correct. It is shown in [13] that the several other variants of that mode of play lead to the same point (x^*, y^*).

One of the most telling criticisms [15] of Cournot's analysis has been that his players learn very slowly. At each stage they change their own allocations assuming the opponent will not change his; and at each stage their assumptions prove wrong because every change provokes an answer. A satisfactory theory should respond to this charge, for if the equilibrium point (x^*, y^*) is to be regarded as the solution of something, it should result from some more enlightened behavior on the players' parts than an infinite sequence of bad guesses!

A related criticism proceeds from the observation that each of Cournot's players calculates his own "reaction function" on the assumption that his opponent's is a constant function. Thus 1 computes $x^*(y)$ by solving

(1.17.4) $$\frac{\partial \pi_1}{\partial x} = \frac{y}{(x+y)^2} - m = 0$$

instead of

(1.17.5) $$\frac{\partial \pi_1}{\partial x} = \frac{y - xy'}{(x+y)^2} - m = 0,$$

tacitly assuming $y' = y'(x) \equiv 0$ in the process. Such an assumption is *irrational*, the argument goes, because the function $y^*(x)$ has a non-vanishing derivative at and near $x = x^*$. Hence Cournot's players persist in behavior which reveals the untruth of the assumptions which prompted the behavior in the first place. Rational players, by comparison, would come quickly to anticipate each other's reactions and would alter their behavior until events confirm (rather than deny) their expectations. We shall return to these points presently; for the moment we observe only that the criticisms are both process-specific in that they object to the way the equilibrium is arrived at rather than to the equilibrium itself. Our own solution dispenses with the Cournot process while preserving his equilibrium.

18. FIRST PRINCIPLES

At the heart of any useful theory of games must lie the "Stoic's dichotomy" between a player's own actions, which he may properly be assumed to control absolutely, and those of his opponents, which he can neither control nor accurately predict. The latter is true, we submit, even in cooperative situations wherein a partner's goodwill is unquestioned and his intentions clearly stated. In particular, the dichotomy must be kept firmly in view when the distinction is drawn between good actions and bad.

An action is not good which promises a desirable reward *only* on the condition that one's opponents' actions may be accurately predicted. Nor, in cooperative situations, is an action good which yields benefit *only* if one's partner's promises are exactly kept. Provision for error and misunderstanding, be it inadvertent or otherwise, must always be made.

Therefore, an action can only be called good whose promise of reward is *robust* in the sense that that promise is, at least in large measure, fulfilled even when one's opponent's actions are not quite as predicted and/or one's partner's are not exactly as agreed upon.

The choice of a saddle-point strategy in a matrix game is, by this view, a good action, for the benefit it promises is only enhanced should the opponent make an unexpected choice. But the action $x = 0$ in the game of Cold War is not a good action because the safety factor (1.11.1) jumps discontinuously from unity (complete safety) to zero (none) if 2 should choose $y = \epsilon > 0$ instead of $y = 0$, as expected. Nor is the action S a good action in Prisoner's Dilemma, because the sentence jumps from one to twelve years if the accomplice plays T instead of S, as (doubtless) agreed upon before the heist.

This fact does not, we wish to emphasize, mean that the action S would never be taken. It might well be, for instance, if the thieves were mother and son. But in the absence of some such relationship, T has much to recommend it. Indeed, it is a very stupid thief who would let himself be forced to play Prisoner's Dilemma with anyone but his own mother. For the zeros in the matrices (1.14.1) can always be replaced with at least the *threat* of a garrotte.

19. THE GAMES PEOPLE PLAY

Prisoner's Dilemma illustrates the rather obvious point that there are games which nobody in his right mind would ever play. Chicken is another obvious example: it is a game wherein two idiots drive their cars toward one another at breakneck speed down a (paved) country road straddling the white line, and the first to pull off it is declared loser and "chicken."

It has been pointed out that, in a sense, one cannot avoid playing because even if you decline a challenge, you've played. But such a declension only makes us chicken players in the sense that we are all merchants without wares, statesmen without constituents, ministers without congregations, and actors without experience.

In the ordinary sense of the verb "to play," it is difficult to imagine that anyone would play in a game with high stakes unless he knew, or thought he knew, of a "good" strategy for doing so. Here a strategy might consist of a single action, or a (possibly randomized) rule for selecting from among several such. A strategy is *good* if it holds forth the promise of substantial reward unless the opponents perform in some quite unexpected manner. That is, a strategy is good only if it is robust in the sense discussed earlier.

This definition is of course imprecise. Yet it is clear from it that there are no good strategies for playing Chicken (better, that is, than not playing), nor for Prisoner's Dilemma, unless five years in jail seem desirable. In the (concocted) bimatrix game (1.19.1), there is no good strategy for player A, though $1/3\,R + 1/3\,S + 1/3\,T$ looks good for B. For A seems certain to lose twice as often as he wins, while B has only to remain inscrutable to go on winning.

(1.19.1)

A \ B	R	S	T
R	1	-1	-1
S	-1	1	-1
T	-1	-1	1

A \ B	R	S	T
R	0	3	6
S	6	0	3
T	3	6	0

Indeed, this seems to be the usual case; if one writes down a game at random, it is likely that at least one of the players will fail to have a good strategy. It is not even clear that there exist games wherein every player has a good strategy.

In fact, there are many such games, and the easiest way to discover them is to build mathematical models of the games people play in real life. In the next several chapters we shall do just that, pointing out in each case that good strategies do exist for all players. We begin with the game of Cold War.

20. MORE ABOUT COLD WAR

Let us consider the symmetric case $m = 1 = \mu$ of Cold War. Then

$$(1.20.1) \qquad \pi_1(x,y) = \frac{x}{x+y} - x,$$

and $x > 1/4$ implies

$$(1.20.2) \qquad \pi_1(x,y) < \pi_1(1/4,y)$$

for every y. So neither player can increase his own payoff by taking an action $x > 1/4$ instead of $x = 1/4$. Nor can he increase his opponent's payoff by such action, since π_1 is a decreasing function of y as π_2 is a decreasing function of x. In short, 1 can have no incentive whatever to choose an $x > 1/4$ over $x = 1/4$, and 2 can have none to choose $y > 1/4$ instead of $y = 1/4$. And in the more general case $m \neq \mu$, one may similarly conclude that there is no incentive for $x > 1/4m$ or $y > 1/4\mu$. On the other hand, the action $x = 0$ yields $\pi_1(0,y) \equiv 0$, and amounts to not playing the game. Every action $x > 0$ renders $\pi_1(x,y)$ positive for small values of y and negative for large ones. So the decision to play (choose $x > 0$) is taken in the hope of faring better than by not playing, and at the risk of faring worse. It remains to assay that risk.

To begin with, observe that

$$(1.20.3) \qquad \frac{\partial \pi_1}{\partial x} = \frac{y}{(x+y)^2} - 1 \quad \text{and} \quad \frac{\partial^2 \pi_1}{\partial x^2} = \frac{-2y}{(x+y)^3} < 0,$$

so $\pi_1(x,y)$ is concave in x for fixed $y > 0$, and is maximized in the interval $0 \leqslant x \leqslant 1/4$ by the choice

$$(1.20.4) \qquad \begin{aligned} x = x^*(y) = \sqrt{y} - y & \quad \text{if} \quad 0 \leqslant y < 1 \\ = 0 & \quad \text{if} \quad y \geqslant 1. \end{aligned}$$

Moreover,

$$(1.20.5) \qquad \begin{aligned} \pi_1^*(y) = \pi_1(x^*(y),y) = (1 - \sqrt{y})^2 & \quad \text{if} \quad 0 \leqslant y < 1 \\ = 0 & \quad \text{if} \quad y \geqslant 1. \end{aligned}$$

The graph of the function $\pi_1^*(y)$ is shown in Figure 1.20A, along with the graphs of $\pi_1(x,y)$ for selected values of x.

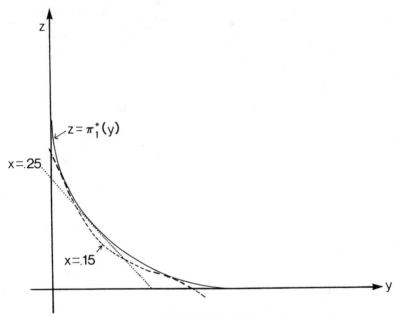

FIGURE 1.20A

It is remarkable how well $\pi_1^*(y)$ is approximated by some of the functions $\pi_1(x, y)$. For it means that 1 can select a single action, say $x = .2$, and do nearly as well as if he knew y in advance and chose $x^*(y)$. Indeed $\pi_1(.2, y) > .98\pi_1^*(y)$ for $.05 < y < .65$ and $\pi_1(.2, y) > .8\pi_1^*(y)$ for $0 \leqslant y \leqslant .05$, so that $x = .2$ is a very good action (strategy) indeed for 1 in the sense discussed earlier. For playing it offers a better payoff than $x = 0$ as long as $y < .8$, and it is robust in the sense that it is near-optimal against a wide variety of 2's possible actions, including all those in the interval $0 \leqslant y \leqslant 1/4$.

A more sensitive examination of the robustness of various actions is possible. In Figure 1.20B a number of the ratios $\pi_1(x, y)/\pi_1^*(y)$ are shown. They all meet the line $z = 1$ twice, at the roots of $x = \sqrt{y} - y$, and cross $z = 0$ at $y = 1 - x$. The curves all rise at first to a point on $z = 1$, dip briefly, rise again to $z = 1$, then plunge to the y-axis. Because the $x = .2$ curve dips only a little between its two peaks (recall that $\pi_1(.2, y) > .98\pi_1^*(y)$ there), the action $x = .2$ is highly robust. But because the $x = .05$ curve falls below $z = 1/2$ between its (sharp) peaks, the action $x = .05$ is not nearly as robust as $x = .2$. It earns less than half of the optimal payoff $\pi_1^*(y)$ against most actions $0 \leqslant y \leqslant 1/2$.

Indeed, the actions $x \leqslant .05$ seem so specialized as to be totally worthless!

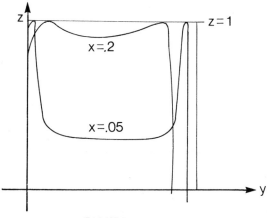

FIGURE 1.20B

They earn a substantial fraction of $\pi_1^*(y)$ only if y is very small or very near one. And, because of the sharpness of the peaks in the graph of $\pi_1(x,y)/\pi_1^*(y)$, they require a very accurate preliminary guess of the value of y to do that. Even if one believes, for instance, that y will be nearly zero, it is probably better to play $x = .2$ and earn $.8\pi_1^*(y)$ if right and $.98\pi_1^*(y)$ if wrong than to play (say) $x = .025$ and earn $.98\pi_1^*(y)$ if right and incur disaster if wrong! So, for practical purposes, it seems reasonable for 1 to ignore the possibility $0 \leqslant y \leqslant .05$.

This suggests that the game of Cold War can profitably be played in a naive and simple fashion. For each player knows that the other will have a defense budget but does not know how large that budget will be. So each should choose an action that is near optimal against a wide variety of possible actions by the other. That is, each should choose a robust strategy, say $x = y = .2$.

If both do, x and y will lie between .05 and .25, and each player's action will be 98 percent optimal against that of his opponent! So each may conclude that his attempt to play well has met with a high degree of success and hope to do as well next year!

(1-7) *Exercise* It is often argued that the probabilities (1.11.1) and (1.11.2) are more properly replaced with $\exp(-y/x)$ and $\exp(-x/y)$ respectively. Are our conclusions regarding the game of Cold War materially affected by such a change? Use a pocket calculator.

(1-8) *Question* What elements of reality are left out of the two models proposed for the Cold War? Would more accurate models yield better quantitative estimates, or would the qualitative nature of the conclusions probably change too?

Any pair (x, y) of robust actions (or strategies) may be regarded as a "solution" of the game, and the equilibrium point $(.25, .25)$ is just one of many such solutions. However, it is a handy *representative* of the set of all such, and we shall often treat it that way.

In the present case, for instance, the actual solution is an ill-defined square in the xy-plane with (x^*, y^*) at its northeast corner. So the dependence of the solutions on the parameters m and μ may be roughly inferred from the fact that

$$(1.20.6) \qquad (x^*, y^*) = \left(\frac{\mu}{(m + \mu)^2}, \frac{m}{(m + \mu)^2} \right)$$

21. THE DECISION PROCESS

No single person chooses the defense budget of a military superpower. Such decisions are made by committee. Moreover each committee member comes equipped with his or her own private estimate of what the opposing nation will do. Those estimates differ as the members enter the committee room and they differ still as they depart. Yet most if not all leave satisfied that a near-optimal choice has been made.

Unlike Cournot's players, these people do *not* deceive themselves! A satisfactory choice *has* been made because a robust action has been taken, one which is near-optimal against a wide variety of the actions available and attractive to the opposition. Such a decision represents a compromise; though the action taken is not what any member would choose alone, it is satisfactory to many if not all of them. Human nature makes compromise necessary, and only the existence of robust actions makes satisfactory compromise possible.

These facts have long been ignored in some circles. A belief has persisted that a rational committee faced with a rational opponent can accurately predict that opponent's action. In some instances the belief is demonstrably false. In the baseball game $(1.1.1)$, for instance, the rational batter cannot (even in consultation with his rational manager and coaches) decide what pitch his rational opponent will throw. In other instances the belief is merely unlikely; Cold War is such an instance.

Reflect that to guess a nation's future defense budget is to venture an economic prediction, and that economic predictions are themselves very predictable. They are very predictably wrong! To construct a theory of games like Cold War which systematically ignores the uncertainty attending the economic predictions the players *must make* seems but folly. One may as easily predict tides by carefully plotting planetary orbits while ignoring the effects of the sun and the moon!

The possibility remains, of course, that someone will someday demonstrate that rational players *must* play games like Cold War in an entirely predictable fashion. When that happens, committees will no longer need to compromise!

The rational committee members will all agree in their estimates of the rational opponent's imminent action, and select the appropriate response. Indeed there will be no further need of committees, since the decision of the whole will be exactly that which any one of the members alone would take.

Until that time, it seems advisable to proceed on the assumption that even rational players are at least a little bit unpredictable. A surprisingly rich and fruitful theory can be built around this apparently awkward hypothesis.

22. CONCLUSION

It would be foolish to attempt to generalize from a single example, and a highly structured one at that. But the structure that we find here will emerge again and again in apparently disparate circumstances, making the above-described mode of play effective in other games as well.

Those games will have at least one thing in common; they will nearly all be simple models of games people actually play, and in which the rewards take the form of large sums of money. But that should surprise no one. For, as pointed out earlier, it seems unlikely that such games could continue to be played year after year by essentially the same players if the players themselves did not believe that certain strategies held promise of substantial reward (better, that is, than not playing) in the face of a wide variety of likely actions by the others. And in each case we shall discover highly robust strategies which do hold such promise. But the promise of reward will always be at the risk of loss, as one would expect in games with high stakes.

REFERENCES

1. Williams, T. S., and John Underwood, *My Turn at Bat: The Story of My Life in Baseball* (New York: Simon and Schuster), 1968, 0 + 129 pp.
2. von Neumann, J., "Zur Theorie der Gesellschaftsspiele," *Math Ann.*, vol. 100 (1928), pp. 295–320.
3. Dresher, M., *Games of Strategy* (Englewood Cliffs, N.J.: Prentice-Hall, 1961), xii + 186 pp.
4. Rapoport, A., *Two-Person Game Theory* (Ann Arbor: Univ. of Michigan Press, 1966), 0 + 229 pp.
5. von Neumann, J., and Morgenstern, *Theory of Games and Economic Behavior* (Princeton, N.J.: Princeton University Press, 1944), xviii + 625 pp.
6. Luce, R. D., and Raiffa, *Games and Decisions* (New York: John Wiley, 1957), xix + 509 pp.
7. Rapoport, A., *N-Person Game Theory* (Ann Arbor: Univ. of Michigan Press, 1970), 0 + 331 pp.

8. Kaufmann, W., *Philosophic Classics* (Englewood Cliffs, N.J.: Prentice-Hall, 1961), ix + 630 pp.

9. Sherman, R. R., *Democracy, Stoicism, and Education* (Gainesville: Univ. of Florida Press, 1973), ii + 69 pp.

10. Edelstein, L., *The Meaning of Stoicism* (Cambridge, Mass.: Harvard Univ. Press, 1966), xiii + 108.

11. Owen, G., *Game Theory* (Philadelphia: W. B. Saunders, 1968), xii + 228 pp.

12. Cournot, A., *Researches into the Mathematical Principles of the Theory of Wealth*, N. T. Bacon, trans., 2d ed. (New York: Kelley, 1927), xxiv + 213.

13. Case, J., and G. Kimeldorf, "On Nash Equilibrium Points and Games of Imperfect Information," *JOTA*, vol. 9, no. 5 (1972), pp. 302-323.

14. Russell, B., *A History of Western Philosophy* (New York: Simon and Schuster, 1945), xxiii + 895 pp.

15. Fellner, W. J. *Competition Among the Few* (New York: Kelley, 1960), xv + 328 pp.

16. Capen, E. C., and R. V. Clapp, "Conflicting Bidding Models in a High Stakes Game," Paper presented to National Meeting of ORSA, Las Vegas, November 16-19, 1975.

17. Capen, E. C., R. V. Clapp, and W. M. Campbell, "Competitive Bidding in High-Risk Situations," *J. Petroleum Technology*, (June 1971), pp. 641-653.

18. Isaacs, R. P., *Differential Games* (New York: J. Wiley, 1965), xxii + 384 pp.

19. Williams, A. C., and M. Oren, "On Competitive Bidding," *Operations Research*, vol. 23, no. 6 (1975), pp. 1072-1080.

Chapter 2

Some Basic Games in Economics

1. COURNOT'S PROBLEM

The problem Cournot originally considered [1] was that facing two well owners in a small village. Since they produce indistinguishable products, he observed, they must charge the same price. And presumably that price will rise or fall in such a way that all the water pumped out of the ground in a given day will be sold that day. Let q_i be the quantity of water pumped by owner i on a given day. Then it is reasonable to assume that the average price p brought by a gallon of water that day will be some decreasing function f of the total quantity $q_1 + q_2$ of water sold. Cournot began a trend in mathematical economics by refusing to specify what function f he had in mind. But in fact little of his meaning is lost if we assume

$$(2.1.1) \qquad p = A - B(q_1 + q_2) = f(q_1 + q_2),$$

the price p being quoted in dollars per quart. Then owner i will earn roughly

$$(2.1.2) \qquad Aq_i - Bq_i(q_1 + q_2) \qquad i = 1, 2$$

dollars that day. And if we substitute

$$(2.1.3) \qquad q_1 = Ax/B \quad \text{and} \quad q_2 = Ay/B,$$

the expressions (2.1.2) become

$$(2.1.4) \qquad \begin{aligned} (A^2/B)\,(x - x(x + y)) &= (A^2/B)\,\pi_1(x, y) \\ (A^2/B)\,(y - y(x + y)) &= (A^2/B)\,\pi_2(x, y). \end{aligned}$$

The functions π_1 and π_2 so defined describe the reward structure of the game G between the two well owners.

The rules of G are that x and y, the players' respective actions, must be non-negative numbers. So G's salient features are all present in the representation

$$(2.1.5) \qquad 1 \underset{x \geqslant 0}{\text{maximize}}\; \pi_1(x, y), \quad 2 \underset{y \geqslant 0}{\text{maximize}}\; \pi_2(x, y).$$

39

Of course the imperatives "maximize" are impossible to perform without collaboration, since the players cannot each have foreknowledge of the other's action. So "maximize" should really be replaced by "make large" in the representation (2.1.5). But, as seen in the last chapter, approximate maximization can sometimes be achieved even though strict maximization cannot. At any rate, (2.1.5) is a compact (if not concise) representation of G, and we shall make frequent use of such representations hereinafter.

This problem may be easily treated by Cournot's method. One calculates

(2.1.6) $$\frac{\partial \pi_1}{\partial x} = 1 - 2x - y \quad \text{and} \quad \frac{\partial \pi_2}{\partial y} = 1 - x - 2y,$$

so that

(2.1.7) $$x^*(y) = (1 - y)/2, \quad y^*(x) = (1 - x)/2,$$

and

$$\pi_1^*(y) = (1 - y)^2/4.$$

The graphs of $x^*(y)$ and $y^*(x)$ are the straight lines shown in Figure 2.1A, and the iterative process described in Chapter I converges to their junction at $(x^*, y^*) = (1/3, 1/3)$. But more to the point, the game may be analyzed as Cold War was, in terms of robust strategies.

To that end, observe that $\pi_1(x, y)$ is a linear function of y for each fixed x,

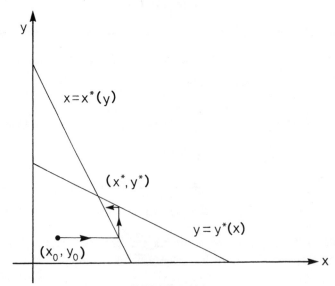

FIGURE 2.1A

since it may be written

(2.1.8) $z = \pi_1(x, y) = x(1 - x) - xy.$

Its graph in the yz-plane is a straight line, which meets the y-axis at $(1 - x, 0)$ and the (vertical) z-axis at $(0, x(1 - x))$. So $x > 1$ implies $\pi_1(x, y) < 0$ for every y, and the actions $x > 1$ are all dominated by $x = 0$. And if $x > 1/2$, then $\pi_1(1 - x, y) > \pi_1(x, y)$ for every y, since their graphs have the same z-intercept and the latter slopes more steeply downward than the former, as indicated in Figure 2.1B. So every action $x > 1/2$ is dominated by some action $0 \leqslant x \leqslant 1/2$. But the latter actions are undominated since each of them is optimal against some y. Indeed the graphs of $\pi_1(x, y)$ and $\pi_1^*(y)$ are tangent to one another at $y = 1 - 2x$, and the graph of $\pi_1^*(y)$ is the envelope of the straight lines (2.1.8) for which $0 \leqslant x \leqslant 1/2$.

Clearly, the straight lines do approximate their envelope over fairly large intervals in the y-axis. For instance (see Table 2.1C), $\pi_1(.3, y) > .75 \; \pi_1^*(y)$ for $0 \leqslant y \leqslant .6$, and $\pi_1(.3, y) > .93 \; \pi_1^*(y)$ for $.2 \leqslant y \leqslant .5$! Indeed, because the dominance relations established earlier make it unlikely that 2 would ever take an action $y > 1/2$, $x = .3$ seems a very robust strategy. On the other hand, the values given in Table 2.1C make it clear that $x = .1$ and $x = .5$ are not particularly robust.

In playing the game, the players may feel quite certain that their opponent will draw some water, but will not know how much. So each should seek a robust action and may assume that his opponent wants one too. Each might take, for instance, the action .3. If both do, their choices will each be 98 percent op-

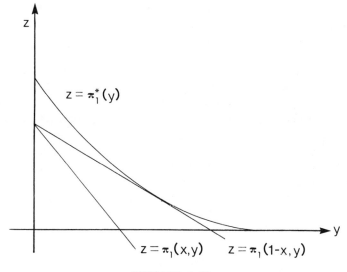

FIGURE 2.1B

TABLE 2.1C

y	$\Pi_1{}^*(y)$	$\Pi_1(.1,y)$	%	$\Pi_1(.3,y)$	%	$\Pi_1(.5,y)$	%
0	.25	.09	36	.21	84	.25	100
.05	.226	.085	38	.195	86	.225	99*
.1	.203	.08	39	.180	89	.200	99
–	.181	.075	41	.165	91	.175	97
.2	.161	.07	43	.150	93	.150	93
–	.141	.065	46	.135	96	.125	87
.3	.123	.06	99	.120	98	.100	81
–	.106	.055	52	.105	99+	.075	71
.4	.090	.05	56	.090	99+	.050	56
–	.076	.045	59	.075	99	.025	33
.5	.063	.04	63	.060	95	0	0
–	.051	.035	69	.045	88	–	–
.6	.040	.03	75	.030	75	–	–
–	.031	.025	81	.015	48	–	–
.7	.023	.02	87	0	0	–	–
–	.016	.015	94	–	–	–	–
.8	.010	.01	99+	–	–	–	–
–	.0056	.005	89	–	–	–	–
.9	.0025	0	0	–	–	–	–
–	.0006	–	–	–	–	–	–
1.0	0	–	–	–	–	–	–

timal against their opponent's. Moreover, their joint earnings will be .240, which is 96 percent of the .250 they could earn together if they became partners. So there is little incentive here to cooperate.

Of course the players could also take the actions $x = 1/3 = y$, which are only a little less robust than $x = .3 = y$, and which are the Cournot-Nash equilibrium strategies as well. But in that case they would together earn only 2/9 instead of the 1/4 they could get by cooperating. And 2/9 is only 89 percent of 1/4. So their quest for exact optimality instead of approximate optimality would result in an actual loss of income, as well as of robustness, in this case.

As in the game of Cold War, the players' uncertainty concerning each other's intentions, and their consequent desire for robustness, leads them to actions quite like the Cournot-Nash equilibrium pair. The fact that those actions are roughly Pareto optimal is of interest, too, but seems incidental to this particular game. The robust actions found earlier for Cold War do *not* approximate Pareto optimality.

(2–1) *Exercise*   Costs of production have been ignored in the present formulation of Cournot's game. To include them, appropriate cost terms $C_i(q_i)$ should be subtracted from the revenue functions (2.1.2). Solve the versions of Cournot's problem which result if $C_i(q_i)$ is (i) a linear function or (ii) a quadratic function of its argument.

Another solution of Cournot's game has been proposed which, because of its popularity [9] over the years, richly deserves mention here. It is the so-called Stackelberg solution, and purports to be the outcome the game would have if one well owner retained the other's assistant as a spy. For then the spying owner would always know his opponent's actions in advance, and could consistently choose his own to be optimal against them.

Let us suppose, for definiteness, that owner 2 retains an agent to spy on 1. Then 2 can arrange that

$$(2.1.9) \qquad y = y^*(x) = (1 - x)/2$$

always. In doing so, 2 becomes the so-called follower, since his action is now chosen after (and in response to) his opponent's. Owner 1 is called the leader, and the best he can do in his "predicament" is to maximize

$$(2.1.10) \qquad \pi_1(x, y^*(x)) = x(1 - x)/2$$

through his choice of x. Then

$$(2.1.11) \qquad x = 1/2 \quad \text{and} \quad y = y^*(1/2) = 1/4.$$

So

$$(2.1.12) \qquad \pi_1 = \pi_1(1/2, 1/4) = 1/8 \quad \text{and} \quad \pi_2 = \pi_2(1/2, 1/4) = 1/16.$$

There is profit indeed in leadership!

But something is terribly wrong with this conclusion, for crime has not paid! It was 2 (the follower) who introduced asymmetry into the game by his industrial espionage, and it is he who has suffered from that asymmetry. One suspects that better use can be made of the information supplied by his agent.

The sensible way to use such extraordinary intelligence is, of course, in *conjunction* with the other weapons at his disposal. And the most powerful of those are his robust actions. The reaction function (2.1.9) is too volatile for a player with robust actions in his arsenal; it allows his opponent to "tool" him about like a monkey on a string. The players of serious games cannot afford to let their opponents rule them so.

While 2 is using the rule (2.1.9), for instance, 1 can force him to reduce his presence in the market from $y = .33$ to $y = .25$ by the substitution of $x = .5$ for $x = .33$. But if 2 elects to react in a more *relaxed* fashion to intelligence received by using, for instance, the less volatile reaction function

$$(2.1.13) \qquad y = .4 - .24x,$$

then the substitution of $x = .5$ for $x = .33$ causes 2 to retreat only from $y = .32$ to $y = .28$. Yet his earnings against the two x-values, namely

(2.1.14)
$$\pi_2(1/2, .28) = .0616 = 1/16 \times .9856$$
$$\pi_2(1/3, .32) = .1109 \ldots = 1/9 \times .998 \ldots$$

compare very favorably with those he could have earned using (2.1.9). Moreover the "hesitant follower" who uses (2.1.13) is not led so *far astray* as the one who chooses (2.1.9). For the maximum of

(2.1.15) $\pi_1(x, .4 - .24x)$

occurs at $x = .395$ and not at $x = .5$. So a modified Stackelberg solution of $x = .395$, $y = .305$ emerges when 2 uses (2.1.13) and 1 maximizes π_1 subject to that constraint.

A more relaxed fashion still of reacting to intelligence is to ignore it entirely while x remains in the interval $.1 < x < .6$, and to play the robust action $y = .3$ steadfastly. Then 2 can still earn

(2.1.16) $\pi_2(1/2, 3/10) = 6/100 = .96 \times 1/16$

against $x = .5$ and provide 1 with an even greater incentive to stop trying to dominate the market. For the maximum of

(2.1.17) $\pi_1(x, 3/10)$

occurs at $x = .35$. In this case, a yet more modified Stackelberg solution emerges at $x = .35$ and $y = .3$, and the leader-follower relationship is virtually obliterated. Indeed, we have returned nearly to the Cournot point $x = 1/3 = y$.

The message here is simple. Because of the robustness of the actions at his disposal, 2 has no need to react violently to intelligence received concerning 1's intent. He is at liberty to "follow" changes in x with much smaller changes in y, if any. Therefore, "leadership" in the extreme sense postulated by Stackelberg can never be established, and the Stackelberg solution will never be observed in any real market.

Actually enterpreneurs realize these things instinctively, and they do *not* capitulate immediately to invasions of their markets. They resist. And robustness is the weapon *wherewith* they resist. Indeed it could be argued that the robustness of a firm's market strategy is the proper measure of its "strength" in the market.

Of course, not all firms have actions to choose from as robust as those in the linear-demand version of Cournot's game. For robustness depends on the *shape* of the demand curve. But there will always be *some* degree of robustness available, for the curves $z = \pi_2(x, y)$ which arise from fixed values of y are tangent to their envelope $z = \pi_2(x, y^*(x)) = \pi_2^*(x)$, so that each undominated y is optimal against some x and *very nearly so* against a host of nearby ones. This fact will quickly become evident to any firm that endeavors to establish the sort of market leadership that Stackelberg suggests is possible.

The Stackelberg solution is an old and beloved fiction of economic theory. But it is only that–a fiction. It is based on ignorance of the most important attribute that a competitor's action can have, namely its robustness. When that attribute is properly accounted for, one sees immediately that the degree of followership that Stackelberg postulates is impossible. Instead a much more limited form of followership presents itself, which leads back to the conclusion that a solution is a pair of robust actions, better likened to Cournot's conception than to Stackelberg's. Robustness, in short, seems to bring order out of chaos in Cournot's game as well as in Cold War.

2. MORE PLAYERS

The same game can be played among any number of well owners. Let their names be $1, \ldots, N$, and let their actions be $x, x_2, \ldots, x_N$ respectively. Write $y = x_2 + \cdots + x_N$. Then player 1's reward is still specified by (2.1.8), and his objectives are (as before) to guess what y will be and to pick an x which will be roughly optimal against it.

Player 1 can no longer assume that $y < 1/2$, though of course the individual inequalities

$$(2.2.1) \qquad x_2 \leqslant 1/2 \quad x_3 \leqslant 1/2 \quad \ldots \quad x_N \leqslant 1/2$$

still follow from the dominance relations. But he knows what y's past values have been, for he has a record of previous days' actions $x(t)$ for $t = 0, -1, -2, \ldots$, and he knows what his earnings $\pi_1(t)$ were on those days. Also

$$(2.2.2) \qquad y(t) = 1 - x(t) - \pi_1(t)/x(t)$$

for $t = 0, -1, -2, \ldots$, so that the sequence $\{y(t)\}_{t=0}^{-\infty}$ can be regarded as known. So if that sequence appears sufficiently regular, player 1 may hypothesize that $y(1)$ will fall in a "confidence interval" $\alpha < y(1) < \omega$. And if that interval is not too large, he can choose a robust action x which is effective against all the y's in it.

There are no guarantees here; the promise of profit is always at the risk of loss even against a single opponent. For player 2 alone can make $y > 1$ which prevents $\pi_1 > 0$. But that is the chance each merchant must take, both in the model and in the real marketplace it seeks to reflect. And the present analysis in terms of robust strategies goes far in explaining the success with which just that chance is so regularly taken. If *something* didn't make it easy, people wouldn't be willing to make their livings at it.

It is worthy of note that Cournot's game has been played rather extensively [12] under laboratory conditions, by juniors, seniors, and graduate students in a well-known school of business administration. Only a brief summary of the experiments and results will be given.

The game the subjects played was not exactly the one described here, since

TABLE 2.2A

Stern's Results

Periods	5	8	9	10	11	12	13	14	15	16	17	18	19	22	25	#
1–5	1	2	2	0	0	2	1	1	1	1	1	6	0	1	1	20
6–10	0	0	0	0	1	1	4	3	3	1	2	5	0	0	0	20
11–15	0	0	1	2	1	1	5	2	2	1	0	4	1	0	0	20
16–20	0	1	0	10	1	5	2	0	0	0	0	1	0	0	0	20
21–25	0	0	0	4	0	2	9	2	3	0	0	0	0	0	0	20
1–25	1	3	3	16	3	11	21	8	9	3	3	16	1	1	1	100

production costs were present, and only integral quantities q_1, q_2 of output were encouraged by the experimenter. But in its essential details, the game was as specified above. In particular, the price law was (2.1.1) with $A = 120$ and $B = 3.158$. The Cournot-Nash equilibrium* for this version of the game occurs at $q_1 = q_2 = 12.667$ and the symmetric Pareto optimum is $q_1 = q_2 = 9.5$. The duopoly data were produced in a pilot study by four subjects who made output decisions in two duopoly markets for twenty-five successive "weeks." The bottom line of Table 2.2A shows the frequency distribution of the 100 quantities produced by the 4 subjects in these 25 time periods; it is a trimodal distribution. A number of things are apparent from the table. To begin with, 25 of the 100 quantities produced exceed 15 units. Of these, 24 occurred in the first 15 weeks and 19 in the first 10. This suggests that an initial learning period was required for the players to discover the need to limit production. Large outputs became increasingly rare as the players gathered experience.

Of the remaining 75 decisions, the most popular choices were 13, 10, and 12. That is about what one would expect, for the choices between $q_i = 9.5$ (the symmetric Pareto optimum) and $q_i = 12.667$ (the Cournot-Nash equilibrium decision) are the most robust actions available to players of this game. So a large number of choices lying outside the interval from (say) 10 through 13 would cast doubt on the validity of the foregoing theory. But a majority of all the decisions taken (51 of the entire 100 and 33 of the final 40) do lie in that interval. So theory and observation are in rough accord.

Something *not* predicted by the theory is the relative unpopularity of the choice $q_i = 11$. Because of it, the frequency distribution has two separate modes in the robust interval $10 \leqslant q_i \leqslant 13$. Perhaps the phenomenon is a real one, and could be observed outside the laboratory as well. But one suspects that the noisy environment of a real marketplace would tend to obscure such narrowly separated peaks and fuse them together into one. In that case it would be impossible

---

*See *exercise* (2-1).

to assert that noncooperative (Cournot-Nash type) behavior is more common than the cooperative (Pareto optimal) kind as it was a little in the experiment. But it would still be possible to assert that robust actions predominate over all others. One may even be able to substantiate such suspicions by running the experiment again, this time replacing the constant A in the price law (2.1.1) with a random variable of moderate variance.

There is much to be learned from experiments of this sort. But it is beside the point to seek precise conclusions from them through the elimination of every source of noise. For the marketplace is a noisy environment, and people's behavior in it is conditioned by the fact. Instead of creating laboratory environments so noiseless as to permit the testing of exact hypotheses, one should devise hypotheses so inexact as to be testable in a noisy environment. The notion of robustness arises naturally in the attempt to phrase such hypotheses.

A second set of experiments are described in [12]. In them, the number of firms per market was permitted to vary. The interesting results concern the variation of the average price prevailing in the various markets with the number of firms in them. The results are exhibited in Figure 2.2B. The lower curve shown there represents the price that would be observed if the players really chose the Cournot-Nash equilibrium actions. And the upper one represents the *average* of the prices that were observed as the different-sized games were repeatedly played. The fact that the observed prices exceed the predicted ones indicates that the unembellished Cournot-Nash non-cooperative theory provides an incomplete explanation at best for the players' behavior. It does, on the other hand, provide a much better explanation than the cooperative theory, according to which the prices will never fall below the monopolist's price no matter

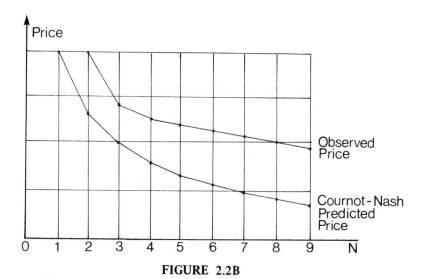

FIGURE 2.2B

how many firms enter the market. Moreover, if one accepts the earlier conclusion that the players should ordinarily produce a little *less* than the equilibrium output in order to gain additional robustness at the expense of but a little additional income, it is possible to account for at least the sign of the observed discrepancy between experimental and theoretical prices on the basis of the refurbished noncooperative theory. For less production does yield higher prices.

In short, prediction and observation are in rough agreement here, both qualitatively and (to a gratifying extent) quantitatively as well. If further experimentation continues to confirm the predictions of the theory to be advanced in this book, the study of games will finally have grown from a backwater of mathematics into a science in its own right. Stern's experiments are but a first step along the path to that goal.

3. SOME FORMAL DEFINITIONS

Cournot's game belongs to a rather noteworthy class of many player games. They may all be abbreviated in the form

$$(2.3.1) \qquad i \max_{x_i \geqslant 0} \pi_i(x_1, \ldots, x_N),$$

since each player's action set is simply the nonnegative real numbers. To play the game (2.3.1) each player $i = 1, 2, \ldots, N$ must choose an $x_i \geqslant 0$. And the reward each i receives is $\pi_i(x_1, \ldots, x_N)$. So $\pi_1, \ldots, \pi_N$ are called the *reward* (or *payoff*) *functions* of the game.

Definition: If each of the payoff functions π_i is unimodal in x_i for fixed x_j $j \neq i$ and monotone decreasing in x_j for each $j \neq i$, then we call (2.3.1) a *simply directed game.*

Definition: The action x_i *dominates* the action x_i' if $x_i < x_i'$ and if the inequality

$$(2.3.2) \qquad \pi_i(\ldots, x_{i-1}, x_i, x_{i+1}, \ldots) > \pi_i(\ldots, x_{i-1}, x_i', x_{i+1}, \ldots)$$

is valid for all $(N-1)$-tuples $(\ldots, x_{i-1}, x_{i+1}, \ldots)$ of nonnegative real numbers.

The latter differs from the notion of dominance introduced in Chapter I for matrix games only in the stipulation that $x_i < x_i'$. Dominance does not have the importance for all games that it does for zero-sum ones, as will be seen from the accompanying example in which each player i must choose between the actions $x_i = 1$ and $x_i = 2$. Here the action $x_1 = 1$ dominates $x_1' = 2$. But it is easy to imagine the choice $x_1 = 2$ anyway. For 2 could offer 1 $100 to sign a con-

(2.3.3)

x_2 \ x_1	1	2
1	20	10
2	30	1

x_2 \ x_1	1	2
1	5	1
2	3	500

tract (iron-clad, of course) promising to choose $x_1 = 2$. So one cannot *ignore* the possibility that $x_1 = 2$ in this game simply because $x_1 = 1$ dominates it.

In simply directed games, however, the notion of dominance (as defined above) does retain the import it has for matrix games. For clearly player i cannot increase his own payoff π_i by substituting the dominated x_i' for x_i. Nor can he expect to be bribed by an opponent or group of opponents for doing so, since all their payoffs are also decreased thereby.

Both Cournot's game and Cold War are simply directed games. Therefore, the above remarks constitute a rigorous proof that the players in Cournot's game will never produce $x > 1/2$, nor will either nation in (the symmetric version $m = \mu$ of) Cold War choose $x > 1/4$. Indeed, most of the games to be found in this book are simply directed games, and dominance arguments are valid for them.

It should be remarked at this time that the game (2.3.1) can be played, as can Cournot's game, by any number of players. Therefore the functions π_1, ..., π_N can have any number of arguments, and equations like

$$(2.3.4) \qquad \pi_1(x, x_2 + \cdots + x_N) = \pi_1(x, x_2, \ldots, x_N),$$

wherein a function of two variables is equated to one of N variables, are natural. Of course (2.3.4) is a blatant abuse of established mathematical notation, but to us it seems easier to perpetuate that abuse than to introduce the additional notation required to correct it. We trust that our meaning will not be irretrievably lost in this way.

Actually the equation (2.3.4) is a special case of another, which will be quite frequently encountered in subsequent chapters.

Definition: Let $\Omega(\cdot, \ldots, \cdot)$ be a function of $N - 1$ variables such that the equation

$$(2.3.5) \qquad \pi_1(x_1, x_2, \ldots, x_N) = \pi_1(x_1, \Omega(x_2, \ldots, x_N))$$

is valid identically for nonnegative $x_1, \ldots, x_N$. Then the game (2.3.1) is called *reducible* and the function Ω is called an *index of opposition* for it.

Cournot's game is of course reducible by the index $\Omega(x_2, \ldots, x_N) = x_2 + \cdots + x_N$. Indeed many of the games we shall meet are reducible, and others are approximately so. The principle fruit of reducibility is that it permits us to interpret two-dimensional figures like Figure 2.1B in the context of N-player games.

The definitions given above merely give names to certain phenomena which are frequently encountered in economic competition, and which appear to simplify the analysis of the games wherein they are present. The variety of circumstances wherein the phenomena recur is striking.

To appreciate the import the phenomena may sometimes have, a preliminary example is helpful. Let us consider the simply directed three-player game

$$(G_3) \qquad i \max_{x_i} \pi_i(x_1, x_2, x_3) = (x_i/(x_1 + x_2 + x_3)) - x_i$$

in which the allowable values of x_i are 0, .25, and .5, $i = 1, 2, 3$. Since (G_3) is obviously symmetric in the three players and has an index of opposition Ω, it is possible to represent the payoff functions in the accompanying tabular (matrix)

x_i \ Ω	0	.25	.5	.75	1
0	0	0	0	0	0
.25	$.75 = \frac{3}{4}$	$.25 = \frac{1}{4}$	$.08 = \frac{1}{12}$	0	$-.05 = \frac{-1}{20}$
.5	$.5 = \frac{1}{2}$	$.17 = \frac{1}{6}$	0	$-.10 = \frac{-1}{10}$	$-.17 = \frac{-1}{6}$

form. It is clear therefrom that $x_i = .25$ dominates $x_i = .5$, so no player has reason to choose $x_i = .5$. Thus, none need fear opposition $\Omega > .5$, and all may safely choose $x_i = .25$, which is optimal against all $\Omega \leqslant .5$. In that case, each player plays $x_i = .25$ against opposition $\Omega = .5$ and earns $\pi_i = .08$. Indeed, since the alternatives are only to play $x_i = .5$ and earn less or to play $x_i = 0$ and earn nothing, it seems natural to call $x_i = .25$ an *optimal action* for player i, the triple $(.25, .25, .25)$ a *solution* of G_3, and the game G_3 itself solvable.

To make these notions precise, further definitions are required.

Definition: In a simply directed and reducible game with index Ω of opposition, a value Ω_0 of Ω is called *dominated* if the inequality $\Omega(\ldots, x_{i-1}, x_{i+1}, \ldots) > \Omega_0$ implies that one of the actions $\ldots, x_{i-1}, x_{i+1} \ldots$ is dominated.

Definition: An action x_i^* is called *optimal* in such a game if it is optimal for i against every undominated value of the index Ω of opposition.

Definition: An N-tuple $(x_1^*, \ldots, x_N^*)$ of optimal actions is called a *solution* of such a game, and the game itself is called *solvable* if it possesses such a solution.

G_3 is of course a solvable game according to the above definitions. But almost all other games are not solvable in the same sense. So our definitions are overly restrictive. On the other hand, Cold War and Cournot's two-player game are almost solvable, since *near-optimal* actions exist for both players in each of them.

Definition: An action x_i^0 is called *robust* if it is near-optimal for i against every undominated value of the index Ω of opposition.

Definition: An N-tuple $(x_1^0, \ldots, x_N^0)$ of robust actions is called an *approximate solution* of such a game, and the game itself is called *approximately solvable* if it possesses an approximate solution.

Whether or not a particular game possesses an approximate solution often depends on the interpretation given the phrase "near-optimal" appearing in the definition of robustness. A major objective in writing this book is to demonstrate that many interesting and important commercial situations are properly modeled as simply directed and reducible games which are approximately solvable.

Any solution, as defined above, is a Cournot-Nash equilibrium point. And approximate solutions are in approximate Cournot-Nash equilibrium. Thus, our approach is in the tradition of noncooperative game theory, but it differs from the usual formulation of that theory in many particulars.

The noncooperative nature of the present solution concept is readily apparent in the game G_3, wherein the players earn .08 when they play "optimally." For 1 and 2 could each agree to pay 3 the sum .08 to choose $x_3 = 0$, thereby doubling everyone's reward. So if 3 is adequately assured that his opponents will each pay him .08 after he has chosen $x_3 = 0$, he should surely do so. It is only when he is forced to act *without* such assurance that we claim $x_3 = .25$ to be his optimal action.

The role of robustness in this theory deserves comment. For robustness and properties like it are well known in other branches of applied mathematics. Problems in partial differential equations, for instance, are called "ill-posed" if their solutions are not in some sense robust. And robustness is all the rage in contemporary statistical theory. Linear programming packages typically permit "postoptimality" or "sensitivity" analyses whereby the dependence of the optimal payoff on various inputs may be determined. Also, "suboptimal strategies" which are insensitive to parameter variations are frequently sought [13] for problems of optimal control. Indeed one often hears it said that some guarantee of the insensitivity of a proposed solution to perturbations of the hypotheses wherefrom it was deduced is the *sine qua non* of applied mathematics. And for no other branch of the subject is that statement as true as it is for game theory, for in no other branch do those hypotheses necessarily relate to the character and behavior of *other human beings*.

4. A GAME BETWEEN FISHERMEN

Games identical in form to Cournot's arise in other ways. Consider, for instance, a group of nations $1, 2, \ldots, N$ bordering an ocean and suppose the ocean to be inhabited by a species of fish whose number varies in accordance with the so-called [10] Verhulst equation

(2.4.1) $\dot{N}(t) = kN(t)[\theta - N(t)]/\theta$

of population growth. Each nation controls the size of its fishing fleet through the sale of licenses, and the international fleet so created "preys" on the fish population in the manner usually postulated [10] for the analysis of predator-prey interactions. So if nation i adopts a policy of issuing x_i licenses each year, the number of fish in the ocean varies as

(2.4.2) $\dot{N} = kN(\theta - N)/\theta - \lambda x N,$

$x = x_1 + \cdots + x_N$ being the total number of predators afloat. Therefore, as t grows large, $N(t)$ tends to be the limit

(2.4.3) $\overline{N} = \theta(1 - \lambda x/k)$

calculated by equating $\dot{N}$ with zero in (2.4.2). In short, $\overline{N}$ depends on the total fleet size as price does on total output in Cournot's game. Moreover, if nation i regards its catch as its reward, we may write

(2.4.4) $\pi_i(x_1, \ldots, x_N) = \theta \lambda x_i [1 - \lambda(x_1 + \cdots + x_N)/k],$

which reduces upon normalization to the form (2.1.4). Hence our earlier results concerning robustness and approximate Pareto optimality for Cournot's game hold in this one as well.

(2-2) *Question* Very different results might be expected if nations were assumed to subtract from the size (2.4.4) of their catch an expression representing the opportunity cost thereof. How does the solution of the problem change if the foregone opportunity has magnitude $C_i(x_i) = c_i x_i/(k_i - x_i)$ for each $i = 1, \ldots, N$?

It should be observed that the reward function (2.4.4) is appropriate only for countries with lots of potential fishermen. For the incentive to limit the number of licenses comes from the danger of overfishing and the consequent scarcity of fish in the future. But only the countries with large fleets need limit the size thereof for fear of overfishing. Smaller nations limit the size of their fleets for other reasons. Indeed it is quite recent that any nation has been forced to consider the possibility of overharvesting such major commercial species as, for instance, the Atlantic cod. But today the major fishing nations do have the capacity to overcrop even the largest commercial fisheries. So games not unlike that discussed above are even now being played.

A rather different sort of game arises if it be supposed that the fish population varies in accordance with the older [10] Gompertz' equation

(2.4.5) $$\dot{N} = -kN \log N/\theta.$$

For then adjoining a predation term and equating $\dot{N}$ with zero gives

(2.4.6) $$N = \theta \cdot \exp(-\lambda x/k),$$

which leads to

(2.4.7) $$\pi_i(x_1, \ldots, x_N) = \lambda \theta x_i \cdot \exp\left(\frac{-x_i \lambda}{k}\right) \cdot \exp\left(\frac{-\lambda}{k} \sum_{\substack{j=1 \\ j \neq i}}^{N} x_j\right),$$

which is maximized at $x_i = k/\lambda$ for any values of $\ldots, x_{i-1}, x_{i+1}, \ldots$ whatever. In short, nation i's optimal (noncooperative) policy is to issue k/λ licenses in all circumstances, without regard to the numbers issued in other countries. And that is directly at variance with the conclusion drawn from the Verhulst model, whereby x_i^* was a decreasing (linear) function of

$$\sum_{\substack{j=1 \\ j \neq i}}^{N} x_j.$$

Clearly a more sensitive and detailed model of the dynamics of a typical fish population will be required before any substantial insight into the nature of competition among fishing fleets can be claimed.

A model proposed recently by Timin and Collier [11] seeks greater detail through the incorporation of additional descriptive variables. These are $N(t)$, the number of animals per unit area, at time t; $E(t)$, the amount of food per unit area at that time; and $W(t)$, the mean amount of stored energy per individual in the population. Both food and the size of the animals in the population are assumed to be expressed in energy units such as calories.

The state variable W is meant to be a crude index of the average age and health of the individual fish. In a single-species population with but little social behavior, the likelihood of an individual giving birth or dying in a brief time is principally dependent on that individual's age and health. Therefore the birth rate per individual b and death rate per individual d may be assumed to be functions of W.

The dynamics of the Timin-Collier system consist of three ordinary differential equations

(2.4.8) $$\begin{aligned} \dot{N} &= (b - d)N - h \\ \dot{W} &= gq - (W + C)b - \mu W \\ \dot{E} &= s - qN - kE, \end{aligned}$$

where

g = the ratio of the quantity (energy ingested—energy not assimilated—energy
    expended to catch, ingest, and assimilate the ingested food) to the amount
    of energy ingested;
q = food ingestion rate per individual;
C = coefficient of energy loss associated with births;
μ = fraction of energy lost by an organism of size W per unit time, due to
    metabolic heat, secretions, molting, etc.;
s = rate of food supply;
k = proportionality constant for rate of food leaving system through decay
    or flushing;
h = total harvest rate.

The quantities q and μ are functions of W and/or E, so there is a high degree of
coupling among the three equations. We shall assume the harvest rate to have the
form

(2.4.9) $h = \lambda N x$

postulated above, x being again the total number of licenses issued in the several
countries.

Because it describes the flow of energy through the population, the Timin-Collier model seems firmly rooted in basic physical concepts. And by the presence of
the state variable W, it permits the basic well-being of the population to vary
somewhat without the extensive data requirements and high dimensionality of
models incorporating age-size structure. A final advantage of the model is that
it can be expressed in terms of dimensionless variables.

To discover these, it is assumed that a stable size distribution will be reached
when food density is maintained at a very high (i.e., non-limiting) level relative
to population density and environmental conditions are held constant. So $W(t)$
will tend to a limiting value W_m. The latter may be obtained by setting $\dot{W}$ equal
to zero in (2.4.8) and solving for W. Let V_m be the effective rate of search per
individual in units of area per unit time, and let μ_m be the value of μ under
those conditions. A new time scale is now defined by

(2.4.10) $\tau = \mu_m t$,

so that $d/d\tau = (1/\mu_m)d/dt$. The new dimensionless state variables are then

(2.4.11) $\eta = (NV_m)/\mu_m$, $F = (EV_m)/(\mu_m W_m)$,   and $\Omega = W/W_m$,

so that population density is given as the number of individuals in an area that
can be searched in a single unit of time, and food density as the ratio of the
amount of food present in that area to W_m. Average health of the population
is the ratio of mean individual mass to W_m. Three dimensionless differential

equations for η, F and Ω are then easily written (where now "$\cdot$" $= d/d\tau$), namely

$$\dot{\eta} = (\bar{b} - \bar{d})\eta - \bar{h}$$

(2.4.12) $$\dot{F} = \bar{s} - \bar{q}\eta - \bar{k}F$$

$$\dot{\Omega} = \bar{g}\bar{q} - (\Omega + \bar{C})\bar{b} - \bar{\mu}\Omega.$$

Here the overbarred quantities are the dimensionless counterparts of the parameters previously introduced. That is,

(2.4.13)

$$\bar{b} = b/\mu_m \qquad\qquad \bar{q} = q/\mu_m W_m$$

$$\bar{d} = d/\mu_m \qquad\qquad \bar{k} = k/\mu_m$$

$$\bar{h} = hV_m/\mu_m^2 \qquad\qquad \bar{g} = g$$

$$\bar{s} = sV_m/\mu_m^2 W_m \qquad \bar{C} = C/W_m$$

$$\bar{\mu} = \mu/W_m.$$

The principal advantage of the dimensionless model (2.4.12-13) derives from the fact that a single set of values may be assigned to the parameters which seem reasonable for a large number of different species. A table of values considered typical by a number of ecologists is given in [11]. From it, Timin and Collier select the forms

(2.4.14)

$$\bar{b} = 3.8\Omega^2 - 3.8\Omega + 0.95 \qquad \bar{k} = .1$$

$$\bar{d} = 0.19/(2\Omega - 1) \qquad\qquad \bar{g} = .2$$

$$\bar{s} = 3 \qquad\qquad\qquad\qquad \bar{C} = .05$$

$$\bar{q} = \frac{F\Omega^{2/3}}{1 + F/10} \qquad\qquad \bar{\mu} = \Omega^{-1/3}$$

as particularly worthy of investigation. We seek to determine the constant solutions of the differential equations obtained by giving the parameters (2.4.13) the values (2.4.14) in the system (2.4.12) and replacing $\bar{h}$ by the predation term $x\lambda\eta$. Clearly λ may be made equal to unity by properly choosing the units in which x (i.e., fishing licenses) are measured.

To find those constant solutions it is necessary to solve the three simultaneous algebraic equations

$$x = A(\Omega) = 3.8(\Omega - .5)^2 - .095/(\Omega - .5)$$

(2.4.15) $$\frac{2F}{10 + F} = 1 + B(\Omega) = 1 + 3.8(\Omega - .5)^2(\Omega + .05)/\Omega^{2/3}$$

$$\frac{F}{10} + \frac{\eta F\Omega^{2/3}}{1 + F/10} = 3.$$

And that is readily accomplished, for the relations

$$\Omega = A^{-1}(x) = 1/2 + \alpha\sqrt{x} \; \cosh\,[(1/3)\cosh^{-1}\gamma x^{-3/2}]$$

$$F = 10(1 + B(\Omega))/(1 - B(\Omega))$$

(2.4.16)

$$\eta = (3 - F/10)(1 + F/10)/F\Omega^{2/3}$$

$$= (1 - 2B)/5\Omega^{2/3} \cdot (1 + B)$$

permit one to solve successively for Ω as a function of x, then F and η as functions of Ω, the constants involved having roughly the values $\alpha = .592349$ and $\gamma = .481135$. Moreover this need be done for only a short interval of x-values. For if the model is to have physical meaning, $\bar{d}$ must be nonnegative. So $\Omega \geqslant 1/2$. But $A(\Omega) = \bar{b} - \bar{d}$ must also be nonnegative, so $\Omega \geqslant .79240 \ldots$. Next η must be nonnegative, so $B(\Omega) \leqslant 1/2$ and $\Omega \leqslant .86152 \ldots$. And finally, $x = A(\Omega)$

TABLE 2.4A

x	Ω	F	η	P	ΔP
.01	.79540	19.70	.0608	.0483	23
.02	.74840	20.01	.0580	.0463	20
—	.80140	20.33	.0551	.0442	21
.04	.80439	20.67	.0522	.0420	22
—	.80734	21.00	.0494	.0399	21
.06	.81038	21.37	.0465	.0377	22
—	.81337	21.73	.0437	.0355	22
.08	.81635	22.11	.0408	.0333	22
—	.81933	22.50	.0380	.0312	22
.10	.82231	22.91	.0352	.0290	22
—	.82528	23.33	.0325	.0268	22
.12	.82824	23.77	.0297	.0246	22
—	.83120	24.22	.0270	.0225	21
.14	.83415	24.68	.0243	.0203	22
—	.83710	25.17	.0216	.0181	22
.16	.84004	25.67	.0190	.0159	22
—	.84297	26.19	.0163	.0138	21
.18	.84590	26.72	.0137	.0116	22
—	.84881	27.28	.0111	.0094	22
.20	.85172	27.86	.0085	.0073	21
—	.85463	28.47	.0060	.0051	22
.22	.85752	29.09	.0035	.00297	21
—	.86040	29.74	.00097	.00083	22
.24	.86328	30.42	−.0015	−.0013	21
.0001	.792431	19.40	.0638	.0506	
0	.7924	19.40			

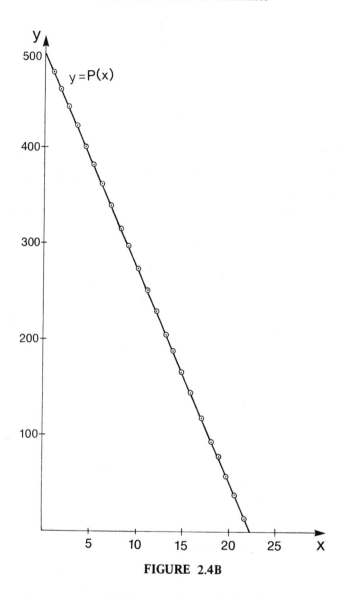

FIGURE 2.4B

increases from zero to .23387 . . . as Ω goes from .7924 . . . to .86152 . . . , so it suffices to examine the interval $0 \leqslant x \leqslant .23387$ of x-values. Larger x's lead to extinction of the population.

The formulas (2.4.16) define functions $\Omega(x)$, $F(x)$, and $\eta(x)$ on that interval. And since the size of the total catch (again measured in calories or other units of energy) is proportional to the product $x \cdot P(x) = x \cdot \eta(x) \cdot \Omega(x)$, while nation i's share thereof is the fraction $x_i/x = x_i/(x_1 + \cdots + x_N)$, one may conclude that i's reward when the nations issue $x_1, \ldots, x_N$ licenses annually is just

$$\pi_i(x_1, \ldots, x_N) = x_i P(x_1 + \cdots + x_N).$$

(2.4.17)
$$= x_i \eta(x_1 + \cdots + x_N) \cdot \Omega(x_1 + \cdots + x_N)$$

A short table of values for $\Omega(\cdot)$, $F(\cdot)$, $\eta(\cdot)$ and $P(\cdot) = \eta(\cdot)\Omega(\cdot)$ appears below, and a few points of the graph $y = P(x)$ are plotted in Figure 2.4B. Obviously those points fit well on the straight line $y = .0506 - .2167x$ which is also shown there. So the reward functions (2.4.17) are well approximated by

(2.4.18) $$\pi_i(x_1, \ldots, x_N) = x_i [A - B(x_1 + \cdots + x_N)],$$

where $A = .0506$ and $B = .2167$. And (2.4.18) is of exactly the form (2.4.4) to which the Verhulst equation led earlier, and which Cournot's game takes when the price law is linear. So our conclusions concerning Cournot's game apply to this one as well.

They suggest, for instance, that fishing treaties between the United States and Canada concerning licensing policy on the Great Lakes should not be necessary. For two players using robust strategies in Cournot's game reap rewards which are 96 percent of Pareto optimal. But on the Grand Banks fisheries off Newfoundland, such treaties should prove helpful because more nations compete for the catch there. We shall not attempt now to analyze the bargaining game which must preceed the signing of such a treaty.

(2-3)   *Question*   Only numerical evidence is currently available to the effect that the function $P(x) = \Omega(x) \eta(x)$ is linear. Is it in fact exactly so, or is the appearance of Figure 2.4B a numerical accident? If $P(x)$ is linear, a proof of the fact should not be difficult.

5. SUPPLY AND DEMAND

Cournot's model of a marketplace would be somewhat more convincing if the linear price law (2.1.1) were replaced by something more realistic. But what? Let us digress briefly on the matter.

Consider a market in which firms X_1 and X_2 compete to sell toothpaste. Let the price of brand X_1 be p_1 cents a tube, the price of X_2 be p_2, and assume the market's demand for toothpaste totally inelastic. Then it is reasonable to expect that the market's demand D_1 for brand X_1 should be a decreasing function of the ratio p_1/p_2. Indeed, some statistical evidence has lately been advanced [2] in behalf of the hypothesis

(2.5.1) $$D_1(p_1, p_2) = \phi(\log m p_2/p_1),$$

ϕ being the normal accumulation function. In [3] we proposed the even simpler hypothesis that

(2.5.2) $D_1(p_1, p_2) = [1 + (p_1/mp_2)]^{-1}$,

which is the form (2.5.1) would take if ϕ were replaced by the logistic function

(2.5.3) $\psi(x) = 1/(1 + e^{-\alpha x})$

and the resulting expression simplified algebraically. The problem of deciding between the demand laws (2.5.1) and (2.5.2) is that of discriminating between two alternative binary response models, namely the logistic and the integrated normal. And this problem has been investigated several times, notably by D. R. Cox and E. A. Chambers. In their paper [5], they discuss the design of an experiment to distinguish between the two models. But they caution that even with so well designed an experiment, "approximately 1,000 observations are needed for even modest sensitivity." Elsewhere [4, p. 28] Cox writes: "For most purposes the logistic and the normal agree closely over the whole range. The only exception is when special interest attaches to the regions where the probability of success is either very small, or very near one. Then the normal curve approaches its limit more rapidly than the logistic." So unless very extensive data are available, statistical evidence for either (2.5.1) or (2.5.2) may be regarded as evidence for the other as well.

The model (2.5.2) has an obvious extension to N-competitor markets. If $X_1, \ldots, X_N$ are N firms competing among themselves to sell like goods, and p_i is the price of brand X_i, we may suppose the demand D_i for brand X_i to be

(2.5.4) $D_i(p_1, \ldots, p_N) = [(m_i p_i/m_1 p_1)^\alpha + \cdots + (m_i p_i/m_N p_N)^\alpha]^{-1}$,

$i = 1, 2, \ldots, N$. Clearly (2.5.4) reduces to (2.5.2) if $N = 2$ and $m = m_2/m_1$. In addition, the demand functions (2.5.4) have the following desirable properties:

(2.5.5)

(i) they depend on the price ratios p_i/p_j alone

(ii) $\sum_{i=1}^{N} D(p_1, \ldots, p_N) = 1$

(iii) $\lim_{p_i \to 0} D_i(p_1, \ldots, p_N) = 1$ for fixed p_j, $j \neq i$

(iv) the functions $D_i(\infty, p_2, \ldots, p_N)$ $(i \neq 1)$ describe an $N - 1$ competitor market of similar type.

The reader should verify the properties (2.5.5) for himself, and observe that m_1 may be put equal to 1 without loss of generality. Hence the functions (2.5.4) describe an N-parameter family of markets characterized by the N-positive numbers $m_2, \ldots, m_N$, and α; $m_2, \ldots, m_N$ describe the consumer's attitudes toward the various brands. Thus if $p_1 = mp_2$ in (2.5.2), each firm will control half the market. Or if $m_1 p_1 = m_2 p_2 = \cdots = m_N p_N$ in (2.5.4), each firm will control an equal share.

The parameter α measures the sensitivity of the market to small price changes. For instance,

$$(2.5.6) \qquad \frac{\partial}{\partial p_1} [1 + (p_1/mp_2)^\alpha]^{-1} \Big|_{p_1 = mp_2} = \frac{-\alpha}{4mp_2} \, ,$$

so that the slope of the demand curve for brand X_1 near $p_1 = mp_2$ is proportional to α. We shall make frequent use of the demand laws (2.5.2) and (2.5.4) throughout the book, because they seem to combine substantial realism with remarkable tractability.

Let us return now to the form the function (2.1.1) ought properly to have. Assume that the well owners produce naturally crystal-clear spring water of the sort that is now sold in bottles and that ordinary drinking water is also available to the consumers in unlimited quantities at a nominal price. Then the demand for spring water should be

$$(2.5.7) \qquad x + y = D_1 = \frac{D}{1 + (p/mp_2)^\alpha} \, ,$$

where D is the total demand for drinking water (here assumed fixed) and mp_2 is the price the well owners must charge to control half the market. It is clear that by choosing units of money and water properly, we can assume $D = mp_2 = 1$. Then, setting $\beta = 1/\alpha$ and solving (2.5.7) for p we may write

$$(2.5.8) \qquad p = p(x + y) = \left(\frac{1}{x+y} - 1 \right)^\beta.$$

This is the form of the price law which follows from (2.5.2). We must ask now if our earlier conclusions concerning Cournot's game change substantially when (2.5.8) replaces (2.1.1).

(2-4) *Exercise*   The form (2.5.8) is hardly the only form the function $p(x+y)$ might take. The alternative

$$p(x+y) = (1 + (x+y)^\alpha)^{-1}$$

also makes sense in some situations. Solve Cournot's problem in this case, α being a positive exponent.

6. COURNOT'S PROBLEM: VERSION II

If Cournot's unspecified price function f has the form (2.5.8), then well owner 1's profit function is

(2.6.1)
$$\pi_1(x,y) = xp(x+y) = x\left(\frac{1}{x+y} - 1\right)^\beta.$$

so

(2.6.2)
$$\frac{\partial \pi_1}{\partial x} = x\frac{\partial p}{\partial x} + p = p - \frac{\beta px}{(x+y)^2\left(\frac{1}{x+y} - 1\right)}.$$

And equating the latter to zero yields a quadratic form in x and y which may be solved for

(2.6.3)
$$x^*(y) = (1 - \beta)/2 + \sqrt{(1 - \beta)^2/4 + \beta y}.$$

Moreover, $x^*(y)$ may be set equal to y to yield

(2.6.4)
$$x^* = y^* = (2 - \beta)/4,$$

the coordinates of the Cournot–Nash equilibrium point.

To investigate robustness, numerical evaluation is required. The results for $\beta = 1/\alpha = 1/4$ are given in Table 2.6A. They show, for instance, that $x = .4$ is

TABLE 2.6A

y	$x^*(y)$	$\Pi_1^*(y)$	$\Pi_1(.2,y)$	%	$\Pi_1(.4,y)$	%	$\Pi_1(.55,y)$	%
0	.75	.57	.28	49	.44	77	.52	91
.05	.72	.54	.26	48	.42	78	.50	93
.1	.68	.50	.25	50	.4	80	.47	94
–	.65	.46	.23	50	.38	83	.45	98
.2	.61	.42	.22	52	.36	86	.42	99+
–	.58	.39	.21	54	.34	87	.39	99+
.3	.54	.36	.20	56	.32	89	.36	99+
–	.50	.32	.19	59	.30	94	.32	99+
.4	.47	.29	.18	62	.28	97	.26	90
–	.43	.26	.17	65	.26	99+	0	0
.5	.39	.23	.16	70	.23	99+		
–	.35	.20	.15	75	.19	95		
.6	.31	.17	.14	82	0	0		
–	.28	.15	.13	87				
.7	.24	.12	.11	92				
–	.20	.10	.10	99+				
.8	.16	.07	0	0				
–	.12	.05						
.9	.08	.03						
–	.04	.01						
1.0	0	0						

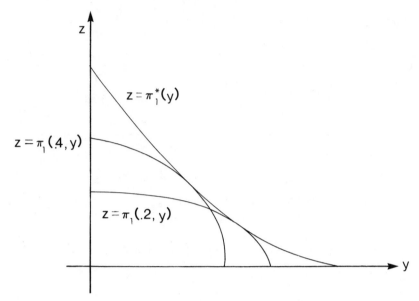

FIGURE 2.6B

a very robust action and that $x = .2$ and $x = .55$ are somewhat less so. The situations is in part explained in Figure 2.6B, wherein the curve $z = \pi_1^*(y)$ and a few of the curves $z = \pi_1(x,y)$ are shown. The latter are almost straight for small values of y but plunge rapidly toward the y-axis to the right of their point of tangency with $z = \pi_1^*(y)$. The game exacts a severe penalty for underestimating y. But our conclusions are not significantly changed by the introduction of the (more) realistic price law (2.5.8); remarkably robust actions exist for both well owners, and they earn very nearly as much by their use as they could through collaboration!

Moreover, the conclusions remain valid as α grows larger. Indeed, as functions of $s = x + y$, the price laws (2.5.8) have roughly the graphs shown in Figure 2.6C; in particular they all pass through the point $(1/2, 1)$ with slope $-4/\alpha$, thus becoming more nearly horizontal as α grows large. And they are well approximated by the piecewise linear functions

$$(2.6.5) \qquad p = \begin{cases} \infty & \text{if } s = 0 \\ 1 + (2 - 4s)/\alpha & \text{if } 0 < s < 1 \\ 0 & \text{if } s \geqslant 1 \end{cases}$$

except near $s = 0$ and $s = 1$, the goodness of fit increasing with α. So the games with price laws (2.5.8) are well approximated by those with price laws (2.6.5), and (2.6.5) is only a truncated form of (2.1.1). Qualitatively, the solutions of

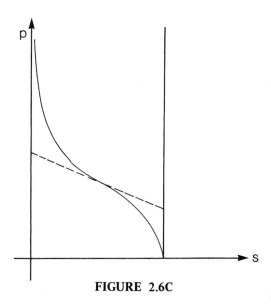

FIGURE 2.6C

the three types of game do not differ markedly, whether they are played by two players or (as discussed in §2) by more.

(2-5) *Question* Two neighborhood massage parlor operators must decide how many masseuses to employ. By choosing appropriate cost and price laws, formulate and solve the version of Cournot' problem confronting these entrepreneurs.

7. BERTRAND

For some forty-five years, Cournot's book received little attention. Then in 1883 it was reviewed in the *Journal des Savants* [6] by the French mathematician Joseph Bertrand. And almost simultaneously Jevons, Walras, Boccardo, and Edgeworth undertook to explain Cournot to the economic community. Bertrand and Edgeworth, in particular, objected that well owners actually control their prices as well as their output levels and accumulate overproduction (output minus actual demand) as inventory. So prices, rather than output levels, determine profit. And today, since mineral water is sold in bottles with brand names printed on the labels (so that brand loyalty plays a role), the criticism is even more justified than it was when Bertrand and Edgeworth advanced it. Let us, therefore, consider some simple market games wherein the players' alternative actions are the various prices each may ask. The simplest such game might be played, for instance, between a pair of truffle cooperatives operating in the French provinces of Périgord and Lorraine.

Truffles are a renowned delicacy, and in times of scarcity they sell at truly astronomical prices. On the other hand, they can be eaten in bulk, and doubtless would be* if they were cheap. So if p_1 is the price (in $ per ounce) of Périgordian truffles and p_2 the price of Lorrentian ones, it is not unreasonable to suppose that the demands for the two are

$$(2.7.1) \qquad D_1(p_1, p_2) = \left(\frac{mp_2}{p_1}\right)^\alpha \quad \text{and} \quad D_2(p_1, p_2) = \left(\frac{p_1}{mp_2}\right)^\alpha,$$

since these are montone functions of the price ratio such that D_i goes to zero as p_i grows large or $p_j (j \neq i)$ small and becomes large as p_i grows small or p_j large.

When demand is described by the laws (2.7.1) and when the on-the-shelf cost of an ounce of truffle is $c, the cooperatives' profit functions are

$$(2.7.2) \qquad \begin{aligned} \pi_1(p_1, p_2) &= (p_1 - c) D_1(p_1, p_2) = (p_1 - c)\left(\frac{mp_2}{p_1}\right)^\alpha \\ \pi_2(p_1, p_2) &= (p_2 - c) D_2(p_1, p_2) = (p_2 - c)\left(\frac{p_1}{mp_2}\right)^\alpha, \end{aligned}$$

respectively. So if p_j is held fixed, i faces a profits curve like that shown in Figure 2.7A, at least if $\alpha > 1$. If $\alpha < 1$, profits do not dip to zero as $p_i \to \infty$, but increase to ∞ instead. Or if $\alpha = 1$, profit increases to a finite limit as $p_i \to \infty$. And since either possibility is absurd, we must assume $\alpha > 1$ in the present discussion.

It is clear from Figure 2.7A that the optimal price $p_i^*(p_j)$ against a particular p_j is that for which $\partial \pi_i / \partial p_i = 0$. So, by the differential calculus,

$$(2.7.3) \qquad \frac{\alpha c - (\alpha - 1) p_i}{p_i^{\alpha+1}}$$

must vanish when $p_i = p_i^*$, and $p_i^* = \alpha c / (\alpha - 1)$ *independent* of p_j!

Thus $p = \alpha c / (\alpha - 1)$ is the epitome of a robust action, for it is optimal against all of the opponent's possible actions. Its promise of reward can be exceeded only through collusion. But there is substantial incentive in this game to collude, since demands remain unchanged as prices are doubled and redoubled. So the present game, while interesting, does not represent reality with great precision.

A better model for some purposes, is obtained by substituting the demand functions (2.5.2) for (2.7.1). That game has been discussed in [3], but suffers from the same deficiency as the previous one; the two players can double and redouble their prices as often as they choose without diminishing the demand for their products.

---

*There is, for instance, a restaurant in Paris whose luncheon specialty is a 100-gram slice of truffle on top of a 100-gram slice of foie gras. So if truffles cost less, say than bologna, the author alone would eat some hundred pounds of them each year.

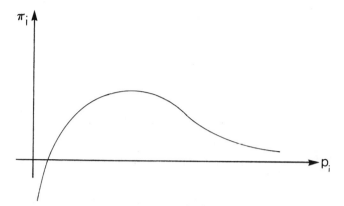

FIGURE 2.7A

8. A BETTER MODEL

A quite satisfactory model may be obtained, on the other hand, by using the demand functions (2.5.4) and considering the prices $p_3, \ldots, p_N$ of the goods $X_3, \ldots, X_N$ which are all the substitutes for X_1 and X_2. For then the demand for X_i may be written

$$(2.8.1) \qquad D_i(p_1, p_2) = \cfrac{1}{1 + \left(\dfrac{m_i p_i}{m_j p_j}\right)^\alpha + m_i^\alpha p_i^\alpha \left[\left(\dfrac{1}{m_3 p_3}\right)^\alpha + \cdots + \left(\dfrac{1}{m_N p_N}\right)^\alpha\right]},$$

where $i, j = 1, 2$ and $i \neq j$. The quantity R defined by the relation

$$(2.8.2) \qquad \frac{1}{m_3^\alpha p_3^\alpha} + \cdots + \frac{1}{m_N^\alpha p_N^\alpha} = \frac{1}{R^\alpha}$$

may be called the market's "receptivity" to the brands X_1 and X_2, and we shall assume it to be a known constant. Large values of R are favorable to the firms 1 and 2, but small ones are not. If $m_1 = m_2 = 1$, for instance, R is the price each must charge to control just a third of the total market. And if $c > R$, neither firm can expect so large a market share.

It is useful to write $p_i = R P_i$ for $i = 1, 2$, so that the demand functions (2.8.1) become

$$(2.8.3) \qquad D_i(P_1, P_2) = \cfrac{1}{1 + m_i^\alpha P_i^\alpha + \left(\dfrac{m_i P_i}{m_j P_j}\right)^\alpha}.$$

Also, we may write $c = RC$, and recall $m_1 = 1$. So in the symmetric case $m_2 = m_1$, the firms' profit functions are

$$(2.8.4) \qquad \pi_i(P_1, P_2) = \frac{R(P_i - C)}{1 + P_i^\alpha + (P_i/P_j)^\alpha}.$$

The graphs of these still have roughly the form indicated in Figure 2.7A, so their maxima are attained when $\partial \pi_i/\partial P_i = 0$ and $P_i^*(P_j)$ is therefore the positive root of

$$(2.8.5) \qquad \frac{P_j^\alpha}{1 + P_j^\alpha} = (\alpha - 1) P_i^\alpha - \alpha C P_i^{\alpha - 1}.$$

The locus of points (P_i, P_j) satisfying (2.8.5) is a curve in the $P_i P_j$-plane which must be determined numerically for specific values of α and C.

A graphical method for doing this is indicated in Figure 2.8A, where the line $l : y = (\alpha - 1) P_i - \alpha C$ and the curve $y = \omega P_i^{1-\alpha}$ are shown. They meet at a single point $Q = Q(\alpha, \omega, C)$ in the positive quadrant, and if $\omega = P_j^\alpha/(1 + P_j^\alpha)$, the ordinate of Q is the desired root of (2.8.5). It is possible, from this construction, to infer the behavior of $P_i^*(P_j) = P_i^*(P_j; \alpha, C)$ as a function of the opponent's price P_j and of the parameters α and C.

As P_j increases from 0 to ∞, for instance, ω increases from 0 to 1 and Q moves upward along l to a limiting position Q_1 on $y = P_i^{1-\alpha}$. And $P_i^*(P_j)$ must simultaneously increase from $P_i^*(0) = \alpha C/(\alpha - 1)$ to the "monopolists' price" obtained by putting $P_j = \infty$ in (2.8.5), then extracting (by some approximate method) the positive root. Thus for any P_j, $P_i^*(P_j)$ always lies between the "lowest competitive price" $P_i^*(0)$ and the monopolists' price $P_i^*(\infty)$.

As C increases, on the other hand, l moves to the right, remaining always parallel to itself, and $P_i^*(\infty)$ is better and better approximated by $P_i^*(0)$. These observations account for the shapes of the sample curves Γ_i shown in Figure

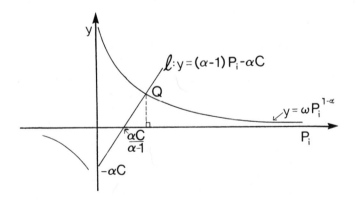

FIGURE 2.8A

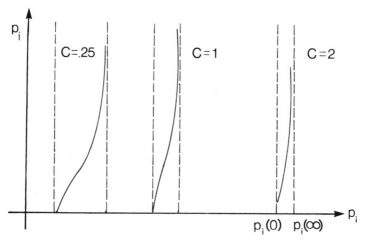

FIGURE 2.8B

2.8B for the parameter values $\alpha = 2$ and $C = .25$, $C = 1$, and $C = 2$. For large values of C there is a price which differs little from the monopolists' price $p_i^*(\infty)$, and which is nearly optimal against any price that one's opponent might charge.

Moreover, for large values of C, there is small incentive for the players to collude in fixing prices. For the solution of the problem

$$(2.8.6) \qquad \underset{P_1, P_2 \geqslant 0}{\text{maximize}} \; \pi_1(P_1, P_2) + \pi_2(P_1, P_2)$$

occurs when $P_1 = P_2$ is the positive root of

$$(2.8.7) \qquad (\alpha - 1) P_i - C P_i^{\alpha - 1} = 2.$$

And the effect of increasing C on the root of (2.8.7) may be inferred from Figure 2.8A by setting $\omega = 2$; that root must also approach $P_i^*(0)$ and $P_i^*(\infty)$ as C becomes large. For instance, if $C = 2 = \alpha$, the root of (2.8.5) is about 4.45, while $P_i^*(0) = 4$ and $P_i^*(\infty) = 4.236. \ldots$ But the players suffer less than a 1 percent loss of profit if they use the robust strategy 4.12 instead of the optimal collusive price 4.24. On the other hand, if C is only 1 and $\alpha = 2$, the incentive to collude is considerably larger. And if C is very small, firms 1 and 2 have almost the unlimited ability to collude that the truffle cooperatives enjoyed earlier.

Very small values of C doubtless do occur from time to time in actual commerce, but only when 1 and 2 are the sole producers of a cheap substitute for a commodity so essential that the demand for it is near perfectly inelastic. For $C < 1$ implies that 1 and 2 can control more than two-thirds of the total market while operating at a profit. And ordinarily one would expect new producers of the cheap substitute to enter the market in such circumstances. Therefore it seems likely that, if and when the present game is actually played out, the parameters are such that very robust strategies are available to the players and there is but small incentive for them to abandon those strategies in favor of more collusive ones.

This likelihood is only increased if one considers also the dependence of $P_i^*(P_j; \alpha, C)$ on α. For clearly $\alpha C/(\alpha - 1)$ and $-\alpha C$ decrease to C and $-\infty$, respectively, as α grows large, so l approaches the vertical line $P_i = C$ as a limiting position. And at least if $C > 1$, the part of $y = \omega P_i^{1-\alpha}$ in the half-plane $P_i > C$ moves steadily downward as α increases. So $P_i^*(0)$, $P_i^*(\infty)$, and the positive root of (2.8.5) all tend to C as α grows large.

It should be remarked in this connection that the monopolists' price, the collusively optimal price, and all robust prices will exceed $\alpha C/(\alpha - 1)$. So unless one has in mind a market wherein competition is so sluggish that 100 percent markups are common, one should expect $\alpha > 2$. Indeed the values $\alpha = 4$, $\alpha = 5$, and $\alpha = 6$, corresponding to minimal markups of $1/3$, $1/4$, and $1/5$, seem typical of a number of retail operations. And discount houses that function on 10 percent markups suggest that α's as large as 11 may sometimes prevail.

Of course the above remarks are purely speculative, for the final determinations of α and C must be empirical. And that has not yet been undertaken. But it may be inferred from Table 2.8C that, even when C and α are quite small highly robust strategies for both players do exist, and those strategies are approximate solutions of (2.8.1) as well. For the price 4.12 is better than 99 percent optimal against $.25 < P_j < \infty$ when $C = 2 = \alpha$. And as remarked earlier, $\pi_i(4.12, 4.12) > .99\pi_i(4.45, 4.45)$, so that the incentive to collude is also small in that case. Similar results are obtained for other large values of C and α, but if both are small, collusion remains attractive.

TABLE 2.8C

P_j	$P_i^*(P_j)$	$\Pi_i^*(P_j)$	$\Pi_i(4.12, P_j)$	%
0	4	0+	0	0
.25	4.01	7.33^{-3}	7.32^{-3}	99+
.5	4.05	.025	.025	99+
.75	4.09	.044	.044	99+
1	4.12	.061	.061	99+
2	4.19	.095	.095	99+
3	4.21	.107	.107	99+
4	4.22	.111	.111	99+
5	4.23	.114	.114	99+
8	4.233	.116	.116	99+
10	4.234	.117	.117	99+
00	4.24	.118	.118	99+

9. ASYMMETRY

It will sometimes happen that $m_2 \neq m_1$, and/or that the two firms will bear somewhat different costs of production. But those complications do not materially affect the foregoing analysis, for robust strategies will still exist and the incentive to collude will remain small. This is most easily seen from an examination of Table 2.8C, wherein it is to be expected in the symmetric case that one's opponent's price will lie between his production cost $C = 2$ and the optimal collusive price of about 4.5.

Clearly $P_i = 4.12$ is nearly optimal against the entire interval $2 < P_i < 4.5$ and is therefore a "good strategy" in the symmetric case. But if one's opponent bears a higher production cost $C_j > C_i = 2$, it can only cause him to raise P_j somewhat. And since $P_i = 4.12$ is more than 99 percent optimal against all large values of P_j, it remains a good strategy when $C_j > 2$. Or if firm j's cost C_j were smaller than 2 (but not smaller than .25), that would not matter either. For 4.12 is nearly optimal against $P_j > .25$ also. But if $C_j < .25$, firm i is at a severe disadvantage and will probably be driven out of the market very quickly, regardless of what strategy it uses.

Similarly, if m_2 is somewhat greater than $m_1 = 1$, firm 2 is at a disadvantage, and must lower its price somewhat. Or if $m_2 < 1$, firm 2 can charge more than 1 can. But if the difference in the m's is great enough to force i to consider P_j's in the interval $0 < P_j < .25$, i will probably be driven out of business anyway.

In short, the earlier conclusions concerning the symmetric case are little altered by small asymmetries in the model. Indeed, the same table of values can be used to evaluate a proposed action (e.g., the action $P_i = 4.12$ in Table 2.8C) in such cases. But gross inequities in the market structure can render the game unprofitable to the disadvantaged player. If a competitor can produce the same item you can at an eighth the cost, no kind of game theory will help.

10. DEPARTURES FROM THE MODEL

Clearly the version of Bertrand's game with which the previous sections have been concerned depends on the assumption (2.8.1) about the demand functions. And in markets described by demands of the form (2.8.1), a plot of D_1 against P_1 while P_2 is held fixed will always have the form shown in Figure 2.10A. But one can just as well imagine curves of other shapes, for instance that in 2.10B. That curve is the graph of a convex combination of two functions of the type (2.8.1), and gives rise to a profits curve of the shape indicated in Figure 2.10C instead of that in Figure 2.7A. The latter is even flatter near its maximum than the former, so robust strategies are even easier to find.

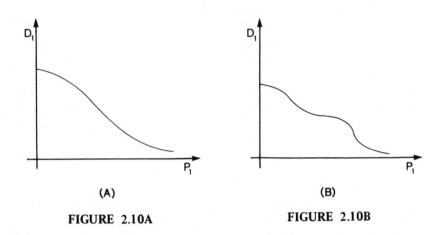

(A)   (B)

FIGURE 2.10A   **FIGURE 2.10B**

(2-6) *Question* The simplest case in which the demand curves have the shape
2.10B would appear to be that in which (2.8.3) is replaced by

$$D_1(P_1, P_2) = \tfrac{1}{2}(1 + P_1^\alpha + (P_1/P_2)^\alpha)^{-1} + \tfrac{1}{2}(1 + P_1^\alpha + (P_1/2P_2)^\alpha)^{-1}$$

$$D_2(P_1, P_2) = \tfrac{1}{2}(1 + P_2^\alpha + (P_2/P_1)^\alpha)^{-1} + \tfrac{1}{2}(1 + (2P_2)^\alpha + (2P_2/P_1)^\alpha)^{-1},$$

so that half the customers rather strongly prefer brand X_1 to X_2 while the rest
are indifferent. Here α must be rather large, and a calculator is indispensable.

We shall not report on the numerical investigation of any market ruled by
such a "composite" demand law as that indicated in Figure 2.10B. We remark
only that a very few such cases have been examined, and that the results have
been as Figure 2.10C suggests; increased robustness and diminished incentive to
collude when compared with markets ruled by "pure" demand laws of the kind
shown in Figure 2.10A and postulated in (2.8.1). The remark is included here
to lend credence to the opinion that robust strategies and small incentive to

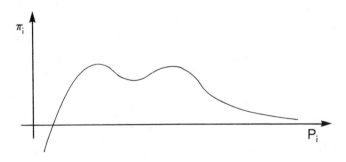

FIGURE 2.10C

collude are genuine market phenomena rather than curiosities to be expected only under certain strained hypotheses on the buyers' choice process.

Substantial support for that opinion must, of course, await empirical evidence concerning the demand laws which actually do prevail in important markets, and extensive numerical investigations based on the results thereof. But such evidence could well fill a book of its own and is far beyond the scope of the present volume. Therefore, for the present, we must content ourselves with the *suggestion* that the conclusions to which we have been led for a narrow class of markets *may in time* prove valid in much less restrictive circumstances.

11. A GAME OF RESOURCE ALLOCATION

It has now been shown that "good strategies" exist for the players in a variety of simple market games. Next to be considered is a game in which the players' decisions concern a single scarce resource, namely labor, of which each has a fixed supply, and which each must divide between two separate activities.

Following Ricardo [7], we consider the trade in wine and wool which passes (or used to pass) between England and Portugal. England, we shall assume, produces wool but no wine, while Portugal makes wine but no wool. Ships sail back and forth between the two countries, according to a prescribed schedule. And for simplicity we shall suppose them to travel fully laden in each direction. For then the rates at which wine arrives in England and wool arrives in Portugal depend only on the number of ships engaged in the trade.

Let a be the rate, in yards per week, at which England produces woolens. And let α be the rate, in barrels per week, at which Portugal produces wine. Also let d be the rate at which wine comes into England and let δ be the rate at which wool arrives in Portugal. Then wine is consumed in England at the rate of d barrels per week and in Portugal at the rate $\alpha - d$. And if it be further assumed that the total supplies of wool in the two countries remain constant, as presumably they would in the long run, wool must get "consumed" in Portugal at the rate δ yards per week and in England at the rate $a - \delta$.

Therefore, let us assume that England's "satisfaction" from the wine-wool trade is proportional to the product

(2.11.1) $$\pi_E = (a - \delta)d,$$

while Portugal's is proportional to

(2.11.2) $$\pi_P = (\alpha - d)\delta.$$

It is each nation's objective to divide its work force between the activities necessary for the trade, namely, production and transportation, in such a way as to make large its own satisfaction.

To see how this may be done, assume that England has a work force of L

men. Each man may be put to work either producing wool or transporting both wine and wool to and fro across the ocean. If he is assigned to production, a man will produce b yards of wool in a day, whereas if he is assigned to transportation he will process r barrels of wine and ρ yards of wool in that time. Similarly, Portugal has a work force of Λ men, each of whom may be assigned either to the production of wine or to transportation. If wine, he will produce at a rate of β barrels per day, while if put to transportation he can (as can an Englishman) process r barrels of wine and β yards of wool in a day. For definiteness, we may think of all transportation workers as sailors. Then our earlier assumptions imply that each nation's capacity to import goods from the other is proportional to the total number of sailors in their combined economy. That is as one would expect, since each ship (and hence each sailor) must spend half its time sailing from England to Portugal, and half returning.

If μ and ν denote the number of English and Portugese laborers, respectively, engaged in production, and if $\mathcal{L} = L + \Lambda$, one may write

$$(2.11.3) \qquad a = b\mu, \quad \alpha = \beta\nu, \quad d = r(\mathcal{L} - \mu - \nu), \quad \delta = \rho(\mathcal{L} - \mu - \nu)$$

The quantities μ and ν are at the nations' disposal, so the game between them may be summarized in the form

$$(2.11.4) \qquad \begin{aligned} &E \max_{0 \leqslant \mu \leqslant L} \quad r(\mathcal{L} - \mu - \nu)[b\mu - \rho(\mathcal{L} - \mu - \nu)] \\ &P \max_{0 \leqslant \nu \leqslant \Lambda} \quad \rho(\mathcal{L} - \mu - \nu)[\beta\nu - r(\mathcal{L} - \mu - \nu)]. \end{aligned}$$

It is convenient, before commencing the search for good strategies wherewith to play the game (2.11.4), to introduce the dimensionless quantities

$$(2.11.5) \qquad s = r/\beta, \quad \sigma = \rho/b, \quad x = \mu/\mathcal{L}, \quad y = \nu/\mathcal{L},$$

in terms of which the functions π_E and π_P may be rewritten

$$\begin{aligned} \pi_E &= (b\beta\mathcal{L}^2)\, s(1 - x - y)\,[x - \sigma(1 - x - y)] \\ &= -(b\beta\mathcal{L}^2)\,[(s + s\sigma)\,x^2 + (s + 2s\sigma)\,xy + s\sigma y^2 \\ &\quad - (2s\sigma + s)\,x - 2s\sigma y + s\sigma] \end{aligned}$$

$$(2.11.6)$$

$$\begin{aligned} \pi_P &= (b\beta\mathcal{L}^2)\,\sigma(1 - x - y)\,[y - s(1 - x - y)] \\ &= -(b\beta\mathcal{L}^2)\,[s\sigma x^2 + (\sigma + 2s\sigma)\,xy + (\sigma - s\sigma)\,y^2 \\ &\quad - 2s\sigma x - (2s\sigma + \sigma)\,y + s\sigma]. \end{aligned}$$

Clearly, strategic decisions in the game are not affected by the factor $b\beta\mathcal{L}^2$ appearing in both π_E and π_P, so we may choose to solve the somewhat simpler game

$$(2.11.7) \qquad \begin{aligned} &E \max_{0 \leqslant x \leqslant L/\mathcal{L}} \quad s(1 - x - y)[x - \sigma(1 - x - y)] \\ &P \max_{0 \leqslant y \leqslant \Lambda/\mathcal{L}} \quad \sigma(1 - x - y)[y - s(1 - x - y)] \end{aligned}$$

instead of (2.11.4). It is clear from (2.11.7) that only a two-parameter family of decision problems is under consideration here.

We begin, as usual, with Cournot's analysis. We discover that $\partial \pi_E / \partial x$ and $\partial \pi_P / \partial y$ vanish along the lines

(2.11.8)
$$l_E: \ Ax + y = 1.$$
$$l_P: \ x + By = 1,$$

where A and B are given in terms of s and σ by

(2.11.9) $\qquad A = (2 + 2\sigma)/(1 + 2\sigma), \quad B = (2 + 2s)/(1 + 2s).$

Those lines intersect at the point

(2.11.10)
$$x^* = (1 - B)/(1 - AB)$$
$$y^* = (1 - A)/(1 - AB),$$

so that if $0 \leqslant x^* \leqslant L/\mathcal{L}$ and $0 \leqslant y^* \leqslant \Lambda/\mathcal{L}$, the point (x^*, y^*) is the unique Cournot-Nash equilibrium of the game (2.11.7). It is also a point of stable equilibrium, since Cournot's iterative procedure converges to it as indicated in Figure 2.11A, whose resemblance to Figure 2.1A should be noted. It remains to consider questions of robustness.

(2-7) *Exercise* As remarked in the text, the coordinates (2.11.10) specify the location of the Cournot-Nash equilibrium so long as those coordinates are feasible. But suppose $x^* > L/\mathcal{L}$. What is the equilibrium then? Does the iterative process depicted in Figure 2.11A still lead to it, irrespective of starting point?

A cursory examination of the matter can be made for the general case, though

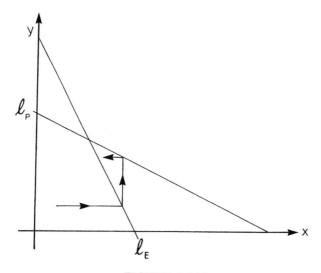

FIGURE 2.11A

a detailed discussion must await the determination of parameters s and σ. To the former end, observe that

$$(2.11.11) \qquad\qquad \pi_E^*(y) = \pi_E(x^*(y), y) = \frac{(1-y)^2}{4(1+\sigma)},$$

while for fixed values of x, the graphs of the functions $\pi_E(x, y)$ are parabolas which open downward in the yz-plane as shown in Figure 2.11B. That figure illustrates, perhaps as dramatically as any can, the inadequacy of Cournot's analysis by itself. For it is concerned only with Figures 2.1A and 2.11A, which are identical. But the Figures 2.1B and 2.11B reveal that the present game is many times more difficult to play than was Cournot's. For the graphs of the several $\pi_E(x, y)$ do not follow that of $\pi_E^*(y)$ in 2.11B as the curves $\pi_1(x, y)$ do $\pi_1^*(y)$ in 2.1B.

The parabolas $z = \pi_E(x, y)$ cross the y-axis in Figure 2.11B at the points $(1 - x, 0)$ and $(1 - x - x/\sigma, 0)$, the distance between them being x/σ. So if σ is very small, these parabolas are fat, and one may choose an x which yields large positive values of $\pi_E(x, y)$ for a wide variety of y's. But if σ is large, the parabolas are narrow and the choice of an appropriate x requires an accurate prediction of y by E.

To guess the orders of magnitude of s and σ, one must observe that together they measure the relative difficulty of production as opposed to transportation. For instance, if $s = \sigma = 0$, sailors can transport no goods between the two countries. Or if $s = \sigma = 1/2$, a given sailor can transport as many goods in a year back and forth between the countries as he could produce if he spent half the year in

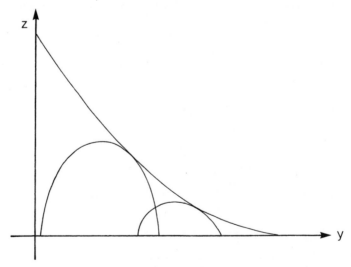

FIGURE 2.11B

TABLE 2.11C

y	$\pi^*(y)$	$\pi(.5, y)$	%	$(\%)^{1/3}$
$0 \leq y < .25$	+	–	–	–
.25	.047	0	0	0
.30	.041	.02	49	79
.35	.035	.03	86	95
.40	.030	.03	100	100
.45	.025	.02	80	93
.50	.021	0	0	0
$1 > y > .50$	+	–	–	–

Portugal making wine and half in England making wool. So one may expect s and σ to exceed $1/2$, for it seems reasonable that a sailor should handle more cargo in a year than a man can make in that time.

Thus it is not possible to find strategies for this game which are nearly as robust as those we have found for the other games we have examined. For instance, Table 2.11C illustrates the situation for $\sigma = 2$. The action $x = .5$, which is exactly optimal against $y = .4$, does not even earn a positive return if $0 \leq y \leq .25$ or if $.5 \leq y \leq 1$. And no other action $0 \leq x \leq 1$ is significantly more robust! But this does not automatically indicate that the game has no good strategies, for the present game differs from those previously considered in one important respect.

In the other games considered in this chapter, the players' actions have been prices or activity levels, which they may be assumed to control absolutely. A price can double or halve overnight and can fluctuate daily over a significant range. A production rate can change nearly as fast. But in the present game, the quantities we so blithely allocated to England's and to Portugal's control were no less than the compositions of their respective populations. In practice, some men are sailors, some shepherds, some vintners, and some weavers. To shift a man from one occupation to another may require a considerable retraining period in addition to real personal sacrifice on his part. So the nations cannot, even if they wish to do so, cause x and y to change rapidly over time, or to fluctuate wildly the way prices and activity levels sometimes can.

In short, the present values of x and y provide much more reliable guides to their future values than (say) the present values of P_1 and P_2 may be supposed to do in the version of Bertrand's game considered earlier. Thus, it seems entirely likely that the very limited robustness evident in Figure 2.11B and in Table 2.11C is *as adequate* to the needs of England and Portugal as the much more strikingly robust actions of the previous games appeared for the players in them.

It is impossible to assert more, for to show that the robust actions available to E and P really are adequate to their needs, more must be known of the nature of those needs. For instance, an examination of the incentive programs available to Portugal for inducing agricultural workers to leave the land and put to sea might reveal that y can be changed by at most 6 percent per annum. And σ might be such that the present value of x is 94 percent optimal against the present y, and any other y that could be reached within the next five years. So the present x is adequate for now but can cease to be if a new incentive program is invented in Portugal.

It is of course possible that a more elaborate dynamic model could exhibit Portugal's alternatives for controlling y explicitly so that the adequacy (or inadequacy) of England's available x's would be apparent from the analysis. (Dynamic models will be discussed in the latter part of this book.) But the present very simple analysis based on Figure 2.11B and Table 2.11C is more basic and should be understood first. It may also prove sufficient for a number of practical purposes.

It should be pointed out, before proceeding to another problem, that the negative entries in Table 2.11C are fictitious. They are the result of exporting more wool from England than is produced there, which is of course impossible because of our requirement that the quantity of wool in use in each country remain constant. All such negative values of π_E or π_P should therefore be replaced by zero. Also, in this regard, it should be mentioned that reasons exist (though we shall not describe them here) for replacing π_E and π_P with $f(\pi_E)$ and $g(\pi_P)$, where f and g are strictly concave real functions of a real variable, possibly the cube-root function. The extent to which that alters the robustness profile of the x's is suggested by the column headed $(\%)^{1/3}$ in Table 2.11C. It does not seem significant, but it does serve to emphasize the difference between the present game, wherein there is no obvious scale against which to measure the degree of satisfaction accruing to the players as a result of their individual actions, and those discussed previously in this chapter wherein the rewards were piles of dollars.

The indeterminacy of the parameters s and σ, functions of f and g, and the multiplicity of Pareto optimum, make it difficult to assess the players' incentive to collude in this game. So we shall not attempt to do so. It seems clear, because of the shape of the curves $z = \pi_E(x, y)$ in Figure 2.11B, that the incentive is greater in the present game than in those examined earlier, but the above-mentioned indeterminacies suggest that an attempt to assess it quantitatively is probably unwise.

(2–8) *Exercise* Calculate the locus of Pareto optimal action pairs (x, y) for this game. How does its shape vary with s and σ?

12. EXCHANGE

Perhpas the most fundamental of all games is that between a man with something to sell and another who wants to buy it. A version of that game was discussed prominently by von Neumann and Morgenstern [8], who offered a solution and compared it with others that had been advanced previously in the economic literature.

Their assumptions were that the object had a value v to the seller and a larger value V to the buyer, so that the transaction could be said to have the value $V - v$ for the two players together. They concluded that rational players would agree on a price p in the interval $v < p < V$, for otherwise the joint benefit $V - v$ of the transaction would not be realized, and that no single p in the interval is more properly called the "fair price" of the object than any other.

A more general problem concerns N potential buyers, to whom the object in question has values $V_1 \geqslant V_2 \geqslant \cdots \geqslant V_N > v$. Each would like to have it for himself, while the seller would like to extract as large a price as he can from the eventual buyer. Such a situation often prevails at an auction and has the rather obvious cooperative solution that the object will always be sold to player 1 if $V_1 > V_2$ and to one of $1, 2, \ldots, L$ if $V_1 = V_2 = \cdots = V_L > V_{L+1}$, though there is disagreement among the several theories as to whether or not the price must exceed V_{L+1} in that case. Again it is impossible that rational players could fail to realize the gain $V_1 - v$, because that is the largest gain possible for them.

It will be shown in the next chapter that certain auctions can, like the market games and allocation model just considered, be analyzed in terms of robust strategies and the like. But that analysis will lead to the conclusion that rational players must, with positive probability, leave deals unmade and property unsold even when substantial profit is to be expected from the transactions. So another area of direct disagreement between the cooperative and noncooperative theories will be revealed. But this time no appeal will be made to first principles for guidance as to which "solution" to accept, for there we have the results of the nickel experiments described in Chapter I to guide us. They strongly suggest that quite sensible people will often leave such profits unrealized and therefore that one should again reject the results of the cooperative theory in favor of the noncooperative ones.

REFERENCES

1. Cournot, A., *Researches into the Mathematical Principles of the Theory of Wealth*, N. T. Bacon, trans. 2d ed. (New York: Kelley, 1971), xxiv + 213.
2. Granger, C., and André Gabor, "Price as an Indicator of Quality; Report on an Enquiry," *Economica*, 33 (1966), pp. 43-70.
3. Case, J., "On the Form of Market Demand Functions," *Econometrica*, vol. 42, no. 1 (1974) pp. 207-210.
4. Cox, D. R., The Analysis of Binary Data, Methuen, London, 1970, pp.
5. Cox, D. R., and E. A. Chambers, "Discrimination Between Alternative Binary Response Models," *Biometrika*, 54 (1967), pp. 573-578.
6. Bertrand, J., "Review of Cournot's Researches," *Journal des Savants*, (September 1883), pp.

7. Taussig, F., *International Trade*. (New York: Macmillan, 1929).

8. von Neumann, J., and O. Morgenstern, *Theory of Games and Economic Behavior* (Princeton, N.J.: Princeton Univ. Press, 1944), xviii + 625 pp.

9. Fellner, W. J., *Competition Among the Few* (New York: Kelley, 1960), xv + 328 pp.

10. Goel, Maitra, and Montroll, *Nonlinear Models of Interacting Populations* (New York: Academic Press, 1971.)

11. Timin, M., and B. Collier, "A Model Incorporating Energy Utilization for the Dynamics of Single-Species Populations," *J. of Theoretical Population Biology*, 2 (1971), pp. 237–251.

12. Stern, D. H., "Some Notes on Oliogopoly Theory and Experiments," *Essays in Mathematical Economics in Honor of Oskar Morgenstern*, M. Shubik, ed., (Princeton, N.J.: Princeton Univ. Press, 1967), xx + 475 pp.

13. Åstrom, K, J., *Introduction to Stochastic Optimal Control Theory* (New York: Academic Press, 1970), xi + 299 pp.

Chapter 3

Auctions

An important feature of any real auction is the uncertainty that prevails concerning the value of the property to be sold. For be it five square miles of oil-bearing sands three miles below the surface of the Gulf of Mexico, a rare object of art at a New York gallery, or a two-year-old tractor at a farm auction in Wisconsin, neither the seller nor any of the prospective buyers can predict with accuracy the future benefits to be expected therefrom.

1. THE MODEL

We assume that the seller (or auctioneer) owns a property from which issues a revenue stream $R(t)$, $0 \leqslant t < \infty$ of present value V. If the property consists of oil sands, $R(t)$ might be measured in (barrels of oil/day) $\times$ ($/barrel of oil) = $/day. Or if it is a tractor, it could be computed as (working hours/day) $\times$ ($/working hour) = $/day. But if it were a Ming dynasty artifact, it is not clear how $R(t)$ might be determined. In any case, it is obvious that neither $R(t)$, $0 \leqslant t < \infty$, nor V can often be estimated with real precision.

V represents the gross profit to be realized from the ownership of the property at auction. It is proportional to the amount of oil the sands contain in the former case, or to the number of working hours left in the tractor in the latter. V is an unknown (but estimable) attribute of the property itself.

In addition, the seller 0 and each of the prospective buyers $1, 2, \ldots, N$ will have conversion factors for extracting profit from the revenue stream, so that player i can earn $$C_i \cdot V$ profit from ownership of the property. Different players can have different conversion factors. For instance, an oil company with a refinery and a chain of retail outlets close by the proposed drilling site can realize more profit from the oil, however much of it is there, than can a company whose operation is based half a continent away. And a farmer whose wife and children drive his tractors can realize more profit from a new one than a farmer who must pay a hired man to operate it. If his land drains quickly in the spring, he is similarly at an advantage. But $C_0, C_1, \ldots, C_N$ are more tangible quantities than V, and we shall assume them known, thus leaving V the only unknown in the equations

(3.1.1) $$V_0 = C_0 V, \ldots, V_N = C_N V$$

for the values to the various players of the property at auction.

The players do not know V, which is a random variable, but they often have real expertise in estimating it. Oil companies devote vast resources to exploration, and farmers spend lifetimes looking at tractors. So each of the players $i = 0, \ldots, N$ can arrive at an estimate E_i of V, and a probability distribution

(3.1.2) $$F_i(t) = \text{prob.} \{E_i \leqslant Vt\}$$

expressing the quality of his estimate, and based on his past estimating record. We assume that the players' estimates are unbiased in the sense that

(3.1.3) $$F_0(1) = F_1(1) = \cdots = F_N(1) = 1/2,$$

so each is as likely to overestimate as to underestimate the property value.

The actions available to the prospective buyers are just the nonnegative real numbers, for any one of them *can* offer to pay (by borrowing if necessary) virtually any price. And the actions available to 0, the present owner, are to accept or reject a given offer. So for $i = 1, \ldots, N$, let P_i be the price offered by prospective buyer i, and let P_0 be the minimum price for which 0 will sell. It is natural to write

(3.1.4) $$P_i = \lambda_i E_i, \quad i = 0, 1, \ldots, N$$

so that the decisions to be made by the players are choices of λ_i rather than of P_i. Then a sale is consummated if and only if

(3.1.5) $$P_i = \lambda_i E_i \geqslant \lambda_0 E_0 = P_0$$

for some $i = 1, \ldots, N$, and i earns

(3.1.6) $$V_i - P_i = C_i V - \lambda_i E_i$$

while 0 earns

(3.1.7) $$P_i - V_0 = \lambda_i E_i - C_0 V$$

herefrom. It is now possible to compute payoff functions for the several players. To do so, observe that the probability with which i offers a price $P_i = \lambda_i E_i$ in "infinitesimal interval" $Vs \leqslant P < V(s + ds)$ while $P_j < sV$ for all $j \neq i$ is

$$\text{prob.} \{Vs \leqslant \lambda_i E_i \leqslant V(s + ds) \quad \text{and} \quad \lambda_j E_j < Vs \quad \forall j \neq i\}$$

$$= \prod_{\substack{j=0 \\ j \neq i}}^{N} F_j(s/\lambda_j) \cdot F_i'(s/\lambda_i) \cdot ds/\lambda_i,$$

provided that the F_i's are all continuously differentiable and the players' estimates are arrived at independently. And if one substitutes

$$(3.1.9) \qquad s = Ct, \quad C_i = \rho_i C \quad \text{and} \quad \lambda_i = Cx_i, \quad i = 1, \ldots, N$$

and integrates (3.1.6)-(3.1.7) over all positive t, one obtains

$$(3.1.10) \qquad \pi_i = CV \int_0^\infty (\rho_i - t) \left(\prod_{\substack{j=0 \\ j \neq i}}^N F_j(t/x_j) \right) \frac{F_i'(t/x_i)}{x_i} \, dt$$

and

$$(3.1.11) \qquad \pi_0 = CV \sum_{i=1}^N \int_0^\infty (t - \rho_0) \left(\prod_{\substack{j=0 \\ j \neq i}}^N F_j(t/x_j) \right) \frac{F_i'(t/x_i)}{x_i} \, dt.$$

The constant C is a convenience parameter; by choosing it equal to some C_i one may arrange that $\rho_i = 1$. It is clear now that, to a prospective buyer $i = 1, \ldots, N$; 0 plays no special role in the auction. His P_0 is just another competing offer (although from himself) that i must beat to obtain the property. For F_0 enters (3.1.10) just as F_j does for each $0 \neq j \neq i$. It is also clear that the constants C and V play no role in the players' decision making; V may be set equal to $1/C$ without loss of generality.

The only parameters that remain in the model are $\rho_0, \rho_1, \ldots, \rho_N$, any one of which may be assumed equal to unity, and the decision variables are x_0, $x_1, \ldots, x_N$. The players choose them in the hope of obtaining large rewards (3.1.10) or (3.1.11).

Now observe that

$$(3.1.12) \qquad \pi_0 + \pi_1 + \cdots + \pi_N = \sum_{i=1}^N (\rho_i - \rho_0) \int_0^\infty \left(\prod_{\substack{j=0 \\ j \neq i}}^N F_j(t/x_j) \right) \frac{F_i'(t/x_i)}{x_i} \, dt$$

is exactly the total net gain to be expected from the transaction. If $\rho_0 \geqslant \rho_i$ for $i = 1, \ldots, N$, then only the auctioneer can expect to gain from the sale of the property whereas, if $\rho_i \geqslant \rho_0$ for some i, then player i can expect a share of the profit resulting from the sale of the property. More detailed information concerning the game can be obtained, it seems, only after the distributions $F_0, F_i, \ldots, F_N$ are specified.

2. BIDDING FOR JARS OF NICKELS

When the property at auction is a jar of nickels, data are available from which to infer the nature of the distributions $F_0, F_1, \ldots, F_N$ of the players' estimates.

For the guesses in table 1.8A of the number of nickels contained in one particular jar follow a simple pattern. Specifically, it may be argued that those data are
well explained by the hypothesis

(3.2.1) $$F(t) = \text{prob. } \{E \leqslant 341\, t\} = t^3/(1 + t^3),$$

E being a "typical estimate." To test that hypothesis, it is convenient to rephrase
it in the equivalent form

(3.2.2) $$\log\,(F(t)/(1 - F(t))) = 3 \log t.$$

For then if t_i be the value of the ith smallest estimate divided by 341, and if
$F(t_i)$ be interpreted as the fraction of the estimates not exceeding t_i, the points
(x_i, y_i) defined by

(3.2.3) $$y_i = \log\,(F(t_i)/(1 - F(t_i))) \quad \text{and} \quad x_i = \log t_i$$

ought all to lie along the straight line $y = 3x$. And, as will be seen from Figure
3.2A, they do for the most part.

Of course more sophisticated tools of the statistician's trade may be brought
to bear on problems like these. For instance, the least-squares estimate of the
slope of the line through the origin which best fits the points shown in Figure
3.2A is $m = 2.47$. And if the leftmost point be ignored as an outlier (as doubtless
it should be, since 42 nickels is a monumentally foolish guess), the least-squares
estimate increases to $m = 2.85$. Moreover, "robust" estimation techniques can
yield [12] all manner of confidence intervals for m, goodness of fit assurance,
and the like. But such sophisticated methods of inference do not seem likely in
the present case to alter the conclusion already apparent from the figure; namely
that it is difficult to reject the hypothesis $y = 3x$ on the evidence supplied by
these data. Thus it may be presumed that a theory of auctions predicated on
the assumption that the underlying uncertainties follow distributions of the
form

(3.2.4) $$F_i(t) = 1/(1 + t^{-\alpha})$$

applies at least to the ones held in classrooms using jars of nickels as properties
of unknown value. In fact it applies to less frivolous kinds of auctions as well.

(3-1) *Exercise*   Test the alternative hypothesis that the logarithms of the estimates are normally distributed, as suggested by Capen, Clapp, and Campbell [2] .

3. A SINGLE PROSPECTIVE BUYER

For simplicity, let us assume that there is but one prospective buyer for the
property at auction and that that property is in fact an offshore oil-drilling site
being offered, not for sale, but for rent, by the U.S. government. In this case

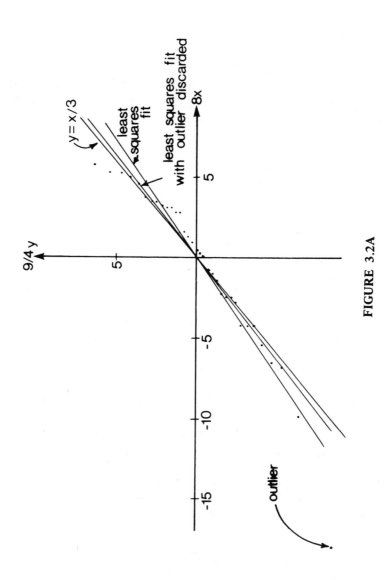

FIGURE 3.2A

there is evidence [1] that the underlying probability distributions (3.2) are in fact the log-normal distribution and that roughly the same quality of information is available to all prospective buyers and to the government. Then, as pointed out in Chapter II, little if anything is lost by replacing log-normal with log-logistic to obtain

(3.3.1) $F_0(t) = 1/(1 + t^{-\alpha_0})$ and $F_1(t) = 1/(1 + t^{-\alpha_1})$.

In fact, there is a suspicion that the oil companies have historically been better guessers than the government, so that $\alpha_0 < \alpha_1$. But that is a secondary effect; the assumption $\alpha_0 = \alpha_1 = \alpha$ seems entirely adequate as a first approximation.

Indeed, under the hypothesis that the random variables $X_i = \log E_i$ are normally distributed for $i = 0, \ldots, N$ about their zero means, Capen, Clapp, and Campbell [2] have suggested that 1.2, .6, and, .3 are appropriate values of their common variance σ^2 in certain situations of practical interest. So if the X_i's are to be logistically distributed, and have the variances observed by the authors named above, the corresponding values of α must be 1.66, 2.34, and 3.31. For the variance of a logistically distributed random variable is

(3.3.2) $\pi^2/3\alpha^2$,

which roughly equals 1.2 when $\alpha = 1.66$, and so on. We shall use these values of α shortly to perform certain numerical experiments. And we shall always assume $\alpha > 1$ to insure the convergence of certain integrals.

(3-2) *Exercise* Imagine that the same jar of nickels were shown to a very large audience and that two are selected from it whose guesses are in fact correct. Tell them both that their guesses are either correct or wrong by a factor of ρ, so that the true value of the jar is with equal likelihood $G, \rho G$, or $G/\rho, G$ being the value of their common guess. Give the jar to one of them and instruct him to sell it to the other if he can expect to profit thereby. Is a sale likely? What prices may be offered? What will the experimenter observe?

(3-3) *Exercise* Consider (3-2) again, but select an infinite sequence $1 < \rho_1 < \rho_2 < \cdots$ of ρ's and tell the guessers that the jar has value $G\rho_i$ or G/ρ_i with probability p_i for each $i = 1, 2, \ldots$ or has value G with probability p_o, where $p_o + 2\Sigma_i p_i = 1$. What property of the information furnished the guessers is responsible for the players' behavior? Is that property shared by the distribution (3.2.1)? The log-normal distribution?

(3-4) *Exercise* Repeat exercise (3-2), giving the seller better information (a value of ρ nearer unity) than the buyer. How does this affect the likely outcome of the experiment?

It is convenient to write, in the case $N = 1$,

(3.3.3) $x_1 = x, x_0 = y$, and $p_0 = p < 1 = p_1$.

Then if we make the hypothesis (3.3.1), the payoff function (3.1.10) takes the form

(3.3.4) $\quad \pi_1(x, y; \alpha) = \int_0^\infty (1 - t)\left(\frac{t^\alpha}{y^\alpha + t^\alpha}\right)\frac{x^\alpha \cdot \alpha t^{\alpha-1}\, dt}{(x^\alpha + t^\alpha)^2}$.

And substituting $\beta = 1/\alpha$, $t = xu^\beta$, and $r = (y/x)^\alpha$, the latter becomes

(3.3.5) $\quad\quad\quad\quad \pi_1(x, r; \beta) = I(r) - x J(r; \beta)$

where

(3.3.6) $\quad\quad\quad\quad J(r; \beta) = \int_0^\infty \left(\frac{u}{r+u}\right)\frac{u^\beta du}{(1+u)^2}$

and $I(r) = J(r; 0)$. Similarly

(3.3.7) $\quad\quad\quad\quad \pi_0(x, r; \beta) = x J(r; \beta) - \rho I(r),$

so that the evaluation of π_0 and π_1 reduces to that of I and J. Clearly

(3.3.8) $\quad \dfrac{t}{(t+r)(1+t)^2} = \dfrac{1}{r-1}\left(\dfrac{r}{(t+r)(t+1)} - \dfrac{1}{(1+t)^2}\right)$

when $r \neq 1$, so that

(3.3.9) $\quad I(r) = \dfrac{r}{r-1}\int_0^\infty \dfrac{dt}{(t+r)(t+1)} - \dfrac{1}{r-1}\int_0^\infty \dfrac{dt}{(1-r)^2} = \dfrac{r \log r}{(1-r)^2} + \dfrac{1}{1-r}$,

and

(3.3.10) $\quad J(r; \beta) = \dfrac{r}{r-1}\int_0^\infty \dfrac{t^\beta\, dt}{(r+t)(1+t)} - \dfrac{1}{r-1}\int_0^\infty \dfrac{t^\beta\, dt}{(1+t)^2}$,

the last two integrals above not being amenable to elementary methods of quadrature. But

(3.3.11) $\quad \int_0^\infty \dfrac{t^\beta\, dt}{(1+t)^2} = B(1 + \beta,\ 1 - \beta) = \Gamma(1 + \beta)\Gamma(1 - \beta)/\Gamma(2)$

$\quad\quad\quad\quad\quad\quad = \beta\Gamma(1 - \beta)\Gamma(\beta) = \beta\pi/\sin \beta\pi,$

where $B(\cdot, \cdot)$ and $\Gamma(\cdot)$ are the classical [3] beta and gamma functions. The remaining integral may be evaluated by contour integration in the complex plane [4, §74], utilizing the contour sketched in figure 3.3A and the Cauchy residue theorem. The details of that computation are omitted. If one writes $\gamma = \pi/\sin \beta\pi$, the result is

(3.3.12) $\quad \int_0^\infty \dfrac{t^\beta\, dt}{(1+t)(r+t)} = \gamma\left(\dfrac{1 - r^\beta}{1 - r}\right),$

which agrees in the limit as $r \to 1$ with (3.3.11). Therefore

(3.3.13) $$J(r; \beta) = \gamma \left(\frac{r^{1+\beta} - r}{(1 - r)^2} + \frac{\beta}{1 - r} \right),$$

if $r \neq 1$. When $r = 1$, the expressions (3.3.10) and (3.3.11) are no longer defined. But then, from (3.3.6)-(3.3.7),

(3.3.14) $\quad I(1) = B(2, 1) = 1/2 \quad$ and $\quad J(1, \beta) = B(2 + \beta, 1 - \beta) = \dfrac{\beta(1 + \beta)\gamma}{2}$,

so that π_1 and π_2 may be evaluated for all positive values of r. Similarly

(3.3.15) $\quad I(0) = B(1, 1) = 1 \quad$ and $\quad J(0, \beta) = B(1 + \beta, 1 - \beta) = \beta\gamma$,

so that

(3.3.16) $\quad \pi_0(x, 0; \beta) = \beta\gamma x - \rho \quad$ and $\quad \pi_1(x, 0; \beta) = 1 - \beta\gamma x$.

It is now possible to search numerically for good actions (or strategies) x and y.

For the fixed value $y = 0$, the buyer's payoff function $\pi_1(x, y; \alpha)$ vanishes when $x = 0$ and agrees with the linear form $1 - \beta\gamma x$ when $x > 0$. Moreover, it

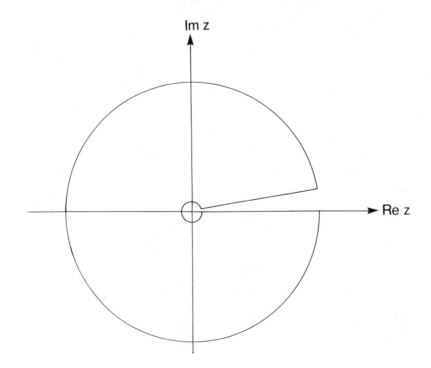

FIGURE 3.3A

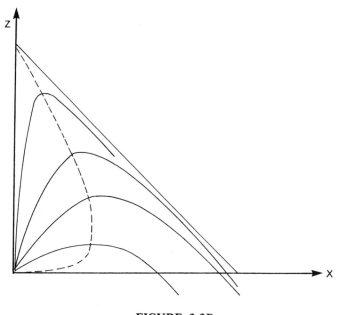

FIGURE 3.3B

seems intuitively obvious that $\pi_1(x, y; \alpha) < \pi_1(x, 0; \alpha)$ when x and y are both positive. So for fixed values of y, the graphs of $z = \pi_1(x, y; \alpha)$ must have roughly the shapes indicated in Figure 3.3B. This was first confirmed numerically by B. T. Smith [5], who performed extensive numerical experiments for the case $\alpha = 2$.

It is true too for the values 1.66, 2.34, and 3.31 of α suggested by the work of Capen, Clapp, and Campbell [2], and certain other values as well.

In particular, the peaks of those graphs all occur along a curve Λ in the xz-plane (the broken curve in Figure 3.3B), which lies near the vertical line $x = .2$ for much of its length when $\alpha = 2.34$. This suggests that $x = .2$ should be a good strategy for the buyer against a wide variety of actions by the seller, an expectation which is confirmed numerically in Table 3.3C.

The action $x = .2$ is apparently a conservative one; Table 3.3C indicates that the game rewards conservative action on the part of the buyer. The effect is further accentuated if one considers relative profit as well as absolute profit in distinguishing good actions from bad. To compute the relative profit to be expected from a pair (x, y) of actions, suppose the players take those actions in each of m auctions. Then if m is large the total profit earned by 1 will be about $m \cdot \pi_1 = m(I - xJ)$, and his total expenditure for the properties he buys will be mxJ. So his relative profit (\$ earned/\$ spent) will be just $(I/xJ) - 1$. And if one plots the latter quantity against x, holding y fixed, one discovers that relative profit is a very rapidly decreasing function of x indeed. A few such plots are shown in Figure 3.3D. They indicate that it is much better for 1 to

TABLE 3.3C

y	π*(y)	π(.1,y)	%	π(.2,y)	%	π(.3,y)	%
.05	.657	.626	95	.637	97	.542	82
.1	.504	.396	79	.504	99+	.462	92
—	.397	.767	67	.390	98	.381	96
.2	.317	.186	59	.301	95	.311	98
—	.255	.135	53	.237	93	.752	99
.3	.206	.101	49	.188	91	.205	99+
—	.167	.078	47	.150	90	.166	99+
.4	.135	.061	45	.121	90	.134	99+
—	.110	.049	45	.098	89	.109	99+
.5	.089	.040	45	.081	90	.088	99+
.6	.059	.036	61	.058	98	.052	88
.75	.032	.021	66	.032	99+	.021	66
.9	.017	.013	76	.017	99+	.003	18

choose $x < x^*(y)$ than $x > x^*(y)$. For if $x > x^*(y)$, there is an $x' < x^*(y)$, which earns 1 the same absolute profit x does, but for a far smaller cash outlay.

This observation provides a strong argument against the choice by 1 of liberal actions, and in particular of dominated actions. For it follows from the shapes

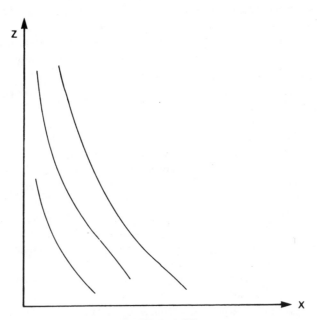

FIGURE 3.3D

of the relative and absolute-profit curves shown in Figures 3.3B and 3.3D that, if x is a dominated action, then the action

(3.3.17) $$x^{**} = \max_{y \geqslant 0} x^*(y)$$

provides a greater absolute return than x does against every $y \geqslant 0$, *and* does so for a lesser initial expenditure.

It is necessary in this game to argue that undominated actions are unwise, because the game itself is obviously not simply directed. While we cannot prove a theorem to the effect that the buyer should *never* take a dominated (ultra-liberal) action, it does seem safe to conclude that he should not do so without some very firm and enforceable commitment on the seller's part to similarly liberal behavior. Indeed, the nature of an adequately firm and enforceable commitment is difficult to foresee.

The seller's situation is quite different, as is clear from Figure 3.3E. There a number of the curves $z = \pi_0(x, y; \alpha)$ are shown for fixed values of x, and for the parameter value $\rho = .6$. They all slope gently downward to the right of their maxima and plunge precipitously to negative values left of it. So 0 suffers little penalty if he chooses $y > y^*(x)$, but much if y is substantially smaller than $y^*(x)$. The seller too is rewarded for conservatism.

The nature of the game is further clarified if we sketch the curves $x = x^*(y)$ and $y = y^*(x)$ in the xy-plane, as is done in Figure 3.3F. There a single point (x^*, y^*) of intersection is shown, and it is a stable equilibrium in Cournot's sense. But more can be said.

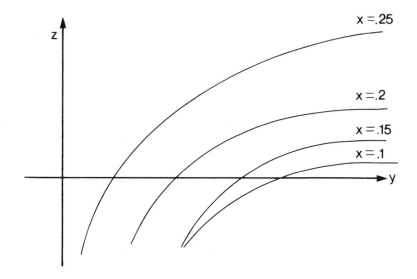

FIGURE 3.3E

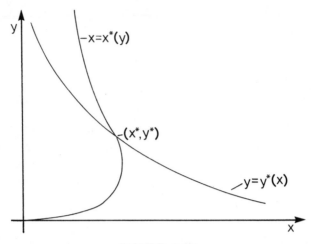

FIGURE 3.3F

The fact that the curves shown in Figure 3.3E move generally upward as x increases reflects the fact that 0 wants high bids from 1. But since the graph of $x = x^*(y)$ is entirely contained in the strip $0 \leqslant x < .3$, there is apparently nothing 0 can do to draw out bids higher than $x = .3$ from 1. Indeed, the values in Table 3.3C indicate that even by announcing the very liberal act $y = .35$ for himself, 0 is unlikely to influence 1 to choose $x > .2$. For with $x = .2$, 1 is 90 percent optimal when $y = .35$, and better still if y is larger. Moreover, there is considerable incentive for y to be larger, since $\pi_0(x, .35; 2.34) < 0$ unless $x > .3$.

Conversely, there is little 1 can do to influence 0 to choose $y \leqslant .9$. For $y = .9$ yields excellent returns against moderate and large values of x without the risk of loss should 1 choose some such conservative action as $x = .1$ or $x = .15$.

In short, conservative actions in this game are large values of y for 0 and small values of x for 1. Overly conservative behavior on either or both their parts makes it unlikely that a sale will take place. For the probability of a sale is $I(r)$, which tends to zero as x gets small or y large. Thus if, as explained above, it is not to be expected that 1 will be more liberal than $x = .2$ or 0 than $y = .9$, then $r \geqslant 33.768 \ldots$ and $I(r) \leqslant .08$. That is, negotiations will lead to no sale at least 92 percent of the time!

The players in such a game are faced with a genuine dilemma, for each would like to close a deal and claim a share of the $\$(1 - \rho)$ profit to be expected therefrom. But only if $y < x$ does the probability $I(r)$ of a sale exceed that of no sale. And it is difficult to arrange that y exceed x because, as explained above, such liberal actions as $x > .2$ and $y < .9$ are fraught with risk.

The nature of that risk is clarified if one observes the close analogy between the dilemma of the present game and the Prisoner's Dilemma discussed in

Chapter I. Indeed, if one considers a simplified version of the present game in which each player has only one conservative action (call it C) and one liberal one (L), the analogy becomes exact. To see this, let the buyer's conservative action C be $x = .2$ and his liberal one L be $x = .45$. The former seems appropriate because it earns a moderate but positive return against a wide variety of y's, while the latter is more risky since

$$\pi_1(.45, y; 2.34) < 0 < \pi_1(.2, y; 2.34)$$

for many y's but greatly facilitates the closing of deals. And let the seller's C be $y = .9$ and his L be $y = .4$ for similar reasons. Then the players' respective reward matrices become as shown in (3.3.18).

(3.3.18)

Buyer's rewards

y \ x	C	L
C	.017	-.042
L	.121	.080

Seller's rewards

y \ x	C	L
C	.015	.142
L	-.021	.138

These exhibit the characteristic trait of the Prisoners' Dilemma, namely the incentive each player has to reach an agreement with the other to play liberally, then dishonor it. But that aspect of the game (3.3.18) plays no role in it, at least as it is ordinarily played. Statements like "I'll offer you 60 percent of what I think it's worth if you'll promise to accept 40% of what you think it's worth" sound so patently absurd that they are never even made, and a player is simply a fool who behaves liberally in this game without obtaining (at the very least) verbal assurance that the other will do likewise.

In short, the game is a noncooperative one, and its solution is the noncooperative solution proposed by Nash and Cournot. Such utopian notions as Pareto optimality have no relevance for it. It will be shown in the following sections that the prospect of playing such games in a noncooperative manner is a less forbidding one than the minuscule rewards in the matrices (3.3.18) might at first suggest.

4. OTHER VALUES OF THE PARAMETERS

The situation is quite different if ρ is smaller than .6, for the seller is then more anxious to dispose of his property. If $\rho = .3$, for instance, the curves $z = \pi_0(x, y; 2.34)$ are as indicated in Figure 3.4A, and 0 has but little reason to fear the action $y = .3$. For it loses money only if $x < .1$ and is near-optimal against the more liberal actions $.2 < x < .3$ to be expected of 1. So here it is to be anticipated that $y \leqslant x$ and that a sale is more likely than no sale.

Finally, if $\rho = .1$, the seller becomes very anxious indeed to sell, since the

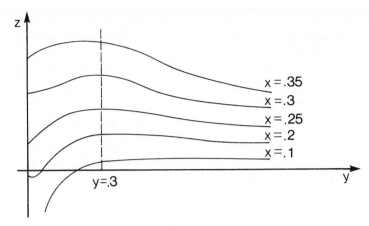

FIGURE 3.4A

curves $z = \pi_0(x, y; 2.37)$ now have the shapes depicted in Figure 3.4B and have negative slope for $y > .05$. Moreover, he has no fear of losing money by the transaction unless $x < .07$, because of (3.3.16). So 0 may safely choose $y = .05$ and expect to close the deal with probability as large as $I(.015) = .95 \ldots$!

It is not, however, wise to reduce y to a value smaller than .05; since the curves are relatively flat in the interval $0 \leqslant y \leqslant .05$, exact optimality against an expected x is of little value. And $x^*(y)$ decreases rapidly to zero in that interval, so that $y < .05$ is merely an invitation to 1 to bid low. It is better to lose one deal in twenty, but claim a substantial share of the total profit $1 - \rho$ to

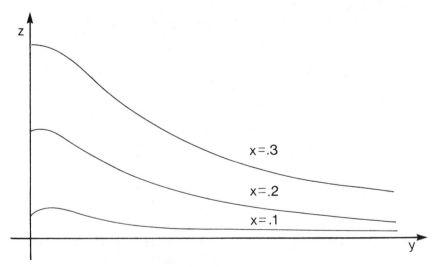

FIGURE 3.4B

be expected from a deal successfully closed, than to close them all (by choosing $y = 0$), thereby leaving all the profit to the buyer. Occasionally farmers *do* have to burn their crops!

This is to be emphasized; each player can unilaterally prevent any deal from going unmade. For 0 can choose $y = 0$, thereby accepting any offer 1 might make, and 1 can choose $x = \infty$ by expressing a willingness to pay whatever price 0 shall ask. But any other actions $0 < x, y < \infty$ yield $0 < I(r) < 1$, so that with some positive probability no sale results.

Better information, in the form of large values of α, is an aid to the closing of deals because better-informed players are less richly rewarded for conservative play. For instance, if $\alpha = 10$, the curves $z = \pi_1(x, y; \alpha)$ have roughly the shapes indicated in Figure 3.4C. Those look much like the ones in figure 3.3B, but they are shifted away from the z-axis, as is the locus Λ of their zeniths. So x's as large as .7 or .8 are perhaps to be expected from 1. Indeed if $\rho = .6$, 0 can do much to encourage such liberal bids. For it is clear from the curves $z = \pi_0(x, y; \alpha)$ sketched in Figure 3.4D that actions as liberal as $y = .6$ are relatively safe ones for 0. They lose money only if $x < .45$, and they earn very nearly an optimal return for x's in the range $.45 < x < .9$. So it is quite easy to imagine even rather cautious players adopting such liberal actions as $x = .75$ and $y = .6$, in which

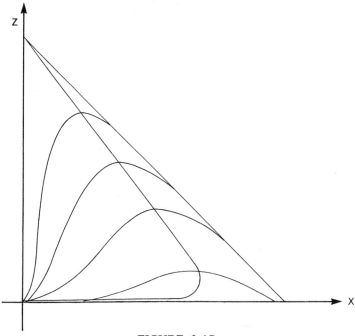

FIGURE 3.4C

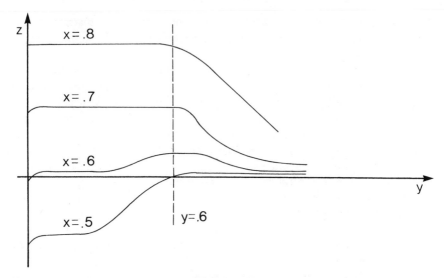

FIGURE 3.4D

case the probability $I(r)$ of closing the deal becomes .820, a far cry from the .08 ... that we found earlier for the case $\alpha = 2.34$.

If we conclude from the examination of Figures 3.4C and 3.4D that $y = .6$ is a relatively liberal action for 0 while $y = .1$ is a conservative one, and that $x = .75$ is liberal for 1 while $x = .25$ is conservative, our attention is directed to the bimatrix game shown in (3.4.1). And no theory is required to see that both

(3.4.1)

Buyer's rewards

y \ x	C	L
C	0	.007
L	.001	.171

Seller's rewards

y \ x	C	L
C	0	.042
L	0	.157

players should play liberally in it! With properly propitious parameters, the dilemma of the game disappears. We consider next two cases in which $\alpha_0 \neq \alpha_1$.

5. DISPARATE INFORMATION

If $\alpha_0 \neq \alpha_1$ in (3.3.1), the evaluation of the functions π_0 and π_1 becomes more difficult. For (3.3.4) must then be replaced by

$$(3.5.1) \quad \pi_1(x, y; \alpha_0, \alpha_1) = \int_0^\infty (1 - t) \left(\frac{t^{\alpha_0}}{t^{\alpha_0} + y^{\alpha_0}} \right) \frac{x^{\alpha_1} \cdot \alpha_1 t^{\alpha_1 - 1} \, dt}{(x^{\alpha_1} + t^{\alpha_1})^2} .$$

And through the substitutions $\beta = 1/\alpha_1$, $t = xu^\beta$, $r = (y/x)^{\alpha_1}$, and $\alpha_0 = \sigma\alpha_1$, the latter gives

(3.5.2) $\pi_1(x, r; \beta, \sigma) = I(r, \sigma) - xJ(r; \beta, \sigma)$

where

(3.5.3) $$J(r; \beta, \sigma) = \int_0^\infty \left(\frac{u^\sigma}{r^\sigma + u^\sigma}\right) \frac{u^\beta \, du}{(1 + u)^2}$$

and $I(r; \sigma) = J(r; 0, \sigma)$. Similarly

(3.5.4) $\pi_0(x, r; \beta, \sigma) = xJ(r; \beta, \sigma) - \rho I(r; \sigma)$.

Moreover, by the further transformation $u = \tan^2 \theta$, J may be reduced to

(3.5.5) $$J(r; \beta, \sigma) = \int_0^{\pi/2} (1 + (r/\tan^2 \theta)^\sigma)^{-1} \tan^{2\beta} \theta \sin \theta \cos \theta \, d\theta,$$

which is singular only if $\beta > 1/2$. For smaller values of β, the integral is easy to evaluate numerically.

Let us examine, for instance, the case in which $\alpha_0 = 2.34$, $\alpha_1 = 4.68$, and $\rho = .6$. It differs from that considered in §3.2 only in that the buyer now has a distinct informational advantage. For his estimates cluster more tightly about the true value of the property at auction than do the seller's.

The curves $z = \pi_1(x, y; \alpha_0, \alpha_1)$ still look much like those in Figure 3.3A, especially for small values of y. That is as one would expect, since the limit as r goes to zero of $J(r; \beta, \sigma)$ does not depend on σ. But for larger values of y, the curves' maxima are shifted slightly to the right, an effect reflected in Figure 3.5A wherein the graphs of $x = x^*(y)$ are shown for several values of α_1. These indicate that the optimal x against a particular y increases slowly as α_1 becomes large, so that better-informed buyers may be expected to behave somewhat more liberally than their less well informed counterparts. But the effect is not dramatic. For even when $\alpha_1 = 11.7$, so that the buyer has the quite remarkable informational advantage indicated by the probability density functions shown in Figure 3.5B, $x^*(y) < .45$ for all y. Indeed, as in the symmetric case discussed earlier, the buyer has always to choose actions in the interval $0 \leqslant x_1 \leqslant .93$ to avoid negative expectations, because of (3.3.16). Moreover, he is strongly motivated to choose undominated actions $0 \leqslant x \leqslant .45$. For the curves

$$z = \pi_1(x, y; 2.34, \alpha_1)$$

slope down and to the right rather abruptly for $x > .45$ when α_1 is large and y fixed.

The seller's payoff curves $z = \pi_0(x, y; 2.34, 4.68)$ also look much like those obtained for the symmetric case, as will be seen from a comparison of Figures

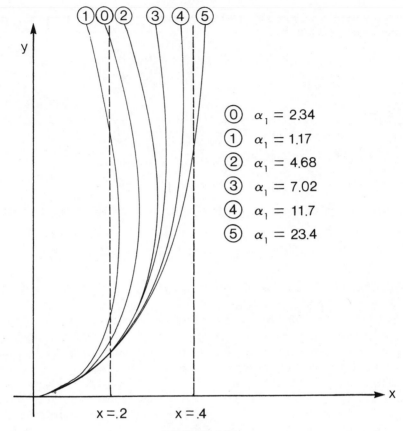

FIGURE 3.5A

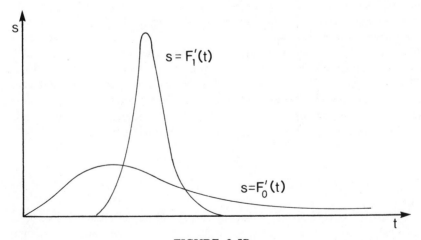

FIGURE 3.5B

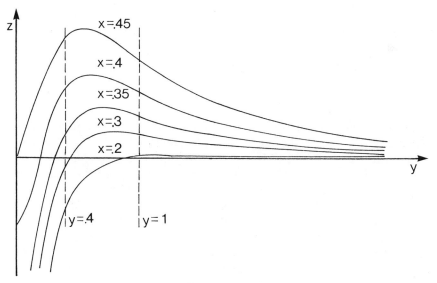

FIGURE 3.5C

3.4D and 3.5C. But they reveal the risk 0 takes in behaving liberally while so handicapped by poor information. For though $x = .2$ is quite a good (if somewhat conservative) action for player 1, 0 can earn a positive expectation against it only by the very conservative actions $y \geqslant .9$. And those actions render the probability of no sale very close indeed to unity. Only if 1 can persuade 0 that $x > .2$ is it at all likely the transaction can be effected to the benefit of both parties.

The point is clarified if we observe from Figure (3.5C) that $y = 1$ is a conservative action for 0, whereas $y = .4$ is a very liberal one. Similarly, $x = .2$ is quite conservative, for 1 and $x = .55$ is liberal. These choices lead to the bimatrix game (3.5.6), which is not an instance of the Prisoner's Dilemma, since the seller

(3.5.6)

Buyer's rewards

y \ x	C	L
C	.013	−.048
L	.107	.068

Seller's rewards

y \ x	C	L
C	.001	.140
L	−.028	.194

would have no incentive to increase y from $L = .4$ to $C = 1$ after the outcome (L, L) had been agreed upon. But the buyer has a definite incentive to decrease x from $L = .55$ to $C = .2$, and that fact alone seems adequate to assure conservative behavior on both players' parts. That the buyer earns more than the seller in that event seems a natural consequence of his informational advantage. And that both players earn so little seems natural too, in view of the fact that the information available to each of them is poor.

An interesting fact emerges from a comparison of the bimatrices (3.3.18) and (3.5.6), namely that the buyer earns more in the symmetric information game than in the present one. For the effect of his extra information is principally to frighten the seller into very conservative behavior. If, on the other hand, he could obtain the information secretly, 0 would not be frightened by it. So he would choose $y \leqslant .9$ as in the symmetric case, and 1 could earn at least $\pi_1(.3, .9; 2.34, 4.68) = .019$ in the game. So the additional information appears valueless to him unless he can obtain it secretly, in which case he can pay as much as 0.2 percent of the value of the property for it. Lest than seem insignificant, recall that offshore oil lands have leased for as much as \$200 million.

Let us also examine a case wherein the advantage lies with the seller. For definiteness, we choose the case $\alpha_0 = 4.68$ and $\alpha_1 = 2.34$. Then the curves $z = \pi_1(x, y; \alpha_0, \alpha_1)$ have again the shapes indicated in Figure 3.3B, but their maxima (and therefore Λ) are somewhat shifted to the right so that much of Λ lies in the strip $.4 < x < .5$. Hence $x = .4$ and $x = .45$ are good strategies for 1. And as in the symmetric case $\alpha_0 = 2.34 = \alpha_1$, $\pi_1(x, y; \alpha_0, \alpha_1) < 0$ when $x > .73$, so it is hard to imagine 1 choosing an $x > .5$ in any circumstances. For the curves $z = \pi_1(x, y; \alpha_0, \alpha_1)$ slope rather steeply downward to the right in the range $x > .5$.

The curves $z = \pi_0(x, y; \alpha_0, \alpha_1)$ are also qualitatively little changed from earlier cases, as will be seen from a glance at Figure 3.5D. But they are not as high as the former, and they all go negative for small values of y. From our examination of them it appears that $y = 1.2$ is a fairly conservative strategy while $y = .5$ is quite a liberal one. As remarked above, $x = .5$ is quite liberal for 1, whereas $x = .25$ is conservative. So with but little loss of content, we may restrict our attention to the bimatrix game (3.5.7), which is not an instance of the Prisoner's Dilemma either; for the buyer would have no reason to decrease x from $L = .5$ to $C = .25$ after (L, L) were agreed upon. But now the seller has rea-

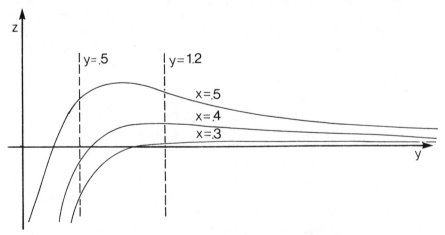

FIGURE 3.5D

(3.5.7)

Buyer's rewards		
$_y$\\$^x$	C	L
C	.014	-.002
L	.053	.160

Seller's rewards		
$_y$\\$^x$	C	L
C	0	.081
L	-.022	.40

son to switch y from L = .5 to C = 1.2. Fear that he might do so is probably sufficient to deter most buyers from such liberal acts as x = .5. We observe in passing that the better-informed player earns more than his opponent when both play conservatively.

6. A COMMENT ON METHOD

Repeatedly in this chapter we have used graphs like (3.3B) and (3.4D) to extract from the continua of possible x's and y's a few which seem representative of whole classes (e.g., the classes of liberal and conservative actions), then studied the bimatrix games obtained by discarding all but the single representative of each class. This is not, of course, to assert that the bimatrix game so obtained is identical with the original game. But it is to be recommended as a quick way to discover difficulties which lie in wait for the players of certain games and to exhibit those difficulties in their most simple and concise form.

It is doubtless even possible (though not particularly desirable) to prescribe rules of thumb for choosing L and C. But most decision makers will find it more satisfying to choose their own L's and C's by examining the graphs $z = \pi_0(x, y; \alpha)$ and $z = \pi_1(x, y; \alpha)$, and so on. Different decision makers will make different choices. Some may even wish to include a middle-of-the-road alternative M as well as an L and a C, thereby constructing a 3×3 bimatrix game instead of a 2×2. But the various choices will lead to similar conclusions unless there is serious disagreement as to what constitutes liberal and what conservative behavior.

If after several attempts, the bimatrices are all of the type (3.4.1), liberal behavior is to be expected from both players and a successful negotiation seems in prospect. But if dilemma games like (3.3.18), (3.5.6), and (3.5.7) persistently appear, substantial difficulties stand in the negotiators' path.

7. A FUNDAMENTAL PRECEPT

One fact has emerged again and again in the foregoing discussion. It may be stated as follows:

In order to achieve the (obviously desirable) transfer of a property from an owner for whom it has small value to another for whom it has more, at least tacit agreement as to what the values are is required. But in the absence of accurate information concerning those values, agreement will be difficult to achieve and hence transfer to effect.

That observation seems a fundamental fact* of economic life. But it has rarely been enunciated as one, and most writers seem to regard it as a paradox that such a transfer might *ever* fail to be made. In particular, it is so treated by the entire cooperative theory of games, whose axiom of Pareto optimality it contradicts. Hopefully, the fact no longer seems paradoxical to the reader.

8. POLICY IMPLICATIONS

The bidding models to which this chapter is devoted were originally developed to facilitate the discovery of good strategies for leasing offshore oil lands. Lease auctions are held regularly by the Bureau of Land Management of the Department of the Interior, and oil companies have historically paid billions of dollars for such leases. We seek now to determine the conditions under which the government should accept or reject a given bid. Since the theory so far developed admits only a single buyer, we must restrict our attention to tracts on which only one bid is received. There were [6, p. 29] 290 single bids received for Louisiana outer continental shelf lands between October 1954 and April 1964, so such tracts are not uncommon.

It seems reasonable to assume that the quality of the information available to both the government and the oil company submitting the bid is the same and is fairly represented by the value $\alpha = 2.34$ suggested earlier. But it is not so clear how the remaining parameter, namely ρ, should be determined. Recall that C_i was defined to be a conversion factor, whereby player i could convert one barrel of oil into $\$C_i$ profit by use of his refining and marketing processes, and that $\rho = C_0/C_1$. But the U.S. government is not active in the oil industry and has therefore no established conversion factor C_0. How, then, is ρ to be determined?

Perhaps the simplest device is to suppose that the United States were to buy an existing oil company with the intent to operate it as a commercial venture. Conventional wisdom has it that the efficiency of the company would then decline, so that the newly created C_0 would be smaller than the C_i's prevailing in the industry at large. Indeed if conventional wisdom is in error on this point, nationalization of the oil industry would appear highly desirable.

We do not quarrel with conventional wisdom. Rather, we assume that the Department of the Interior has been able, in some fashion, to arrive at a figure for C_0 and that in fact $C_0 < C_1$. Indeed, we assume for definiteness that $C_0 = .6C_1$, so that $\rho = .6$. One would doubtless prefer to believe ρ larger so that a bureaucrat could earn as much, say, as 3/4 of a capitalist. But our conclusions are largely unchanged if ρ lies elsewhere in the interval $.6 < \rho < 1$.

---

*Return to exercise 3-2.

If $\alpha = 2.34$ and $\rho = .6$, our parties sit squarely on the horns of the dilemma of the game (3.3.18). Liberal behavior is so riskly for both players that it is hard to imagine $y < x$, as required for the probability of no sale to be less than a half.

The game (3.3.18) has only four outcomes, namely CC, LC, CL, and LL. In the latter case, many tracts are leased and brought into production, which benefits the public because it increases the fuel supply and the government's nontax revenues. But as remarked earlier, the outcome LL is difficult to achieve. In the case CL, wherein the seller remains liberal but the buyer grows conservative, the public suffers because the government's nontax revenues decline and fewer new lands are developed. But the oil companies prosper. Indeed in this case, the public interest would be better served if the woefully inept ($\rho = .6$, remember) government went into the oil business and developed the lands itself. In the case CC each party receives a fair share of the profit from the tracts leased, but to the public's despair most offerings result in no sale. Finally, in the case LC, the oil companies fall victim, as the matrices (3.3.18) show.

In short, only the difficult outcome LL offers benefit to all parties concerned, and even that results in no sale with probability .455. Can the rules of the game be changed so as to improve the outlook for all concerned?

It seems quite possible that they can, for if the government employed disinterested parties to engage in exploratory drilling on the lands in question and to make their findings available well in advance of the date of the auction, the participants' information would be more reliable than the geophysical data they now typically have. Perhaps even the level $\alpha = 10$ could be achieved, so that the game to be played would resemble (3.4.1) instead of (3.3.18).

The details of how such an end may be achieved will not be pursued here. Who the "disinterested parties" are to be, and how their findings are to be distributed, require careful consideration. But so obvious are the advantages of (3.4.1) over (3.3.18) for all, that quite likely an agreement could be reached concerning them. In short, the public (i.e., the government) is at liberty to change the rules of the game, and the foregoing analysis suggests that substantial benefit could result from such change.

9. RECURRENT NEGOTIATIONS

Certain agreements expire after a specified time, and have to be renewed periodically. Labor union contracts and arms limitation pacts are familiar examples. Moreover the precise benefits of a particular commitment are doubtful at the time it is agreed to, for those benefits are distributed over the full term of the treaty or contract. Their value remains unknown until the time of their realization, which is often far in the future. Clearly, then, the winner's curse is a feature of such negotiations.

When an agreement is reached in a situation wherein lurks the winner's curse, it is usually because one or both of the parties involved overestimate the benefit to themselves. Moreover it is typically clear, at renewal time, that the originally expected benefits have not materialized. Thus, the negotiators on either side are motivated to drive an even harder bargain next time, making subsequent agreement more elusive still. Consequently, the effect of the winner's curse is not dissipated but *compounded* by the recurrent nature of these agreements.

10. SEVERAL PROSPECTIVE BUYERS

The word "auction" ordinarilly suggests a plurality of prospective buyers, and it is time now to deal with that aspect of the problem. In doing so, we shall focus our attention first on the decision to be made by a typical prospective buyer. For to him the auctioneer's P_0 is, as pointed out in §3.1, just another competing offer which he must beat to obtain the property at auction. F_0 enters (3.1.10) just as does F_j for each $0 \neq j \neq i$. Only after we have analyzed a typical bidder's prospects shall we return to ask how 0 shall choose P_0.

It will be convenient, in what follows, to assume that each π_i save π_0 is a decreasing function of x_j for $j \neq i$ and a unimodal function of x_i. Extensive numerical evidence indicates that these assumptions are indeed correct, but as yet analytic proofs have not been found.

If the assumptions are correct and if x_0 is given some fixed (unalterable by 0) value, the game played by the remaining players is simply directed. So there is no reason for the bidders to take dominated actions. Or if x_0 is restored to 0's control, $i \neq 0$ has only one motive to take a dominated action; namely the promise of a side payment from 0. For 0 is the only player who can benefit by such action on i's part.

Side payments by an auctioneer to a bidder are commonly known as kickbacks; they are widely frowned upon by the auctiongoing public and are punishable by law in most states. Therefore, we shall assume that a rule against them is enforceable and in force. Hence, no bidder has cause ever to take a dominated action.

It shall be pointed out that while the bidders should not collaborate to secure large bids they may well do so (either overtly or otherwise) to secure low ones. This aspect of the problem is investigated at length in [7], where it is shown how two rival bidders may collude tacitly to secure vastly improved profits for themselves. But we shall not pursue the notion here, as it is felt that a sufficiently active auctioneer can and normally will deny that strategy to the bidders.

It will be convenient also to adopt the notational conventions

$$(3.10.1) \quad \rho_1 = 1, \quad x_1 = x, \quad x_0 = y_1, \quad x_2 = y_2, \ldots, \quad \text{and} \quad x_N = y_N,$$

to assume for simplicity that all F_j's have the form (3.3.1) and also that the α_j's all have the common value α for $j = 0, 1, \ldots, N$. Then the integral (3.10.1) takes the form

$$\pi_1(x, y_1 \ldots, y_N; \alpha)$$

(3.10.2)
$$= \int_0^\infty \frac{(1-t)}{[1+(y_1/t)^\alpha] \cdots [1+(y_N/t)^\alpha]} \frac{x^\alpha \cdot \alpha t^{\alpha-1} \, dt}{(x^\alpha + t^\alpha)^2},$$

which reduces to

(3.10.3) $$\pi_1(x, y; \alpha, N) = \int_0^\infty (1-t) \left(\frac{t^\alpha}{y^\alpha + t^\alpha} \right)^N \frac{x^\alpha \cdot \alpha t^{\alpha-1} \, dt}{(x^\alpha + t^\alpha)^2}$$

when $y_1 = \cdots = y_N = y$. Moreover, the familiar substitutions $\beta = 1/\alpha$, $t = xu^\beta$, and $r = (y/x)^\alpha$ now yield

(3.10.4) $$\pi_1(x, r; \beta, N) = I_N(r) - x J_N(r; \beta)$$

where

(3.10.5) $$J_N(r; \beta) = \int_0^\infty \left(\frac{u}{r+u} \right)^N \frac{u^\beta \, du}{(1+u)^2},$$

$I_N(r) = J_N(r; 0)$, and $J_1(r; \beta) = J(r; \beta)$ because of (3.3.6). The integrals $J_N(\cdot; \cdot)$ can of course be evaluated directly as J was. But another method is available. For the identity

(3.10.6) $$\left(\frac{u}{u+r} \right)^N = \sum_{K=0}^{N-1} \binom{N-1}{K} \frac{r^K}{K!} \frac{\partial^K}{\partial r^K} \left(\frac{u}{u+r} \right)$$

permits one to write

$$P_N(D) J(r; \beta) = \sum_{K=0}^{N-1} \binom{N-1}{K} \frac{r^K}{K!} D^K J(r; \beta)$$

$$= \sum_{K=0}^{N-1} \binom{N-1}{K} \frac{r^K}{K!} D^K \int_0^\infty \left(\frac{u}{u+r} \right) \frac{u^\beta \, du}{(1+u)^2}$$

(3.10.7)

$$= \int_0^\infty \sum_{K=0}^{N-1} \binom{N-1}{K} \frac{r^K}{K!} \left(\frac{\partial}{\partial r} \right)^K \left(\frac{u}{u+r} \right) \frac{u^\beta \, du}{(1+u)^2}$$

$$= \int_0^\infty \left(\frac{u}{u+r} \right)^N \frac{u^\beta \, du}{(1+u)^2} = J_N(r; \beta),$$

where $D = d/dr$, $\binom{N-1}{K}$ is a binomial coefficient, and the operators $P_N(D)$ are defined for $N = 1, 2, \ldots$ by

(3.10.8)
$$P_N(D) = \sum_{K=0}^{N-1} \binom{N-1}{K} \frac{r^K}{K!} D^K .$$

Thus, to evaluate the expectations (3.10.4), one need only apply the operators (3.10.8) to the integrals I and J evaluated earlier. The results are

$$I_N(r) = P_N(D) \cdot I(r)$$

(3.10.9)
$$= \left(\frac{1}{1-r}\right)^N + \left(\frac{1}{1-r}\right)^2 \sum_{j=0}^{N-1} \theta(j) \sum_{l=0}^{N-1-j} \binom{N-1}{l+j} (r+l) \left(\frac{r}{1-r}\right)^l$$

and

$$J_N(r;\beta) = P_N(D) \cdot J(r;\beta)$$

(3.10.10)
$$= \frac{\beta - (\beta + N)r}{(1-r)^{N+1}} + \frac{\delta r^{1+\beta}}{(1-r)^2} \sum_{j=0}^{N-1} \frac{M_j(1+\beta)}{j!}$$

$$\sum_{l=0}^{N-1-j} \binom{N-1}{l+k} (l+1) \left(\frac{r}{1-r}\right)^l ,$$

where

(3.10.11)
$$M_j(\lambda) = \lambda(\lambda - 1) \cdots (\lambda - j + 1)$$

and

(3.10.12)
$$\theta(j) = \log r \qquad \text{if} \quad j = 0$$
$$= \frac{(-1)^{j+1}}{j} \qquad \text{if} \quad j = 1, 2, \ldots .$$

The expressions (3.10.9) and (3.10.10) of course become quite ungainly if N is at all large, but they are eminently suitable for machine computation. In particular, from (3.10.5)

(3.10.13)
$$I_N(0) = 1 \quad \text{and} \quad J_N(0;\beta) = \beta\gamma$$

as before, so that

(3.10.14)
$$\pi_1(x, 0; \beta, N) = 1 - \beta\gamma x,$$

and

(3.10.15)
$$I_N(1) = B(N+1, 1) = \frac{1}{N+1}$$
$$J_N(1;\beta) = B(\beta + N + 1, 1 - \beta) = \gamma\beta(\beta+1) \cdots (\beta+N)/(N+1)!$$

Also it is clear from (3.10.3) that for positive x, $\pi_1(x, y; \alpha, N)$ is a decreasing function of y and continuous at $y = 0$. So the curves $z = \pi_0(x, y; \alpha, N)$ must

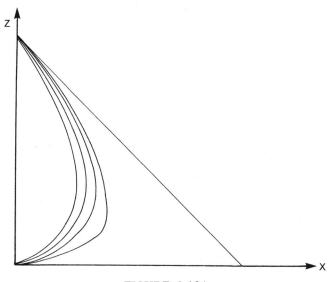

FIGURE 3.10A

still have much the shape indicated in Figure 3.3B. This is confirmed by extensive computation, the functions having been evaluated for the values $N = 1$, $2, \ldots, 10$. In particular, the curves Λ_N whereon the graphs $z = \pi_1(x, y; \alpha, N)$ attain their zeniths have been determined with some accuracy. A number of them are shown in Figure 3.10A. They move steadily outward from the z-axis as N increases, apparently toward some limiting curve Λ_*. It is of interest to determine Λ_*.

To that end, suppose that bidder I's N opponents agree among themselves to choose the action y/N^β. Then 1 will earn $\pi_1(x, y/N^\beta; \beta, N)$. Does the limit of that quantity, as N grows large, exist? Clearly if y is replaced by y/N^β, then $r = (y/x)^\alpha$ is replaced by r/N, since $\alpha\beta = 1$. So the limit in question exists if

$$(3.10.16) \qquad \lim_{N \to \infty} J_N(r/N; \beta) = J_*(r; \beta)$$

does for each $0 \leqslant \beta < 1$ and each $r \geqslant 0$. But

$$\lim_{N \to \infty} J_N(r/N; \beta) = \lim_{N \to \infty} \int_0^\infty \left(\frac{t}{t + r/N}\right)^N \frac{t^\beta \, dt}{(1 + t)^2}$$

$$(3.10.17) \qquad = \int_0^\infty \lim_{N \to \infty} \left(\frac{1}{1 + r/Nt}\right)^N \frac{t^\beta \, dt}{(1 + t)^2} = \int_0^\infty e^{-r/t} \frac{t^\beta \, dt}{(1 + t)^2}$$

$$= \int_0^\infty \frac{e^{-ru} \, du}{u^\beta (1 + u)^2} = J_*(r; \beta),$$

the next-to-last equality being obtained from the substitution $u = 1/t$. Thus $J_*(r; \beta)$ is the Laplace transform of $t^{-\beta} (1 + t)^{-2}$, and

(3.10.18) $I_*(r) = J_*(t; 0) = 1 - re^r E_1(r)$

where $E_1(r)$ is the so-called exponential integral [8]. Equation (3.10.18) is essentially #29.3.127 of [8]. For $\beta > 0$, the transform $f(r)$ of $t^{-\beta} (1 + t)^{-2}$ does not appear in the tables. However, it follows from elementary properties of the transform that

(3.10.19) $f''(r) - 2f'(r) + f(r) = \Gamma(1 - \beta) r^{\beta-1}$.

Moreover,

(3.10.20) $f(0) = \int_0^\infty \frac{t^{-\beta} dt}{(1 + t)^2} = \beta\gamma$ and $f'(0) = -\int_0^\infty \frac{t^{1-\beta} dt}{(1 + t)^2} = \beta\gamma - \gamma$,

so that $f(r)$ is the solution of the differential equation (3.10.19) meeting the side conditions (3.10.20). Therefore

(3.10.21) $f(r) = (r - \beta) e^r (\Gamma(1 - \beta) \cdot \gamma(\beta, r) - \gamma) + \Gamma(1 - \beta) r^\beta$,

where $\gamma(\cdot, \cdot)$ is the well-known "incomplete gamma function" [8]. And because excellent polynomial and rational approximations are available [9] for $E_1(\cdot)$ and $\gamma(\cdot, \cdot)$, $I_*(r)$ and $J_*(r; \beta)$ are readily evaluable for all positive r. Hence, one may determine Λ_* with some accuracy; it too is shown in Figure 3.10A. On it the functions

(3.10.22) $\pi_1^*(x, y; \alpha) = I_*(r) - x J_*(r; \beta)$

attain their maxima. And in the crescent-shaped region R between $\Lambda_1 = \Lambda$ and Λ_*, the functions (3.10.3) attain theirs for $N = 1, 2, \ldots$.

If 1's opponents take different actions, so that $y_1, y_2, \ldots, y_N$ are all distinct, one may perform the partial fraction expansion

(3.10.23) $\dfrac{1}{(1 + y_1^\alpha/t^\alpha) \cdots (1 + y_N^\alpha/t^\alpha)} = \dfrac{A_1 t^\alpha}{y_1^\alpha + t^\alpha} + \cdots + \dfrac{A_N t^\alpha}{y_N^\alpha + t^\alpha}$,

where

(3.10.24) $A_i = y_i^{\alpha(N-1)} \Bigg/ \prod_{\substack{j=1 \\ j \neq 1}}^N (y_i^\alpha - y_j^\alpha)$.

And from that follows

$\pi_1(x, y_1, \ldots, y_N; \alpha) = A_1 \pi_1(x, y; \alpha) + \cdots + A_N \pi_1(x, y_N; \alpha)$,

(3.10.25)

so (3.10.2) may be evaluated when $y_1, \ldots, y_N$ are either all equal or all distinct. Of course a combination of the two methods permits evaluation when some though *not* all of the y_i's are distinct if the occasion requires it.

Capen, Clapp, and Campbell have observed [10] that in their model, the curves $z = \pi_1(x, y_1, \ldots, y_N; \alpha)$ tend to look alike if the numbers $y_1, \ldots, y_N$ are allowed to vary while their power mean

$$(3.10.26) \qquad \left(\frac{y_1^{1/2} + \cdots + y_N^{1/2}}{N} \right)^2$$

is held constant. And more to the point, the maxima of those curves tend to fall near a common vertical line when plotted in the xz-plane. So the optimal x against one set of y's tends to be nearly optimal against any other set having the same power mean (3.10.26). That effect is observed for the present model, too, as one would expect.

Such observations are clearly important to the decision maker. Instead of guessing who his opponents are going to be and what individual y's they are likely to choose, he need only guess a single number, namely the power mean of all his opponents' y's. Since those y's are in reality random variables, their mean is easier to estimate than are their individual values.

Of course it may be doubted that either can meaningfully be estimated, but in practice it would seem that they can. For instance, Capen, Clapp, and Campbell [2] have written, "Some believe that the input requirements for a competitive bidding model are quite severe—that reliable input is impossible to obtain. We do not think so. Unless one successfully engages in espionage, he is not going to know his opponent's bid. But he does not need to. *We have found* that by studying the behavior of companies in past sales, we can get a fair clue as to what they will do in the future—close enough to make the model results meaningful [italics added]." And they have described their procedure for "studying the behavior of companies in past sales" in some detail (on pp. 648–649) there.

Clearly the operative part of their conclusion is the final clause thereof, "—close enough to . . . ." For behind it lurks the notion of robustness, without which there can be no thought of meaningful application. The fact that their analysis is widely imitated in the industry bears ample witness that their beliefs are not ill-founded.

Let us return now to the examination of the crescent-shaped region R in the xz-plane which is bounded by the curves Λ and Λ_*. All the functions (3.10.3) attain their maxima in it. And it appears from extensive empirical evidence that the functions (3.10.2) do too, though we know at present no analytic proof of the fact. The lower portion of R appears in Figure 3.10B, together with a few of the curves $z = \pi_1(x, y_1, \ldots, y_N; \alpha)$. Note the flatness of the latter as they pass through R. All the curves look much alike, and in particular, much like the curve $z = \pi_1(x, y; \alpha)$, which crosses R at the same height. The simplicity of

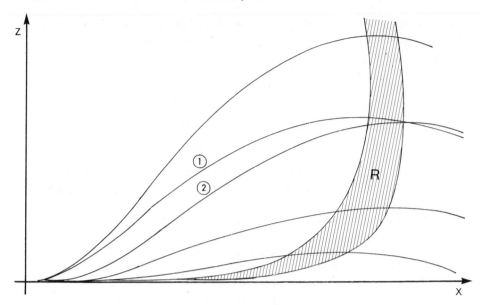

FIGURE 3.10B

their geometry permits a very simple procedure for choosing good actions in this game.

(3-5)   *Question*   An analytic proof that the curves $z = \pi(x, y_1, \ldots, y_N; \alpha)$ all attain their zeniths at points of R would be most welcome.

11. A PROCEDURE FOR CHOOSING ACTIONS

The easiest way to exhibit the utility of a decision procedure is to demonstrate its use. Let us, therefore, consider an individual (the "client") about to bid on a particular property. We assume that the client has already estimated the value of the property and has decided that from one six other bids on it will be forthcoming. He has also decided that the other bidders will, if they bid at all, offer about a quarter of their estimates of the property's worth.

To help the client choose his own bid, we plot each of the curves

$$z = \pi_1 (x, .25; 2.34, N)$$

for $N = 1, 2, \ldots, 6$, on a single sheet of paper, as is done in Figure 3.10C. Then it is apparent, for instance, that $x = .4$ is a poor bid, for it loses money if even five of the six prospective bidders decide to participate. But $x = .25$ is a good action, because it is near-optimal against all of the likely possibilities. Moreover, it is clear that because of the general flatness of the curves near the vertical line $x = .25$, further efforts of maximization are probably not worthwhile even if the exact number of opponents could be known.

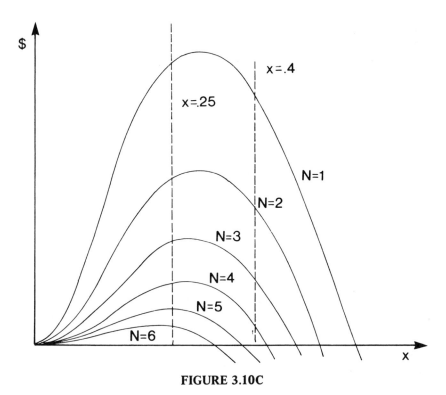

FIGURE 3.10C

Such analyses are easy to perform because a computer can be programmed to plot Figures like 3.10C for several dozen likely scenarios in a matter of seconds, though numerical integration is required if players with different information quality parameters $\alpha_1, \ldots, \alpha_N$ are to be included. The result is not always as encouraging, however, as was Figure 3.10C.

If, for instance, it is expected that the opponents who participated will bid 35 percent of their value estimates instead of 25 percent, the curves $z = \pi_1(x, .35; 2.34; N)$ must be plotted for $N = 1, \ldots, 6$. They are as shown in Figure 3.10D. They look much like those in 3.10C except that they are lower. Once again $x = .4$ is a bad action, as it loses money unless $N = 1$ or $N = 2$. And again $x = .25$ is a fairly good one as it earns money unless $N = 5$ or $N = 6$, in which case every $x \geqslant .025$ will also lose money. No action is guaranteed to earn a positive return in all of these cases, but if one does choose to bid in such an adverse situation, as well one may, $x = .2$ seems a good choice. It is relatively near-optimal in the cases $N = 1, 2, 3, 4$, wherein it makes money and loses but little when it does not.

Other expectations on the client's part lead, of course, to other figures. But the others can never look very different from 3.10C and 3.10D, because of the simple geometry of the curves $z = \pi_1(x, y_1, \ldots, y_N; \alpha_0, \ldots, \alpha_N)$. And typically only a few of those curves need be shown because of the monotone fash-

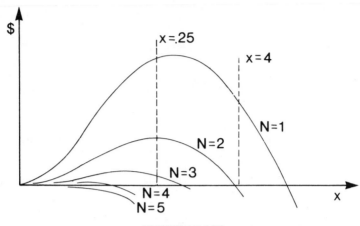

FIGURE 3.10D

ion in which π_1 depends on each y_i, $i = 1, \ldots, N$. Thus, such figures provide a very compact summary of the outcomes likely to result from the choice of a particular action x. And it is possible to select, from the continuum of possible x's, a short list thereof which seem as worthy as any of the client's considera-tion. From Figure 3.10D, for instance, one might submit the values $x = .1, .15,$ $.2, .25$, with $x = .2$ especially recommended. For $x = .1$, while involving but small risk of loss, earns less than half the return possible if $N \leqslant 3$. And $x = .25$ suffers twice the loss that $x = .2$ does when loss is inevitable, while earning only marginally more in the more favorable cases.

Precise decision rules do not seem possible, because of the uncertainty which surrounds the values of $y_1, y_2, \ldots, y_N$. Nor does precision even seem particu-larly desirable, in view of the flatness of the curves as they cross R. Finally, it is impossible to give rules for predicting $y_1, \ldots, y_N$, though Capen, Clapp, and Campbell [2] describe procedures for determining their historical values.

The point to be emphasized is that with *only the vaguest of guesses* concern-ing the nature of the opposition likely to be encountered, one can eliminate a large number of possible x's from consideration and choose from among the remainder one likely to be effective if not in any sense optimal. It is an im-portant point because it is not an obvious one. Indeed, it appears that so com-pletely has the nature of the auction environment been misunderstood in the past that $x = 1$ has been seriously advocated [11] as a bidding strategy! Small wonder, then, that adherents of the present sort of bid selection are almost uniformly enthusiastic about the results to be obtained therewith.

A natural question to ask at this point concerns the dependence of our con-clusions on the assumption of log-normality, which we transmuted slightly into log-logisticality. Capen, Clapp, and Campbell [2] have spoken briefly to this question; they have pointed out that the log-normal distribution does not ac-curately describe the uncertainty that exists concerning a tract likely to have negative value. The present theory can be augmented to comprehend the possibility of tracts of negative value, but due to limitations of space, we have chosen not to do so here. Such augmentation would have considerable practical value, for many tracts of doubtful promise will be offered at auction in the next few years.

On the positive side, it does appear that considerable relaxation of our hypotheses is possible without materially affecting the conclusions. For the factor in the integrand of (3.5.7) involving $y_1, \ldots, y_N$ is nothing more than a distribution function. And it may be reached by *any other* distribution approximable by functions of the form (3.10.23). Moreover, a rather rich variety of shapes may be attained by functions of that form, as the reader may easily convince himself in a few minutes at a computer console.

In addition, the term involving x may be replaced by a convex combination of several such terms, the result being to replace the curve

$$z = \pi_1(x, y_1, \ldots, y_N; \alpha)$$

with a convex combination of several such curves. If all the individual ones peak in the vertical portion of R, so must their convex combination. Thus, while it is hardly clear what changes can be made in the model and what cannot, one can at least say that *some* changes have very little effect on the conclusions.

12. OTHER KINDS OF AUCTIONS

To this point, only sealed-bid auctions have been discussed. It is time now to examine certain other common variants of the auction process, namely ordinary (audible) auctions and so-called Dutch auctions wherein prices are bid down instead of up. These variations, in contrast to the sealed-bid one, take place gradually over time, so the bidders have the opportunity to think, to bluff, and to revise initial estimates as such auctions progress. The implications of the fact are substantial.

Let it be assumed, to begin with, that each bidder can separate the set of all potential prices into two subsets, consisting respectively of those prices he will pay if given the opportunity and those he will not. Moreover, if he is willing to pay one price for the property in question, he is willing to buy it too at any lesser price. And if unwilling to pay one price, he is likewise unwilling to pay a higher one. From these it follows that each bidder i has a *critical price* P_i which separates the prices he will pay from those he won't.

Critical prices can vary with time, as new information concerning the property at auction is received. For surely, P_i is related to, if not identical with, i's best estimate E_i of the property's monetary value. And E_i is subject to change as additional facts become available. Moreover, as the ratio $x_i = P_i/E_i$ is again subject to i's control, it is apparent that P_i can change in response to changes in i's intent as well as in his evaluation of the property at auction. Temporarily, x_i will be called i's "tactic."

It is conceivable that a player might extract information regarding the value of the property to be sold by listening to rival bids as they are called out at an audible auction. Indeed, some students have tried to do just that during the classroom experiments described in Chapter I. But because no reliable way of doing it has yet been proposed, and because the students who tried it in the classroom usually fell victim to the "winner's curse," the attempt appears a foolish one. Accordingly, the strategies sought hereinafter do not require revision of value estimates while the auction is in progress.

It is also conceivable that information concerning other bidders' tactics can be obtained by observing their behavior during an auction. But again, no reliable way has been proposed for doing it, and none seems likely to be. Every auctiongoer knows how to bluff and can effectively disguise his intent by doing so. Some feign lack of interest while the bidding goes on around them, so not to inflate the others' value estimates or otherwise goad them to liberal action. Others pretend extraordinary interest, knowing that the "winner's curse" falls most heavily on him whose misfortune it is to outbid really determined opposition, and hoping the others present fear to do just that. Jump bids or frequent loud dones are indicative of such intent. But really these transparent ploys serve only to emphasize what every experienced auctiongoer already knows, namely that a man's early bids (or lack thereof) on a property reveal little or nothing about his final one.

In short, it seems only folly to await the receipt of information during the course of an auction which justifies revision, either of one's value estimate or of one's assessment of opposing intentions. If one need not revise one's assessment of opposing tactics, one need not alter one's own tactic either. Therefore, it may be assumed that auctiongoers will maintain *constant* value estimates E_i and *constant* tactics x_i during a typical auction. Consequently their critical prices P_i will remain constant too.

(3-6) *Question* Consider (3-2) again, but admit several buyers with disparate information (i.e., values of ρ). Is there any way one of them can improve his information by listening to his opponents' bids? Does he need to know their ρ's to do it?

If such were not the case, a strategy for an ordinary or a Dutch auction would consist of a rule for revising one's tactic in response to information received. But once it is accepted that reliable information will not be forthcoming, strategies for such auctions reduce to single tactics, *chosen (or choosable) before the bidding opens.* Thus, a strategy for either of the present sorts of auction, as for sealed-bid auctions, consists of a single number x_i chosen in advance by player i. And as the "winner's curse" is as much a feature of ordinary and Dutch auctions as of sealed-bid ones, it is to be expected that $0 \leqslant x_i < 1$.

13. EXPECTED SALE PRICES

Once it is understood that the bidders' critical prices $P_0, P_1, \ldots, P_N$ remain constant during the course of an auction, its outcome is easy to discern. If the auction is Dutch, the auctioneer starts by asking a high price, then gradually reduces his asking price until it equals the *largest* of the critical prices. At that instant, the bidder whose critical price is largest has the opportunity to buy the property at a figure acceptable to him and does so. The sale price is the largest critical price. Or if the auction is ordinary, the auctioneer begins by asking a nominal amount and increases the asking price until it is exceeded by just one critical price. Then only a single bidder remains willing to pay the asking price, and he is permitted to do so, but he does not pay his own critical price, since the asking price never goes that high. It grows only until it exceeds the *next-highest* critical price by some small amount. For practical purposes, the sale price *is* the next-largest critical price.

The consequences of this fundamental fact are noteworthy. To discover them, reflect that the "best strategy" for an ordinary or a Dutch auction (should such a thing exist) must be the same for each bidder because of the symmetry assumed earlier. Call it x^* for an ordinary auction and y^* for a Dutch one. As mentioned earlier, both numbers must be between zero and one. But there is no reason to suppose them equal. If the values of x^* and y^* were widely known, each bidder i's critical price would be $P_i = x^*E_i$ at an ordinary auction and $P_i = y^*E_i$ at a Dutch one. The several critical prices at an auction of either kind would be just the value estimate, deflated by an appropriate factor. The *statistics* of the critical prices would be exactly those of the value estimates.

To explore the nature of those statistics, the value estimates recorded in Table 1.8A are a ready guide. There are, for instance, 376,992 ways of selecting five women from among the thirty-six who guessed how many nickels the jar in question contained. And among the 376,992 "five-person auctions" that can be so formed, the woman who guessed 900 is present in 52360. So the probability that 900 be the largest of five randomly chosen estimates is just $52360/376992 = .139$. And similarly, the probability that the Kth-largest of the thirty-six estimates received be also the largest of five randomly chosen ones is the binomial coefficient

$$(3.13.1) \qquad \binom{K-1}{4}$$

divided by 376992. The vertically shaded histogram of Figure 3.13A indicates the relative frequencies with which the largest of five estimates randomly chosen from among the thirty-six received lie in the seven intervals $t_{j-1} \times 341 \leqslant E < t_j \times 341$ for which

$$(3.13.2) \qquad t_j = .4j, \quad j = 1, \ldots, 7.$$

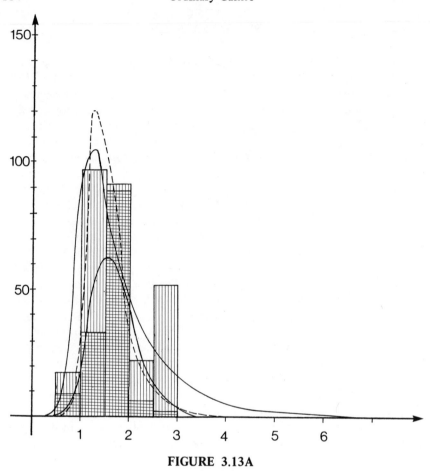

FIGURE 3.13A

The horizontally shaded histogram, by contrast, indicates the relative frequencies with which the next largest of the same five estimates fell in those intervals. Those frequencies are easily computed too, since the probability that the Kth-largest of the thirty-six estimates be also the next largest of five randomly chosen ones is

$$(3.13.3) \qquad (36 - K)\binom{K - 1}{3}\Big/376992.$$

Three effects are evident in the histograms. First, nearly all the shaded area lies to the right of the vertical line $t = 1$. This is the familiar "winner's curse" phenomenon and reflects the fact that both the highest and next highest of five randomly chosen estimates are likely to be overestimates rather than underestimates. Second, the horizontally shaded area lies nearer the vertical axis than does the other, as it must since the next largest of five estimates cannot exceed the largest. Finally, the horizontally shaded histogram shows more *central tendency* than the vertically shaded one, having only three tall columns (including the tallest) as opposed to four.

The last observation is the only possibly surprising one, and likely the most important. For it suggests that, at a long series of ordinary auctions, the sale price should vary less about its expected value than at a similar series of Dutch auctions. Both windfall profits and fiscal disasters should be less frequent. Indeed, because the horizontally shaded histogram looks as the vertically shaded one might if it were somehow made easier to guess the values of jars of nickels, the former histogram appears to advertise a substantially less risky commercial undertaking than does the latter.

Perhaps continuous theoretical distributions illustrate the effects more clearly. It was remarked in § 13.2 that the data of Table 1.8A are well explained by the hypothesis (3.2.1). So let $E_1, E_2, \ldots, E_N$ be N random variables distributed according to a particular probability distribution function $F(t)$. Then the probability that the largest of those random variables not exceed t is the probability of the event

(3.13.4) $E_1 \leqslant t$ and $E_2 \leqslant t$ and $\ldots$ and $E_N \leqslant t$,

namely $[F(t)]^N$. Similarly, the probability that the next largest not exceed t may be computed as the probability that only the first exceed t or only the second exceed t or $\ldots$ or only the last exceed t *or none* exceed t. It is

(3.13.5) $N[F(t)]^{N-1} - (N-1)[F(t)]^N$.

When, in particular, $N = 5$ and $F(t)$ is as defined in (3.2.1), the distributions are

(3.13.6) $\left(\dfrac{t^3}{1+t^3}\right)^5$ and $5\left(\dfrac{t^3}{1+t^3}\right)^4 - 4\left(\dfrac{t^3}{1+t^3}\right)^5$,

respectively, and their derivatives or "frequency functions" are

(3.13.7) $\dfrac{15t^{14}}{(1+t^3)^6}$ and $\dfrac{60t^{11}}{(1+t^3)^6}$.

These are the smooth curves appearing in Figure 3.13A, the taller, steeper one being the theoretical analogue of the horizontally shaded histogram and the lower, flatter one corresponding to the vertically shaded one. Obviously, the comments made earlier regarding the location and dispersion of the histograms apply as well to their theoretically derived counterparts.

Admittedly one can imagine histograms more closely adherent to their theoretical ideals. In particular, the rightmost two columns of the vertically shaded histogram depart noticeably from their continuous analogue. But it must be recalled that those two columns reflect only the contributions of the *largest three* of the thirty-six guesses received. So substantially better agreement between theory and observation must await experiments involving more numerous respondents. Except for those two columns of the vertically shaded histogram, the agreement between the rectilinear histograms and the smooth frequency functions seems rather good.

The dotted curve in Figure 3.13A is the graph of the derivative of the distribution function

(3.13.8) $$\left(\frac{t^5}{1+t^5}\right)^5,$$

which *would govern* the statistics of the largest of five randomly chosen guesses *if* the information-quality parameter α were increased from three to five. Plainly it more nearly resembles the taller and steeper of the two solid curves than the other one. In particular, the *tail* of the dotted curve more nearly resembles that of the taller solid curve. And the "winner's-curse" phenomenon resides primarily in the tails of the related distributions, since, for instance, the probability of overvaluing the property by a factor of more than two is the area under the relevant frequency curve and to the right of the vertical line $t = 2$.

In sum, the three curves in Figure 3.13A depict the risks inherent in three different kinds of five-person auctions. The lower solid curve and the dotted one correspond to Dutch auctions, wherein the information quality parameters are, respectively, $\alpha = 3$ and $\alpha = 5$. Plainly the latter is less risky than the former. The taller solid curve corresponds to an ordinary auction with $\alpha = 3$. Since it more nearly resembles the dotted curve than the lower solid one, one may conclude that the risk of an ordinary auction where $\alpha = 3$ is comparable to that at a Dutch auction where $\alpha = 5$, and *much smaller* than that at a Dutch auction where $\alpha = 3$. Therefore, the advantages to buyer and seller alike of ordinary auctions instead of Dutch auctions are as great and as indubitable as the advantages of information quality $\alpha = 5$ instead of $\alpha = 3$. To the seller, these advantages are the incentive to more aggressive bidding on the buyers' parts, resulting in higher expected sale prices. And to the buyers the advantage is a more predictable sale price; a reduced threat from the "winner's curse"! It is not surprising, then, that ordinary auctions *are* ordinary and Dutch ones comparatively rare.

14. DUTCH AUCTIONS

Actually, Dutch auctions are more common than most people realize. For in a sense, sealed-bid auctions are Dutch auctions. To see this, observe that bidder i at a Dutch auction wins the property and pays a price in the "infinitesimal interval" $Vt < P < V(t + dt)$ only in the event that

(3.14.1) $Vt < P_i < V(t + dt)$ and $P_j < P_i$ $\forall j \neq i.$

Moreover, assuming without loss of generality that $V = 1$ and recalling that $P_i = x_i E_i$ for every i, it follows that the event (3.14.1) occurs with probability

(3.14.2) $$\left[\prod_{\substack{j=0 \\ j \neq i}}^{N} F_j(t/x_j)\right] \cdot [F_i'(t/x_i)dt/x_i].$$

So, integrating over all positive values of t, one concludes that i's expected earnings from participation in the Dutch auction are

$$(3.14.3) \qquad \pi_i = \int_0^\infty (1-t) \left[\prod_{\substack{j=0 \\ j \neq i}}^{N} F_j(t/x_j) \right] \cdot F_i'(t/x_j)\, dt/x_i,$$

which is obviously a special case of (3.1.10). It is in this sense that sealed-bid auctions can be said to *be* Dutch auctions; the set of strategies x_i available to each player i is the same in both sorts of auction, as is the payoff

$$\pi_i(x_0, x_i, \ldots, x_N)$$

resulting from the choice of the strategy x_0 by the auctioneer, x_1 by bidder $1, \ldots,$ and x_N by bidder N.

Because of this equivalence between Dutch and sealed-bid auctions, the comparisons of the previous sections between Dutch and ordinary auctions are valid comparisons too between sealed-bid and ordinary auctions. In particular it may be concluded that, while good strategies for sealed-bid auctions are good ones for Dutch auctions as well, those strategies will be markedly too conservative for use at an ordinary auction. It remains to be seen which strategies *are* the good ones at ordinary auctions.

15. ORDINARY AUCTIONS

There are N ways for bidder i to win an ordinary auction and pay a price P in the infinitesimal interval $Vt < P < V(t + dt)$, since that is the outcome of any of the events

$$(3.15.1) \qquad \begin{aligned} & P_i > V(t + dt) \quad \text{and} \quad Vt < P_k < V(t + dt) \\ & \qquad \text{and} \quad P_j < Vt \quad \forall j \neq i, k, i \neq k = 0, 1, \cdots, N. \end{aligned}$$

So assuming once again without loss of generality that $V = 1$ and recalling once more that $P_i = x_i E_i$, the probability of a typical one of those events is

$$(3.15.2) \qquad [1 - F_i(t/x_i)] \cdot [F'(t/x_k)\, dt/x_k] \cdot \left[\prod_{\substack{j=0 \\ j \neq i, k}}^{N} F_j(t/x_j) \cdot \right]$$

Then integrating over all positive values of t and summing over $k \neq i$, one concludes that i's expected earnings from participation in the auction are

$$(3.15.3) \quad \pi_i = \sum_{\substack{k=0 \\ k \neq i}}^{N} \int_0^\infty (1-t)\,[1 - F_i(t/x_i)] \left[\prod_{\substack{j=0 \\ j \neq i, k}}^{N} F_j(t/x_j) F_k'(t/x_k)\, dt/x_k \right]$$

for $i = 1, 2, \ldots, N$. The derivation of a similar expression for π_0 is left as an exercise to the interested reader.

The special case wherein all participants have the same quality of information, that is, in which $F_0 = F_1 = \cdots = F_N = F$, and in which i's opponents all use the same strategy $x_j = y$ for $j \neq i$, seems a simple one worthy of separate consideration. For then all N summands in the expression (3.15.3) are equal, and writing $x_i = x$ gives

$$(3.15.4) \quad \pi_i = N \int_0^\infty (1 - t) [1 - F(t/x)] \cdot [F(t/y)]^{N-1} \cdot F'(t/y) \ dt/y,$$

a function of only the two variables x and y. And when the distribution F is a tractable one, the integration may be explicitly performed. So ordinary auctions may be analyzed numerically, as sealed-bid ones already have been, for the determination of robust strategies and the like.

Indeed, if the assumptions (3.2.4) again are made, obvious substitutions reduce (3.15.4) to the form

$$(3.15.5) \quad \pi_i = N \cdot K_N(r) - Ny L_N(r; \beta),$$

where now $r = (x/y)^\alpha$, $K_N(r) = L_N(r; 0)$, and

$$(3.15.6) \quad L_N(r; \beta) = \int_0^\infty \left(\frac{r}{r+u} \right) \left(\frac{u}{1+u} \right)^{N-1} \frac{u^\beta \ du}{(1+u)^2}.$$

Moreover the Cauchy residue theorem [4], applied as before about the contour of Figure 3.3A, again permits the evaluation of the integral $L_N(\cdot ; \cdot)$. The result is

$$L_N(r; \beta)$$

$$(3.15.7) \quad = \frac{\gamma}{(r-1)^{N+1}} \left(r \sum_{K=0}^N \frac{(N-1+\beta) \cdots (N-K+\beta)}{K!} (r-1)^K - r^{N+\beta} \right)$$

whenever $r \neq 1$ and $0 < \beta < 1$, the constant γ having again the value $\pi/\sin \beta\pi$. If $\beta = 0$, the expression (3.15.7) is clearly without meaning, but in that case the integration may be carried out by elementary means. One obtains

$$K_N(r) = \frac{r}{r-1} \left[\frac{\log r}{1-r} + \sum_{K=1}^{N-1} \frac{(-1)^K}{K} \right.$$

$$(3.15.8)$$

$$\left. \cdot \binom{N-1}{K-1} \left(\frac{1}{r^K} - 1 \right) + \frac{(-1)^N}{N} \left(\frac{1}{r^N} - 1 \right) \right].$$

Finally, when $r = 1$ and $0 < \beta < 1$,

$$L_N(1; \beta) = \int_0^\infty \frac{u^{N-1+\beta}\, du}{(1+u)^{N+2}} = B(N + \beta, 2 - \beta)$$

(3.15.9)

$$= \frac{(1 - \beta)\beta(\beta + 1) \cdots (\beta + N - 1)}{(N + 1)!}\, \gamma,$$

and

(3.15.10) $$K_N(1) = B(N, 2) = 1/N(N + 1)$$

when $r = 1$, $\beta = 0$. Here $B(\cdot, \cdot)$ again denotes the classical beta function [3]. The expressions (3.15.7)–(3.15.10) permit the evaluation of $\pi_i(x; y, N)$ for all positive values of x, y, and integers N. So extensive plotting of the curves obtained by holding y and N fixed is possible once more, with the aid of an automatic computer.

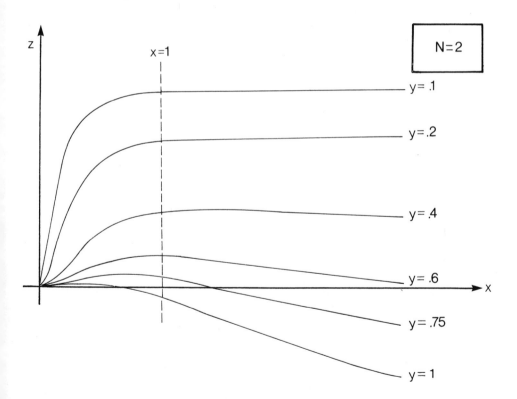

FIGURE 3.15A

The payoff curves so obtained are quantitatively not unlike the one sketched in Figure 3.3B. In particular they are unimodal. But as y tends to zero, they tend asymptotically to the horizontal line $Z = 1$ rather than to one having negative slope. Figures 3.15A–3.15C exhibit some sample curves for the value $\alpha = 2.34$ of the information-quality parameter, $N = 2, 3,$ and 5, and likely alternatives for y. Though the curves shown differ only quantitatively from those of Figure 3.3B, they demonstrate nonetheless a fundamental qualitative difference between ordinary and Dutch (i.e., sealed-bid) auctions.

The difference lies in the gentle downward slope of the curves to the right of the vertical line $x = 1$. It suggests little incentive to bid conservatively against other conservative bidders. If y is known to be small, then the best x's are large ones. This is in direct contrast to the Dutch, or sealed-bid, case, wherein large

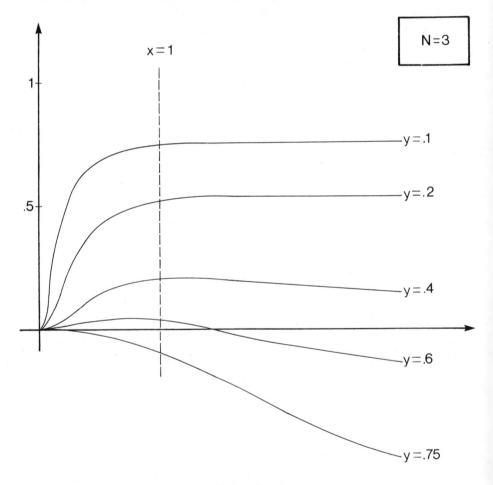

FIGURE 3.15B

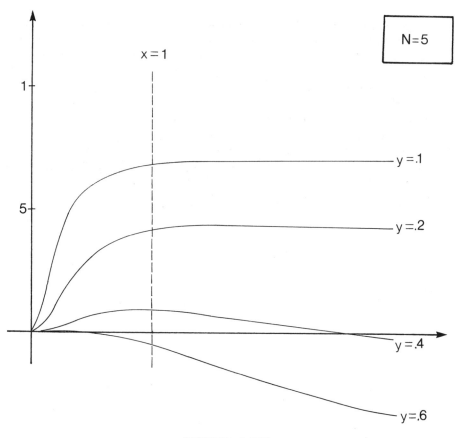

FIGURE 3.15C

x's are dominated. While bidders at sealed-bid auctions are thus *directly* motivated to conservative action, their counterparts at ordinary auctions have only
the *indirect motivation* thereto which derives from the knowledge that liberal
action by one will eventually necessitate like actions by all. The forces that tend
to produce uniformly moderate action are subtler here. Yet the fact that many
people, for instance dealers in cattle, tobacco, and oriental rugs, earn substantial
portions of their income at auctions suggests that the forces are effective nonetheless.

16. EQUILIBRIA

It was asserted earlier that, because the reduced risks encountered by bidders
at ordinary auctions should motivate them to more aggressive actions than they
would take at a Dutch or sealed-bid one, the expected sale price, at an ordinary

auction should be higher. But such an assertion cannot be substantiated without assumptions about the bidders' behavior.

Because robust strategies are available in both games, we assume the players choose them. Then each plays near optimally against his foes, provided there are not too many of them. Indeed, it is convenient to assume that each plays exactly optimally against the rest, so that together the players' strategies are in Nash equilibrium. In practice one would perhaps expect them to be a bit more conservative than that, but as a first approximation the Nash assumptions will do. Only symmetric equilibria are sought (those, that is, for which $x_1 = x_2 = \cdots = x_N$) from a belief that no others are likely to exist and because symmetric ones are easy to compute.

Observe first that for Dutch and sealed-bid auctions the payoff functions have the form

$$(3.16.1) \qquad \pi = F(r) - xG(r),$$

where $r = (y/x)^\alpha$. So

$$(3.16.2) \qquad \frac{\partial \pi}{\partial x} = F'(r) \frac{\partial r}{\partial x} - G'(r) \frac{\partial r}{\partial x} - G(r).$$

And the simultaneous vanishing of $\partial \pi / \partial x$ and equality of x with y imply that $r = 1$ and

$$(3.16.3) \qquad \alpha G'(1) - G(1) = \alpha F'(1)/x,$$

so that finally

$$(3.16.4) \qquad x^* = y^* = F'(1)/(G'(1) - \beta G(1)),$$

β being equal to $1/\alpha$ as always. Next, one observes that the integrals defining $F(\cdot)$ and $G(\cdot)$ may be differentiated with respect to r for

$$(3.16.5) \qquad \begin{aligned} F'(1) &= -NB(N-1, 2) \\ G'(1) &= -NB(N+1+\beta, 2-\beta) \\ G(1) &= B(N+1+\beta, 1-\beta). \end{aligned}$$

So standard procedures for evaluating the beta function yield finally

$$(3.16.6) \qquad x_D^* = \frac{1}{\gamma \left(1 + \dfrac{2\beta}{N}\right)} \; \frac{N!}{\beta(\beta+1)\cdots(\beta+N)}$$

as the symmetric Nash equilibrium strategy for the $N+1$ bidder Dutch or sealed-bid auction.

Similarly the payoff functions for an ordinary auction have the form

$$(3.16.7) \qquad \pi = F(r) - yG(r)$$

where now $r = (x/y)^\alpha$. So

(3.16.8)
$$\frac{\partial \pi}{\partial x} = F'(r) \frac{\partial r}{\partial x} - yG'(r) \frac{\partial r}{\partial x} .$$

And the conditions $x = y$ and $\partial \pi / \partial x = 0$ together imply that $r = 1$ and

(3.16.9)
$$x^* = y^* = F'(1)/G'(1).$$

Moreover the integrals defining $F(\cdot)$ and $G(\cdot)$ may again be differentiated to yield

(3.16.10)
$$F'(1) = NB(N + 1, 2)$$
$$G'(1) = NB(N + 1 + \beta, 2 - \beta),$$

wherefrom it follows that

(3.16.11)
$$x_0^* = \frac{1}{(1 - \beta)^\gamma} \cdot \frac{N!}{\beta(\beta + 1) \cdots (\beta + N)}$$

is the symmetric Nash equilibrium strategy for an ordinary auction. Comparison of (3.16.11) with (3.16.6) indicates that more aggressive behavior is indeed called for at ordinary auctions than at Dutch or sealed-bid ones.

To compare the resultant expected sale prices under equilibrium play in the two kinds of auctions, one observes first that the expected value of the largest of $N + 1$ estimates of the property's value is

(3.16.12)
$$J_N(1;\beta) = \left(1 + \frac{\beta}{N - 1}\right) \frac{\beta(\beta + 1) \cdots (\beta + N - 2)}{(N - 2)!} \gamma,$$

while the expected value of the next-largest guess is

(3.16.13)
$$L_N(1;\beta) = (1 - \beta) \frac{\beta(\beta + 1) \cdots (\beta + N - 2)}{(N - 2)!} \gamma.$$

And the expected sale price is just the expected highest (respectively next-highest) guess deflated by the appropriate equilibrium strategy (3.16.6) or (3.16.11). Therefore, the expected sale price at a Dutch or sealed-bid auction is

(3.16.14)
$$x_D^* J_N(1;\beta) = (N - 1)/(N - 1 + 2\beta),$$

while that at an ordinary auction is

(3.16.15)
$$x_0^* L_N(1;\beta) = (N - 1)/(N - 1 + \beta).$$

Since the latter exceeds the former for all $0 < \beta < 1$ and integers N, the expected sale prices are, as anticipated, higher at ordinary auctions than at Dutch or sealed-bid ones.

To estimate the magnitude of the discrepancies involved, Table 3.16A has been prepared. In it, N has been allowed to vary from 1 to 12, and various quan-

TABLE 3.16A

N	J_N	L_N	x_0^*	x_D^*	P_0^*	P_D	ratio
1	1.97	.79	.89	.27	.70	.54	1.30
2	2.39	1.13	.73	.29	.82	.70	1.18
3	2.73	1.37	.64	.28	.88	.78	1.12
4	3.02	1.56	.58	.27	.90	.82	1.09
5	3.28	1.73	.53	.26	.92	.85	1.08
6	3.52	1.88	.50	.25	.93	.88	1.07
7	3.73	2.01	.47	.29	.99	.89	1.06
8	3.93	2.14	.44	.23	.95	.90	1.05
9	4.11	2.25	.42	.22	.95	.91	1.05
10	4.29	2.36	.41	.21	.96	.92	1.04
11	4.46	2.46	.39	.21	.96	.93	1.04
12	4.62	2.55	.38	.20	.97	.93	1.03

tities of interest have been recorded. The rows correspond to values of N. The column headed J_N contains the values of $J_N(1; \beta)$ for $\beta = \alpha^{-1} = 1/2.34$, and that headed L_N lists those of $L_N(1; \beta)$. The columns topped by x_0^* and x_D^* give the equilibrium strategies for ordinary and Dutch auctions, respectively, while those headed P_0 and P_D contain the expected sale prices under equilibrium play. Note that $P_0 = X_0^* L_N$ and $P_D = X_0^* J_N$ to within round-off error, and that $P_0 > P_D$ in every row. The column headed "ratio" contains the quotients P_0/P_D for convenience.

Of course the quantities given in Table 3.16A are not to be taken too literally. For the whole idea of robustness is that players have considerable latitude in selecting their strategies, and variation of strategies causes variation too in expected prices. In particular, it is reasonable to expect somewhat more conservatism from the bidders at either sort of auction than the values of x_0^* and x_D^* would indicate. But belief that the comparisons of the table are reliable, at least as first approximations, seems justified. Further corroboration is probably better sought experimentally than through additional theoretical development.

(3.7) *Question* Bidding for construction contracts has not been discussed here. In it, each competitor estimates the cost of doing the job in question and tenders an offer to do it for somewhat more than that. Strategies are simply markup rates. Such auctions can be analyzed much as ordinary and sealed-bid ones have been.

17. CHOOSING AN AUCTION FORMAT

A number of comparisons between ordinary and Dutch or sealed-bid auctions are now apparent. Risks are smaller at ordinary ones, so bidding is more aggressive and sale prices a trifle higher. But the foolishly aggressive bidder is more a menace at ordinary auctions than at sealed-bid ones, because it takes longer for the mechanism to expose the error of his ways. This reflects the fact that liberal actions (all $x \geqslant 1$, for instance) are dominated at Dutch and sealed-bid auctions, while all are indomitable at ordinary ones. Other comparisons, plausible at first glance, have occasionally been suggested.

One is that Dutch auctions proceed more quickly than ordinary ones, and are therefore a better way to dispose of a large number of essentially similar properties, like bushel baskets of fruit or vegetables at a farmer's market. It is plausible because the first bidder to speak wins the property, thus eliminating much of the dialogue that makes ordinary auctions so picturesque. But it is probably not a valid comparison, because wholesale tobacco auctions are conducted in the ordinary fashion and are said to average a sale every twenty-eight seconds.

Another charge of more consequence is that ordinary auctions are inappropriate for disposing of extremely valuable properties, such as offshore oil lands. The argument usually presented is that no individual can properly be asked to bear the responsibility of bidding such sums as $200 million. But that argument is without force once it is accepted that no information can be received during an ordinary auction which justifies the alteration of one's critical price. For then bidder i, now a representative of firm i, can be supplied with instructions not to bid more than P_i and not to let the property be sold for less. He can even be given written guarantees relieving him of legal responsibility for his action, so long as he does not disobey orders. Then the responsibility falls, not on the bidder himself, but on the firm which chose the critical price P_i prior to the auction date. Presumably, P_i would be chosen by the same person or committee thereof who would choose the bid B_i to be entered at a sealed-bid auction. So the responsibility is the same in either case. The *risk* is smaller in the former circumstance, however, for the reasons presented earlier.

It is possible, of course, that some firm could seize an advantage if ordinary auctions should replace sealed-bid ones for such purposes by adopting a strategy whereby its critical price rises gradually as opposing bids are called out. It has not been *proved* that information justifying the increase of either x_i or E_i is unobtainable from observation of the other bidders' behavior. It has only been argued that such information is hard to come by. Indeed, the lack of an impossibility proof appears to be the primary gap that remains in our present understanding of ordinary auctions. It is, for the moment, only *improbable* that an informational advantage could be seized.

In order to secure the advantages of low risk to the bidders which render ordinary auctions more attractive than Dutch or sealed-bid ones, Vickrey [13] has proposed a modification of the sealed-bid process. It is to solicit sealed bids and sell to the highest bidder, but to charge him only the next-highest-price bid. Clearly this proposal has the dual virtues or reducing the bidders' risks as an ordinary auction would, while precluding the possibility that an opponent gain useful information by observing some individual's behavior. And therefore it deserves more consideration than it has heretofore received, as, for instance, a vehicle for disposing of publicly owned oil and mineral rights. It holds excellent promise of generating higher rents on those properties while reducing both the lessor's risk and the probability that a marginal property will go unsold.

Actually, from the auctioneer's point of view, any auction format that reduces bidders' risks would appear to be a good one. For reduced risk means more aggressive bidding and consequently higher sale prices. Thus, either the standard or Vickrey form of the sealed-bid process would appear to be improved from the auctioneer's (or public's) point of view, by allowing the bidders to submit conditional bids, conditioned on the number of competitors who choose to take part in the auction. An envelope containing a particular bidder's sealed offer would include a promise to pay one sum of money if his were the only bid received, another if just two bids were received, . . . , and a last if ten or more bids were forthcoming. Then each would be protected, in part, from the submission of bids by unexpected rivals, and less deterred from aggressive action. This proposal, like Vickrey's, would appear advantageous to buyers and sellers alike.

18. CONCLUSIONS

As stated at the outset, the present chapter on auctions is by far the most significant of this entire book. So it is appropriate to dwell briefly on the nature of that claimed significance.

In part, the claim is based on the obvious fact that important managerial decisions involving hundreds of millions of dollars are being made, and have been made for some time, by essentially the reasoning set forth here. And the decision makers seem almost uniformly enthusiastic about the results! To this extent, the significance of the theory of auctions is commercial. But the chapter has theoretical significance, too, in that it provides an unparalleled opportunity to test an hypothesis underlying all of noncooperative game theory.

Cournot proposed in 1838 that entrepreneurs can, should, and do compete by attempting first to guess their opponents' likely behavior and then choosing their own as would be optimal (or nearly so) should their initial guesses prove correct. In other words

(C)   There is no better way to compete than the obvious way.

Indeed Cournot treats the statement (C) as an axiom in his theory of competition, though he never states it explicitly. It may properly be called "Cournot's axiom," therefore, though few in this century have been willing to regard it as axiomatic, or even to believe it true.

There is, in fact, no shred of evidence to contradict (C). In particular, von

Neumann's theory of matrix games can never contradict it, since his saddle-point solutions are the same as the Cournot-Nash equilibria for such games. But many have declared their *faith* that (C) is false. Indeed the entire cooperative theory of games is founded on such a declaration. For it is an axiom of that theory that "rational players" will find a way to play that is not only better than the obvious way but "best" in the sense of Pareto optimality.

Nothing in the present chapter implies that the axiom is either true or false. But the fact that so many highly motivated (and talented and compensated) people have for years devoted their best efforts to the choice of bidding strategies lends a degree of plausibility to (C) that perhaps it previously lacked. In subsequent chapters, other familiar forms of competition will be considered at which years of play by similarly thoughtful players have likewise failed to reveal a "better way" to play than Cournot's obvious one. But in no case will either the promise of reward or the effort expended equal that which auction problems have called forth. Indeed it may well be that (C) will *never again* sustain so determined an assault from the combined forces of ingenuity and self-interest. And having withstood these many attempts to disprove it by discovering better ways to play, (C) seems moderately likely to survive future attempts as well.

In short, Cournot's axiom appears to possess exactly those attributes which an axiom should. A degree of plausibility is conferred upon it by relevant experience, and it seems impossible to deduce from other more primitive assumptions. Moreover, it seems to lead (rather directly in fact) to worthwhile conclusions. It is a strong axiom, destined perhaps to remain controversial, so its assumption should never go unacknowledged. But until a better one comes along, Cournot's axiom seems an appropriate foundation for theories of economic competition.

Appendix

Formulas (3.10.6), (3.10.9), and (3.10.10) were obtained by direct, but rather lengthy, calculation. Those calculations are reproduced here to spare the reader the tedium of performing them for himself. From the binomial theorem

$$(A1) \qquad 1 = [Z + (1 - Z)]^n = \sum_{k=0}^{n} \binom{n}{k} Z^{n-k}(1 - Z)^k,$$

so

$$(A2) \qquad 1/Z^n = \sum_{k=0}^{n} \binom{n}{k} (-1)^k \left(\frac{Z-1}{Z}\right)^k.$$

And substituting $Z = 1 + r/t$ gives

$$(A3) \qquad \left(\frac{t}{t+r}\right)^{n+1} = \sum_{k=0}^{n} \binom{n}{k} (-1)^k \frac{tr^k}{(t+r)^{k+1}}.$$

But since

(A4)
$$\frac{t}{(r+t)^{k+1}} = \frac{(-1)^k}{k!}\frac{\partial^k}{\partial r^k}\frac{t}{t+r},$$

one has

(A5)
$$\left(\frac{t}{t+r}\right)^{n+1} = \sum_{k=0}^{n}\binom{n}{k}\frac{r^k}{k!}\frac{\partial^k}{\partial r^k}\frac{t}{t+r},$$

from which (3.10.6) follows when $n = N - 1$ also

(A6)
$$\frac{r^k}{k!}\frac{d^k}{dr^k}\frac{1}{1-r} = \frac{1}{1-r}\left(\frac{r}{1-r}\right)^k$$

(A7)
$$\frac{r^k}{k!}\frac{d^k}{dr^k}\frac{1}{(1-r)^2} = \frac{k+1}{1-r}\left(\frac{r}{1-r}\right)^k$$

and

(A8)
$$\frac{r^k}{k!}\frac{d^k}{dr^k}\frac{r}{1-r} = \frac{r+k}{(1-r)^2}\left(\frac{r}{1-r}\right)^k.$$

Then by Leibnitz's formula for the derivatives of a product,

$$\frac{r^k}{k!}\frac{d^k}{dr^k}\frac{r\log r}{(1-r)^2}$$

(A9)
$$= \frac{r^k}{k!}\sum_{j=0}^{k}\binom{k}{j}\frac{d^j}{dr^j}\log r\,\frac{d^{k-j}}{dr^{k-j}}\frac{r}{(1-r)^2}$$

$$= \frac{r^k}{k!}\left[(\log r)\frac{k!(r+k)}{(1-r)^{k+2}} + \sum_{j=1}^{k}\frac{k!}{j!(k-j)!}\right.$$

$$\left.\cdot(-1)^{j+1}(j-1)!\,r^{-j}\,\frac{(k-j)!(r+k-j)}{(1-r)^{k-j+2}}\right]$$

$$= \frac{1}{(1-r)^2}\left[(\log r)(r+k)\left(\frac{r}{1-r}\right)^k\right.$$

$$\left.+ \sum_{j=1}^{k}\frac{(-1)^{j+1}}{j}(r+k-j)\left(\frac{r}{1-r}\right)^{k-j}\right]$$

And if $\theta(j)$ be as defined in (3.10.11),

(A10)
$$\frac{r^k}{k!}\frac{d^k}{dr^k}\frac{r\log r}{(1-r)^2} = \sum_{j=0}^{k}\theta(j)(r+k-j)\left(\frac{r}{1-r}\right)^{k-j}.$$

Similarly, if $M_j(\lambda)$ be as defined in (3.10.11), Leibnitz's rule also gives

$$\frac{r^k}{k!} \frac{d^k}{dr^k} \frac{r^\lambda}{(1-r)^2}$$

(A11)

$$= \frac{r^k}{k!} \sum_{j=0}^{k} \binom{k}{j} \frac{d^j}{dr^j} r^\lambda \cdot \frac{d^{k-j}}{dr^{k-j}} \frac{1}{(1-r)^2}$$

$$= \sum_{j=0}^{k} M_j(\lambda) r^{\lambda-j} \cdot \frac{(k-j+1)!}{(1-r)^{k-j+2}} \frac{k!}{j!(k-j)!} \frac{r^k}{k!}$$

$$= \frac{r^\lambda}{(1-r)^2} \sum_{j=0}^{k} \frac{M_j(\lambda)(k-j+1)}{j!} \left(\frac{r}{1-r}\right)^{k-j}.$$

Formulas (A10) and (A11) greatly facilitate the application of $P_N(D)$ to $I(\cdot)$ and $J(\cdot\,;\cdot)$. Indeed

$$P_n(D)I(r) = \sum_{k=0}^{n} \binom{n}{k} \frac{r^k}{k!} \frac{d^k}{dr^k} I(r)$$

$$= \sum_{k=0}^{n} \binom{n}{k} \frac{r^k}{k!} \frac{d^k}{dr^k} \frac{r\log r}{(1-r)^2} + \sum_{k=0}^{n} \binom{n}{k} \frac{r^k}{k!} \frac{d^k}{dr^k} \frac{1}{1-r}$$

$$= \frac{1}{(1-r)^2} \sum_{k=0}^{n} \binom{n}{k} \sum_{j=0}^{k} (r+k-j)\theta(j) \left(\frac{r}{1-r}\right)^{k-j}$$

(A12)

$$+ \frac{1}{1-r} \sum_{k=0}^{n} \binom{n}{k} \left(\frac{r}{1-r}\right)^k$$

$$= \frac{1}{(1-r)^2} \sum_{j=0}^{n} \theta(j) \sum_{k=j}^{n} \binom{n}{k} (r+k-j) \left(\frac{r}{1-r}\right)^{k-j}$$

$$+ \frac{1}{1-r} \left(1 + \frac{r}{1-r}\right)^n$$

$$= \left(\frac{1}{1-r}\right)^{n+1} + \frac{1}{(1-r)^2} \sum_{j=0}^{n} \theta(j) \sum_{l=0}^{n-j} \binom{n}{l+j} (r+l) \left(\frac{r}{1-r}\right)^l,$$

from which (3.10.9) follows by setting $n = N - 1$. Finally

$$P_n(D)J(r;\beta)$$

$$= \sum_{k=0}^{n} \binom{n}{k} \frac{r^k}{k!} \frac{d^k}{dr^k} J(r;\beta)$$

$$= \beta\gamma \sum_{k=0}^{n} \binom{n}{k} \frac{r^k}{k!} \frac{d^k}{dr^k} \frac{1}{1-r} - \gamma \sum_{k=0}^{n} \binom{n}{k}$$

$$\cdot \frac{r^k}{k!} \frac{d^k}{dr^k} \frac{r}{(1-r)^2} + \gamma \sum_{k=0}^{n} \binom{n}{k} \frac{r^k}{k!} \frac{d^k}{dr^k} \frac{r^\lambda}{(1-r)^2}$$

$$= \beta\gamma \sum_{k=0}^{n} \binom{n}{k} \frac{1}{1-r} \left(\frac{r}{1-r}\right)^k$$

(A13)
$$- \gamma \sum_{k=0}^{n} \binom{n}{k} \frac{r+k}{(1-r)^2} \left(\frac{r}{1-r}\right)^k$$

$$+ \gamma \sum_{k=0}^{n} \binom{n}{k} \frac{r^\lambda}{(1-r)^2} \sum_{j=0}^{k} \frac{M_j(\lambda)(k-j+1)}{j!} \left(\frac{r}{1-r}\right)^{k-j}$$

$$= \frac{\gamma\beta}{(1-r)^{n+1}} - \frac{\gamma r}{(1-r)^{n+2}} - \frac{\gamma}{(1-r)^2} \cdot \frac{nr}{1-r} \left(\frac{1}{1-r}\right)^{n-1}$$

$$+ \frac{r^\lambda}{(1-r)^2} \sum_{k=0}^{n} \sum_{j=0}^{k} \binom{n}{k} \frac{M_j(\lambda)(k-j+1)}{j!} \left(\frac{r}{1-r}\right)^{k-j}$$

$$= \frac{\beta\gamma - \gamma(n+\lambda)r}{(1-r)^{n+2}} + \frac{\gamma r^\lambda}{(1-r)^2} \sum_{j=0}^{n} \sum_{l=0}^{n-j} \binom{n}{l+j} \frac{M_j(\lambda)}{j!} (l+1) \left(\frac{r}{1-r}\right)^l,$$

which is exactly (3.10.10) if $n = N - 1$ and $\lambda = \beta + 1$. As remarked earlier, the expressions are clumsy if $N > 1$, but they are ideally suited for machine computation.

REFERENCES

1. Crawford, P. B., "Texas Offshore Bidding Patterns," *J. Petroleum Technology* (March 1970), pp. 283-289.
2. Capen, E. C., R. V. Clapp, and W. M. Campbell, "Competitive Bidding in High-Risk Situations," *J. Petroleum Technology* (June 1971), pp. 641-653.

3. Widder, D. V. *Advanced Calculus*, 2d ed. (Englewood Cliffs, N.J.: Prentice-Hall, 1961), xvi + 520.

4. Churchill, R. V., *Complex Variables and Applications*, 2d ed., (New York: McGraw-Hill, 1960), ix + 297 pp.

5. Smith, B. T., "Nash Equilibria in a Sealed Bid Auction," unpublished Ph.D. thesis, The Johns Hopkins University, June 1973.

6. Brown, K. C., *Bidding for Offshore Oil* (Dallas: Southern Methodist Univ. Press, 1969), 0 + 76 pp.

7. Smith, B. T., and J. Case, "Nash Equilibra in a Sealed Bid Auction," *Management Science*, Management Science, Vol. 22, No. 4 (1975).

8. Abramowitz, M. and I. A. Stegun, eds., *Handbook of Mathematical Functions* (New York, Dover), xiv + 1046 pp.

9. Luke, Y. L., *The Special Functions and Their Approximations*, vol. 2, (New York: Academic Press, 1969), xx + 485 pp.

10. Capen, E. C., R. V. Clapp, and W. M. Campbell, "Competitive Bidding in High Risk Situations," Paper presented to National Meeting of ORSA, San Diego, Nov. 12-14, 1973.

11. Capen, E. C., and R. V. Clapp, "Conflicting Bidding Models in a High Stakes Game," Paper presented to National Meeting of ORSA, Las Vegas, November 16-19, 1975.

12. Hollander, M. and D. A. Wolfe, *Nonparametric Statistical Methods* (New York: John Wiley, 1973), xvii + 503 pp.

13. Vickery, W., "Counterspeculations, Auctions, and Competitive Sealed Tenders." *J. of Finance*, Vol. 16 (1961), pp. 8-37.

Chapter 4

Inventory Decisions

In this chapter and the next, we consider a class of decisions which confront nearly all merchants, namely inventory decisions. An extensive literature is already available on inventory theory, [1], [3], and [4] being perhaps typical. But existing analyses disregard the effect of competition on inventory decisions, and in many businesses competition does more to determine the efficacy of a particular inventory policy than any other factor. Liquor stores, appliance outlets, clothing establishments, and automobile dealers tend to make sales primarily from stock on hand. So if they do not have the item or variety a particular customer wants, or if another dealer has one he prefers, they stand to lose the customer's trade. And that fact alone accounts for the hundreds of thousands of dollars even moderate-sized liquor stores keep tied up in inventory, or the five hundred-odd cars typically found on suburban auto dealers' lots. Let us see how, in a properly simplified situation, competition does explain the observed phenomenon of *gigantic* inventories.

1. THE AUTO DEALER'S GAMES

Consider a city in which the demand for cars is known to be constant and equal to D cars per week. Several dealers $1, 2, \ldots, N$ compete for shares of this market. Typically, each potential buyer visits a number of their showrooms before making a purchase. In each he is greeted by a salesman and asked to describe the type of car he wishes to own. Then the salesman "introduces" the buyer (if he can) to one or more such cars.

If n_i is the number of potential buyers who visit i's showroom each week, and if s_i is the number of cars (assumed constant) that i keeps on hand, we may assume that such introductions take place at a rate of $kn_i s_i$ introductions per week. Then if dealer i's share of the market is equal to his share of the introductions made within the market, the demand for his cars is

$$(4.1.1) \qquad D_i = \frac{Dn_i s_i}{n_1 s_1 + \cdots + n_N s_N}.$$

We assume that dealer i sells cars for P_i dollars more than he pays for them, and faces a carrying cost of C_i dollars per car per week for the maintenance of his inventory. Thus, his profit from a week's operation is

$$(4.1.2) \qquad \pi_i(s_1, \ldots, s_N) = \frac{DP_i n_i s_i}{n_1 s_1 + \cdots + n_N s_N} - C_i s_i$$

dollars. The function π_i of the variables $s_1, \ldots, s_N$ is the payoff function for player i in an N-player game G_N. Each dealer i is a player and must choose a strategy $s_i \geqslant 0$ to secure for himself a large reward.

G_N is simply directed, since π_i is obviously a decreasing function of each s_j, $j \neq i$, and since the fact that $\partial^2 \pi_i / \partial^2 s_i < 0$ implies π_i is concave (and therefore unimodal) in s_i. Therefore no player can have any incentive to use a dominated strategy. Also the identifications $N = 2, D = P_1 = P_2 = n_1 = n_2 = 1, s_1 = x, s_2 = y$, $C_1 = m$, and $C_2 = \mu$ show that the game of Cold War discussed in Chapter I is a special case of G_2.

If we introduce the dimensionless variables

$$(4.1.3) \qquad \sigma = \frac{C_i s_i}{DP_i} \quad \text{and} \quad \omega = \frac{C_i}{n_i P_i D} \sum_{\substack{j=1 \\ j \neq i}}^{N} n_j s_j,$$

we may take

$$(4.1.4) \qquad \pi = \frac{\pi_i}{DP_i} = \frac{\sigma}{\omega + \sigma} - \sigma$$

to be player i's reward function, σ his action variable, and ω his index of opposition. The latter is of course beyond i's control but not, perhaps, beyond his power to effectively predict.

In reality, the game is repeated many times over a succession of weeks. So i has a record of his own past sales $D_i(t)$ and his own past decisions $\sigma(t)$ for $t = 0, -1, -2, \ldots$. Therefore, he can solve the equation

$$(4.1.5) \qquad D_i(t) = \frac{D\sigma(t)}{\omega(t) + \sigma(t)}$$

for the history $\{\omega(-t)\}_{t=0}^{\infty}$ of his opponents' "opposition." And if that time series appears regular, he can endeavor to predict future values $\omega(1), \omega(2), \ldots$. Three questions thus present themselves: (i) How predictable is a typical dealer's history of opposition $\{\omega(-t)\}_{t=0}^{\infty}$? (ii) What is the proper response $\sigma^*(\omega)$ if ω could be adequately predicted? (iii) How sensitive is i's payoff to small inaccuracies in his prediction? We have no answer to the first, as most dealers seem to regard the information necessary for the computation of that time series as highly confidential. But we can give complete answers for the other two.

To answer (ii), we observe that if $\sigma > 1/4$, then

(4.1.6) $$\pi(\sigma, \omega) < \pi(1/4\ \omega)$$

for every ω. Therefore i should never use a strategy $\sigma > 1/4$; such strategies are all dominated by the strategy $\sigma = 1/4$. Moreover

(4.1.7) $$\frac{\partial \pi}{\partial \sigma} = \frac{\omega}{(\omega + \sigma)^2} - 1 \quad \text{and} \quad \frac{\partial^2 \pi}{\partial \sigma^2} = \frac{-2\omega}{(\omega + \sigma)^3} < 0,$$

so $\pi(\sigma, \omega)$ is concave in σ for fixed $\omega > 0$ and is maximized over the interval $0 \leqslant \sigma \leqslant 1/4$ by the choice

(4.1.8)
$$\sigma = \sigma^*(\omega) = \sqrt{\omega} - \omega \quad \text{if} \quad 0 < \omega < 1$$
$$= 0 \qquad\qquad\quad \text{if} \quad \omega \geqslant 1.$$

The case $\omega = 0$ is of no interest.

To treat (iii), observe that

(4.1.9)
$$\pi^*(\omega) = \pi(\sigma^*(\omega), \omega) = (1 - \sqrt{\omega})^2 \quad \text{if} \quad 0 < \omega < 1$$
$$= 0 \qquad\qquad\qquad\qquad\quad \text{if} \quad \omega \geqslant 1.$$

The graph of this function is shown in Figure 4.1A, along with the graphs of $\pi(\sigma, \omega)$ for selected values of σ.

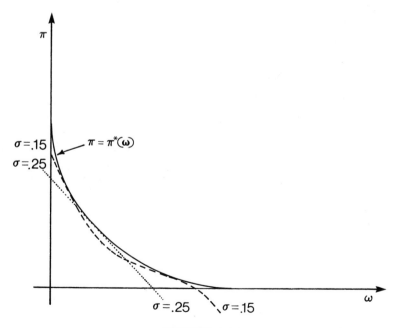

FIGURE 4.1A

It is of course the graph of the same function discussed in Chapter I in the analysis of Cold War. So the same strategies are robust in this game as were robust in that. But now the possible values of ω are more numerous, since we can no longer assume $y < 1/4\mu$. For instance if G_N is symmetric in the sense that $n_i = n_j$, $P_i = P_j$, and $C_i = C_j$ for all $i \neq j$, then the fact that G_N is simply directed and the strategies $\sigma > 1/4$ are dominated, together with the definitions (4.1.3) of σ and ω together imply that

$$(4.1.10) \qquad\qquad \omega \leqslant (N-1)/4.$$

So for G_2, G_3, and G_4 we have the upper bounds $\omega \leqslant .25$, $\omega \leqslant .5$, and $\omega \leqslant .75$, respectively. But for G_5 we can conclude only that $\omega \leqslant 1$, which by itself is of no help.

This constitutes an undeniable difference between the games G_N for which $N < 5$ and those for which $N \geqslant 5$. But we doubt that the distinction is important practically, for it is precisely when N becomes large that one expects the time series $\{\omega(-t)\}_{t=0}^{\infty}$ to be most regular, and therefore $\omega(1)$ and $\omega(2)$ to be most predictable. Nor is this entirely a wishful expectation on our part; there are natural "restoring forces" at work to make it so!

We attempt no more than a qualitative description of those forces. The key to their understanding is the notion of robustness. For when inventories grow so large that ω is nearly one, the profits to be made are very small. Moreover, the robustly efficient strategies all lose money against such values of ω, so it becomes necessary to use nonrobust strategies just to avoid incurring losses. And when the players are all playing nonrobust strategies, the small errors they must inevitably make in predicting ω will cause many of them to maintain inventories which are either too large or too small. In the latter case $(\sigma < \sigma^*(\omega))$ they earn only a small fraction of the already small sum $\pi^*(\omega)$, while in the former $(\sigma > \sigma^*(\omega))$ they incur actual losses. So if ω remains close to 1 for an appreciable period, a number of the participants will become discouraged (or bankrupt) and drop out of the market, thereby reducing the magnitude of the opposition faced by the remaining players.

It is of interest to note the effect of these forces on the behavior of the Cournot-Nash equilibrium, as more and more dealers enter the market. We consider only the symmetric case $n_i = n_j$, $P_i = P_j$, and $C_i = C_j$ for all $i \neq j$. In that case it is natural to look for a positive symmetric equilibrium $s_1^* = s_2^* = \cdots = s_N^* > 0$; such equilibria may be found by writing

$$(4.1.11) \qquad \omega = (N-1)\sigma \quad \text{and} \quad \frac{\partial\pi}{\partial\sigma} = \frac{\omega}{(\omega+\sigma)^2} - 1 = 0.$$

The only possibility is

$$(4.1.12) \qquad\qquad \sigma^* = (N-1)/N^2 = s_i^* C_i/P_i D,$$

which yields in consequence

(4.1.13) $\omega = (N - 1)^2/N^2$.

So as N grows large, the players in the game experience opposition more and more nearly approaching unity, and are forced to adopt less and less robust strategies to avoid losing money, which must eventually lead to bankruptcies and so on.

In short, it seems that only the situation wherein most dealers face levels of opposition in the central portion of the interval $0 < \omega < 1$ can long persevere. So most of them can safely settle on a single robust strategy, subject only to occasional adjustment as suggested by observed trends in the series $\{\omega(-t)\}_{t=0}^{\infty}$ or in the values of the parameters P_i, C_i, and D. The latter are, in reality, perhaps as able to change significantly over time as $\omega(t)$ itself!

When all behave thus, all play near- optimally against one another and so are collectively in a rough sort of Cournot-Nash equilibrium. The restoring forces described above, which tend to perpetuate that state of equilibrium, make it seem a very stable kind of equilibrium indeed.

(4-1) *Exercise* It may be argued that real carrying costs are convex, rather than linear, so that $C_i s_i^2$ should replace $C_i s_i$ in (4.1.2).

(4-2) *Exercise* Suppose that a rising interest rate causes carrying costs to increase. What effect does this have on "optimal" inventory levels?

(4-3) *Exercise* Solve the auto- dealers' game again, assuming arbitrary convex cost functions $C(s_i)$. What determines whether the cost increase reflected by the replacement

$$C(s_i) \to C(s_i) + \alpha f(s_i)$$

raises or lowers "optimal" inventory levels.

2. AN ANALOGY

There are remarkable similarities between the auto dealers' game and the auction games considered in Chapter III. Perhaps the most obvious is the similarity between the reward curves $Z = \pi(x, y; \alpha)$ shown in Figure 3.3B for the auction game and the curves $Z = \pi(\sigma, \omega)$ shown below in Figure 4.2A for the auto dealers'. It was precisely the geometry of the reward curves which lent effectiveness to the procedure proposed for choosing auction bids. And that geometry is repeated here, so the same procedure can be used by auto dealers as well.

Suppose, for example, that "Dealer Dave" is in competition with four similar dealers, each of whom may be expected to choose either $\sigma = .1$ or $\sigma = .2$. Then

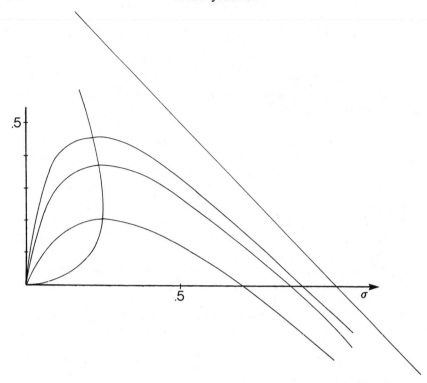

FIGURE 4.2A

Dave will face a level ω of opposition equal to .4, .5, .6, .7, or .8. The five relevant curves $Z = \pi(\sigma, \omega)$ appear in Figure 4.2B. Clearly any strategy $0 < \sigma < .2$ makes money in each of the scenarios he envisages, while any $\sigma > .2$ loses money when $\omega = .8$. So while it is perhaps not possible to choose an *optimal* strategy, one may surely choose an effective one given Dave's expectations. In particular, $\sigma = .15$ should serve him well, being better than 71 percent optimal against $\omega = .8$ and at least 89 percent against the other candidates.

The procedure is a natural one, and almost anyone who knows whom his opponents are and holds specific beliefs concerning their likely actions would use some form of it. The possibility of such a procedure does *not* require assertion. What does need to be pointed out is its remarkable effectiveness, due to the existence of robust actions, in games of such fundamental importance as the present one and the auction games of Chapter III. Indeed, it seems likely often to perform even more effectively than it does in Dave's behalf, for many dealers are likely more accurate guessers than Dave thought himself to be. The procedure is an alternative to monitoring the time series $\{\omega(-t)\}_{t=0}^{\infty}$ and seems preferable to that approach when there are but a few opponents and when data concerning their past behavior are available. Otherwise, the time-series approach holds more promise.

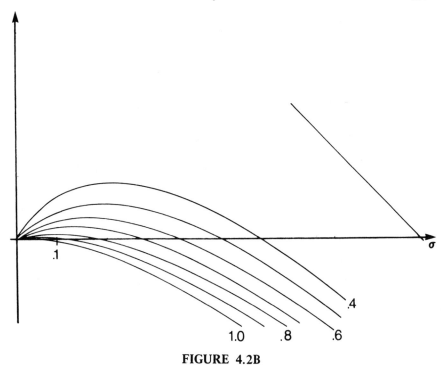

FIGURE 4.2B

Finally, to complete the analogy, it should be pointed out that the time-series method is applicable to auction games as well as to the dealers'. For the curve $Z = \pi_1(x, y; \alpha)$ crossing R at height $Z = h$ looks much like any other

$$Z = \pi_1(x, y_1, \ldots, y_N; \alpha)$$

crossing R at that height. The curves $Z = \pi_1(x, .4; 2.34)$ and $Z = \pi_1(x, .16, .16, .16, .16; 2.34)$, for instance, are shown (curves ① and ② respectively) in Figure 3.10B looking much alike for $x \geqslant .25$, but less so for $.05 < x < .2$. And the similarity permits the definition of an "approximate index of opposition" $\Omega(y_1, \ldots, y_N)$ to play the role of $\omega = \omega(s_1, \ldots, s_N)$ defined in (4.1.3).

To that end, let $P(y_1, \ldots, y_N)$ be the point at which $Z = \pi_1(x, y_1, \ldots, y_N; \alpha)$ crosses Λ_2 (which lies in the interior of R as indicated in Figure 3.10A), and let $\Omega(y_1, \ldots, y_N)$ be that value of y for which $Z = \pi_1(x, y; \alpha)$ passes through $P(y_1, \ldots, y_N)$. There is exactly one such y because exactly one of the curves $Z = \pi_1(x, y; \alpha)$ passes through every point of the wedge-shaped region

(4.2.1) $\{(x, Z) : x \geqslant 0 \quad \text{and} \quad Z \leqslant 1 - \beta\gamma x\}.$

Ω is only an approximate index of opposition because the two functions of $N + 2$ variables $\pi_1(x, y_1, \ldots, y_N; \alpha)$ and $\pi_1(x, \Omega(y_1, \ldots, y_N); \alpha)$ are not equal. They merely appear, on the basis of empirical evidence, to approximate one another.

Actually, better approximations result if $\pi_1(x, y, y; \alpha)$ is used instead of $\pi_1(x, y; \alpha)$ in the definition of $\Omega(\cdot, \ldots, \cdot)$, but we shall not exploit the fact. We know of no analytic expression for $\Omega(\cdot, \ldots, \cdot)$, though it is easy to compute iteratively because of the monotonicity of $\pi_1(x, y; \alpha)$ in y. The power mean (3.10.26) is of course another approximate index of opposition, though not so good a one as Ω. The existence of an index (or approximate index) of opposition simplifies the task of bid selection considerably. For the level Ω of opposition that has prevailed in the past may then be determined from historical data, and x chosen to maximize $\pi_1(x, \Omega; \alpha)$.

The simplest way to estimate Ω is probably to guess the total value V of some large number of properties recently sold, as one may do with some accuracy if many were, and to set

(4.2.2) $$\Omega = M/V,$$

where M is the actual proceed from the past sales. For then Ω is roughly the fraction of true property value that the opposition bids at auction. Or if the auctions are truly numerous, one may compute an $\Omega(t)$ for each time period $t = -1, -2, \ldots$ in the past and seek to analyze the time series $\{\Omega(-t)\}_{t=0}^{\infty}$.

The analogy between these two seemingly disparate games is of course interesting for its own sake, but it is not dwelt upon here for that reason. Rather, it seems that procedures of the sort proposed above have been used to good advantage in the oil industry's lease auctions. And it seems almost certain that those procedures can be used to equal advantage by auto dealers, who play so similar a game. We shall encounter more games with essentially the same structure as we proceed.

3. FLUCTUATIONS

In the last section we considered inventories that remain (roughly) constant, without marked fluctuations. It was not unduly restrictive to do this while discussing automobile dealers, for most of them do attempt to maintain a fairly steady influx of new cars to offset demands as they occur. But many other goods have to be bought in large lots, then sold off gradually, due to the presence of a substantial fixed ordering cost payable each time an order is placed, and independent of the order size. Indeed, it is with such goods that conventional (i.e., noncompetitive) inventory theory has [1] most often been concerned.

Consider, then, a number of merchants $1, 2, \ldots, N$ each selling the same good X. Let $x_i(t)$ be the amount of X merchant i has on hand at time t, and let the demand on him for X be

(4.3.1) $$D_i(t) = \frac{D n_i x_i(t)}{n_1 x_1(t) + \cdots + n_N x_N(t)}$$

by analogy with (4.1.1). Let P_i be the profit i earns from the sale of a unit of X, and C_i be the cost to i of maintaining a unit of X in inventory for one week. Also, let K_i be the cost of placing a single order for X. We emphasize that this cost is independent of order size. Finally, let us denote by $N_i(T)$ the number of orders placed by i during the period $0 \leqslant t \leqslant T$. Then i's profit during that period is

$$(4.3.2) \qquad J_i(T) = -K_i N_i(T) + P_i \int_0^T D_i(t)\, dt - C_i \int_0^T x_i(t)\, dt.$$

As before, each of the competitors $i = 1, \ldots, N$ is a player in a game, which we may again call G_N. Each i must decide when to reorder, and how much, in order to make J_i large.

If we assume the game to be of long duration, it seems reasonable to assume too that each merchant will adopt an (s, S) policy. That is, i will wait until $x_i(t) = s_i$, then reorder $q_i = S_i - s_i$ additional units of X in order to boost his sales.

When the players have all chosen their strategies $(s_1, S_1), \ldots, (s_N, S_N)$, and the initial stocks $x_{10} = x_1(0), \ldots, x_{N0} = x_N(0)$ are known, the quantities $x_i(t)$, $N_i(t)$, and $D_i(t)$ are all determined for the duration. So one may in principle evaluate the limits

$$(4.3.3) \qquad \pi_i(s_1, S_1, \ldots, s_N, S_N) = \lim_{T \to \infty} \frac{J_i(T)}{T}, \quad i = 1, \ldots, N.$$

The result is

$$(4.3.4) \qquad \pi_i = \frac{P_i D n_i (S_i - s_i) - n_i D K_i - C_i (S_i - s_i) \left[\dfrac{n_i(S_i + s_i)}{2} + \displaystyle\sum_{\substack{k=1 \\ k \neq i}}^{N} \dfrac{n_k(S_k - s_r)}{\log (S_k/s_k)} \right]}{\log\left(\dfrac{S_i}{s_i}\right) \displaystyle\sum_{k=1}^{N} \dfrac{n_k(S_k - s_k)}{\log (S_k/s_k)}}$$

as is demonstrated in the appendix to this chapter with the aid of Birkhoff's ergodic theorem. And upon substituting

$$(4.3.5) \qquad \Omega_i = \frac{1}{n_i} \sum_{\substack{k=1 \\ k \neq i}}^{N} \frac{n_k(S_k - s_k)}{\log (S_k/s_k)},$$

we obtain

$$(4.3.6) \qquad \pi_i = \frac{P_i D(S_i - s_i) - D K_i - C_i (S_i - s_i)[(1/2)(S_i + s_i) + \Omega_i]}{(S_i - s_i) + \Omega_i \log\left(\dfrac{S_i}{s_i}\right)},$$

wherefore it is clear that the strategies (s_k, S_k), $k \neq i$ of i's opponents affect his payoff π_i only through their contribution to Ω_i. For this reason we shall call Ω_i the "opposition" faced by i. He cannot know Ω_i at the time he chooses (s_i, S_i), for it is controlled by his opponents. But he can probably predict it with some degree of accuracy, just as automobile dealer i was able to predict ω_i in the nonfluctuating situation. For from (2.6) one obtains

$$(4.3.7) \qquad \Omega_i = \frac{P_i D(S_i - s_i) - DK_i - (1/2) C_i (S_i^2 - s_i^2) - (S_i - s_i)\pi_i}{C_i(S_i - s_i) + \log\left(\dfrac{S_i}{s_i}\right)\pi_i},$$

so that a historical record of $\{\Omega_i(t)\}_{t=0}^{\infty}$ may be calculated from the three known time series $\{s_i(-t), S_i(-t), \pi_i(-t)\}_{t=0}^{\infty}$. Hence, as in the simpler (nonfluctuating) model, i must guess that Ω_i will lie in some confidence interval $a < \Omega_i < b$, and try to choose a good strategy (s_i, S_i) against those levels of opposition.

If K_i is very small, the difference $q_i = S_i - s_i$ should be small too, compared with s_i or S_i. So we may use the approximation

$$(4.3.8) \qquad \log \frac{S_i}{s_i} = \log\left(1 + \frac{q_i}{s_i}\right) = q_i/s_i$$

to write

$$(4.3.9) \qquad \pi_i = \frac{P_i D - DK_i/q_i - C_i(s_i + \Omega_i + q_i/2)}{1 + \Omega_i/s_i}.$$

And (4.3.9) is maximized with respect to q_i (regardless of the values of s_i and Ω_i) only if

$$(4.3.10) \qquad q_i = \sqrt{\frac{2DK_i}{C_i}},$$

which is to say, of course, that the strategies (s_i, S_i) on the line $S_i - s_i = \sqrt{2DK_i/C_i}$ dominate all others. Equation (4.3.10) is the classic "square root law" for order quantities, which has been discovered many times before [3], [4] in non-competitive situations. Its reappearance here is just one more affirmation of its remarkable "robustness." When q_i is given the constant value (4.3.10) in expression (4.3.9), the latter becomes

$$(4.3.11) \qquad \pi_i = \frac{A_i s_i - C_i s_i(s_i + \Omega_i)}{s_i + \Omega_i},$$

where

$$(4.3.12) \qquad A_i = P_i D - \sqrt{2DK_i C_i}.$$

And since (4.3.11) is of the form (4.1.2), the present problem may be said to reduce to the previous one if K_i is sufficiently small.

If K_i is not small, the analysis becomes more complicated. The introduction of the dimensionless variables

(4.3.13)
$$x = \frac{C_i s_i}{P_i D}, \quad y = \frac{C_i S_i}{P_i D}, \quad \omega = \frac{C_i \Omega_i}{P_i D},$$

$$\mu = \frac{K_i C_i}{P_i^2 D}, \quad \text{and} \quad \pi = \frac{\pi_i}{P_i D}$$

is helpful. In terms of these, (4.3.6) becomes

(4.3.14)
$$\pi = \frac{(1 - \omega)(y - x) - \mu - (1/2)(y^2 - x^2)}{y - x + \omega \log \dfrac{y}{x}} = \frac{1 - \dfrac{\mu}{y - x} - \dfrac{y + x}{2} - \omega}{1 + \dfrac{\log y - \log x}{y - x} \omega}.$$

Again i's objective is to guess ω to within some sort of confidence interval, then choose values of x and y which earn large profits against the ω's therein. Clearly π is negative if $\omega \geqslant 1$.

Indeed π is positive only if

(4.3.15)
$$(y - x)[(1 - \omega) - (x + y)/2] \geqslant \mu,$$

which is the case for $y > x > 0$ only when (x, y) lies in the shaded region R of the plane indicated in Figure 4.3A. If μ and ω are small, R can fill nearly the entire triangle whose vertices are $(0, 0)$, $(1, 1)$, and $(0, 2)$. But if $\omega \geqslant 1$, or if $\mu \geqslant 1/2$, R is entirely empty. Therefore, we shall assume that $0 < \omega < 1$ and $0 < \mu < 1/2$ in what follows. A firm for which $\mu \geqslant 1/2$ is doomed to lose money, as is one which consistently faces opposition of magnitude $\omega \geqslant 1$.

Next, we examine the behavior of the function $\pi(x, y; \mu; \omega)$ near the boundary of the region $0 < x < y$, for fixed values of μ and ω. We observe that, as y decreases to any fixed positive value of x, the numerator of the second of the two quotients (4.3.14) representing π decreases to $-\infty$ while the denominator approaches $1 + \omega/x \neq 0$, so that

(4.3.16)
$$\pi(x, x; \mu; \omega) = -\infty \quad \text{if} \quad x > 0.$$

This fact has the natural interpretation that, if y is only infinitesimally greater than x, i will have to reorder infinitely often, and his reorder costs will outweigh whatever profit he might otherwise have earned.

Similarly, if x should tend to zero while μ, ω, and $y - x$ are held constant, the numerator of the first of the quotients (4.3.14) for π remains bounded while its denominator tends to $+\infty$. So

(4.3.17)
$$\pi(0, y; \mu; \omega) = 0 \quad \text{if} \quad y > 0.$$

This fact too has a natural interpretation. It is a consequence of the form (4.3.1) of the demand law governing the merchants' sales.

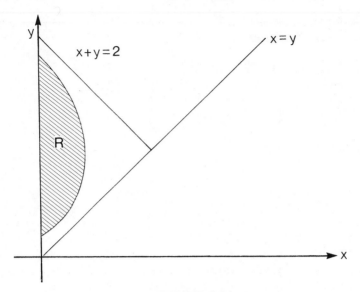

FIGURE 4.3A

Let us discuss that demand law in the case $N = 2$. Then (4.3.1) tells us that the players' inventories $x_1(t)$ and $x_2(t)$ will evolve according to the differential equations

$$(4.3.18) \qquad \frac{dx_i(t)}{dt} = \frac{-Dn_ix_i(t)}{n_1x_1(t) + n_2x_2(t)} \, , \ i = 1, 2,$$

during periods $a < t < b$ wherein neither player reorders. The system (4.3.18) clearly has a unique solution curve through every point (x_{10}, x_{20}) in the positive quadrant of the $x_1x_2 =$ plane. Indeed, those solution curves are just the straight lines directed toward the origin. Hence, if player 1 adopts a strategy $0 < s_1 < S_1$ while 2 adopts $0 = s_2 < S_2$, their joint inventory vector $(x_1(t), x_2(t))$ will evolve as shown in Figure 4.3B. Player 1 sells the quantity $S_1 - s_1$ of X infinitely many times, while 2 never even sells his initial stock x_{20}. So for him

$$(4.3.19) \qquad \lim_{T \to \infty} \frac{P_2}{T} \int_0^T D_2(t) \, dt = \lim_{T \to \infty} \frac{P_2x_{20}}{T} = 0,$$

and $N_2(T) \equiv 0$. And since the third integral in the expression (4.3.2) is bounded as $T \to \infty$, 2's average payoff is zero when he uses $s_2 = 0$ against $s_1 > 0$.

This argument, incidentally, shows why the cooperative solution $s_1 = 0 = S_2$ (or $s_1 = s_2 = \cdots = s_N = 0$ in the general case) is not a realistic proposal for this game; infinitesimally little cheating on the part of even a single player destroys the profits of all his opponents. That is, if $s_1 > 0$ while $s_2 = \cdots = s_N = 0$, then

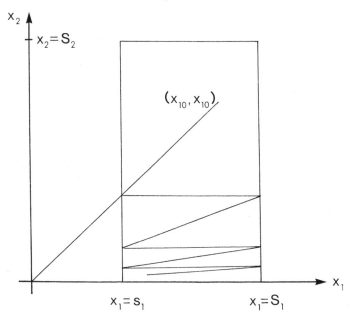

FIGURE 4.3B

$\pi_2 = \cdots = \pi_N = 0$, no matter how small s_1 might be. The proof of this fact is the multidimensional analogue of the argument suggested by Figure 4.3B.

We know now that π vanishes everywhere on the boundary of R, and attains a positive maximum in the interior of that set whenever it is nonempty. We wish to locate that maximum. Observe from (4.3.14) that π is of the form

$$(4.3.20) \qquad\qquad \pi = \frac{\alpha - \omega}{1 + \beta\omega}.$$

where α and β are functions of position in the xy-plane. Their level curves have been sketched in Figure 4.3C, π cannot attain even a local maximum at a point P in R where the level curves of α and β cross. For from any such P one may move along a β-level curve in the direction of increasing α until one reaches a point P' at which the α- and β-level curves meet tangentially. Then clearly π is greater at P' than at P for every value of ω. Let Γ be the curve whereon the α and β-level curves are tangent to one another. We have shown that every strategy $(x, y) \notin \Gamma$ is *dominated* by at least one strategy on Γ, much as the strategies (s_i, S_i) not on the line $q_i = S_i - s_i = \sqrt{2DK_i/C_i}$ were dominated, in the approximated version of the game, by strategies on it. This implies that the dimension of i's strategy space may be reduced to one in this game too. For Γ is the graph of a function $y = Y(x), 0 \leqslant x < \infty$, so i need only solve the problem

$$(4.3.21) \qquad\qquad \underset{x}{\text{maximize}}\ \pi(x, Y(x), \omega)$$

for appropriate values of ω, though we shall make no essential use of this fact.

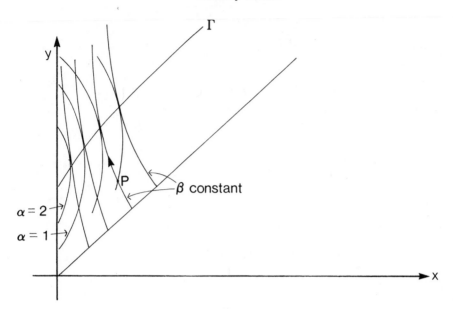

FIGURE 4.3C

It may be shown in the usual fashion that Γ is the solution set of an equation which becomes

(4.3.22) $t^2 - s^2 - 2st \log (t/s) - 2 = 0$

upon the substitutions

(4.3.23) $x = s \sqrt{\mu}$ and $y = t \sqrt{\mu}$.

(4.3.22) defines a function $t = T(s)$, $0 \leqslant s < \infty$ from which the values of $Y(x)$ may be computed for any given μ. Table 4.3D gives values of $T(s)$. Additional values may most easily be calculated by introducing polar coordinates in the st-plane. Therefore, since μ is a known constant, i can determine the appropriate curve Γ to any desired degree of accuracy. We assume in what follows that he has done so. A second condition is needed to locate the precise point in R at which π attains its maximum.

There are, of course, many other necessary conditions independent of (4.3.22). A particularly simple one is obtained from the observation that, at a local

TABLE 4.3D

s	T(s)	s	T(s)	s	T(s)	s	T(s)
0	1.41	.80	2.99	3.10	6.36	30.50	36.40
.06	1.62	1.42	3.90	4.54	7.85	68.40	75.90
.16	1.88	1.86	4.50	6.42	10.08		
.42	2.35	2.47	5.30	9.58	13.68		

maximum of the quotient,

(4.3.24) $Q(x, y) = N(x, y)/D(x, y),$

the first-order conditions

(4.3.25)
$$N_x D - D_x N = 0$$
$$N_y D - D_y N = 0$$

must hold. But this pair of homogeneous linear equations can have solutions (N, D) for which $D \neq 0$ only if the determinant

(4.3.26) $D_x N_y - N_x D_y$

is zero. Applying this condition to the first of the quotients (4.3.14) yields

(4.3.27) $(x - y)(xy + (x + y - 1)\omega + \omega^2) = 0,$

which is satisfied for $0 < x < y$ only if

(4.3.28) $y = \dfrac{1 - \omega - x}{\omega + x}\, \omega.$

The expression (4.3.28) defines a rectangular hyperbola $H(\omega)$ which cuts the co-ordinate axes and the line $x = y$ at the points $(0, 1 - \omega), (1 - \omega, 0),$ and $(\sqrt{\omega} - \omega,$

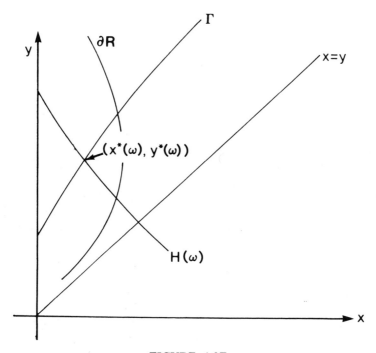

FIGURE 4.3E

$\sqrt{\omega} - \omega$), respectively, for $0 < \omega < 1$. Therefore if $0 < \omega < 1 - \sqrt{2\mu}$, the curves $H(\omega)$ and Γ cross inside R, as shown in Figure 4.3E, and the coordinates $(x^*(\omega), y^*(\omega))$ of their point of intersection describe the optimal strategy for i against ω. But if $\omega \geqslant 1 - \sqrt{2\mu}$, the region R has no interior, positive profits are impossible, and the optimal strategies are all those for which $x = 0$, since these give zero payoff.

It is now possible for i, having guessed the level ω of his opposition, to compute $x^*(\omega)$ and $y^*(\omega)$ and therefore to play optimally against his opponents. But his guesses must in practice be (at least slightly) inaccurate. Therefore it should be verified that robustly efficient strategies exist in this game too. We shall do in the next section for a single value of the parameter μ.

4. A NUMERICAL EXAMPLE

Let us consider the case $\mu = .125$. This lies well within the interval $0 < \mu < 1/2$ wherein a profit can be earned and yet is large enough (as we soon shall see) to require large order quantities. Our objective is to compare the profits

(4.4.1) $\pi^*(\omega) = \pi(x^*(\omega), y^*(\omega), \omega)$

earned by using the optimal strategies $x^*(\omega)$ and $y^*(\omega)$ against various values of the opposition index ω with the quantity

(4.4.2) $\bar{\pi}(\omega) = \pi(.025, .582, \omega)$

which results from the use of the strategy $\bar{x} = .025, \bar{y} = .582$ against all opposition.

It is clear that no profit can be earned unless $0 \leqslant \omega < 1/2 = 1 - \sqrt{2\mu}$. Therefore, we computed the values of $x^*(\omega)$ and $y^*(\omega)$ for the levels $\omega = .02, .05,$ .10, .125, .15, .2, .25, .3, .35, .4, .45, and .5 of opposition. These are very easily approximated, incidentally, if Γ is replaced by a straight line in the strip $0 < x < .1$. For Γ is nearly straight in that interval, and the intersection of $H(\omega)$ with any straight line may be calculated from the quadratic formula. However, we chose a slightly more sensitive graphical method as better suited to our present purposes. The results appear in Table 4.4A, wherein the column headings are self-explanatory except for the one marked "efficiency." The entries in that column are simply the ratios $\bar{\pi}(\omega)/\pi^*(\omega)$, which seem useful for purposes of comparison. The values shown for $x^*(\omega)$ and $y^*(\omega)$ are not particularly accurate, but those of $\pi^*(\omega)$ are much more so because of the considerable flatness of the payoff near its optimum. Clearly the strategy $(\bar{x}, \bar{y}) = (.025, .582)$ is very nearly optimal against almost any opposition, performing poorly only if $\omega < .02$ or if $\omega > .45$. So even more robust strategies are available for the game $\mu = .125$ than were there for the auto dealers' game discussed earlier! Arguments concerning the existence of forces tending to prevent the escape of ω from the central portion of the region $0 < \omega < 1 - \sqrt{2\mu}$ may also, of course, be advanced in the case $\mu = .125$. But we shall not pause here to do

TABLE 4.4A

W	x*(w)	y*(w)	π*(w)	$\bar{\pi}$(w)	efficiency
.02	.015	.558	.410	.406	.99
.05	.028	.594	.330	.329	.99
.10	.039	.621	.241	.238	.99
.125	.041	.627	.207	.202	.98
.15	.042	.630	.178	.174	.98
.20	.041	.628	.131	.128	.98
.25	.038	.619	.094	.092	.99
.30	.032	.605	.065	.064	.98
.35	.024	.585	.041	.041	.99
.40	.016	.561	.023	.022	.98
.45	.007	.534	.008	.006	.75
.50	0	.500	0	---	---

so, because the issue of ω's central tendency cannot properly be settled without the examination of actual series

$$\{\omega(-t)\}_{t=0}^{\infty}$$

by those who have access to such series.

Much more, of course, remains to be said on the subject of robustness, both for the present game and for those characterized by other values of μ. But further numerical investigation seems better left to the potential user, who presumably will know which values of μ concern him. The data of Table 4.4A at least suggest that satisfactory strategies exist for other values of μ as well.

(4-4) Actually, $\int_0^T D_i(t)\,dt$ can be evaluated by elementary means. The ergodic theorem is needed only to evaluate $\int_0^T x_i(t)\,dt$. Evaluate the former without the aid of ergodicity.

(4-5) Suppose $\int_0^T x_i(t)\,dt$ were replaced by $\int_0^T [x_1(t)]^2\,dt$ in (4.3.2). How would this affect (4.3.4)? Refer to the appendix.

(4-6) In reality $D = D(t)$ is a random variable, and dealers must predict it roughly three months in advance to get their orders filled in time. Assume that $D(t+1) = D(t) + \Delta(t)$; here $\{\Delta(t)\}$ is a sequence of independent identically distributed *normal* random variables. Does this fact alone place an upper bound on the number of players who can play the auto dealers' game indefinitely? Assume zero reordering costs $K_1, \ldots, K_N$.

Appendix: The Derivation of Equation 4.3.4

It is to be shown that the result of performing the limit operation indicated in (4.3.4) is the function π_i of the positive arguments $s_1, S_1, \ldots, s_N, S_N$ exhibited in (4.3.4). That will be done with the aid of Birkhoff's ergodic theorem [5].

One may begin with the observation that

$$(A1) \quad (N_i(t) - 1)(S_i - s_i) \leqslant \int_0^T D_i(t) \, dt$$

$$\leqslant (N_i(T) + 1)(S_i - s_i) \leqslant 2(S_i - s_i) + \int_0^T D_i(t) \, dt,$$

wherefrom it follows that

$$(A2) \quad (S_i - s_i) \lim_{T \to \infty} \frac{N_i(T)}{T} = \lim_{T \to \infty} \frac{1}{T} \int_0^T D_i(t) \, dt = \overline{D}_i.$$

Thus the evaluation of (4.3.3) reduces to the computation of the time averages of $D_i(t)$ and $x_i(t)$ over long periods.

The dynamic system governing the depletion of inventories during periods $a < t < b$ during which no reorders are placed may be written

$$(A3) \quad \dot{x}_i(t) = -D_i(t) = -Dn_i x_i(t)/I(t),$$

$i = 1, \ldots, N$, where

$$(A4) \quad I(t) = n_1 x_1(t) + \cdots + n_N x_N(t).$$

The laws (A3) hold in the N-dimensional rectangle

$$(A5) \quad R = \{x = (x_1, \ldots, x_N): \ 0 < s_i < x_i < S_i\},$$

while $x_i(t)$ is supposed to jump instantaneously from s_i to S_i at instants τ for which

$$(A6) \quad \lim_{t \to \tau} x_i(t) = s_i.$$

The faces F_i of R whereon $x_i = s_i$ will be said to constitute the *near boundary* of R, while the opposite faces F_i' whereon $x_i = S_i$ form the *far boundary*. Thus, the *state vector* $x(t)$ obeys the law (A3) until it reaches a point of the near boundary of R, then jumps to a point of the far one.

For $N = 2$, the motion is as depicted in Figure 4.3B, except that $s_2 > 0$ implies $x_2(t) = S_2$ from time to time. But, simple as that picture is, it will prove useful to develop even simpler representations of the motion. To that end, define new variables $y_1, y_2, \ldots, y_N$ by the relations

$$(A7) \quad \begin{aligned} y_1 &= x_1 + x_2 + \cdots + x_N \\ y_i &= (1/n_1) \log x_1 - (1/n_i) \log x_i, \quad i = 2, 3, \ldots, N. \end{aligned}$$

The Jacobian of this coordinate transformation is

$$J(x_1, \ldots, x_N) = \frac{\partial(y_1, \ldots, y_N)}{\partial(x_1, \ldots, x_N)}$$

$$\text{(A8)} \quad = \begin{vmatrix} 1 & 1 & 1 & \cdots & 1 \\ (-1/n_1 x_1) & (1/n_2 x_2) & 0 & \cdots & 0 \\ (-1/n_1 x_1) & 0 & (1/n_3 x_3) & \cdots & 0 \\ \vdots & \vdots & \vdots & & \vdots \\ (-1/n_1 x_1) & 0 & 0 & & (1/n_N x_N) \end{vmatrix} = \frac{\displaystyle\sum_{i=1}^{N} n_i x_i}{\displaystyle\prod_{i=1}^{N} n_i x_i}.$$

It is positive throughout R, since the products $n_1 x_1, \ldots, n_N x_N$ all are.

It is clear that $y_2(t), \ldots, y_N(t)$ all remain constant during periods $a < t < b$ wherein (A3) holds, while $y_1(t) = y_1(a) - D(t - a)$ for such t, as the equations (A3) imply

$$\text{(A9)} \quad \begin{aligned} \dot{y}_1 &= \dot{x}_1 + \cdots + \dot{x}_N = -D \\ \dot{y}_i &= \dot{x}_1/n_1 x_1 - \dot{x}_i/n_i x_i = 0, \quad i = 2, 3, \ldots, N. \end{aligned}$$

Similarly the vector $y(t) = (y_1(t), \ldots, y_N(t))$ jumps discontinuously from y to $y + v^i$ at instants τ for which $x_i(t)$ diminishes to s_i, the vectors $v^1, \ldots, v^N$ being defined by

$$\text{(A10)} \quad \begin{aligned} v^1 &= ((S_1 - s_1), (1/n_1) \log (S_1/s_1), \ldots, (1/n_1) \log (S_1/s_1)), \\ v^i &= ((S_i - s_i), \ldots, (1/n_i) \log (s_i/S_i), \ldots, 0) \end{aligned}$$

for $i = 2, \ldots, N$, the only nonzero components of v^i being the first and the ith.

It is instructive to draw the histories of a few of the evolutions in y-space defined by the laws (A9)-(A10), even though such can conveniently be done only for $N = 2$. Clearly the motion is confined to the compact set R^* in that space which is the image under the transformation (A7) of the hyperrectangle R. The near boundary of R^* is composed of the images $F_1^*, \ldots, F_N^*$ of the near faces $F_1, \ldots, F_N$ of R, while the far boundary consists of the images $F_1'^*, \ldots, F_N'^*$ of its opposite faces.

The first few stages of such an evolution are shown in Figure A1, beginning from the initial position y. It is to be emphasized that the horizontal portions are traversed at the uniform rate $-D$, while the oblique ones are negotiated instantaneously.

Beginning at y, the state moves steadily westward (in the direction of decreasing y_1) until it reaches the near boundary of R^* at $y^1 \in F_1^*$. Thence it is translated instantaneously to $y^1 + v^1 \in F_1'^*$, and resumes its westward motion until again striking the near boundary of R^*, this time at $y^2 \in F_2^*$. Thence it goes immediately to $y^2 + v^2 \in F_2'^*$ and again resumes its westward drift, and so on. If a point of $F_1^* \cap F_2^*$ is ever reached, say at y^k, gradual movement is resumed from $y^k + v^1 + v^2$.

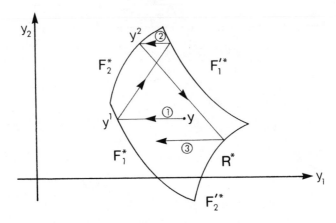

FIGURE A1

The motion seems even simpler if one imagines the entire $y_1 y_2$-plane to be "tiled" with infinitely many copies (i.e., translates) $R^* - m_1 v^1 - m_2 v^2$ of R^* itself, as shown in Figure A2. For then the state of the system moves forever along the ray r pointing west from y. The kth horizontal segment of the path shown in Figure A1 is just the image of the segment of r lying in the kth translate of R^* west of y in Figure A2, when that translate is carried back to R^*.

Exactly the same constructions may be carried out in any number of dimensions, though the pictures corresponding to A1 and A2 are hard to draw if

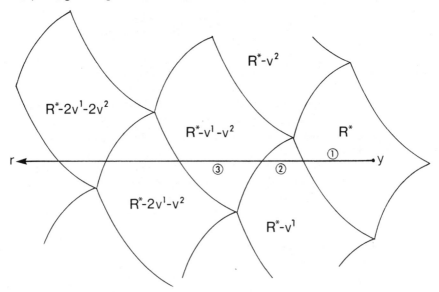

FIGURE A2

$N = 3$ and impossible when N is larger. The motion may always be regarded as a uniform one through a space subdivided into an infinite number of translates of R^*. Such subdivision is always possible because, since the opposite faces of R^* are translates of one another, every point in the space lies in one and only one translate of R^*.

If y be any point in E_N, and if e_1 be the vector $(1, 0, \ldots, 0)$ in that space, one may define

(A11) $$T_t(y) = y - Dt\, e_1.$$

The group $\{T_t\}$ of transformations thus defined for all real t clearly has the properties

(A12) $$T_{s+t}(y) = T_s(T_t(y)) = T_t(T_s(y)),$$

t and s being real and y an element of E_N. It also preserves Lebesgue measure, since the latter is translation invariant. That is

(A13) $$\mu(T_t(A)) = \mu(A)$$

for every Lebesgue measurable subset A of E_N. Finally, it may be observed that, for almost every vector $(s_1, S_1, \ldots, s_N, S_N)$ in E_{2N} the transformations T_t are all *ergodic* in the sense that

(A14) $$T_t(A) = A$$

for some $t \neq 0$ and some measurable $A \subset R^*$ implies

(A15) $$\mu(A) = 0 \quad \text{or} \quad \mu(A) = \mu(R^*).$$

For if A is a subset of R^* such that

(A16) $$0 < \mu(A) < \mu(R^*) \quad \text{and} \quad T_t(A) = A,$$

then

(A17) $$T_t(A) = A - Dte_1 = A - m_1 v^1 - m_2 v^2 - \cdots - m_N v^N$$

for some integers $m_1, m_2, \ldots, m_N$ not all zero. So all components of $m_1 v^1 + \cdots + m_N v^N$ save the first must be zero. That is

(A18) $$(m_1/n_1) \log (S_1/s_1) + (m_j/n_j) \log (s_j/S_j) = 0$$

for $j = 2, 3, \ldots, N$. And since such an equation fails to hold for almost every quadruple (s_1, S_1, s_j, S_j), the transformations T_t are almost surely ergodic.

When a commutative group $\{T_t\}$ of transformations are measure preserving and ergodic, Birkhoff's theorem asserts that

(A19) $$\lim_{t \to \infty} \frac{1}{t} \int_0^t f(T_s(y))\, ds = \frac{1}{\mu(R^*)} \int_{R^*} f(y)\, d\mu(y) \quad \text{a.e. } (y)$$

for every real-valued and integrable function f defined on R^*. So one may compute the time average of f along trajectories $\{T_s(y)\}_{s>0}$ as a space average over the compact region R^*. And since this permits the computation of those time averages when the trajectories are *unknown*, it is a very great saving indeed. For the explicit integration of the system (A9)–(A10) for the trajectories $\{T_t(y)\}_{t>0}$ appears exceedingly tedious if not impossible, while the evaluation of time averages via (A19) is easy.

To begin, it is necessary to evaluate the area $\mu(R^*)$ of R^*. It is just

$$\mu(R^*) = \int_{R^*} dy_1, \ldots, dy_N = \int_R J(x_1, \ldots, x_N)\, dx_1, \ldots, dx_N$$

$$(A20) \qquad = \int_{S_1}^{S_1} \int_{S_2}^{S_2} \cdots \int_{S_N}^{S_N} \left[\left(\sum_{i=1}^{N} n_i x_i \right) \middle/ \left(\prod_{i=1}^{N} n_i x_i \right) \right] dx_1 dx_2 \ldots dx_N$$

$$= \sum_{i=1}^{N} (S_i - s_i) \prod_{\substack{j=1 \\ j \neq i}}^{N} (1/n_j) \log (S_j/s_j) \ ,$$

$J(x_1, \ldots, x_N)$ being the Jacobian defined by (A8). Next one must know the time averages

$$(A21) \qquad \overline{D}_i = \lim_{T \to \infty} \frac{1}{T} \int_0^T D_i(t)\, dt \quad \text{and} \quad \overline{x}_i = \lim_{T \to \infty} \frac{1}{T} \int_0^T x_i(t)\, dt.$$

To compute them via (A19), one observes first that the coordinate transformation (A7) is invertible for

$$(A22) \qquad x_1 = X_1(y_1, \ldots, y_N), \ldots, x_N = X_N(y_1, \ldots, y_N).$$

Therefore one may write

$$\overline{x}_i = \frac{1}{\mu(R^*)} \int_{R^*} X_i(y_1, \ldots, y_N)\, dy_1 \ldots dy_N$$

$$= \frac{1}{\mu(R^*)} \int_R x_i J(x_1, \ldots, x_N)\, dx_1 \ldots dx_N$$

$$(A23)$$

$$= \frac{(S_i - s_i)\left[n_i(s_i + S_i)/2 + \displaystyle\sum_{\substack{j=1 \\ j \neq i}}^{N} (n_j(S_j - s_j)/\log (S_j/s_j)) \right]}{\log (S_i/s_i) \displaystyle\sum_{j=1}^{N} (n_j(S_j - s_j)/\log (S_j/s_j))} \ ,$$

and similarly

$$\bar{D}_i = \frac{1}{\mu(R^*)} \int_{R^*} \left[Dn_i X_i(y_1, \ldots, y_N) \middle/ \sum_{j=1}^{N} n_j X_j(y_1, \ldots, y_N) \right] dy_1 \ldots dy_N$$

$$= \frac{1}{\mu(R^*)} \int_{R} \left[Dn_i x_i \middle/ \sum_{j} n_j x_j \right] J(x_1, \ldots, x_N) \, dx_1 \ldots dx_N$$

(A24)
$$= \frac{1}{\mu(R^*)} \int_{s_1}^{S_1} \cdots \int_{s_N}^{S_N} \left[Dn_i x_i \prod_{j=1}^{N} n_j x_j \right] dx_1 \ldots dx_N$$

$$= \frac{n_i D(S_i - s_i)}{\log(S_i/s_i) \sum_{j=1}^{N} (n_j(S_j - s_j)/\log(S_j/s_j))} .$$

Finally, combining the results (A2), (A23), and (A24), (4.3.4) is obtained immediately.

REFERENCES

1. Naddor, E., *Inventory Systems* (New York: J. Wiley, 1966).
2. Case, J., and J. Donelson III, "On the Evaluation of the Payoff Functions in a Game of Inventory Control," Paper presented to 4th Meeting of ORSA, March, 1974.
3. Magee, J. F., *Production Planning and Inventory Control* (New York: McGraw-Hill, 1958).
4. Sasieni, A. Yaspan, and L. Friedman, *Operations Methods and Problems* (New York: John Wiley, 1959).
5. Birkhoff, G. D., "A Proof of the Ergodic Theorem," Proc. Nat'l. Acad. Sci., Vol. 17, pp. 656-60 (1931).

Chapter 5

Investment Games and Customer Behavior

The market models discussed earlier in this book have all proceeded from rather gross assumptions concerning the law of supply and demand. Such assumptions, while appropriate sometimes, often ignore the best information that an entrepreneur has, for his most reliable information may well be that which he acquires himself from daily contact with his customers: who they are, their feelings on logistical matters, and his own ability to meet their usual requirements. Thus it is desirable to construct models of customer behavior which reflect at least the more obvious aspects of it, such as brand loyalty, memory span, and shopping schedules. A number of such models, all of a simplistic nature, have been constructed and analyzed by J. Coleman Kitchen [2], [3].

1. INVESTMENT GAMES

In Kitchen's models, N competitors coexist in a certain market. Each chooses a single number, which represents the size of his investment in the satisfaction of his customers. The money thus spent may determine the range of varieties of a product that he sells, the competence of his service personnel, or the choice of films and frequency of showings at a cinema owned by him.

The market in which the N players (stores) operate contains D consumers. Each of them acts independently of the others. The probability p, controlled by storekeeper i, that a consumer investigating his store will (be satisfied with what he finds there and) make a purchase is the same for each consumer and is independent of past history. (Properly, p should be written p_i, but subscripts on this and other variables will be omitted when there is no apparent ambiguity as to which store is meant.) The cost per month (in dollars) to the storekeeper of maintaining this probability is a function $C(p)$ such that

$$(5.1.1) \qquad C(0) = 0, \quad C(1) = \infty, \quad 0 < C'(p) < \infty$$

for $0 \leqslant p < 1$. Also $C''(p)$ is assumed to exist and be continuous for $0 \leqslant p < 1$; the functions $C(\cdot)$ may differ from store to store by at most a multiplicative constant.

If a customer is satisfied at store i on a given shopping trip, he returns there on his next trip; if he is not, he goes home and randomly selects a store to visit next time. As will be explained presently, the timing of his next trip is independent of the results of his previous ones and may be governed by any of a certain class of probability laws. It is assumed also that the store earns a "raw profit" (retail price–wholesale price) of c from each sale. Thus the "net profit" in a month is c times the number of items sold in that month minus the "overhead" cost $C(p)$.

2. A MOTIVATING EXAMPLE

Suppose that each of the D consumers shops once each month. There are N stores in town carrying various varieties of a certain product (perhaps comic books), and each person visits exactly one store each shopping trip. Such would be natural if the stores were far apart, the individuals had little time for shopping, or their interest in the product were more casual than urgent.

The profit earned from the sale of a single item is c, and the cost h of carrying a single variety for a month is the same for all varieties in any given store. Each variety might, for instance, be stored in a rack or bin of fixed size.

Suppose that each consumer seeks to purchase a single variety every month and that $f(t)$ is the probability with which he chooses variety t. If it is assumed that $f(t)$ is a decreasing function of t, $f(\cdot)$ serves as a measure of the popularity of the various varieties. Each consumer purchases the chosen variety at the store he visits if it is available there; in this case he will return there next month. If what he wants is unavailable, he makes no purchase that month, and next month chooses randomly a new store to visit.

If the number of varieties is large, it is useful to think of a continuum of product varieties. The popularity function $f(\cdot)$ introduced above must then be replaced by a probability density function $f(t)$ defined for $t \geqslant 0$ such that

$$(5.2.1) \qquad \int_s^t f(u)\, du$$

is the probability that a particular consumer's choice for a given month will lie in the interval $s < u \leqslant t$. Of course, since f is a probability density function it must satisfy

$$(5.2.2) \qquad \int_0^\infty f(u)\, du = 1.$$

In reality, $f(t)$ is a step function with jumps only at the integer values of t, but we approximate it by a smooth function positive for all finite t.

If the manager stocks all varieties from 0 to a, then each entering customer will make a purchase with probability

$$(5.2.3) \qquad\qquad p = F(a) = \int_0^a f(u)\, du$$

and the monthly inventory cost associated with the "selection" $[0, a)$, and therefore with the probability p, is $C(p) = ha$. Hence

$$(5.2.4) \qquad\qquad C(p) = hF^{-1}(p),$$

where $F(\cdot)$ is the cumulative distribution associated with the density f and defined by (5.2.3).

It is easy to show that the function $C(p)$ so defined meets the requirements (5.1.1) proposed earlier. On the other hand, differentiation of (5.2.4) yields

$$(5.2.5) \qquad\qquad f(t) = h/C'(C^{-1}(ht))$$

and permits the recovery of f from C, whenever the latter satisfies (5.1.1). In particular, the fact that C is convex implies C' is increasing, and therefore that f is decreasing as earlier postulated.

(5-1) *Exercise* Show that the function $C(p)$ defined by (5.2.4) does meet the requirements (5.1.1).

Possible choices of $C(p)$ are

$$(5.2.6) \qquad\qquad \frac{kp}{1 - p}, \; k \tan\left(\frac{\pi p}{2}\right), \quad \text{and} \quad -\left(\frac{h}{a}\right)\ln(1 - p),$$

where $k = C(1/2)$ and $a > 0$. The corresponding popularity densities are

$$(5.2.7) \qquad\qquad \frac{k/h}{(k/h + t)^2}, \; \frac{2}{\pi}\frac{h/k}{1 + (th/k)^2}, \quad \text{and} \quad ae^{-at},$$

respectively. Of course it is entirely possible to envisage functions $C(\cdot)$ which are not convex, but such will not be discussed here.

(5-2) *Exercise* Derive (5.2.5) from (5.2.3).

(5-3) *Exercise* Verify the asserted correspondence between (5.2.6) and (5.2.7).

The model presented above is only one of a seemingly endless variety which relate entrepreneurial investment to consumer behavior in a more or less concrete fashion. More elaborate explanations of observed consumer behavior will suggest themselves to even the most casual reader, doubtless lie nearer the truth than the present rudimentary one, and deserve considerable attention. But Kitchen's was a pilot study, designed to discover the sorts of information to be extracted from models of a certain general type. So rather than become involved with complicated behavioral assumptions, he chose to bury as many as possible of the details of consumer activity within the abstract cost functions $C(\cdot)$. The model described above is only *one of many* leading to cost functions of the same general type. Kitchen's remaining behavioral hypotheses lead to the study of a certain Markov process, to be described in the next section.

3. CONSUMERS' SHIFTING ALLEGIANCES

Let it be said of a given consumer that he is in state j if he has made a purchase at store j this month, and is in state 0 if he has failed to make a purchase. It was explained earlier that if he is in state $j \neq 0$ this month he will return to store j next month and make a purchase there with probability p_j. So the probability of a transition from state $j \neq 0$ to state i in any month is

$$(5.3.1) \qquad p_{ji} = \begin{array}{ll} p_j & \text{if } i = j \\ 1 - p_j & \text{if } i = 0 \\ 0 & \text{if } i \neq j \ \text{ and } \ i \neq 0. \end{array}$$

And if he is in state 0 this month, he will visit store i with probability $1/N$ and be satisfied with probability p_i or disappointed with probability $1 - p_i$. So the probability of a transition from state 0 to state i in any month is

$$(5.3.2) \qquad \begin{array}{ll} p_{0i} = p_i/N & \text{if } i \neq 0 \\ = 1 - (1/N) \sum_j p_j & \text{if } i = 0. \end{array}$$

Thus if $\pi_i(t)$ be the probability that a given customer is in state $j = 0, 1, \ldots, N$ during month t, the recurrence relations

$$(5.3.3) \qquad \pi_i(t + 1) = p_i \pi_i(t) + p_i \pi_0(t)/N$$

must hold for $i = 1, \ldots, N$. Moreover, one must have

$$(5.3.4) \qquad \pi_0(t) + \cdots + \pi_N(t) = 1.$$

Thus, one might compute the probabilities $\pi_0(t), \ldots, \pi_N(t)$ for $t = 1, 2, \ldots$ if one were given their values for $t = 0$. Moreover, it is known from the elementary theory of Markov processes [1] that the limits

$$(5.3.5) \qquad \pi_i = \lim_t \pi_i(t)$$

exist for $i = 0, 1, \ldots, N$, and satisfy the $N + 1$ equations obtained by set-ting $\pi_i(t) = \pi_i(t + 1) = \pi_i$ in (5.3.3) to (5.3.4). Thus if one defines, for each $i = 1, \ldots, N$,

$$(5.3.6) \qquad\qquad s_i = p_i/(1 - p_i),$$

one may write

$$(5.3.7) \qquad\qquad \pi_i = \frac{\pi_0 p_i}{N(1 - p_i)} = \frac{\pi_0 s_i}{N}.$$

So the fact that

$$(5.3.8) \qquad 1 = \pi_0 + \pi_1 + \cdots + \pi_N = \pi_0 \frac{N + s_i + \cdots + s_N}{N}$$

yields finally

$$(5.3.9) \qquad \pi_0 = \frac{N}{N + s_1 + \cdots + s_N} \quad\text{and}\quad \pi_i = \frac{s_i}{N + s_1 + \cdots + s_N}$$

for $i = 1, \ldots, N$. The quantity s_i is simply the "odds" that a customer visiting store i in a given month will be satisfied there, and is controlled directly by storekeeper i. And $\pi_i(s_1, \ldots, s_N)$ is the steady-state probability that a given customer will buy from him in a given month if each keeper $j = 1, \ldots, N$ takes action s_j every month. So $D\pi_i(s_1, \ldots, s_N)$ is the fraction of all customers who buy from i in a typical month, and $cD\pi_i(s_1, \ldots, s_N)$ is the revenue he may ex-pect from their purchases. If one writes finally $C(s_i) = C(p_i(s_i))$ for $C(s_i/(s_i + 1))$, one may express storekeeper i's expected monthly profit* as

$$(5.3.10) \qquad P_i(s_1, \ldots, s_N) = \frac{cDs_i}{N + s_1 + \cdots + s_N} - K_i C(s_i).$$

Therefore the storekeepers are engaged in the game

$$(5.3.11) \qquad\qquad i \max_{s_i \geq 0} P_i(s_1, \ldots, s_N),$$

which differs from the auto dealers' game discussed in the previous chapter only because of the constant N appearing in the denominator of the fractional part of (5.3.10), and because $C(s_i)$ may not be proportional to s_i itself.

Clearly $P_i(s_1, \ldots, s_N)$ is decreasing in each $s_j (j \neq i)$ and unimodal in s_i when-ever $C(s_i)$ is convex in s_i. So the game (5.3.11) is simply directed when $C(s_i)$ is convex, and there is no possibility that the players will collude to bring dominated actions into use. Moreover, from its similarity to the auto dealers' game, one

---

*The K_i's appearing here are simply (positive) constants of proportionality, introduced to furnish a notion of "efficiency," which may differ somewhat from player to player.

would expect robust strategies to exist for the storekeepers' game unless $C(\cdot)$ is violently nonlinear. They do, as will be shown presently. First, however, certain comments seem in order.

It should be observed, for instance, that the present game has a cooperative aspect that others (like the auto dealers' game) do not. The number of items the market is willing to buy is no longer a fixed constant but a variable depending on the entire vector $(p_1, \ldots, p_N)$. So there is doubtless a cooperative solution for the game whereby one store (the one with least overhead, i.e., the smallest of the constants K_i mentioned above) maintains a large inventory and the rest accept side payments from the most efficient in return for going out of business. Such transactions are observed from time to time when one store owner buys out another and closes the less profitable site. They are the exception rather than the rule, however, as the new owner usually continues to operate both stores for reasons of location. Those reasons cannot properly be explained in terms of the present model, though, since location plays no explicit role in it. It suffices to observe that rarely are there enough such sales to permit one store (or one owner) to exercise a real monopoly in any single market.

It should be observed too that the model (5.3.11) is appropriate in rather more general circumstances than those for which it was derived. Kitchen shows, under certain conditions on the function $p_\alpha(I)$, that [2] the expression (5.3.10) is appropriate if a typical store's gain from a sale is not a fixed constant c, but one of $0 = c_0 < c_1 < c_2 < \cdots < c_r$, the probability of gain c_α being $p_\alpha(I)$ when I is the store's monthly investment in consumer satisfaction. For then c may be taken to be a certain linear combination of $c_0, c_1, \ldots, c_r$.

Likewise, the model is appropriate if each customer shops (returns to the market), not once each month, but according to some stochastic arrival process with jumps of size one whereby the number N_t of his visits in t months is (almost surely) asymptotic to t for large t.

Finally, it is possible to extend the above results to two apparently different models of customer behavior. In both, it is assumed that each of the D customers maintains a list of preferred stores. If a given customer is satisfied at a particular store he returns to it each trip until it fails to satisfy him. When that happens (as almost surely it must), he strikes that store from his list and on his next trip selects a store to visit as follows: with probability $1 - \epsilon$ he randomly selects a store from his current list, and with probability ϵ he randomly chooses a store not on that list. If he is satisfied with the store so chosen, he adds it to his list and returns there next trip; otherwise he drops it from (or leaves it off) the list and on his next trip randomly selects a store in the manner described above.

The models differ only in their treatments of the empty list. The first supposes that when a customer's list is empty, he randomly visits stores until eventually he is satisfied at one and is obliged to return there next trip. Thereafter, he will always have either an empty list or one containing a single store to which he is committed to return. It is inevitable that the customer will eventually reach this state. Once he does, his behavior is exactly what it was in the original model. So the same long-term conclusions apply.

For the second model it is supposed that a customer with an empty list simply reinstates all N stores to his list and begins again. And in this model too, though it involves a different set than (5.3.3) of Markov transition relations, the steady-state probabilities (5.3.9), and hence the payoff functions (5.3.10), are appropriate.

In short, there are a number of alternate hypotheses under which the game (5.3.11) mirrors accurately the effects of the store owners' various decisions. Doubtless there are others under which their game differs but little from (5.3.11). Let us now, therefore, proceed to the analysis of that game.

4. LINEAR COST FUNCTIONS

Having established the validity of the model (5.3.11) under a variety of assumptions concerning consumer behavior, we must ask how the players ought to behave in it. We consider first the case in which $C(s) \equiv s$, as that one seems the simplest in which $C(p) = C(s/(1 + s))$ has the properties required in §1.

Since the essential features of the game are unchanged when the payoff functions (5.3.10) are multiplied by positive constants, we may consider for simplicity the game

$$(5.4.1) \qquad i \max_{s_i \geqslant 0} P_i(s_1, \ldots, s_N) = \frac{s_i}{s_i + w_i} - T_i s_i$$

where $T_i = K_i/cD$ and $w_i = N + \Sigma_{j \neq i} s_j$. It is, but for the fact that $w_i \geqslant N$, identical to the auto dealers' game. In particular, P_i is a concave function of s_i for fixed w_i and T_i. So there is a unique maximizing value s_i^* for each pair (w_i, T_i) given by

$$(5.4.2) \qquad \begin{aligned} s_i^* &= \sqrt{w_i/T_i} - w_i \quad \text{if} \quad 0 \leqslant w_i \leqslant 1/T_i \\ &= 0 \qquad\qquad\qquad \text{otherwise.} \end{aligned}$$

And the largest value of P_i^* in that case is

$$(5.4.3) \qquad \begin{aligned} P_i^*(w_i) &= (1 - \sqrt{T_i w_i})^2 \quad \text{if} \quad 0 \leqslant w_i \leqslant 1/T_i \\ &= 0 \qquad\qquad\qquad\quad \text{otherwise.} \end{aligned}$$

Clearly both s_i^* and P_i^* are continuous in w_i and in T_i over the relevant ranges $w_i \geqslant N$ and $T_i > 0$. It is clear too that relatively robust values of s_i are available for values of $w_i T_i < .85$ or so, because of the similarity of the present game with the auto dealers'. But for values of $w_i T_i$ nearer one, s_i must be very near $s_i^* = s_i^*(T_i, w_i)$ to yield a near-optimal return. More will be said about robustness

presently. First, however, we point out that in Rosen's terms [4] the game
(5.4.1) is "diagonally strictly concave" and therefore possesses a unique Nash
equilibrium $(s_1^*, \ldots, s_N^*)$ which is *stable* in the sense that the solutions of the
ordinary differential equations

$$\dot{s}_i = \partial P_i(s_1, \ldots, s_N)/\partial s_i$$

all converge to $(s_1^*, \ldots, s_N^*)$ from starting points $(s_{10}, \ldots, s_{N0})$ in the positive
orthant of $s_1 \ldots s_N$-space provided suitable conventions are in force at the
boundaries thereof. The nature of those equilibria is of interest.

To compute them, suppose $T_1 \leqslant \cdots \leqslant T_N$ and define

$$(5.4.4) \qquad S = \sum_j s_j \quad \text{and} \quad S_i = S - s_i$$

and

$$(5.4.5) \qquad W = \sum_j T_j \quad \text{and} \quad W_i = W - T_i.$$

If $\bar{s} = (s_1, \ldots, s_N)$ is a positive Nash equilibrium, it must satisfy the N equations

$$(5.4.6) \qquad s_i = \sqrt{(S_i + N)/T_i} - S_i - N,$$

or

$$(5.4.7) \qquad N + S = \sqrt{(S_i + N)/T_i},$$

so the quantities $(S_i + N)/T_i$ have a common value C independent of i. So

$$(5.4.8) \qquad s_i = \sqrt{C} - CT_i,$$

and summing these over all $j \neq i$ gives

$$(5.4.9) \qquad S_i = (N - 1)\sqrt{C} - CW_i$$

so that, from the definition of C,

$$(5.4.10) \qquad CW - (N - 1)\sqrt{C} - N = 0.$$

This quadratic equation may be solved for

$$(5.4.11) \qquad \sqrt{C} = ((N - 1) + \sqrt{(N - 1)^2 + 4NW})/2W,$$

which value may be inserted in (5.4.8) to yield

$$(5.4.12) \qquad s_i = \frac{(N - 1)^2 + \sqrt{(N - 1)^2 + 4NW}}{2W}$$
$$- \frac{T_i((N - 1)^2 + 2NW + (N - 1)\sqrt{(N - 1)^2 + 4NW})}{2W^2}.$$

The latter may be simplified, in the case $T_1 = \cdots = T_N = T$, to

(5.4.13) $s_i = (N - 1)/2N^2T - 1 + ((N - 1)^2 + 4N^2T)^{1/2}/2N^2T,$

and it may also be shown that the equilibrium payoff to player i is

(5.4.14) $P_i^* = (1 - T_i\sqrt{C})^2.$

Thus if $s_1 > 0, \ldots, s_N > 0$ is a Nash equilibrium, it must be that the s_i's have the values (5.4.12). Conversely, those values constitute an equilibrium if and only if they are all positive. Moreover, (5.4.8) reveals that all will be positive iff s_N is positive. Manipulation of the expression (5.4.11) for C then yields the condition

(5.4.15) $W \geq NT_N^2 + (N - 1)T_N,$

which is both necessary and sufficient for (5.4.12) to represent an equilibrium.

Next, suppose that (5.4.15) is violated, so that (5.4.12) does not represent an equilibrium. Then some of the s_i, presumably the ones corresponding to the largest T_j (for those are the least efficient operators) must vanish at equilibrium. The presumption is correct, as it can be shown that $T_j \geq T_k$ implies $s_j \leq s_k$ at equilibrium. If (5.4.15) is violated, one may seek an equilibrium by setting equal to zero all those s_i which are made nonpositive by the formula (5.4.12), and trying again to find positive values of the remaining s_i which satisfy (5.4.6). Failing that, one puts equal to zero all those s_i which were nonpositive at either earlier attempt, and continues. The process fails only if $T_1 > 1/N$, in which case $(0, \ldots, 0)$ is the desired equilibrium because no player can earn a positive profit even against null opposition. It is emphasized that null opposition differs from no opponents, since a store with $s_j = 0$ still attracts a few customers; it just doesn't get repeat customers! No justification for the procedure outlined above will be given. Rather, we return to the matter of robustness. As usual, when discussing that subject, we fix attention on a particular player i, and suppress the subscript i for the duration.

Any discussion of robustness must begin with the elimination of whatever dominated actions there may be. In the present game one may establish that

>   (i) if $0 < T \leq 1/4N$ then each $s > 1/4T$ is dominated, and

(5.4.16)

>   (ii) if $1/4N \leq T \leq 1/2$ then each $s > \sqrt{N/T} - N$ is dominated.

Such facts are essential because they eliminate certain actions from further consideration *and* because they limit the degree of opposition w to be encountered.

We assume for the present that T is the same for all players and that $T < 1/N$; then a symmetric equilibrium in positive values of s exists and yields to each player a positive profit. Motivated by our findings for previous games, we look for robust actions in the neighborhood of the symmetric equilibrium action s^*.

Let $R(w, T)$ denote, for a given strategy $\hat{s}$, the ratio of the payoff to a player i using $\hat{s}$ against opposition w to that earned using $s^*(w)$ against w. The shape of the graph of $z = R(w, T)$ for fixed $\hat{s}$, T is familiar from the discussion in Chapter IV of the auto dealers' game. Typically, it equals unity for two values of w, is nearly unity for small w (if $\hat{s}$ is at all robust), and becomes negative for excessively large w. Finally we denote by w_{max} the value of w realized when each opposing player simultaneously chooses his largest undominated action, and by R_{min} the least value of $R(w, T)$ in the interval $N \leqslant w \leqslant w_{max}$. Then we determine R_{min} for various values of N and T and various actions $\hat{s}$. If R_{min} is nearly unity for a particular pair (N, T), then $\hat{s}$ is a robust strategy for the game specified by that parameter pair.

If, for example, $N = 2$ and $T = .01$, the Nash equilibrium lies at (24.96, 24.96). So choosing $\hat{s} = 24.96$, we calculate that $R(2, .01) = .917$ and that R increases to 1, reaching it at about $w = 23$, then decreases to .999999 and increases back to 1 when the opposing player's action is 24.96, which is near $w_{max} - 2 = 25$. But one can do even better overall using $\hat{s} = 21.22$, since then R exceeds .95 on the entire interval $2 \leqslant w \leqslant w_{max} = 27$. Kitchen [3] offers in Table 5.4A often highly robust strategies for various values of N and T. These

TABLE 5.4A

T	N	S	R_{min}
.00025	2	999.9	.78
.00025	2	599.9	.89
.00025	3	888.4	.82
.00025	3	599.9	.89
.00025	4	749.3	.69
.00025	4	599.5	.9
.001	2	249.9	.81
.001	2	149.9	.9
.001	3	221.7	.86
.001	3	149.5	.9
.001	4	186.8	.68
.001	4	149.5	.9
.01	2	25.	.92
.01	2	20.6	.96
.01	3	21.7	.97
.01	3	20.6	.98
.01	4	18.1	.44
.01	4	15.4	.74
.06	2	4	.99
.06	3	3.15	.93
.06	4	2.4	-677
.06	4	.083	.05

TABLE 5.4B

N = 2

T	P*	Value of P_{min} for Nash strategy	$\bar{P}/N$	(P/N)/P*
.00025	.250	.78	.478	1.9
.001	.248	.81	.456	1.8
.01	.231	.92	.369	1.6
.06	.16	.99	.214	1.3
		N = 3		
.00025	.111	.82	.315	2.8
.001	.110	.86	.298	2.7
.01	.102	.97	.228	2.2
.06	.064	.93	.111	1.7
		N = 4		
.00025	.062	.69	.234	3.8
.001	.062	.68	.219	3.5
.01	.056	.44	.16	2.9
.06	.033	-677	.065	2.0

indicate that robust strategies exist in profusion for a wide variety of games of this type and provide a handy guide for prospective players of the games.

These games contain considerable incentive to collude, for if S be the sum of all s_i, the optimal total profit available to the N players together is the maximal value of $S/(S + N) - TS$, and any vector of s_i such that $S = \sqrt{N/T} - N = \bar{S}$ will yield it. The total payoff when $\bar{S}$ is played is then $\bar{P} = (1 - \sqrt{NT})^2$. So it is possible to compare the payoff P^*, which the players get at the game's Nash equilibrium, with $\bar{P}/N$, a single player's share of the optimal pot. Kitchen has done exactly that for a number of values of (N, T); the results appear in Table 5.4B. Observe that the ratios $(\bar{P}/N)/P^*$ are large, and increase with efficiency, that is, as T decreases.

Actually, there is an even stronger form of cooperation which the players may contemplate. For $\bar{P}$ is the most they can earn if all remain in business. If only one remains open, while the rest all close their doors, the remaining store could earn $(1 - \sqrt{T})^2 > \bar{P}$ and pay the others even more that $\bar{P}/N$ in side payments.

We do not dwell on these matters at length, because agreements of the sort described above seem prohibitively hard to reach and to maintain. Under the latter arrangement, the "retired" storekeepers would find it difficult to prevent the remaining operator from missing occasional payments. Even under the former (simpler) cooperative arrangement, there is substantial incentive for individuals to cheat! Only when relying on a robust strategy does a player seem to possess a measure of protection against unexpected acts by his competitors and yet retain a more or less reasonable expectation of profit.

5. CONVEX COST FUNCTIONS

Many of the results obtained for linear cost functions may be extended to the case in which $C(s)$ is strictly convex. For instance, the games (5.3.11) remain diagonally strictly concave in that case and therefore possess unique equilibria which are stable in the sense described earlier. Also, the games remain simply directed, so there is no incentive to introduce dominated strategies. Finally, robust strategies may well be present.

To demonstrate robustness, it is of course necessary to choose a specific cost function so that numerical experiments may be performed. The function

$$(5.5.1) \qquad C(s) = T(s + 1)^3 - T$$

is convex but not linear. If it be assumed that (5.5.1) holds, then the optimal response $s^*(w)$ to the level w of opposition is

$$
(5.5.2) \quad
\begin{aligned}
s^*(w) &= (-1/2)[(w + 1) + ((w - 1)^2 + 4(w/3T)^{1/2})^{1/2}] \quad \text{if} \quad w \leqslant 1/3T \\
&= 0 \qquad \text{otherwise.}
\end{aligned}
$$

No profit can be made if $N > 2$ and $T > 1/6$.

The Nash equilibrium actions, as in the linear model, are often robust. Table 5.5A illustrates the fact for various (N, T).

TABLE 5.5A

N = 2

T	R_{min} for Nash Strategy	T	R_{min} for Nash Strategy
10^{-3}	.99	10^{-9}	.93
10^{-4}	.99	10^{-10}	.92
10^{-5}	.97	10^{-11}	.92
10^{-6}	.96	10^{-12}	.92
10^{-7}	.94	10^{-13}	.92
10^{-8}	.93		

N = 3

T	R_{min} for Nash Strategy
10^{-3}	.99
10^{-4}	.99
10^{-6}	.97
10^{-9}	.94
10^{-12}	.93
10^{-13}	.93

(5-4) *Exercise* Find the Cournot-Nash equilibrium if $T_i s_i$ is replaced by an arbitrary common cost function $C(s_i)$ in (5.4.1). What will be the effect of a regulatory decision that causes a cost increase

$$C(s_i) \rightarrow C(s_i) + \alpha f(s_i)$$

in this industry. What property of f determines whether the level of consumer services will increase or decrease as a result of that decision?

(5-5) *Question* Estimate the benefits of cooperation to be obtained should the players agree to form a coalition of the whole and distribute profits equally. Do the benefits increase or decrease as their efficiencies improve?

6. POSSIBLE EXTENSIONS

Two limitations of the present models should be immediately apparent: the customers have ridiculously short memories, and they exhibit an unnatural willingness to drive all over town. More elaborate models should be constructed wherein other visits than the most recent play a role in customers' choice processes, and wherein they are more likely to visit stores near home than others far away. Doubtless such models will in time be constructed, analyzed, and fitted to available market data.

Moreover, two other primary determinants of customer behavior must be accounted for, namely price levels and advertisement. It will be shown in the next chapter how these effects may be introduced into the auto dealers' game without rendering the model intractable. Doubtless they may be introduced into investment games too, though not in the same manner.

Before such deeds are accomplished, however, it is tempting to speculate that the results will follow the pattern established here; the more complex games will also have payoff functions which may be calculated with the aid of the theory of finite *ergodic* Markov processes, they will be simply directed, and they will possess robust strategies. If so, the methods of this book should permit a fairly thorough comprehension of those games.

REFERENCES

1. Cinlar, Erhan, *Introduction to Stochastic Processes* (Englewood Cliffs, N.J.: Prentice-Hall, 1975).
2. Kitchen, J. Coleman "On a Class of Investment Games," Ph.D. thesis in the mathematical sciences, The Johns Hopkins University, 1975.
3. Kitchen, J. Coleman, *Competitive Investment Games*, to appear
4. Rosen, J. B., "Existence and Uniqueness of Equilibrium Points for Concave *N*-person Games," *Econometrica*, vol. 33, no. 3 (July 1965), pp. 520-534.

Chapter 6

Ad Games and a Cab Game

The game-theoretic nature of a considerable variety of prototypical managerial decisions has been discussed within these pages, but the one managerial activity that seems to intrude most into daily life has yet to be mentioned. Advertising strategy has not engaged our attention. To discuss advertising in quantitative terms, a model of customer reaction to it is required.

1. THE MODEL

Let us consider firms (breweries, cosmetic manufacturers, and automobile makers are familiar examples) who compete for the trade of a fixed pool of customers. Call the firms $1, 2, \ldots, N$ and let $x_i(t)$ be the fraction of the total customer pool who trade at time t with firm i. Then $1 - x_i(t)$ is the fraction of customers who do not. Assume first that if i spends at a rate of \$$u_i$/week on his advertising campaign during a period $[t, t + h)$ of time wherein the other firms do not advertise, $x_i(t)$ will increase by a quantity

$$(6.1.1) \qquad \alpha_i h f(u_i) (1 - x_i(t)) + o(h)$$

roughly proportional to the duration h and to the fraction $1 - x_i(t)$ of the customers not already committed to brand i, but depending in a possibly non-linear fashion on the expenditure rate u_i. Since the pool of customers is of fixed size, those i gains must be lost by the firms $j \neq i$. Assume that the fraction j loses is proportional to the fraction j has at time t, namely $x_j(t)/(1 - x_i(t))$. So $x_j(t)$ will decrease by a quantity

$$(6.1.2) \qquad \alpha_i h \cdot f(u_i) \cdot x_j(t) + o(h)$$

in the period $[t, t + h)$. And if it be assumed that the effects of simultaneous advertising by all parties are additive, the net change in $x_i(t)$ during the period due to their combined efforts is

$$(6.1.3) \qquad \Delta x_i(t) = \alpha_i h \cdot f(u_i)(1 - x_i(t)) - h x_i(t) \sum_{\substack{j=1 \\ j \neq i}}^{N} \alpha_j f(u_j) + o(h).$$

So passing to the limit as $h \to 0$ we obtain

$$(6.1.4) \quad \dot{x}_i = \alpha_i f(u_i) - (\alpha_1 f(u_1) + \cdots + \alpha_N f(u_N)) x_i, \quad i = 1, \ldots, N.$$

The N equations (6.1.4) constitute a very simple system of ordinary differential equations, trivially solvable if $u_1, \ldots, u_N$ are specified constants or functions of time.

The positive numbers $\alpha_1, \ldots, \alpha_N$ may be termed "effectiveness coefficients," for an advertiser with a large α can win converts more cheaply than one whose α is small. And the function $f(\cdot)$ may be called the "response function," since it describes customers' response rate to various levels of expenditure. We assume it to be the same for every firm, to have derivatives of all orders including an everywhere positive first derivative, and a second derivative which is negative or zero at least for large values of the argument. The latter restriction of course implies that a law of diminishing returns is in effect. It may also be assumed that $f(1) = 1$, as any other value could be absorbed into the constants $\alpha_1, \ldots, \alpha_N$; $f(0) = 0$ is natural too.

If $u_1, \ldots, u_N$ take constant positive values, $x_i(t)$ tends rapidly to its steady-state value

$$(6.1.5) \qquad X_i(u_1, \ldots, u_N) = \frac{\alpha_i f(u_i)}{\alpha_1 f(u_1) + \cdots + \alpha_N f(u_N)},$$

which clearly is positive and less than unity. Moreover, if it is assumed that

$$(6.1.6) \qquad X_i(\lambda u_1, \ldots, \lambda u_N) = X_i(u_1, \ldots, u_N)$$

for every $\lambda > 0$, it is possible to infer the form of the function f. For then the fraction (6.1.5) is unchanged if one either divides top and bottom by $f(u_i)$ or divides every argument by u_i. So

$$(6.1.7) \quad \alpha_1 \left(\frac{f(u_1)}{f(u_i)} \right) + \cdots + \alpha_N \left(\frac{f(u_N)}{f(u_i)} \right) = \alpha_1 f \left(\frac{u_1}{u_i} \right) + \cdots + \alpha_N f \left(\frac{u_N}{u_i} \right),$$

because $f(1) = 1$. And if (6.1.7) is to hold as an identity in $\alpha_1, \alpha_2, \ldots, \alpha_N$, then necessarily

$$(6.1.8) \qquad \frac{f(u_j)}{f(u_i)} = f \left(\frac{u_j}{u_i} \right)$$

must hold for positive values of u_i and u_j. Moreover, (6.1.8) is equivalent to the functional equation

$$(6.1.9) \qquad f(xy) = f(x) \cdot f(y),$$

wherefore $F(x) = \log f(x)$ must obey

$$(6.1.10) \qquad F(xy) = F(x) + F(y).$$

And since (6.1.10) has no other [1] continuous solutions than $F(\cdot) = \gamma \log (\cdot)$, we may conclude that

(6.1.11) $$f(x) = x^\gamma$$

for some constant γ. Finally the restrictions placed earlier on the derivatives of $f(\cdot)$ imply $0 < \gamma \leqslant 1$. One may now formulate the basic advertising game very quickly.

2. THE AD GAME

Assume that the firms $1, \ldots, N$ have constant monthly advertising budgets $u_1, \ldots, u_N$ and that their revenues are proportional to the number of customers they have. The latter numbers will then be constant too, and be given by (6.1.5). So the total rewards accruing firm i during a given month will be about

(6.2.1) $$\pi_i(u_1, \ldots, u_N) = \frac{K_i \alpha_i u_i^\gamma}{\alpha_1 u_1^\gamma + \cdots + \alpha_N u_N^\gamma} - u_i,$$

K_i being a positive constant. Hence when $\gamma = 1$, the identifications $\alpha_i = n_i$, $K_i = P_i D$, and $C_i = 1$ show that the Ad Game is, like Cold War before it, simply another instance of the auto dealers' game. So it too can be expected to yield to the techniques which have already proven their worth in bidding games. However, it seems likely that the cases $\gamma < 1$ are of more interest in the present context than $\gamma = 1$. So we should examine at least a few of those games before jumping to conclusions about the applicability of bidding techniques to advertising decisions.

If one defines

(6.2.2) $$\sigma = (u_i/K_i)^\gamma \quad \text{and} \quad \omega = \frac{1}{K_i^\gamma \alpha_i} \sum_{\substack{j=1 \\ j \neq i}}^{N} \alpha_j u_j^\gamma,$$

then one may regard σ as i's normalized action variable, ω as his index of opposition, and

(6.2.3) $$\pi = \frac{\pi_i}{K_i} = \frac{\sigma}{\sigma + \omega} - \sigma^{1/\gamma}$$

as his normalized payoff function. The curves $Z = \pi(\sigma, \omega)$ for fixed ω look much like those from previous games, except of course that they are now bounded above by the strictly concave $Z = 1 - \sigma^{1/\gamma}$ instead of by the straight line $Z = 1 - \sigma$. A few examples appear in Figure 6.2A, wherein the line Λ of

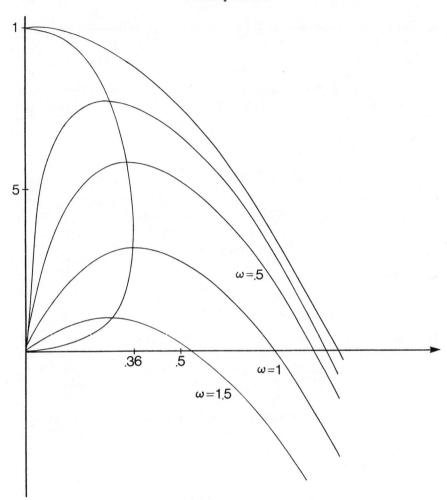

FIGURE 6.2A

zeniths is also shown, for the case $\gamma = 1/2$. The game differs from others we have studied in that, for any fixed value of ω, $\partial\pi/\partial\sigma$ can be made positive by choosing σ small enough. So against *any* level of opposition, a positive reward may be earned. Of course if ω is very large, the rewards to be earned are small and only very conservative actions will earn them. But robust strategies do exist, as Figure 6.2A suggests. They are found by eye, choosing a vertical line $\sigma = $ constant to approximate Λ, and they earn near-optimal returns against a wide variety of ω's.

To appreciate how wide the range of ω's is against which $\sigma = .3$ earns a good reward, observe from Figure 6.2A that values of $\sigma > .36$ are dominated. So in the symmetric games $\alpha_1 = \alpha_2 = \cdots = \alpha_N$, a player whose opponents all choose $\sigma < .36$ will experience levels of opposition $\omega < (N-1) \times .36$. Thus, as many as five or even six opponents providing maximal opposition may be admitted to the competition without fear of driving ω to levels that cause $\sigma = .3$ to perform poorly. In short, the diminishing returns to advertising expenditure implied by $\gamma = 1/2$ bring even more robustness to the present game than was found in the auto dealers', or in the auction games considered earlier. The effect is further magnified if γ is again decreased.

3. WHEN AUTO DEALERS ADVERTISE

Various of the models heretofore described may be assembled into larger models, wherein each participant chooses, not one, but several distinct actions. For example, we may put the previous advertising model together with the auto dealers' game to obtain one in which each dealer chooses both his inventory level and his advertising budget. One might expand the model to include the effect of price variations as well if it seemed desirable to do so. In practice, however, there seems to be a rather well defined "price" for a given automobile (ordinarily distinct from the "sticker price") from which significant deviation is rare, and it seems more realistic to regard the prices as fixed and to consider reductions below them to be advertising costs.

To construct the desired model, assume that the number n_j of potential customers visiting i's showroom each week is governed by advertising. That is, assume that

(6.3.1) $$n_i = X_i(u_1, \ldots, u_N),$$

where $X_i(\cdot, \ldots, \cdot)$ is defined by (6.1.5). Then the value of advertising is in bringing customers to the showroom, and the value of inventory is in satisfying those who come. Player i's reward function is

(6.3.2)
$$\pi_i(s_1, u_1, \ldots, s_N u_N) = \frac{P_i D s_i X_i}{s_1 X_1 + \cdots + s_N X_N} - C_i s_i - u_i$$

$$= \frac{P_i D s_i \left(\dfrac{\alpha_i u_i^\gamma}{\alpha_1 u_1^\gamma + \cdots + \alpha_N u_N^\gamma} \right)}{\left(\dfrac{s_1 \alpha_1 u_1^\gamma + \cdots + s_N \alpha_N u_N^\gamma}{\alpha_1 u_1^\gamma + \cdots + \alpha_N u_N^\gamma} \right)} - C_i s_i - u_i$$

$$= \frac{P_i D s_i \alpha_i u_i^\gamma}{s_1 \alpha_1 u_1^\gamma + \cdots + s_N \alpha_N u_N^\gamma} - C_i s_i - u_i$$

Therefore, if one defines the dimensionless quantities

(6.3.3)   and
$$\sigma = (C_i s_i / P_i D), \quad \mu = (u_i / P_i D)^\gamma,$$

$$\omega = \frac{C_i}{(P_i D)^{1+\gamma}} \sum_{\substack{i=1 \\ j \neq i}}^{N} \frac{\alpha_j}{\alpha_i} s_j u_j^\gamma,$$

one may regard σ and μ as normalized action variables belonging to i, ω as his normalized opposition, and

(6.3.4) $$\pi = \frac{\pi_i}{P_i D} = \frac{\sigma\mu}{\sigma\mu + \omega} - \sigma - \mu^{1/\gamma}$$

as his normalized reward. Clearly he would like to make π as large as he can. And that requires

(6.3.5) $$\mu^{1/\gamma} = \gamma\sigma,$$

for his choices μ and σ have clearly to solve the problem

(6.3.6)
$$\text{minimize} \quad \sigma + \mu^{1/\gamma}$$
$$\text{subject to} \quad \mu\sigma \; = \; \text{constant.}$$

Hence, substituting (6.3.5) into (6.3.4) yields

(6.3.7) $$\pi(\sigma, \omega) = \frac{\gamma^\gamma \sigma^{1+\gamma}}{\gamma^\gamma \sigma^{1+\gamma} + \omega} - (1 + \gamma)\sigma.$$

The further substitutions of

(6.3.8) $$x = (1 + \gamma)^{1+\gamma} \sigma^{1+\gamma} \quad \text{and} \quad y = \omega/\gamma^\gamma (1 + \gamma)^{1+\gamma}$$

into (6.3.7) yield finally

(6.3.9) $$\pi(x, y) = \frac{x}{x + y} - x^{\frac{1}{1+\gamma}},$$

which is a reward function of exactly the form (6.2.3) considered earlier, in relation to the pure advertising problem. But the reward curves $Z = \pi(x, y)$, y fixed, look differently because they are bounded above by the strictly convex graph $Z = 1 - x^{1/1+\gamma}$ instead of by a concave or a linear one.

Figures 6.3A and 6.3B show the curves obtained for the parameter values $\gamma = 1$ and $\gamma = .5$, respectively. They differ from families encountered earlier in that they are not unimodal, they all have negative slope near the origin, and hence local maxima at $x = 0$. The implication is that even if so much opposition is anticipated that breaking even may prove impossible, highly conservative actions do not pay for $x = .2$ loses less against near-break-even levels of opposition in either case ($\gamma = 1/2$ or $\gamma = 1$) than does $x = .05$, as is clear from Figures 6.3A and 6.3B. Such phenomena are hardly unusual in business situations, but they have not previously been evident in the models presented here.

In these games, even more than in most, there is a "proper level" at which to run the dealership if it is to be run at all. For example, $x = .2$ is very nearly optimal in either game for a wide range of y's (including the critical ones near the break-even point) for $x = .2$ yields a near-optimal profit against almost

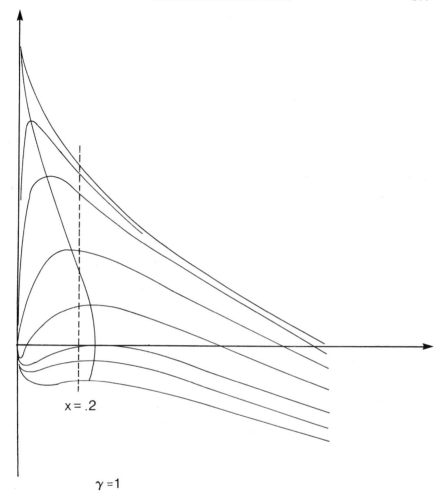

FIGURE 6.3A

any opposition (save very small opposition) which permits profit. Very small opposition allows such large profits that optimality is of little importance. Moreover, against opposition too large to permit profit, $x = .2$ is effective in reducing (though not minimizing, for $x = 0$ does that) losses!

To determine how much opposition is required to render breaking even impossible, it is helpful to consider the symmetric game $P_1 = \cdots = P_N = P$, $C_1 = \cdots = C_N = C$, $\alpha_1 = \cdots = \alpha_N = \alpha$, and to suppose that i's opponents take the same action $(s_j, u_j) = (s, u)$ for all $j \neq i$. Then

$$(6.3.10) \qquad \omega = (N - 1)\left(\frac{Cs}{PD}\right)\left(\frac{u}{PD}\right)^{\gamma}.$$

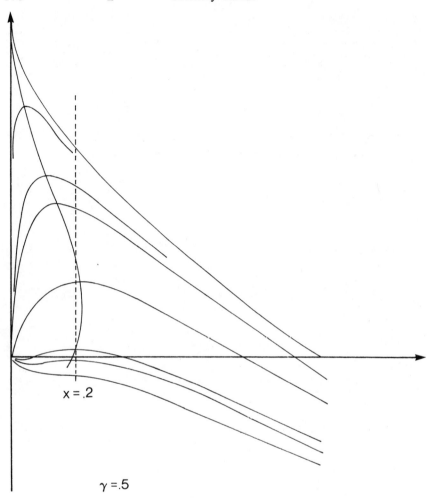

x = .2

γ = .5

FIGURE 6.3B

So if $u = C\gamma s$ in accordance with (6.3.5) and if $Cs/PD < 1/4$ so that the opponents actions are undominated, the inequality

(6.3.11) $y < (N - 1)/(4 + 4\gamma)^{1+\gamma}$

must hold. Therefore break-even is possible in the game for which $\gamma = 1$ unless
$N > 17$, because the break-even value of y in that case is about $y = .25$. Break-
even is possible when $\gamma = .5$ unless $N > 6$, because the break-even value of y is
about .35 in that case.

In short, the compounding of the two games (Ad Game + Auto Dealer's
Game) into one has produced a third that is even better behaved than the

originals, in the sense that it can be played by more players without necessitating reduced activity levels or otherwise complicating the fundamental decisions to be made. Indeed, once the decision to play the game is taken (thereby proclaiming the belief that opposition will be small enough to allow profit), there seems little reason to play at any other level that $x = .2$.

4. MANY, MANY PLAYERS

The Baltimore City Yellow Pages list eleven pages of automobile dealers. So on the face of it, N can be very large indeed and inequalities like (6.3.11) little help in establishing upper bounds on the level of opposition to be anticipated. But in reality the outlook is not so bleak, for each buyer visits only a few showrooms, and the dealers he does not visit do not compete for his trade.

To incorporate this notion into the formulation of the basic Auto Dealer's Game, let $S_1, \ldots, S_L$ be the "small subsets" of the set $S = \{1, 2, \ldots, N\}$ of all dealers, and for $l = 1, \ldots, L$, let D_l be the number of customers who visit just those dealers in the subset S_l of S. Also as in (4.1.2), let

$$(6.4.1) \qquad \omega_l = \sum_{\substack{j \in S_l \\ j \neq i}} s_j.$$

Then dealer i's profit is

$$(6.4.2) \qquad \pi_i(s_1, \ldots, s_N) = \left(\sum_l \frac{P_i D_l s_i}{s_i + \omega_l} \right) - C_i s_i,$$

the sum being taken over all l such that $i \in S_l$. Moreover if we let D^i be the total number of customers visiting dealer i, and set $\rho_l = (D_l / D^i)$, we may write

$$(6.4.3) \qquad \pi_i = \sum_l \rho_l \left(\frac{P_i D^i s_i}{s_i + \omega_l} - C_i s_i \right) = \sum_l \rho_l \pi_i^l(s_1, \ldots, s_N),$$

which exhibits the reward function π_i as a convex combination of payoff functions of the form (4.1.2), defines π_i^l for $l = 1, \ldots, L$, and shows that dealer i may regard himself as a player in several small games simultaneously. The sums in (6.4.3) are again to be taken over all l for which $i \in S_l$.

Then the fact that liberal actions are dominated provides upper bounds for ω_l in each of the subgames S_l in which i is a participant. Thus, the fact that most customers visit a relatively small number of dealers can be expected to yield *useful* upper bounds of the form (6.3.11) for most, if not all, of the subgames in which a given dealer takes part. The present game, incidentally, illustrates another way in which robustness is practically important. Big-city auto dealers really must play in a number of small games simultaneously, and the levels of opposition will presumably be different in the different games. Hence the action s_i can be good in each of them only if it is robust.

5. A CAB GAME

Occasionally in a game with very many players, each is equally in competition with all the rest. It is in this instance that the classical theory of "perfect competition" is most nearly relevant, but even then robustness can be a dominant factor.

Consider the game between all the taxicab drivers in a large city with a single major airport located far from the downtown area. Cabs circulate throughout the city, picking up passengers and carrying them to their destinations. Occasionally a passenger wants to go to the airport, and the taxi driver has no choice but to take him there. On arrival at the airport, the driver is faced with a decision; he may go empty back to the city immediately, or he may wait there for a passenger who is city bound.

For simplicity, let us assume that all cabs at the airport at a given time form a single queue. A cab driver's only options on leaving a customer at the airport are to join the queue to await a return fare, or to "deadhead" back to the city without one. Pure chance governs the taxi drivers' discovery of customers in the city, so the only decisions drivers make in this model are those described above, made at the airport. Thus, a complete "strategy" for a driver in this "game" consists of a single number. Call it K. If he finds on arrival no more than K cabs already in the airport queue, he joins it. Otherwise he deadheads back to town.

The essential features of the model are exhibited in the graph in Figure 6.5A, wherein the several vertices correspond to "events" in the life of a taxi and the connecting edges represent "conditions" that exist between events. One might indicate the current status of a particular cab, for instance, by a poker chip placed on the graph. If the chip is on the arc DA, the cab is en route to the airport (a condition) with a customer. At A, the cab reaches the airport and drops

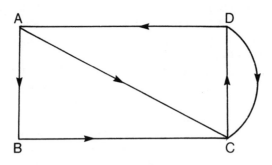

FIGURE 6.5A

its passenger (an event). Then it may choose either traveling to the city without a passenger, the condition represented by the arc AC, or waiting in the airport queue for a city-bound one, symbolized by the arc AB. The vertex B represents the event whereby such a passenger enters the cab. After it the two proceed together to a destination in the city. Vertex C represents arrival at any such destination, while D represents discovery of a new passenger in the city by the cab driver. Finally, the arcs CD and DC represent, respectively, searching in the city for a customer and carrying him or her to an in-city destination.

Arcs AC, BC, and DA all require t_A hours to traverse, while DC requires t_C hours. Presumably t_A and t_C are smaller than one. The remaining conditions (arcs) are of variable duration, because the airport queue may be either long or short, and because passengers are located in the city by a search process wherein chance is often decisive.

We shall assume that passengers turn up at the airport seeking cabs to take them to the city according to some sort of stochastic arrival process and that their mean rate of arrival is λ passengers per hour. Similarly, passengers are generated by another such process at a mean rate of θ per hour in the city. Of these, a fraction π choose in-city destinations, while the rest wish to go to the airport. Write

(6.5.1) $$\mu = (1 - \pi)\theta \quad \text{and} \quad \nu = \pi\theta.$$

If we denote by $N_{AB}(T)$ the number of complete traversals of the arc AB by taxis during the interval $0 \leqslant t \leqslant T$ of time, and so on, we may write

$$N_{BC}(T) = \lambda T + o(T) \qquad \text{a.s.}$$
(6.5.2) $$N_{DA}(T) = \mu T + o(T) \qquad \text{a.s.}$$
$$N_{DC}(T) = \nu T + o(T) \qquad \text{a.s.}$$

Here, as usual, the symbol $o(T)$ denotes an otherwise unspecified function of T having the property

(6.5.3) $$\lim_{T \to \infty} \frac{o(T)}{T} = 0.$$

It may be observed that

(6.5.4) $$N_{DA}(T) = N_{AB}(T) + N_{AC}(T) + o(T),$$

since every cab that traverses DA during $0 \leqslant t \leqslant T$ must also traverse either AB or AC too, though possibly not until after $t = T$. In this instance, $o(T)$ stands for the number of cabs on either of arcs AB or AC when $t = T$, and cannot exceed the total number M of taxis serving the city and its environs. Clearly that number, though we do not know what number it is, satisfies condition (6.5.3).

By similarly considering the arcs incoming and outgoing at vertices B, C, and

D, we may write four such equations altogether. These are:

$$N_{DA}(T) = N_{AB}(T) + N_{AC}(T) + o(T)$$
$$N_{AB}(T) = N_{BC}(T) + o(T)$$
(6.5.5)
$$N_{AC}(T) + N_{BC}(T) + N_{DC}(T) = N_{CD}(T) + o(T)$$
$$N_{CD}(T) = N_{DA}(T) + N_{DC}(T) + o(T).$$

The system (6.5.5) is redundant in the sense that any three of them contain all the information that the four together do, but the first, second, and fourth of them may be solved for

$$N_{AB}(T) = \lambda T + o(T) \qquad \text{a.s.}$$
(6.5.6)
$$N_{AC}(T) = (\mu - \lambda) T + o(T) \qquad \text{a.s.}$$
$$N_{CD}(T) = (\mu + \nu) T + o(T) \qquad \text{a.s.},$$

so that (6.5.2) *and* (6.5.6) describe the mean rates of taxi flow across *all* arcs of the graph.

Next, let $T_{AB}(T)$ denote the total time spent by all cabs in condition AB during $0 \leqslant t \leqslant T$, and let $T_{CD}(T)$ have like meaning for CD. Moreover, assume that of the total of M cabs available, just σM of them are in service at any given time, where $o < \sigma < 1$. Then one may write

$$[N_{AC}(T) + N_{BC}(T) + N_{DA}(T)] \cdot t_A + N_{DC}(F) \cdot t_C + T_{AB}(T) + T_{CD}(T) + o(T)$$

(6.5.7)

$$= 2\mu T \cdot t_A + \nu T \cdot t_C + \frac{T_{AB}(T)}{N_{AB}(T)} N_{AB}(T) + \frac{T_{CD}(T)}{N_{CD}(T)} N_{CD}(T) + o(T) = M\sigma T,$$

the terms $o(T)$ being included to account for traversals not yet complete at the instant $t = T$. But the limits

(6.5.8) $\qquad \overline{W}_A = \lim_{T \to \infty} \dfrac{T_{AB}(T)}{N_{AB}(T)}$ and $\overline{W}_C = \lim_{T \to \infty} \dfrac{T_{CD}(T)}{N_{CD}(T)},$

which are the average waiting times for the conditions AB and CD, respectively, may be shown to exist under very mild assumptions on the various passenger-arrival processes. So dividing equation (6.5.7) through by T and passing to the limit as T becomes large, one obtains

(6.5.9) $\qquad \overline{W}_C = (\sigma M - \lambda \overline{W}_A)/\theta - 2(1 - \pi) t_A - \pi t_C.$

Equation (6.5.9) expresses a necessary relationship between waiting times at the airport and in the city. It gives precise form to the intuitively obvious fact that the more cabs choose to wait at the airport, the longer will be the queue there, and consequently the waiting time in it.

The average waiting time at the airport, $\overline{W}_A$, depends on the particular strategies adopted by the individual cab drivers. Before computing it, however, we observe that the special nature of the present graph conveys further relevant information. To this end, let us focus attention on one particular taxicab, hereinafter called the "green cab," and let us denote by $n_{AB}(T)$ the number of complete traversals of AB by the green cab during $0 \leqslant t \leqslant T$, and so on. Let us also write $n(T) = n_{CD}(T)$ for notational convenience.

The probability p that the green cab enters AB after DA is a function of the strategy K chosen by its driver, whom we shall call Green, and of the strategies $K_2, K_3, \ldots, K_M$ chosen by the drivers of all the other cabs. It can be zero if Green refuses ever to pick up passengers at the airport, one if he never returns to the city without a passenger, or it can assume various intermediate values. In terms of the probabilities p and π, one may write

$$n_{DC}(T) = \pi n(T) + o(T)$$
$$n_{DA}(T) = (1 - \pi) n(T) + o(T)$$
(6.5.10)
$$n_{AB}(T) = p(1 - \pi) n(T) + o(T)$$
$$n_{AC}(T) = (1 - p)(1 - \pi) n(T) + o(T)$$
$$n_{BC}(T) = p(1 - \pi) n(T) + o(T)$$

If Green be presumed to work throughout the period $0 \leqslant t \leqslant T$, he must spend all of that time in one of the six states $AB, BC, CD, DA, DC,$ or AC. So

$$[n_{AC}(T) + n_{BC}(T) + n_{DA}(T)] \cdot t_A + n_{DC}(T) \cdot t_C + t_{AB}(T) + t_{CD}(T) + o(T)$$

(6.5.11)

$$= \left[2(1 - \pi) t_A + \pi t_C + \frac{t_{AB}(T)}{n_{AB}(T)} p(1 - \pi) + \frac{t_{CD}(T)}{n_{CD}(T)} \right] n(T) + o(T)$$

$$= [2(1 - \pi) t_A + \pi t_C + p(1 - \pi) \overline{w}_A + \overline{w}_C] n(T) + o(T) = T,$$

where $t_{AB}(T)$ and $t_{CD}(T)$ denote the number of hours spent by the green cab in states AB and CD between the times $t = 0$ and $t = T$, and

(6.5.12)
$$\overline{w}_A = \lim_{T \to \infty} \frac{t_{AB}(T)}{n_{AB}(T)}, \qquad \overline{w}_C = \lim_{T \to \infty} \frac{t_{CD}(T)}{n_{CD}(T)}.$$

Also, Green's revenues during the period would be

$$J(T) = F_A [n_{DA}(T) + n_{BC}(T)] + n_{DC}(T) F_C$$
(6.5.13)
$$= [(1 + p)(1 - \pi) F_A + \pi F_C] n(T).$$

Actually, of course, Green works only oT hours during the period $0 \leqslant t \leqslant T$ and earns $oJ(T)$ dollars. In either case, his earnings rate is roughly

$$(6.5.14) \quad \lim_{T \to \infty} \frac{J(T)}{T} = \frac{(1+p)(1-\pi) F_A + \pi F_C}{2(1-\pi) t_A + \pi t_C + \overline{w}_C + p(1-\pi) \overline{w}_A} \qquad \text{a.s.,}$$

provided only that T is large. This is to be compared with the industry's earning rate of

$$(6.5.15) \qquad \frac{(\mu + \lambda) F_A + \nu F_C}{\sigma M}$$

dollars per hour, the latter being the total fares collected during a typical hour, divided by the number of cab-hours worked. It is interesting to observe that if all drivers including Green adopt the same strategy, then

$$(6.5.16) \qquad \overline{w}_A = \overline{W}_A, \quad \overline{w}_C = \overline{W}_C, \quad \text{and}$$
$$p = \lim_{T \to \infty} \frac{n_{AB}(T)}{n_{DA}(T)} = \lim_{T \to \infty} \frac{N_{AB}(T)}{N_{DA}(T)} = \frac{\lambda}{\mu},$$

so the expression (6.5.14) reduces to the simpler one (6.5.15) because of (6.5.1) and (6.5.8), as plainly it must.

The symmetry of the situation suggests that, if indeed there is an "optimal strategy" for the "taxi driver's game," it is the same for each player. So one may attempt to "solve" the game by setting the opponents' strategies K_2, $K_3, \ldots, K_M$ equal to some common value $N - 1$ (so that Green never encounters a queue containing more than N other cabs), thereby rendering the ratio (6.5.14) dependent on just the two numbers K and N which determine p, $\overline{w}_A$, and $\overline{w}_C$, then seeking N such that $K = N - 1$ is an optimal strategy for Green. This task is made easier by the observation that while Green exercises great control over his average airport waiting time, $\overline{w}_A$, he is unable to materially affect his waiting times in the city, $\overline{w}_C$. Indeed, $\overline{w}_C = \overline{W}_C$ if Green chooses $K = N - 1$, and the two differ only imperceptibly if $K \neq N - 1$. The city is a large place, with many cabs competing for the fares generated in it, and the trouble of finding them is altered little by the duration of Green's excursions beyond. Thus one may, for practical purposes, replace $\overline{w}_C$ by $\overline{W}_C$ in (6.5.14). In view of (6.5.1) and (6.5.8), one is left finally with

$$(6.5.17) \qquad f(K, N) = \frac{(1+p)\mu F_A + \nu F_C}{\sigma M - \lambda \overline{W}_A + p\mu \overline{w}_A}.$$

If Green knew N, he would surely choose K so as to maximize his long-run average earning rate $f(K, N)$. But to determine the value of K which achieves this, one must know the exact nature of the dependence of p, $\overline{w}_A$, and $\overline{W}_A$ on K and N. And to know that, one must consider in detail the genesis of the airport queue under the assumptions that Green plays the strategy K while all the $M - 1$ other drivers play $N - 1$.

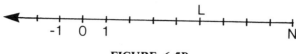

FIGURE 6.5B

First, let us determine the probability $P_L(t)$ that the airport queue has length L at time t, Green being newly arrived at A. At such an instant, Green has long been absent from the airport, so $P_L(t)$ is virtually what it would be if $K = N - 1$. Hence it suffices to compute $P_L(t)$ under the additional assumption that $K = N - 1$. In this context, it is clear that L can have any of the values $L = 0$, $1, \ldots, N$. We shall allow L to assume negative integer values as well, by adopting the convention that a queue of $-L$ cabs means that no cabs are present and L passengers are waiting for them. Cabs and passengers can never be waiting simultaneously, as it is assumed that a passenger can enter a cab and be on his or her way to the city instantaneously. The totality of possible states of the queue is thus as indicated in Figure 6.5B. If the various arrival processes are in fact Poisson processes, the queue can be in state $L < N$ at time $t + dt$ iff it was in one of the states $L - 1, L, L + 1$ at time t. Thus

$$(6.5.18) \quad P_L(t + dt) = P_L(t)(1 - \lambda \, dt)(1 - \mu \, dt) + P_{L-1}(t)\mu \, dt + P_{L+1}(t)\lambda \, dt,$$

which implies

$$(6.5.19) \qquad P_L'(t) = \mu P_{L-1}(t) - (\mu + \lambda)P_L(t) + \lambda P_{L+1}(t).$$

So the limits as $t \to \infty$ of the functions $P_{L-1}(\cdot), P_L(\cdot), P_{L+1}(\cdot)$ must be solutions of the finite difference equation

$$(6.5.20) \qquad \alpha P_{L-1} - P_L + \beta P_{L+1} = 0.$$

Similarly, because the queue can be in state N at time $t + dt$ iff it was in one of the states N or $N - 1$ at time t, one has

$$(6.5.21) \qquad P_{N-1} = \rho P_N,$$

where the constants appearing in (6.5.20) and (6.5.21) have the values

$$(6.5.22) \qquad \alpha = \frac{\mu}{\mu + \lambda}, \quad \beta = \frac{\lambda}{\mu + \lambda}, \quad \text{and} \quad \rho = \frac{\lambda}{\mu} = \frac{\beta}{\alpha}.$$

As is well known, the solutions of (6.5.20) are all of the form

$$(6.5.23) \qquad P_L = A + B\rho^{-L}, \quad L < N.$$

But since

(6.5.24) $$\sum_{L=-\infty}^{N} P_L = 1,$$

A must vanish. Thus (6.5.20), (6.5.22), and (6.5.23) together imply that

(6.5.25) $$P_L = (1 - \rho) \rho^{N-L}$$

for every integer L less than or equal to N. Consequently the probability p that the queue contain no more than K cabs on Green's approach is

(6.5.26) $$p = p(K, N) = \sum_{L=-\infty}^{K} P_L = \rho^{N-K}.$$

Similarly Green's expected waiting time in the queue is

(6.5.27)
$$\overline{w}_A = \overline{w}_A(K, N) = \sum_{L=0}^{K} \left(\frac{L+1}{\lambda}\right) P_L = \frac{\rho^N(1-\rho)}{\lambda} \sum_{L=0}^{K} (L+1) \rho^{-L}$$
$$= \frac{\rho^N}{\lambda(1-\rho)} [(K+1) \rho^{-K} - (K+2) \rho^{1-K} + \rho^2],$$

while everyone else's is

(6.5.28) $$\overline{W}_A = \overline{w}_A(N-1, N) = \frac{\rho^2}{\lambda(1-\rho)} [N/\rho - (N+1) + \rho^N].$$

Substitution of (6.5.26)–(6.5.28) into (6.5.14) now gives $f(K, N)$ as an explicit function of its arguments K and N. For economy we put $K = N - J$ and write

$$f(K, N) = f(N - J, N)$$

(6.5.29)
$$= \frac{(1 + \rho^J) \mu F_A + \nu F_C}{\sigma M - \rho N + (N + J - 1) \rho^{2J-1} + [\rho^2 (1 - \rho^N) - (\rho^{2J} - \rho^{N+J-1})] (1 - \rho)^{-1}}.$$

From (6.5.29) it is apparent that, unless either N or J is small, $f(.\,,.)$ is well approximated by the simpler function

(6.5.30) $$\phi(K, N) = \phi(N - J, N) = \frac{\mu F_A + \nu F_C}{\sigma M - \rho N + \rho^2/(1 - \rho)},$$

because $\rho < 1$. The significance of this fact will be discussed presently. For the moment we point only to obvious computational convenience.

The conditions that $K = N - 1$ be an optimal strategy for Green against his opponents' common choice of $N - 1$ are just

(6.5.31) $$f(N - 2, N) < f(N - 1, N) > f(N, N),$$

which reduce to

(6.5.32)

$$\frac{2\mu F_A + \nu F_C}{\sigma M - 1/\rho - 1 - \rho + N(1/\rho - \rho) + \left(\dfrac{1/\rho - \rho^2}{1 - \rho}\right)\rho^N} < \frac{(\mu + \lambda) F_A + \nu F_C}{\sigma M}$$

$$\frac{(1 + \rho^2)\,\mu F_A + \nu F_C}{\sigma M + \dfrac{\rho^2}{1 - \rho}(1 + \rho - 2\rho) + N\rho(\rho^2 - 1) + \dfrac{\rho}{1 - \rho}(1 + \rho)\,\rho^N} < \frac{(\mu + \lambda) F_A + \nu F_C}{\sigma M},$$

according to (6.5.29). It is frequently easy to solve the inequalities (6.5.32) for the values of N which satisfy them, since those N's are typically large, and the terms involving ρ^N negligible in consequence. Let us do this now for appropriate values of the several parameters indigenous to the model.

Professor de Vany finds [2] that the constants $\lambda = 35, \theta = 435, \pi = .8, \mu = 87$, $\nu = 348, \rho = .4023, t_A = .5, t_C = .2, F_A = 11, F_C = 4, M = 750$, and $\sigma = .6$ are reasonable descriptions of the taxi traffic between one city and its suburban airport. Using them (and ignoring the terms in ρ^N) reduces the inequalities (6.5.32) to

(6.5.32′)

$$\frac{3306}{446.11 + 2.08N} < 6.08 > \frac{2503.87}{450.34 - .337N},$$

which imply that the values of N between 47 and 114 inclusive satisfy the equilibrium conditions (6.5.31)!

So large a variety of equilibria is confusing, for classical analyses do not often deal with questions of multiplicity. Yet it is important to do so here, because the prospect of 50 cabs waiting typically at the airport is so different from that of 110.

Figure 6.5C exhibits the graphs of several of the curves $y = f(K,N)$, for fixed values of N in the interval $47 \leqslant N \leqslant 114$. The graphs actually consist of finitely many discrete points, but these are connected with straight-line segments in the figure to illustrate certain repetitive patterns more clearly. For each N in the interval, the functions $f(K, N)$ are constant for $K > N$, and virtually so for $K < N$. Moreover, $f(K,N)$ does not exceed the industry average (6.5.15) for any K and attains it only for $K = N - 1$. To play against a large number of opponents, all of whom behave identically, one must play exactly as they do. Otherwise one earns markedly less than the industry's average rate of return while the opponents earn a little more.

In practice, it is *impossible* to play exactly as one's opponents do because (a) they do *not* all behave identically, (b) one cannot measure their strategies precisely even if they are all the same, and (c) real strategies are subject to future change. It seems safe to assume, moreover, that working taxi drivers are entirely cognizant of these facts. Consequently the strategies they choose doubtless exhibit a degree of "robustness" in the sense that they yield desirable rates of re-

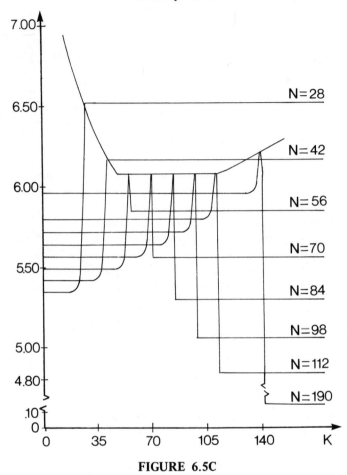

FIGURE 6.5C

turn against a *considerable variety* of the opponents' possible choices, rather than being effective only against the single choice that seems most likely.

Table 6.5D compares the rates of return obtained from the strategies $K = 12$, 48, 69, 111, and 150 against various values of N with the rate

(6.5.33) $$f^*(N) = f(K^*(N), N)$$

that Green would obtain if he knew his opponents' common strategy $N - 1$ in advance and chose the optimal response $K = K^*(N)$ against it. It reveals, for instance, that the choice $K = 69$ is at least 92 percent optimal against virtually any value of N the opponents might choose. But it shows also that $K = 48$ is at least 90 percent optimal against those same values of N, while $K = 98$ is 87 percent optimal against them. And even the seemingly quite ridiculous strategies $K = 12$ and $K = 150$ are better than 72 percent optimal. So from a taxi driver's

TABLE 6.5D

N	f*(N)	f(12,N)	%	f(48,N)	%	f(69,N)	%	f(98,N)	%	f(150,N)	%
7	$7.17	$7.17	100	$7.17	100	$7.17	100	$7.17	100	$7.17	100
14	6.95	5.62	81	6.95	100	6.95	100	6.95	100	6.95	100
21	6.71	5.32	79	6.71	100	6.71	100	6.71	100	6.71	100
23	6.52	5.35	82	6.52	100	6.52	100	6.52	100	6.52	100
35	6.33	5.39	85	6.33	100	6.33	100	6.34	100	6.33	100
42	6.17	5.42	88	6.17	100	6.17	100	6.17	100	6.17	100
49	6.08	5.46	90	6.08	100	6.00	99	6.00	99	6.00	99
56	6.08	5.49	90	5.49	90	5.85	96	5.85	96	5.85	96
63	6.08	5.53	91	5.53	91	5.70	94	5.70	94	5.70	94
70	6.08	5.56	91	5.56	91	6.08	100	5.56	91	5.56	91
77	6.08	5.60	92	5.60	92	5.60	92	5.43	89	5.43	89
84	6.08	5.64	93	5.64	93	5.64	93	5.30	87	5.30	87
91	6.08	5.68	93	5.68	93	5.68	93	6.08	100	5.18	85
98	6.08	5.72	94	5.72	94	5.72	94	5.72	94	5.06	83
105	6.08	5.76	95	5.76	95	5.76	95	5.76	95	4.95	81
112	6.08	5.80	95	5.80	95	5.80	95	5.80	95	4.85	80
119	6.10	5.84	96	5.84	96	5.84	96	5.84	96	4.75	78
126	6.14	5.88	96	5.88	96	5.88	96	5.88	96	4.65	76
133	6.18	5.92	96	5.92	96	5.92	96	5.92	96	4.56	75
140	6.21	5.96	96	5.96	96	5.96	96	5.96	96	4.47	74
147	6.25	6.01	96	6.01	96	6.01	96	6.01	96	4.38	72
154	6.29	6.05	96	6.05	96	6.05	96	6.05	96	6.11	97

point of view, there is virtually nothing to choose between strategies in the interval $48 \leqslant K \leqslant 98$, and nothing so terribly bad either about those a great deal larger or smaller. Moreover, qualitatively similar conclusions are valid if Green owns (and chooses the strategy for), not a single cab, but a small fleet of them.

From all that has now been demonstrated, the underlying nature of the competition between the taxi drivers in question is readily apparent. It is not a contest with high stakes, for strategies abound which guarantee at least 90 percent of the industry's average return. But the drivers would like to do better if they could. Since not all of them actually do behave alike, it is plain that some will earn a little more than the industry average, while their competitors get a little less.

If, for instance, a small fleet of green cabs using strategy K competes against a much larger fleet of otherwise colored ones using a common strategy $N - 1 \neq K$ in the interval $47 \leqslant N - 1 \leqslant 114$, green cabs will earn less than the industry average and the others more. The driver of an independent cab belonging to neither fleet can also earn more than the industry average if he guesses which of the strategies $K, N - 1$ is the more successful and adopts it himself.

The same is true if more than two strategies are simultaneously in use; some will be more effective than others, and there will be an incentive for the less successful players to imitate the more successful ones until all behave and fare alike. But the strategy that emerges in this fashion seems as likely to be a matter of historical accident as to be the result of coherent economic forces. In particular, consensus seems as likely to settle on the strategy $K = 47$ as any other in the admissible interval.

For other values of the system parameters, a similar analysis is possible. In particular, an interval $N_* \leqslant N \leqslant N^*$ of numbers N may be found satisfying the equilibrium conditions (6.5.32), N_* being the least positive integer for which the first of those inequalities holds, and N^* being the greatest for which the other does. Almost certainly, then, all cabs will join queues of length $K = N_* - 1$ or less, and the probability that there are no cabs waiting at the airport at a given instant may be estimated from (6.5.29) using $N = N_*$. That probability remains ridiculously small for a wide variety of parameter values, suggesting that taxi service at the airport will remain excellent despite wide variations in the parameters of the system. Especially noteworthy is the fact that F_A, the fare to or from the airport, can be substantially reduced without diminishing service quality appreciably.

6. OBSERVATIONS

We have now considered a wide variety of the games of commerce and have found at least approximate solutions (in the sense of Chapter II) for all of them. Most of the games have been simply directed ones, but even those that were not (the cab game and the auction games wherein the auctioneer was a player, for instance) possessed approximate solutions and distinctly robust strategies. That is because it is *easy* to discover games in which these phenomena occur; every trip to the corner grocery, movie theater, or gas station reveals at least one of them. It would be possible to continue almost indefinitely in this fashion, formulating the games of daily commerce in some simple manner, then calculating robust strategies for the players in them. But the reader is now familiar with this process and knows both how to go about it and what sorts of information he may expect to gain thereby. It is time to pass on to other matters.

Problems

(6-1) *Question* Consider two different kinds of advertising, for instance, radio advertising and TV advertising. How should these enter the formulation of the Ad Game, and what does its solution become?

(6-2) *Question* To construct a market model wherein both advertising decisions and pricing decisions play a role, one may begin with the so-called better model of Bertrand's game examined in Chapter II. As the constants $m_i^{-\alpha}$ measure the "public image" of brand i, it seems natural to write

$$m_i^{-\alpha} = X_i(u_1, \ldots, u_N).$$

Can the game so constructed be reduced to a previous case?

(6-3) *Question* Do there exist other equilibria in the cab-drivers' game whereby different drivers adopt different decision rules?

REFERENCES

1. Dieudonné, J., *Foundations of Modern Analysis* (New York: Academic Press, 1960).
2. De Vany, A., "Alternative Ground Transportation Systems for Dallas/Ft. Worth Regional Airport," a report prepared for the Federal Trade Commission, (1977).

Part II

Differential Games

Chapter 7

Information and Its Uses

In the games considered to this point, there has rarely been any need to distinguish strategies from actions. Except in a few matrix games wherein the optimal strategies involved randomization over two or more actions, the best strategies have seemed always to consist of a single robust action. But managerial decisions are not often so simple, since there is usually available a stream of information (in the form of stock market quotations, current sales data, and market survey results, for instance) bearing on the decisions to be made. Moreover, actions are typically taken, not once and for all, but periodically, and the opportunity often exists to adjust one's action even in the middle of a period. For instance, a supermarket manager typically sets his prices for the week on Monday morning, but he can alter them at any time on instructions from the chain's headquarters. A brewery truck may visit a given bar once weekly but make extra stops when supplies run unexpectedly low. Thus, the best strategies do not typically consist of a single action but of a rule for choosing actions appropriate to whatever information has been received prior to the moment of choice. The (s, S) policies discussed in Chapter IV were examples of such rules, being based on inventory histories. It is now time to begin the systematic study of *decision rules* in general.

The classic result concerning such rules is known as the *perfect information theorem*. It was proved in its original form by Zermelo [6], in 1912, who was primarily interested in chess. It was given its present most general form by Kuhn [3] in 1950. As usual, we begin with an example.

1. GAMES IN EXTENSIVE FORM

The perfect information theorem concerns games in which at most a finite number of actions (or "moves") are allowed each player, and in which the players play in turn. Such games are conveniently represented graphically and are called *games in extensive form*. For instance, Figure 7.1A represents a game in which player *I* has a single move, while both nature and player *II* have either one or none. Player *I*'s move is represented by the point of the graph labeled *I*.

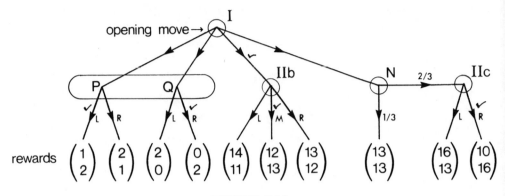

FIGURE 7.1A

When his turn comes to play, he may choose any of the lines emanating from point I. If he chooses the one leading to N, it will be nature's turn to move next; nature will end the game with probability 1/3 by choosing the line emanating from N marked with that fraction or allow II to move with probability 2/3 by choosing the other line starting at N.

If the others' choices allow him to make the move marked IIc, II will presumably choose the line leading to the ultimate point (or "outcome") at which the reward vector is $\binom{10}{16}$. For the reward of 16 which he gets there is better than the 13 he gets if he chooses the line leading to the ultimate point marked $\binom{16}{13}$. The fact that I gets just 10 in the former event instead of the 16 he earns in the latter is presumably irrelevant to II. Similarly if I forces him to the point IIb, II will choose the line M leading to $\binom{12}{13}$.

The points P and Q together constitute a single *information set*, called IIa, as indicated in the figure. The significance of this stipulation is that II is not allowed to know if he is at point P or point Q when I forces him to move from IIa. And the uncertainty complicates his decision. For if he were at P, he would doubtless choose the line marked L emanating from it, whereas he would surely pick the line marked R if he knew he were at Q. Indeed, the situation is just as if both players chose simultaneously in the bimatrix game shown in the accompanying diagram and that bimatrix game has no immediately obvious solution.

I II	P	Q
L	1	2
R	2	0

I II	P	Q
L	2	0
R	1	2

Games in which each information set consists of a single point are called *games of perfect information*, and they can be "solved" by a simple labeling procedure. We shall first illustrate the procedure for the variant of the game depicted in Figure 7.1A wherein P and Q are distinct information sets.

First we label P with the reward vector $\binom{1}{2}$, since that is the one II would choose if given the choice P. Then we label Q with $\binom{0}{2}$, IIb with $\binom{12}{13}$, and IIc with $\binom{10}{16}$ for similar reasons. Next label N with the expectation vector $\frac{1}{3}\binom{13}{13} + \frac{2}{3}\binom{10}{16} = \binom{11}{15}$, since that is what the players may expect to receive if nature is given the choice N. And finally, we label point I with $\binom{12}{13}$, since that is a better reward for I than the $\binom{1}{2}$ he can get by going to P, the $\binom{0}{2}$ he can get at Q, or the $\binom{11}{15}$ he can get at N. So the value of the game to I is 12, while to II it has value 13. Moreover, I's "optimal strategy" is to choose IIb, while II's is to choose L at P, R at Q, M at IIb, and R again at IIc. It is easily verified that the above pair of strategies, which we shall hereinafter denote $(IIb, (L, R, M, R))$, is in Cournot-Nash equilibrium in the sense that each is optimal against the other. Such strategies constitute decision *rules* because they are of the form "upon arrival at position ___ choose action ===." The rules can of course be considerably more elaborate when the game tree is larger.

To describe the labeling procedure in general, certain terminology is useful. A *graph* is a finite collection of *points* and *lines*, each of the latter being incident on exactly two of the former. A *path* is a line or sequence of lines connecting two or more points. A *rooted tree* is a graph in which at most one path connects any pair of points, and in which some point O is connected by a path to every other point. A point Q is called a *successor* of P if the path joining O to Q passes through P. Point Q is an *immediate* successor of P if the path joining P to Q consists of a single line. Finally, a point of a tree is called *ultimate* if it has no successors, and it is cited *penultimate* if all of its successors are immediate.

An N-player game in extensive form having perfect information may now be said to consist of

(i) a rooted tree (like that in Figure 7.1A);

(ii) a reward function, assigning a payoff vector to each ultimate point of the tree;

(iii) a partition of the points of the tree into those representing nature's moves, player I's moves, etc.; and

(iv) for each point P of the tree representing one of nature's moves, a probability distribution over the lines emanating from P.

One may envisage the playing of the game as follows: the game tree is drawn on a tabletop and a poker chip is placed at its root O. If O represents a move belonging to nature, a random device is activated which chooses a line emanating therefrom in accordance with the probability distribution prescribed by (iv), and the chip is slid along the line chosen to an immediate successor of O. Or if O represents a move belonging to player i, then i simply chooses an immediate successor of O and slides the chip to it. In either case the chip passes from O to one of its immediate successors, say P. And from P it passes, in similar fashion, to an immediate successor Q of P, and so on. Continuing in this manner, the chip comes in time to rest at an ultimate point, and each player $i = 1, 2, \ldots, N$ is awarded the ith component of the payoff vector assigned thereto by (ii).

A strategy for player i is a function which assigns to each point of the tree representing one of i's moves a line emanating therefrom. For instance, II's equilibrium strategy for the game depicted in Figure 7.1A is to choose, at each of the points P, Q, IIb and IIc, the line emanating therefrom which is marked with a $\sqrt{}$. It is better than the strategy whereby he chooses the line marked L in every case. It is possible to find a Cournot-Nash equilibrium N-tuple of strategies for any finite game in extensive form having perfect information by the labeling procedure illustrated above. To prove as much, we first describe the procedure in full generality.

Observe that in any finite rooted tree either (a) O is ultimate or (b) some point is penultimate. For if O is not ultimate, there is a "longest path Γ in the tree (i.e., one consisting of at least as many lines as any other) composed of $n \geqslant 1$ lines. And on that Γ there is a "last" point (which is, of course, ultimate) and a "next-to-last" point, which is penultimate. If it were not, the tree would contain a path of length $n + 1$ and Γ would not be a longest path. Observe, too, that when a game in extensive form is fully prescribed, all its ultimate points are labeled (as in Figure 7.1A) with payoff vectors.

To carry out the labeling procedure, choose a penultimate point P. If P represents one of nature's moves, label it with the expected value of the payoff vectors wherewith its successors are labeled, using the probability distribution furnished by (iv). Or if P represents one of player i's moves, choose from among the payoff vectors labeling its successors the one whose i^{th} component is largest, and label P with it. In case of ties, any such vector will do. If Q is the successor of P whose label now labels P as well, record the fact that at P, player i should choose the line joining P to Q. Finally delete the successors of P from the tree, thereby creating a smaller tree wherein P is both labeled and ultimate. This process may be continued until O becomes ultimate, at which time it will be labeled as well. Since all successors of O will then have been deleted, the records kept will completely specify a strategy for each player. Call those strategies $\sigma_1^*, \ldots, \sigma_N^*$. It remains only to show that they are in Cournot-Nash equilibrium.

The case $N = 1$ is trivial, for then player 1 has no other opponent than nature, and the procedure obviously produces an optimal strategy σ_1^* for him. And if $N > 1$, the procedure produces the same σ_i^* it would produce in the game against nature played over the same tree, wherein nature behaves according to the rules (iv) at points of the tree representing its own moves, and according to the rule σ_j^* at points representing moves of player $j \neq i$. Therefore, each σ_i^* is optimal against $\ldots, \sigma_{i-1}^*, \sigma_{i+1}^*, \ldots$ (and nature), and the N-tuple $\sigma_1^*, \ldots, \sigma_N^*$ is indeed in Cournot-Nash equilibrium.

The perfect information theorem is a very important one for two-player zero-sum games (i.e., those for which the components of each payoff vector are two in number and add up to zero) because a Cournot-Nash equilibrium pair for such a game is a saddle-point pair as well. However, its import for other games is much less because it often ignores important facets of their structure. In the game of Figure 7.1A, for instance, the players might reach an agreement that I

will push the chip to N and pay 2 to II on the condition that II choose L instead of R in the event that nature allows him to move. Or they might not, depending on I's willingness to believe that II will not double-cross him by playing R after all on arrival at IIc. So a question arises as to whether the Cournot-Nash pair $(IIb, (L, R, M, R))$ or the Pareto optimal pair $(N, (L, R, M, L))$ is more properly regarded as the "solution" of the game in question. That is hardly surprising in view of our accumulated experience with Cournot-Nash equilibria; such equilibria *do* sometimes constitute (either exact or approximate) noncooperative solutions of the sort defined in Chapter II; but more often, as in the case of the equilibrium at the origin in Cold War, they do not. In the latter event, it is probably a mistake to regard equilibrium points as solutions of games.

Indeed the relationship between equilibria and noncooperative solutions for games in extensive form is quite as it was for the games in normal form discussed in Part I of the book. Some games in extensive form do have exact noncooperative solutions, but most do not. Of those which do not, a few have approximate noncooperative solutions, and again, most do not. If a particular game does have either an exact or an approximate noncooperative solution, that solution will be in (at least approximate) Cournot-Nash equilibrium. So a method of computing all equilibria will also compute all noncooperative solutions. If none of the latter exist, the method may still yield approximate solutions. Finally, by perturbing equilibria slightly, additional approximate solutions may be generated.

An additional subtlety appears here and deserves mention. A game in extensive form may have additional Cournot-Nash equilibria not found by the labeling procedure described earlier. For instance, all of the strategy pairs $(IIb, (\cdot, \cdot, M, R))$ are equilibria in the game depicted in Figure 7.1A, though the labeling procedure produces only one of them.

To see the reason for this, let P be a point in a tree and delete from the tree all points and lines save P, its successors, and the lines joining same. The figure so produced is called a subtree of the original tree, and the game whose first move is represented by P may be called the subgame associated therewith. It is easy to see that at the moment of labeling P in the original tree the procedure will have produced a Cournot-Nash equilibrium for the subgame starting at P. So the procedure yields equilibria which are in equilibrium for the whole game *and* for every subgame as well. It could never produce $(IIb, (L, L, M, R))$, for instance, which is in equilibrium for the whole game but not for the subgame starting at Q.

Equilibria which remain in equilibrium when restricted to any subgame have been called "perfect equilibria" by Selten [4]. It should be observed that if no player has dominated strategies, then every noncooperative solution $\sigma_1^*, \ldots, \sigma_N^*$ is, in particular, a perfect equilibrium. For each σ_i^*, $i = 1, \ldots, N$ must be optimal against every $(N-1)$-tuple $\ldots, \sigma_{i-1}, \sigma_{i+1}, \ldots$ available to the opponents and therefore optimal in the whole game and in every subgame thereof. So every noncooperative solution can be found among the perfect equilibria obtained from the use of the labeling procedure.

If some player has a dominated strategy, there may be points in the game tree which cannot be reached unless one or more of the players employ dominated strategies. P and Q, for instance, are such points in the graph of Figure 7.1A. In that case, a noncooperative solution $\sigma_1^*, \ldots, \sigma_N^*$ need not be a perfect equilibrium, for σ_i^* need not be optimal for subgames starting at points P of the above-described sort. But σ_i^* must still be optimal for the game which remains when all such points, and the lines incident upon them, have been deleted from the tree. Hence, even if dominated strategies are present, one may discover whatever noncooperative solutions exist by means of the labeling algorithm. If such solutions exist, the algorithm will find some, and the rest may be generated from these by assigning moves arbitrarily at the points reachable only by means of dominated strategies. In short, to find noncooperative solutions of games in extensive form, it suffices to have an algorithm for producing perfect equilibria. If such solutions exist at all, some of them *are* perfect equilibria and the rest differ from such only at an "unimportant" set of points.

Of course, games in extensive form, like those in normal form, rarely have exact noncooperative solutions. Indeed the game of Figure 7.1A has no such solution. But we shall discover that, as was the case for games in normal form, a fascinating variety have approximate ones. The games for which we shall do this are indeed games in extensive form. But they differ from those we have encountered heretofore in that their graphs include an infinitude, indeed a continuum, of points. So one must think, not in terms of a poker chip being slid first by one player, then by another, from point to point of a discrete network, but of one sliding continually under the simultaneous influence of all the players across a plane or higher dimensional Euclidean space. Such games are in fact simpler computationally than their discrete analogues because they permit recourse to the tools of the calculus. The two-player Ad Game will serve as a first example.

(7-1)   *Question*   Construct the tree for the game that remains when tick-tack-toe has progressed to the state

How many strategies has x in that game? Is there a winning strategy for o at this point? Use a *large* sheet of paper; a xerox helps too!

2. THE SIMPLE AD GAME: VERSION II

In that game, let $x(t)$ be the fraction of all customers who trade at time t with brewer 1; $1 - x(t)$ is then the fraction trading with 2. Assume as before that $x(t)$

varies according to the law, or *kinematic equation*, as Isaacs [2] has called it,

$$(7.2.1) \qquad \dot{x}(t) = (1 - x(t)) \sqrt{u(t)} - \alpha x(t) \sqrt{v(t)}.$$

The response function $f(\cdot) = \sqrt{\cdot}$ is chosen once more for simplicity.

Since revenue is proportional to market share, the brewers' instantaneous profits are

$$(7.2.2) \qquad \pi_1(t) = P \cdot x(t) - u(t) \quad \text{and} \quad \pi_2(t) = Q \cdot (1 - x(t)) - v(t)$$

dollars per week, respectively. So each player i earns, not a pile of dollars, but a *profit stream* $\pi_i(t), 0 \leqslant t < \infty$. And to distinguish "large" profit streams from "small" ones, one must specify what is meant by the "size" of such a stream.

A natural definition is of course the *"average profit"*

$$(7.2.3) \qquad \bar{\pi} = \lim_{T \to \infty} \frac{1}{T} \int_0^T \pi(t) \, dt.$$

But for a number of reasons, ably presented by Wagner [5, Chapter 11] in a discrete-time setting, it is more usual to discount future profits relative to current ones, and therefore to describe the size of an income stream by its *present value*

$$(7.2.4) \qquad \text{P.V.} (\pi(\cdot)) = \int_0^\infty e^{-\rho t} \pi(t) \, dt.$$

If in particular $\pi(t) \equiv \pi$, a constant, its present value is π/ρ. Or if $\pi(t)$ is not itself a constant, there is a single number π called the *equivalent average return* of $\pi(\cdot)$ and denoted

$$(7.2.5) \qquad \pi = \text{E.A.R.} (\pi(\cdot)) = \int_0^\infty \rho e^{-\rho t} \pi(t) \, dt,$$

such that the constant income stream of \$$\pi$/week has the same present value as does $\pi(\cdot)$.

Clearly $\pi(\cdot)$ has a larger present value than $\pi'(\cdot)$ iff it has a larger equivalent average return, so the two notions of size induce the same preference relation on income streams. But the integral (7.2.5) seems a more tractable definition of size than does (7.2.4) because typically it tends to a finite limit as ρ decreases to zero though (7.2.4) does not. Indeed the equation

$$(7.2.6) \qquad \lim_{\rho \to 0} \int_0^\infty \rho e^{-\rho t} \pi(t) \, dt = \lim_{T \to \infty} \frac{1}{T} \int_0^T \pi(t) \, dt$$

appears valid whenever the limit on the right exists. Moreover, the limit on the left often exists (when $\pi(t) = t \cos t$, for instance), though that on the right does not. Hence, we shall assume that brewer i will choose his advertising strategy in such a way as to render the expected average return of his profit stream $\pi_i(t)$, $0 \leqslant t < \infty$, namely

$$(7.2.7) \qquad\qquad J_i = \int_0^\infty \rho e^{-\rho t}\, \pi_i(t)\, dt,$$

as large as possible.

The game the brewers play is called a *differential game* because of the differential nature of the law (7.2.1). Its salient features are apparent from the representation

$$1 \quad \max_{u \geqslant 0} J_1(x; u(\cdot), v(\cdot)) = \int_0^\infty \rho e^{-\rho t}\, [P \cdot x(t) - u^2(t)]\, dt$$

(DG) $$2 \quad \max_{v \geqslant 0} J_2(x; u(\cdot), v(\cdot)) = \int_0^\infty \rho e^{-\rho t}\, [Q \cdot (1 - x(t)) - v^2(t)]\, dt$$

subject to $\dot{x} = (1 - x)u - \alpha xv$,

wherein the square roots in the kinematic equations have been replaced by squares in the payoff integrals for convenience.

One *may* play the game as though the time element were not present. For if one adopts a strategy $u = $ constant that is near-optimal against constants v in an interval, it will also be near-optimal against a $v(\cdot)$ which varies in some fashion over that interval. Indeed if both players choose constant strategies u and v, $x(t)$ approaches the steady state

$$(7.2.8) \qquad\qquad X(u, v) = \frac{u}{u + \alpha v}$$

rapidly as t grows large. So J_1 and J_2 will be approximately

$$(7.2.9) \qquad \pi_1(u, v) = \frac{Pu}{u + \alpha v} - u^2 \quad \text{and} \quad \pi_2(u, v) = \frac{Q\alpha v}{u + \alpha v} - v^2,$$

the approximations being exact if ρ is decreased to the limit 0. Hence the same robust strategies which make π_1 and π_2 large make J_1 and J_2 large as well. But new possibilities present themselves, because of the evolutionary nature of DG.

Through market research, for instance, most brewers know their current shares in the principal markets in which they compete. So it may safely be assumed that each observes the current value of $x(t)$. Therefore player 1 can employ an advertising policy $u(x(t))$ which varies as a function of his market share. Indeed it is possible so to choose the function $u(\cdot)$ that 1 is assured of an optimal return against any constant policy $v(\cdot) \equiv v$ for 2.

To see how this may be done, observe that $x(t)$ tends to a solution $x = a$ of

$$(7.2.10) \qquad\qquad (1 - x)u(x) - \alpha xv = 0$$

whenever 1 chooses the variable advertising policy $u(x)$ while 2 chooses the constant one $v(x) \equiv v$. So knowing his own $u(x)$, and observing that $x(t) \to a$, 1 can deduce 2's budget v. And he already knows that, to earn a maximal return against v, it is necessary to drive $x(t)$ to the position $X(u^*(v), v)$, which results from using the constant budget

$$(7.2.11) \qquad u^*(v) = (2\alpha v/3) \cdot \left\{ \cosh \left[\left(\frac{1}{3} \right) \cosh^{-1} \left(1 + \frac{27P}{2\alpha^2 v^2} \right) \right] - 1 \right\}$$

which is optimal against v. So a positional strategy $u_1(x)$ is optimal against every v (at least in the limit as $\rho \to 0$) only if the solution of equation (7.2.10) is exactly $x = a = X(u^*(v), v) = \phi(v)$. Hence the relation

$$(7.2.12) \qquad (1 - \phi(v)) u_1(\phi(v)) = \alpha v \phi(v)$$

must hold identically in v. Moreover $x = \phi(v)$ may be solved explicitly for $v = \phi^{-1}(x)$. So (7.2.12) gives finally

$$u_1(x) = [\alpha x/(1 - x)] \cdot \phi^{-1}(x)$$

$$(7.2.13)$$
$$= \frac{x}{1 - x} \sqrt{\frac{27P/4}{\cosh \left[3 \cosh^{-1} \left(\frac{1 + x/2}{1 - x} \right) \right] - 1}}$$

It is of interest that the expression (7.2.13) does not depend on α. Several values for $u_1(x)$ appear in Table 7.2A. It is not clear whether its values are exactly symmetric about $x = 1/2$ or only approximately so. But it does appear that the strategy (7.2.12) yields the optimal return against all constant budgets $v(\cdot) \equiv v$. Substantial numerical evidence supports this claim.

(7-2) *Question* In the light of the discussion of Stackelberg solutions found at the end of §2.1, how advisable does the strategy $u_1(x)$ seem?

TABLE 7.2A

x	$u_1(x)$	x	$u_1(x)$	x	$u_1(x)$
.001	.063	.35	.954	.75	.866
.01	.199	.4	.980	.8	.800
.05	.436	.45	.995	.85	.714
.1	.600	.5	1	.9	.600
.15	.714	.55	.995	.95	.436
.2	.800	.6	.980	.99	.199
.25	.866	.65	.954	.999	.063
.3	.917	.7	.917		

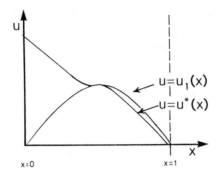

FIGURE 7.2B

Even granting the truth of the claim, however, it is not clear that $u_1(x)$ is a good strategy to use. For if so much is to be gained from the use of position-dependent policies, it must be presumed that one's opponent will use one too.

The strategy $u^*(x)$, indicated graphically in Figure 7.2B, roughly approximates $u_1(x)$ for large values of x, though not for small ones. When playing it, player 1 spends heavily on advertising if his market share is small and less so if it is large, as one might expect. The function $u^*(x)$ is tabulated briefly in Table 7.2C for the symmetric parameter values $P = 8 = Q$ and $\alpha = 1$. An account of its discovery is deferred for the moment. It is a highly robust strategy against an opponent who plays only constant strategies $v(x) \equiv v > 0$, though not as robust of course as $u_1(x)$.

To see that such is the case, observe that $x(t)$ must tend to a zero of

$$(7.2.14) \qquad f(x) = (1 - x)u^*(x) - \alpha x\, v(x)$$

as t grows large, for $f(0) = u^*(0) > 0$ and $f(1) = -\alpha v(1) < 0$. Let $x = a$ be such a zero, and suppose that $\lim_t x(t) = a$. Then J_i is approximately $\pi_i(u^*(a), v)$, the approximation being again exact in the limit as $\rho \to 0$. So one may associate with the strategy pair $(u^*(\cdot), v)$ a payoff $\pi_i(u^*(\cdot), v)$, $i = 1, 2$, and compare $\pi_1(u^*(\cdot), v)$ with $\pi_1^*(v)$, as has been done previously to determine robustness.

TABLE 7.2C

x	u*(x)	x	u*(x)	x	u*(x)
.05	1.616	.4	.973	.75	.459
.1	1.501	.45	.986	.8	.346
.15	1.386	.5	1	.85	.246
.2	1.273	.55	.975	.9	.156
.25	1.165	.6	.884	.95	.075
.3	1.069	.65	.741		
.35	.999	.7	.592		

TABLE 7.2D

v	x	$\pi_1(u*(\cdot), v)$	$\pi_1*(v)$	%	$\pi_2(u*(\cdot), v)$
.005	.944	7.55	7.78	97	.45
.05	.840	6.66	7.03	95	1.27
.1	.788	6.17	6.51	95	1.68
.2	.724	5.52	5.76	96	2.17
.3	.682	5.04	5.19	97	2.45
.5	.623	4.30	4.34	99	2.77
.6	.597	3.99	4.00	99+	2.86
1	.5	3	3	100	3
2	.336	1.66	1.67	99+	1.31
2.1	.328	1.57	1.59	99	.96
2.3	.313	1.41	1.44	98	.21
2.5	.299	1.25	1.31	96	-.65
2.7	.288	1.11	1.19	93	-1.59
2.9	.277	.98	1.09	90	-2.63

No entries appear in Table 7.2D for values of v between .6 and 2 except $v = 1$, because $\pi_1(u*(\cdot), v) > .99\, \pi_1*(v)$ in that range. And values $v > 2.9$ do not appear because $v > \sqrt{Q} = 2.828 \ldots$ implies $\pi_2(u, v) < 0$ for all u, so constant strategies $v > \sqrt{Q}$ on 2's part entail infinite loss.

It should also be remarked that if 2 thinks as 1 does, and adopts $v*(x) = u*(1 - x)$ instead of a constant strategy, then $x = 1/2$ is the sole zero of (7.2.14) and each player earns the largest payoff possible against the strategy of his opponent, namely

$$(7.2.15) \qquad 3 = \max_{v \geqslant 0} \pi_2(u*(\cdot), v) = \max_{u \geqslant 0} \pi_1(u, v*(\cdot)).$$

That is, each of the strategies $u*(x)$ and $v*(x)$ is optimal against the other and they form a Cournot-Nash equilibrium pair. Indeed, the equilibrium is exact; and they are optimal against other things as well, for if the graph of $u*(\cdot)$ indicated in Figure 7.2A is perturbed in any such way that $x = 1/2$ remains the sole zero of (7.2.14), the profits $\pi_i(u(\cdot), v(\cdot))$ do not change. Or if the change in $u(\cdot)$ produces only a small change in the location of the zero $x = a$, $v*(\cdot)$ will remain approximately optimal against $u(\cdot)$, because of its robustness. In short, the strategies $u*(x)$ and $v*(x)$ are optimal, or nearly so, in a wide range of circumstances.

But it is not to be supposed that $u*(\cdot)$ is near-optimal against every $v(\cdot)$, for it loses money against the (suicidal) $v \equiv 10$, and it is far from optimal against

$$(7.2.16) \qquad \begin{aligned} v(x) &= 2 \quad \text{if} \ \ x \leqslant 1/2 \\ &= .002 \quad \text{if} \ \ x > 1/2 \end{aligned}$$

unless $x(0) > 1/2$. All of the above statements concerning $u^*(\cdot)$ are true in the limit as $\rho \to 0$ and approximately so for small positive values of ρ. It is natural to deal extensively with the limiting case of DG because, as will presently become clear, it is computationally the simplest.

Two propositions have now been established concerning the strategy pair $(u^*(\cdot), v^*(\cdot))$. Each is (A) approximately optimal against all potentially profitable constant strategies available to the opponent, and (B) exactly optimal against the other for every initial position $x(0) = x_0$. Proposition (B) of course asserts that the pair is in perfect Cournot-Nash equilibrium, while (A) seems a natural extension of the robustness concept into the realm of differential games. Its verification is a step toward showing that the pair $(u^*(\cdot), v^*(\cdot))$ constitutes an approximate noncooperative solution of the game. Certain of our other remarks provide corroboration for this view, but it is not clear that convincing arguments to the effect that particular pairs (or triples or N-tuples) constitute approximate noncooperative solutions, like those offered previously for games with one-dimensional strategy spaces, are possible for differential games; strategy spaces are now of infinite dimension, and it is not even certain that one may meaningfully define dominance relations on them.

Rather, it seems likely, one shall probably be forced to make do with the knowledge that particular strategy pairs $(u^*(\cdot), v^*(\cdot))$ have some key property or properties in common with the idealized solution concept lingering always at the back of the mind. Properties (A) and (B) are offered here as especially appropriate "key" properties. The latter is recommended because every exact noncooperative solution will always have it, and approximate ones will have it approximately. And the former appeals because it was the verdict of Chapter VI that constant strategies of the form $u(x) \equiv$ robust action were very good ones indeed for the Ad Game; so good, in fact, that one need not be surprised if either or both advertiser chooses to disregard his information and pursue a constant advertising policy.

(7-3) *Question* Conventional wisdom has it that a constant fraction of sales should be turned back into advertising. How does a conventional v-player fare against one who chooses $u = u^*(x)$? It may be helpful to approximate $u^*(x)$ by a cubic form.

In the next chapter a method will be presented for discovering strategy pairs $(u^*(\cdot), v^*(\cdot))$ for which propositions (A) and (B) both are true. First, however, we shall examine one possible use of information in another of the games discussed earlier in a purely static context.

3. A DIFFERENTIAL GAME OF RESOURCE ALLOCATION

In some situations, action variables are not merely real numbers but must be chosen from specified intervals on the real line. For instance, it might be postulated that workers are trained, in the game of resource allocation discussed in Chapter II, at the time they enter the work force either as sailors or as factory hands, but not both. Then the composition of a nation's work force changes at a rate which cannot exceed that at which its citizens attain working age. If the population has achieved a stable age distribution, it may be assumed that citizens attain retirement age at roughly the same rate. So if a man works on the order of five hundred months during his working life, only the five hundredth part of a nation's work force can be converted from transportation to production or vice versa in any given month. Accordingly, it seems more accurate to assert that the nations $1 = E$ and $2 = P$ do not play the game (2.45) described earlier, but the differential game

$$1 \quad \max J_1 = \int_0^\infty \rho e^{-\rho t}(1 - x(t) - y(t))[x(t) - \sigma(1 - x(t) - y(t))] \, dt$$

$$(7.3.1) \quad 2 \quad \max J_2 = \int_0^\infty \rho e^{-\rho t}(1 - x(t) - y(t))[y(t) - s(1 - x(t) - y(t))] \, dt$$

$$\text{subject to} \quad \dot{x}(t) = u(t), \qquad \dot{y}(t) = v(t),$$

$$\text{and} \qquad |u| \leqslant m, \qquad |v| \leqslant \mu,$$

wherein m and μ have roughly the values $L/500\mathcal{L}$ and $\Lambda/500\mathcal{L}$, respectively.

Certain terminology will be useful for the discussion of this game. We shall call the rectangle

$$(7.3.2) \quad E = E(m, \mu) = \{(x, y): \ 0 \leqslant x \leqslant L/\mathcal{L} \quad \text{and} \quad 0 \leqslant y \leqslant \Lambda/\mathcal{L}\}$$

the *playing space* of the game. The intersection of E with any vertical line $x \equiv$ constant will be called a vertical section of E. Then if the deletion of a curve C from the xy-plane separates each vertical section of E into just two nonempty disjoint line segments, it will be said that C *vertically separates* E. Horizontal sections and the horizontal separation of E are similarly defined.

To understand the game (7.3.1), one must know the extent to which the players in it can govern their own fate. To this end, we define a closed subset S of E to be an *attainable goal for player 2* if there exists a strategy $v(x, y)$ for him such that the pair of equations

$$(7.3.3) \qquad \dot{x}(t) = u(t) \qquad \dot{y}(t) = v(x(t), y(t))$$

has a unique solution for every measureable and admissible $u(t), 0 \leqslant t < \infty$, if that solution reaches S, and if it has the property that $(x(t), y(t)) \in S$ implies $(x(t'), y(t')) \in S$ for every $t' > t$. Then player 2 can drive the moving point $(x(t), y(t))$ into S and keep it there indefinitely.

Let S be an attainable goal for 2. Then S must clearly meet every vertical section of E. We shall call $P \in S$ a *lower boundary point of S* if P is the lowest point in the intersection of S with some vertical section of E. Then the lower boundary of S is the graph of a function $\phi(\cdot)$ defined on the interval $0 \leqslant x \leqslant L/\mathcal{L}$. The *upper boundary* of S is similarly defined. It too is the graph of a function ψ defined on $0 \leqslant x \leqslant L/\mathcal{L}$.

If ϕ does not satisfy the one-sided Lipschitz condition

$$(7.3.4) \qquad \phi(x + h) \leqslant \phi(x) + \frac{\mu}{m}|h|$$

for every $x \in [0, L/\mathcal{L}]$ and $h \in [-x, L/\mathcal{L} - x]$, S is not an attainable goal for 2, for then there are points on the lower boundary of S from which 1 may drive $(x(t), y(t))$ at least temporarily out of S. Nor is S an attainable goal for 2 if ψ does not satisfy

$$(7.3.5) \qquad \psi(x + h) \geqslant \psi(x) - \frac{\mu}{m}|h|.$$

But if ϕ and ψ do satisfy (7.3.4) and (7.3.5), respectively, and if $\phi(x) < \psi(x)$ for each $0 \leqslant x \leqslant L/\mathcal{L}$, then S is an attainable goal for 2. To prove it, one need only exhibit an appropriate strategy $v(x, y)$.

The reader will verify that the strategy defined by

$$(7.3.6) \qquad v(x, y) = \begin{cases} 1 & \text{if } y < \phi(x) \\ -1 & \text{if } y > \psi(x) \\ 2p - 1 & \text{if } y = p\phi(x) + (1 - p)\psi(x) \end{cases}$$

satisfies a uniform Lipschitz condition in E. Therefore, the equations (7.3.3) are uniquely solvable in E, and clearly each solution of (7.3.3) must reach S in finite time and remain there indefinitely. These conclusions follow readily from the standard theorems [1] concerning the existence and uniqueness of solutions of ordinary differential equations. In particular, S might be a closed ϵ-neighborhood of the graph C of a function ϕ satisfying the two-sided Lipschitz condition

$$(7.3.7) \qquad -\frac{\mu}{m}h \leqslant \phi(x + h) - \phi(x) \leqslant \frac{\mu}{m}h.$$

And if we further agree that a set is an attainable goal if every ϵ-neighborhood of it is one, then C itself is an attainable goal.

Now if (x, y) is a position in E which is unfavorable to 2, he can arrange that the point $(x(t), y(t))$ never remain at (x, y) by selecting an attainable goal S which does not contain (x, y), then driving $(x(t), y(t))$ into S. And the smaller the attainable goal he chooses, the more unfavorable positions he will thus avoid.

Thus we define a *minimal attainable goal* for 2 to be an attainable goal which contains no other such as a proper subset. Then one may state

Theorem A: A closed subset S of E is a minimal attainable goal for player 2 iff S is the graph of a function ϕ satisfying (7.3.7).

The minimal attainable goals for 1 are obtained in a similar fashion, so theorem A completely characterizes the minimal attainable goals in the game (7.3.1),

Now let C be the graph of a function $F(x)$ satisfying (7.3.7). Suppose that C separates E vertically, and let S be an ϵ-neighborhood thereof. Then the lower boundary of S is the graph of $\phi(x) = F(x) - \epsilon$ and its upper boundary is the graph of $\psi(x) = F(x) + \epsilon$. Moreover, the strategy $v(x, y)$ defined by (7.3.6) drives $(x(t), y(t))$ into S and keeps it there, against any strategy $u(x, y)$ that 1 may choose. Similarly, if Γ separates E horizontally, is the graph of a function $G(y)$ such that

$$(7.3.8) \qquad -\frac{m}{\mu} h \leqslant G(y + h) - G(y) \leqslant \frac{m}{\mu} h,$$

and if S' is a δ-neighborhood of the graph of Γ, then the strategy $u(\cdot, \cdot)$ defined by $u(x, y) = v(y, x)$ and (7.3.6) drives $(x(t), y(t))$ into S' and keeps it there. So when the players 1 and 2 choose C and Γ as their goals, $(x(t), y(t))$ is driven into $S \cap S'$ and kept there. And if ϵ, δ are small, $S \cap S'$ is a small neighborhood of the point P at which C and Γ meet. Hence the players will receive about

$$(7.3.9) \qquad \pi_1(x, y) = (1 - x - y)[x - \sigma(1 - x - y)]$$

and

$$\pi_2(x, y) = (1 - x - y)[y - s(1 - x - y)],$$

respectively, when the above-described strategies are played, where (x, y) are the coordinates of P. And π_1, π_2 are, of course, exactly the payoff functions (2.45) considered in Chapter II, wherein the static version of the game was examined. It was pointed out there that $\partial \pi_1 / \partial x$ and $\partial \pi_2 / \partial y$ vanish along the lines

$$(7.3.10) \qquad \begin{aligned} l_1 &: Ax + y = 1 \\ l_2 &: x + By = 1 \end{aligned}$$

where A and B are given in terms of s and σ by

$$(7.3.11) \qquad A = (2 + 2\sigma)/(1 + 2\sigma), \qquad B = (2 + 2s)/(1 + 2s)$$

so that π_1 is maximized against a particular value of y iff $x = x^*(y) = (1 - y)/A$ and π_2 is maximized against a particular value of x by $y = y^*(x) = (1 - x)/B$. Moreover, the function $y^*(\cdot)$ satisfies (7.3.7) iff $\Lambda \leqslant AL$. So the players can choose the graphs of $x^*(\cdot)$ and $y^*(\cdot)$ for their respective goals in the game iff the inequalities

$$(7.3.12) \qquad L/B \leqslant \Lambda \leqslant AL$$

both hold. They will if L and Λ are equal or nearly so. That is, each country can adopt a training policy whereby its current labor-force allocation is always instantaneously optimal against that of the other country, provided that the inequalities (7.3.12) both hold. Otherwise one of the countries, due to its larger population and the additional flexibility of allocation afforded thereby, can prevent the other from achieving perpetual instantaneous optimality, for then one player's ability to utilize his information is significantly exceeded by that of his opponent. Such inequities often result from constraints of the form $|u| \leqslant m$ and $|v| \leqslant \mu$ in differential games.

(7-4)   *Question*   In the light of the discussion of Stackelberg solutions found at the end of §2.1, how advisable do the attainable goals $x = x^*(y)$ and $y = y^*(x)$ seem?

The purpose of the present chapter has been to introduce the reader to games in which a strategy is not a number or short list of numbers but an entire decision rule. Such games may be incorporated into the conceptual framework developed earlier for games with strategy spaces of low dimension. In particular, the same notion of noncooperative solutions may be adopted for the new sort of game. But because of the enormity of the function spaces from which strategies may now be chosen, it no longer seems possible to offer brute-force demonstrations that particular N-tuples constitute approximate noncooperative solutions. Rather, it would seem, it will be necessary to proceed by showing that particular N-tuples have certain carefully chosen properties in common with whatever exact or approximate solutions may happen to exist.

It was suggested earlier that the properties (A) and (B) have much to recommend them. And they do. But it is entirely possible that other investigators may propose other properties with as much or more to be said in their behalf. We have settled on the present pair for their tractability and apparent intuitive appeal. The next chapter will be devoted to strategy N-tuples which possess either or both of them.

REFERENCES

1. Coddington, E. A. and N. Levinson, *Theory of Ordinary Differential Equations* (New York: McGraw-Hill, 1955).
2. Isaacs, R., *Differential Games* (New York: John Wiley, 1965).
3. Kuhn, H. W., "Extensive Games and the Problem of Information," in *Contributions to the Theory of Games II*, H. W. Kuhn and A. W. Tucker, eds. Annals of Mathematics Studies, no. 28 (Princeton, N.J.: Princeton Univ. Press., 1953).
4. Selten, R., "A Simple Model of Imperfect Competition, Where Four Are Few and Six Are Many, *Int'l. J. Game Theory* (1973), pp. 141–201.

5. Wagner, H. M., *Principles of Operations Research* (Englewood Cliffs, N.J.: Prentice-Hall, 1969).
6. Zermelo, E., "Uber eine Anwendung der Mengenlehre und der Theorie des Schacspeils," *Proceedings of the Fifth International Congress of Mathematicians*, Cambridge, Mass. II (1912) pp. 501-504.

Chapter 8

Solving Differential Games

1. EQUILIBRIA FOR MANY-PLAYER DIFFERENTIAL GAMES

The salient features of the two differential games with which the reader is now familiar may be displayed* thus:

$$i \text{ maximize} \qquad J_i = \int_0^\infty e^{-\rho t} L_i(x(t), u_1(t), \ldots, u_N(t)) \, dt$$

(8.1.1)

$$\text{subject to} \qquad \dot{x}(t) = f(x(t), u_1(t), \ldots, u_N(t))$$

$$\text{and} \qquad u_i(t) \in U_i, \qquad x(t) \in S,$$

the constraints being assumed to hold for all $t \geqslant 0$ and $i = 1, \ldots, N$. Here $x(t) = (x_1(t), \ldots, x_n(t))$ is an n-dimensional "state vector" whose instantaneous value is always known to all the players $1, \ldots, N$, while $u_i(t) = (u_i^1(t), \ldots, u_i^{m_i}(t))$ is an m_i-dimensional control vector chosen at each instant by player i. The evolution of $x(t)$ is governed by the players' choices of $u_1(t), \ldots, u_N(t)$. S is the set of all possible "states of information" and U_i is the set of control vectors available to player i. In the examples of current interest, the sets $S, U_1, \ldots, U_N$ have simple geometrical shapes and lie in spaces of low dimension. It is suggested that the reader identify the abstract quantities $x(t), u_1(t), \ldots, u_N(t)$, $S, U_1, \ldots, U_N, L_1, \ldots, L_N$, and f with their counterparts from the two differential games of the previous chapter.

A strategy (or policy) for player i is a function $\phi_i(\cdot)$ assigning a control vector in U_i to each possible information state $x \in S$. To play it, i simply chooses

(8.1.2) $$u_i(t) = \phi_i(x(t))$$

---

*As remarked in the previous chapter, it makes no difference when $\rho > 0$ if the players' objectives are phrased in terms of *equivalent average returns* ($\rho e^{-\rho t}$) or *present values* ($e^{-\rho t}$). Both produce the same preference relation. We therefore choose the latter convention ($e^{-\rho t}$) for its computational simplicity throughout Chapter VIII, except in situations wherein it becomes necessary to discuss limits as $\rho \to 0$.

at each instant $t \geqslant 0$. Ordinarily, the choice of a strategy by each player determines the evolution of $x(t)$ for all $t \geqslant 0$, and therefore the "control histories" $u_i(t) = \phi_i(x(t))$ as well. Finally, when $x(t), u_1(t), \ldots, u_N(t)$ are all known, the integrals $J_1, \ldots, J_N$ may be evaluated. And when that is done for every starting point $x(0) = \xi \in S$, N functions

(8.1.3) $$J_1(\xi; \phi_1, \ldots, \phi_N), \ldots, \mathcal{J}_N(\xi; \phi_1, \ldots, \phi_N)$$

result. $J_i(\xi, \phi_1, \ldots, \phi_N)$ represents the reward accruing to player i if the game starts in position ξ and the players all adhere to the strategies $\phi_1, \ldots, \phi_N$, respectively. An N-tuple of strategies $\phi_1^*, \ldots, \phi_N^*$ is said to constitute a *perfect equilibrium* if the inequalities

(8.1.4) $$J_i(\xi; \ldots, \phi_{i-1}^*, \phi_i, \phi_{i+1}^*, \ldots) \leqslant \mathcal{J}_i(\xi, \phi_1^*, \ldots, \phi_N^*)$$

all hold for every $\xi \in S$ and $i = 1, \ldots, N$.

Our first objective is to discover a test whereby one may determine whether or not a given strategy N-tuple does or does not constitute an equilibrium. For that, it suffices to have a test which distinguishes optimal strategies for the one-player game

(8.1.5)

$$\text{maximize} \qquad J = \int_0^\infty e^{-\rho t} L(x(t), u(t))\, dt$$

$$\text{subject to} \qquad \dot{x}(t) = f(x(t), u(t))$$

$$\text{and} \qquad u(t) \in U, \qquad x(t) \in S,$$

since the latter test may then be applied N-times to see if each ϕ_i is indeed optimal against the rest.

We shall say that $\phi(x)$ is an "admissible strategy" for (8.1.5) if $\phi(\cdot)$ is defined and continuously differentiable on an open set containing S, and if no solution $\chi(t; \xi)$ of the initial value problem

(8.1.6) $$\dot{x} = f(x, \phi(x)), \qquad x(0) = \xi$$

that starts in S ever escapes from S. Hereinafter, we abuse notation to the extent that we write $\phi(t, \xi)$ for $\phi(\chi(t, \xi))$. The question is whether a given ϕ is optimal for (8.1.5) in the sense that

(8.1.7) $$\int_0^\infty e^{-\rho t} L(\chi(t, \xi), \phi(t, \xi))\, dt \geqslant \int_0^\infty e^{-\rho t} L(x(t), u(t))\, dt$$

for every pair $(x(t), u(t))$ of functions defined on $0 \leqslant t < \infty$ for which $x(0) = \xi$ and the constraints

(8.1.8) $$x(t) \in S, \quad u(t) \in U, \quad \dot{x}(t) = f(x(t), u(t))$$

hold for almost every positive t.

Suppose first that ϕ is admissible and that L is *simple* in the sense that

(8.1.9)
$$L(x,u) \leqslant 0 \qquad \forall (x,u) \in S \times U$$
$$L(x, \phi(x)) = 0 \qquad \forall x \in S.$$

Then ϕ is optimal because the integral on the left of (8.1.7) vanishes while that on the right is not positive.

Now suppose that L is not simple, and define

(8.1.10)
$$H(x,u,p) = L(x,u) + p \cdot f(x,u)$$

for all vectors p in the n-dimensional Euclidean space E_n. The function H is known as the Hamiltonian function, and has a long and interesting history [8]. Next suppose that there exists a function $\hat{u}(x,p)$ defined on $S \times E_n$ such that

(8.1.11)
$$H(x, \hat{u}(x,p), p) > H(x, u, p)$$

for all $u \neq \hat{u}(x,p)$ in U. Also let $V(x)$ be *any solution at all* of the Hamilton-Jacobi equation

(8.1.12)
$$H(x, \hat{u}(x, \nabla V(x)), \ \nabla V(x)) = \rho V(x)$$

which is defined on all of S. Then the new integrand

(8.1.13)
$$\hat{L}(x,u) = L(x,u) + \nabla V(x) \cdot f(x,u) - \rho V(x)$$

is simple in the sense of (8.1.9), since the strategy

(8.1.14)
$$\phi^*(x) = \hat{u}(x, \nabla V(x))$$

has the properties

(8.1.15)
$$\hat{L}(x, \phi^*(x)) = L(x, \hat{u}(x, \nabla V(x))) + \nabla V(x) \cdot f(x, \hat{u}(x, \nabla V(x))) - \rho V(x)$$
$$= H(x, \hat{u}(x, \nabla V(x)), \ \nabla V(x)) - \rho V(x) \equiv 0,$$

because V solves (8.1.12), and

(8.1.16)
$$\hat{L}(x,u) = L(x,u) + \nabla V(x) \cdot f(x,u) - \rho V(x) = H(x, u, \nabla V(x)) - \rho V(x)$$
$$< H(x, \hat{u}(x, \nabla V(x)), \ \nabla V(x)) - \rho V(x) = 0$$

by assumption (8.1.11). Therefore, the inequality (8.1.7) holds when L is replaced by $\hat{L}$ and ϕ^* is defined by (8.1.14). Finally,

$$\int_0^\infty e^{-\rho t} \hat{L}(x(t), \ u(t)) \, dt$$

$$= \int_0^\infty e^{-\rho t} L(x(t), \ u(t)) \, dt + \int_0^\infty e^{-\rho t} [\nabla V(x(t)) \cdot f(x(t), \ u(t)) - \rho V(x(t))] \, dt$$

$$= \int_0^\infty e^{-\rho t} L(x(t), u(t))\, dt + \int_0^\infty \frac{d}{dt}[e^{-\rho t} V(x(t))]\, dt$$

(8.1.17)

$$= \int_0^\infty e^{-\rho t} L(x(t), u(t))\, dt - V(\xi) + \lim_{t \to \infty} e^{-\rho t} V(x(t))$$

for every pair $(x(t), u(t))$ satisfying $x(0) = \xi$ and the constraints (8.1.8). And for similar reasons

$$\int_0^\infty e^{-\rho t} \hat{L}(\chi(t; \xi), \phi^*(t, \xi))\, dt$$

(8.1.18)

$$= \int_0^\infty e^{-\rho t} L(\chi(t; \xi), \phi^*(t; \xi))\, dt - V(\xi) + \lim_{t \to \infty} e^{-\rho t} V(\chi(t; \xi)).$$

Therefore, the inequality (8.1.7) holds for L as well as $\hat{L}$ whenever the limits appearing in (8.1.17) and (8.1.18) vanish. In particular (8.1.7) must hold whenever S is compact and $V(\cdot)$ is defined on all of S.

Therefore one may test a given ϕ for optimality by replacing $\hat{u}(x, \nabla V(x))$ with $\phi(x)$ in (8.1.12), solving the resultant *linear* partial differential equation for V, and comparing the $\hat{u}(x, \nabla V(x))$ so obtained with $\phi(x)$. Or one may compute an optimal strategy ϕ^* by solving the (usually nonlinear) Hamilton-Jacobi equation (8.1.12) for V and using (8.1.14). An exactly *analogous* procedure can be made to yield perfect equilibria $\phi_1^*, \ldots, \phi_N^*$ for the many-player game (8.1.1).

Before examining that procedure, we pause to encapsulate our results concerning the single player game (8.1.5) in the form of

Theorem A: Suppose that S_0 is an open subset of S in n-space and that $V(x)$ is a continuously differentiable function defined everywhere in S_0. Suppose too that $V(\cdot)$ satisfies equation (8.1.12) everywhere in S_0, that $\phi^*(\cdot)$ is defined by (8.1.14), and that no solution of (8.1.6) starting in S_0 ever leaves it. Then $\phi^*(\cdot)$ is an optimal strategy in the class of all ϕ for which the solutions of (8.1.6) do not escape from S_0.

The content of the theorem is illustrated in Figure 8.1A. In it are shown the set S, the subset S_0, and some sample trajectories arising from the strategy $\phi^*(\cdot)$. The theorem asserts that the trajectory Γ^* belonging to ϕ^* and starting at x_0 yields a greater reward than does Γ^0, which never leaves S_0. But it does not preclude the possibility that some third Γ, which escapes for a while from S_0, may yield a still greater one.

It should be mentioned here that single-player differential games are more

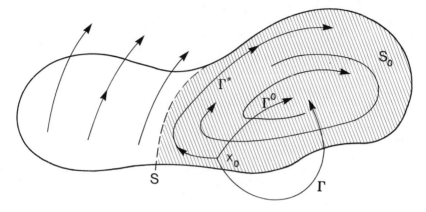

FIGURE 8.1A

commonly known as problems of optimal control, or sometimes, of the calculus of variations. So theorem A is, in reality, a theorem about optimal control. While we are not aware that this particular theorem appears in the literature, others quite like [2] it certainly do. Indeed, the first theorem relating the calculus of variations and the Hamilton-Jacobi equation, which was known earlier in another connection, appears to be due to Carathéodory [3]. We shall illustrate the application of the theorem to problems of many-player differential games shortly. First, however, we shall pause to state a corollary of theorem A which will prove useful in what follows:

Corollary: If the function $V(\cdot)$ of theorem A fails to satisfy (8.1.12), but is instead a solution of any of the related equations

$$(8.1.12')\qquad H(x, \hat{u}(x, \nabla V(x)),\ \ \nabla V(x)) = \rho V(x) + C$$

where C is an arbitrary (real) constant, the conclusions of the theorem remain valid.

The proof of the corollary is trivial, since $(8.1.12')$ is the Hamilton-Jacobi equation associated with the control problem $(8.1.5')$ derived from (8.1.5) when the integrand is $L(x, u)$ is replaced by $L'(x, u) = L(x, u) - C$. But the control problems (8.1.5) and $(8.1.5')$ are obviously "equivalent" in the sense that any strategy optimal for one is optimal for the other too, since the admissible strategies are the same for the two problems and the relation $J' = J - C/\rho$ between their objective functionals is independent of the strategy chosen. The impact of the corollary is simply that it is a little easier to find a solution for one of the several equations $(8.1.12')$ than for the single equation (8.1.12).

The solution procedure itself begins with the definition of N Hamiltonian functions

$$H_i(x, u_1, \ldots, u_N, p) = L_i(x, u_1, \ldots, u_N) + p \cdot f(x, u_1, \ldots, u_N)$$

(8.1.19)

and the discovery of N control functions $\hat{u}_1(x, p_1, \ldots, p_N), \ldots, \hat{u}_N(x, p_1, \ldots, p_N)$ which are in equilibrium for the auxiliary game

(8.1.20) $\qquad i \max_{u_i \in U_i} \text{imize } H_i(x, u_1, \ldots, u_N, p_i)$

and therefore satisfy the inequalities

$$H_i(x, \hat{u}_1(x, p_1, \ldots, p_N), \ldots, \hat{u}_N(x, p_1, \ldots, p_N), p_i)$$

(8.1.21) $\quad > H_i(x, \ldots, \hat{u}_{i-1}(x, p_1, \ldots, p_N), u_i, \hat{u}_{i+1}(x, p_1, \ldots, p_N), \ldots, p_i)$

for every $u_i \neq \hat{u}_i(x, p_1, \ldots, p_N)$ in U_i. If such functions $\hat{u}_1(\cdot), \ldots, \hat{u}_N(\cdot)$ can be found, the N Hamilton-Jacobi equations

$$H_i(x, \hat{u}_1(x, \nabla V^1(x), \ldots, \nabla V^N(x)), \ldots, \hat{u}_N(x, \nabla V^1(x), \ldots,$$

(8.1.22) $\qquad\qquad\qquad\qquad\qquad \nabla V^N(x)), \nabla V^i(x)) = \rho V^i(x)$

may be written. If they can also be solved for the N unknown functions $V^1(x), \ldots, V^N(x)$, strategies may be defined by the relations

(8.1.23) $\qquad \phi_i^*(x) = \hat{u}_i(x, \nabla V^1(x), \ldots, \nabla V^N(x)).$

And each of the strategies (8.1.23) is, by the manner of its construction, optimal against the rest for every starting point $x(0) = \xi$ in S. So $\phi_1^*, \ldots, \phi_N^*$ is a perfect equilibrium if it is obtained in the above-described manner. Let us illustrate the procedure as it applies to the two-player Ad Game.

2. THE TWO-PLAYER AD GAME

This game has been discussed at some length in previous chapters. Its principal features are displayed below:

$$1 \text{ maximize} \qquad \int_0^\infty e^{-\rho t}[P \cdot x(t) - u^2(t)] \, dt$$

(8.2.1) $\quad 2 \text{ maximize} \qquad \int_0^\infty e^{-\rho t}[Q - Q \cdot x(t) - v^2(t)] \, dt$

$$\text{subject to} \qquad \dot{x}(t) = (1 - x(t))u(t) - \alpha x(t)v(t)$$

$$\text{and} \qquad 0 \leqslant x \leqslant 1, \quad u \geqslant 0, \quad v \geqslant 0.$$

So S here is the unit interval, while U_1 and U_2 are positive half lines. The Hamiltonian functions are

$$(8.2.2) \quad \begin{aligned} H_1(x, u, v, p_1) &= Px - u^2 + p_1(1 - x)u - p_1\alpha xv \\ H_2(x, u, v, p_2) &= Q - Qx - v^2 + p_2(1 - x)u - p_2\alpha xv, \end{aligned}$$

and setting $\partial H_1/\partial u = 0 = \partial H_2/\partial v$, one finds

$$(8.2.3) \quad \begin{aligned} \hat{u}_1(x, p_1, p_2) &= p_1(1 - x)/2 \\ \hat{u}_2(x, p_1, p_2) &= -p_2\alpha x/2. \end{aligned}$$

Then making the identifications $p_1 = \nabla V = V'$ and $p_2 = \nabla W = W'$ and substituting the control functions (8.2.3) into (8.2.2), one obtains the Hamilton-Jacobi equations

$$(8.2.4) \quad \begin{aligned} Px + (1/2)(1 - x)^2 V'^2(x) + (1/2)\alpha^2 x^2 V'(x)W'(x) &= \rho V(x) + C \\ Q(1 - x) + (1/2)(1 - x)^2 V'(x)W'(x) + (1/4)\alpha^2 x^2 W'^2(x) &= \rho W(x) + \gamma. \end{aligned}$$

They constitute, in the present example, a pair of ordinary differential equations without (as yet) side conditions, and in nonstandard form. If solved for the unknown functions $V(x)$ and $W(x)$, they yield the equilibrium strategies $u^*(x)$ and $v^*(x)$ through the relations

$$(8.2.5) \quad \begin{aligned} u^*(x) &= \hat{u}(x, V'(x), W'(x)) = (1/2)(1 - x)V'(x) \\ v^*(x) &= \hat{v}(x, V'(x), W'(x)) = -(1/2)\alpha x W'(x). \end{aligned}$$

If one defines the quantities

$$(8.2.6) \quad A = (1 - x)/\alpha x, \quad B = 4(Px - \rho V - C)/\alpha^2 x^2, \quad C = 4(Q - Qx - \rho W - \gamma)/(1 - x)^2$$

one may write

$$(8.2.7) \quad \begin{aligned} V' &= (1/A\sqrt{3})(2C - B + 2(B^2 - BC + C^2)^{1/2})^{1/2} = f(x, \rho V, \rho W) \\ W' &= (A/\sqrt{3})(2B - C + 2(B^2 - BC + C^2)^{1/2})^{1/2} = g(x, \rho V, \rho W). \end{aligned}$$

System (8.2.7) constitutes an equivalent system of ordinary differential equations for $V(x)$ and $W(x)$, but one which is in standard form. So the usual [6] existence and uniqueness results hold in the interval $0 < x < 1$. In particular, the solutions must depend analytically on the parameter ρ, since f and g both do. In short, the system (8.2.7) is an equivalent form of (8.2.4), which seems amenable to the standard tools of analysis. It is convenient for our present purposes, however, to consider yet another equivalent system.

If one solves (8.2.5) for $V'(x)$ and $W'(x)$, integrates once, and substitutes the result in (8.2.4), one obtains upon simplification

(8.2.8)
$$\psi_1(x, u, v) = \frac{u^2}{2} - \left(\frac{\alpha x}{1 - x}\right) uv + \frac{Px}{2} - \rho \int^x \frac{u(s) \, ds}{1 - s} - c = 0$$

$$\psi_2(x, u, v) = \frac{v^2}{2} - \left(\frac{1 - x}{\alpha x}\right) uv + \frac{Q(1 - x)}{2} - \frac{\rho}{\alpha} \int^x \frac{v(s) \, ds}{s} - \gamma = 0.$$

Moreover, it is shown in the appendix to this chapter that for $c = \psi_1(x_0, u_0, v_0)$, $\gamma = \psi_2(x_0, u_0, v_0)$, and for ρ sufficiently small, the equations (8.2.8) have unique solutions $u(x; \rho)$, $v(x; \rho)$ such that $u(x_0; \rho) = u_0$ and $v(x_0; \rho) = v_0$. Indeed these solutions are differentiable in x and satisfy the equations

(8.2.9)
$$[(1 - x)u - \alpha xv] u' - \alpha xuv' = \rho u - P(1 - x)/2 + \alpha uv/(1 - x)$$

$$(1 - x) vu' + [(1 - x)u - \alpha xv] v' = \rho v - Q\alpha x/2 + uv/x,$$

which because of the uniqueness asserted above are entirely equivalent to the integral equations (8.2.8). Moreover, if one defines anew

(8.2.10)
$$A = (1 - x)u - \alpha xv, \qquad B = \rho u - P(1 - x)/2 + \alpha uv/(1 - x)$$

$$C = \rho v - Q\alpha x/2 - uv/x,$$

one may solve (8.2.9) for u' and v', obtaining

(8.2.11)
$$u' = (AB + \alpha xuC)/(A^2 + \alpha x(1 - x)uv) = F(x, u, v; \rho)$$

$$v' = (AC - (1 - x)vB)/(A^2 + \alpha x(1 - x)uv) = G(x, u, v; \rho).$$

They, like (8.2.7), constitute a pair of ordinary differential equations in standard form to which the usual results apply. In particular, they have a unique analytic solution $(x, u(x; \rho), v(x; \rho))$ through each (x_0, u_0, v_0) in the positive octant of xuv-space, such that $u(x; \rho)$ and $v(x; \rho)$ both depend analytically on ρ. In particular, the solutions for small values of ρ are well approximated by those for $\rho = 0$, at least locally. Moreover, the equations (8.2.11) are particularly easy to solve when $\rho = 0$, since the functions ψ_1 and ψ_2 defined in (8.2.8) are then "integrals of the motion," and any curve $(x, u(x), v(x))$ whereon ψ_1 and ψ_2 have [10] the constant values $\psi_1(x, u, v) = c$ and $\psi_2(x, u, v) = \gamma$ is a solution curve. So if we define

(8.2.12) $R = \alpha x/(1 - x), \quad S = Px + 2c, \quad \text{and} \quad T = Q(1 - x) + 2\gamma,$

the solutions may be written

(8.2.13)
$$u(x) = (1/\sqrt{3})(2TR^2 - S + 2(T^2R^4 - STR^2 + S^2)^{1/2})^{1/2}$$

$$v(x) = (1/\sqrt{3})(2S/R^2 - T + 2(S^2/R^4 - ST/R^2 + T^2)^{1/2})^{1/2}.$$

They are well defined for $0 < x < 1$, since the quantities in parentheses can never be negative and constitute a two-parameter family because c and γ appear in S and T.

Indeed, if (x_0, u_0, v_0) lies on the surface Σ defined by

$$(8.2.14) \qquad\qquad (1 - x)u - \alpha xv = 0,$$

it suffices to choose

$$(8.2.15)$$
$$-2c = u_0^2 + Px_0 - \frac{2\alpha x_0}{1 - x_0} u_0 v_0 = Px_0 - u_0^2$$

$$-2\gamma = v_0^2 + Q(1 - x_0) - \frac{2(1 - \gamma_0)}{\alpha x_0} u_0 v_0 = Q(1 - x_0) - v_0^2$$

to obtain a solution curve $(x, u(x), v(x))$ of (8.2.8) through (x_0, u_0, v_0). So the functions $u(x)$ and $v(x)$ obtained from (8.2.13) constitute perfect equilibrium pairs for the limiting case $\rho = 0$ of the game, and the solutions of (8.2.8) provide a like multiplicity of equilibria for the games $\rho > 0$. In short, there are a host of strategy pairs $(u^*(x), v^*(x))$ which share the property (B) of a solution. Let us now seek those among them which also share property (A).

Observe first that if $u(x) \geqslant 0$ is any continuous function on $0 < x \leqslant 1$, the equation

$$(8.2.16) \qquad\qquad (1 - x)u(x) - \alpha xv = 0$$

has at least one solution in the unit interval, so if 1 chooses the stationary strategy $u(\cdot)$ and 2 chooses the constant one v, $x(t)$ will be driven to a solution $x = a$ of (8.2.16). The resulting rewards will be $Pa - u^2(a)$ to 1 and $Q(1 - a) - v^2$ to 2 if $\rho = 0$, and approximately that if ρ is small but positive. So if $u(\cdot)$ is to be optimal against v, it must drive $x(t)$ to the same position* $X(u^*(v), v)$ that the optimal constant strategy $u^*(v)$ does. Similarly, a variable $v(\cdot)$ must drive $x(t)$ to the same position* $X(u, v^*(u))$ as $v^*(u)$ does. So if $u(\cdot)$ is to be (at least approximately) optimal against constant v's, and vice versa, they must together equilibrate the same position $X(u^*, v^*)$ as would Cournot's optimal response functions $u^*(v)$ and $v^*(u)$ if *they* could be played simultaneously. Thus the desired curve $(x, u(x), v(x))$ must pass near (if not through) the point $(X(u^*, v^*), u^*, v^*)$ of the surface Σ in xuv-space. Σ, incidentally, may be described as the union of all horizontal lines which meet both the (vertical) x-axis in xuv-space and the line segment joining $(1, 1, 0)$ with $(0, 0, 1/\alpha)$.

The mysterious strategies $u^*(x)$ and $v^*(x)$ introduced in the previous chapter were calculated in exactly this way. For the parameter values $P = 8 = Q$ and $\alpha = 1$, the corresponding static equilibrium pair is $u^* = 1 = v^*$ and leads to the market share $x = 1/2$. So $u^*(x)$ and $v^*(x)$ were obtained from (8.2.13) and (8.2.15)

---

*The symbols $X(u, v)$ and $u^*(v)$ were defined in the discussion of the two-player game in Chapter VII.

with $(x_0, u_0, v_0) = 1/2, 1, 1)$; the curve $(x, u^*(x), v^*(x))$ therefore crosses Σ at $(1/2, 1, 1)$ and, as it turns out, nowhere else.

To summarize, the Hamilton-Jacobi equations ordinarily characterize perfect equilibria and lead to a plethora of such in the present case. So an additional condition is required to single out those which more nearly resemble solutions. Condition (A) of the previous chapter seems appropriate for that purpose here.

Of course the strategy pairs $(u^*(x), v^*(x))$ obtained in this way satisfy (B) exactly and (A) only approximately. One might, on balance, prefer other strategies $u(\cdot)$ which more nearly satisfy (A) while satisfying (B) only approximately, but such a $u(\cdot)$ is easily obtained as a convex combination of $u^*(\cdot)$ and the $u_1(\cdot)$ obtained in Chapter VII which satisfied (A) exactly and (B) only approximately. Or one might choose to investigate approximate solutions of the Hamilton-Jacobi equations in some systematic fashion. For the moment, we shall *not* undertake any such investigation. Rather, we shall rest content with our discovery of strategy pairs $(u^*(x), v^*(x))$ which have at least approximately the properties (A) and (B) of a real solution. Such strategies may seem "good" to a particular player faced with a particular opponent, or they may not, depending on the nature of his expectations concerning that opponent's behavior. At least they provide reasonable candidates. Before employing one of them, a prospective player would probably wish to try it out in a few "preseason" games against friends playing devil's advocate, and using play money. He obviously can not try it against all strategies available to his opponent, but he can in this way test it against a number of the likely ones.

The roles of (A) and (B) in finding those candidates are to be emphasized. To discover strategy pairs (or N-tuples) possessing (B), it is necessary to solve certain differential equations. To single out those which also have property (A), one must impose side (typically initial) conditions on those solutions. The pattern will be repeated later on in other games.

3. ONE AND SEVERAL PLAYERS

We found, in the two-player Ad Game, a plethora of perfect equilibria. We shall endeavor to explain now why that it is to be expected in nonzero-sum games, but not in zero-sum or single-player ones. To that end, suppose $L(x, u)$ to be an increasing function of x and consider again the single-player game (8.1.5). Consider too the static optimization problem

(8.3.1)
$$\begin{array}{ll} \underset{x,\,u}{\text{maximize}} & L(x, u) \\ \text{subject to} & f(x, u) \geqslant 0 \end{array}$$

which it suggests. The direction of the inequality is prescribed by the monoticity of L in x. The Kuhn-Tucker conditions which hold at a solution $(\bar{x}, \bar{u})$ of (8.3.1) are

$$H_x(\bar{x}, \bar{u}, p) = 0$$
(differential conditions)
$$H_u(\bar{x}, \bar{u}, p) = 0$$

(8.3.2) $$p \cdot f(\bar{x}, \bar{u}) = 0$$ (orthogonality)

$$p \geqslant 0$$ (positivity)

$$f(\bar{x}, \bar{u}) \geqslant 0$$ (feasibility),

where H is now the so-called Lagrangian function

(8.3.3) $$H(x, u, p) = L(x, u) + p \cdot f(x, u).$$

and p an undetermined multiplier. These may be compared with the Hamilton-Jacobi conditions (8.1.11) and (8.1.12). Identifying again $p = p(x) = \nabla V(x) = V'(x)$, the latter are

$$H(x, u^*(x), p(x)) = \rho V(x)$$

(8.3.4) $$H_u(x, u^*(x), p(x)) = 0$$

$$p(x) \geqslant 0,$$

the first being the Hamilton-Jacobi equation (8.1.12) itself, the second a consequence of (8.1.11), and the third following from the monotonicity of L in x. If the optimal strategy $u^*(x)$ is such as to drive $x(t)$ to a limiting value x_∞, then $f(x_\infty, u^*(x_\infty))$ must vanish. So at x_∞, feasibility and orthogonality prevail too. Indeed all the conditions (8.3.2) hold there, for differentiating (8.1.12) with respect to x gives

(8.3.5) $$\frac{\partial H}{\partial x} + \frac{\partial H}{\partial u} \frac{du^*(x)}{dx} + \frac{\partial H}{\partial p} \frac{dp(x)}{dx} = \rho V'(x),$$

and the latter yields

(8.3.6) $$-\partial H/\partial x = p' - \rho p = p'(x) \cdot f(x, u^*(x)) - \rho p(x),$$

since $\partial H/\partial u$ is known already to vanish. Also the right-hand side of (8.3.6) tends to zero as $x(t) \to x_\infty$, $\rho \to 0$. In short, the Hamilton-Jacobi conditions together with $f(x, u^*(x)) = 0$ imply the Kuhn-Tucker conditions for (8.3.1), and the pair $(x_\infty, u_\infty) = (x_\infty, u^*(x_\infty))$ may be expected to furnish a maximum therefor. So only a relatively few strategies $u^*(\cdot)$ can be optimal; a similar result obtains for two-player zero-sum games, since (8.3.6) is valid for them as well.

The situation for non-zero-sum games, however, is very different. To see how, we consider the two-player version of (8.1.1) and assume L_1 increasing in x while L_2 decreases therewith. We also consider the related static game

(8.3.7)
$$i \, \max \quad L_i(x, u_1, u_2)$$
$$\text{subject to} \quad f(x, u_1, u_2) = 0, \quad i = 1, 2.$$

To find an equilibrium for it, we may seek three numbers $(\bar{x}, \bar{u}_1, \bar{u}_2)$ such that $(\bar{x}, \bar{u}_1)$ solves

(8.3.8)

$$\underset{(x, u_1)}{\text{maximize}} \quad L_1(x, u_1, \bar{u}_2)$$

$$\text{subject to} \quad f(x, u_1, \bar{u}_2) \leqslant 0.$$

and $(\bar{x}, \bar{u}_2)$ solves

(8.3.9)

$$\underset{(x, u_2)}{\text{maximize}} \quad L_2(x, \bar{u}_1, u_2)$$

$$\text{subject to} \quad f(x, \bar{u}_1, u_2) \geqslant 0.$$

The Kuhn-Tucker conditions for these problems are, of course,

(8.3.10)

$$H_{1x}(\bar{x}, \bar{u}_1, \bar{u}_2, p_1) = 0 \qquad H_{2x}(\bar{x}, \bar{u}_1, \bar{u}_2, p_2) = 0$$

$$H_{1u_1}(\bar{x}, \bar{u}_1, \bar{u}_2, p_1) = 0 \qquad H_{2u_2}(\bar{x}, \bar{u}_1, \bar{u}_2, p_2) = 0$$

$$p_1 \cdot f(\bar{x}, \bar{u}_1, \bar{u}_2) = 0 \qquad p_2 \cdot f(\bar{x}, \bar{u}_1, \bar{u}_2) = 0$$

$$p_1 \geqslant 0 \qquad p_2 \leqslant 0$$

$$f(\bar{x}, \bar{u}_1, \bar{u}_2) \geqslant 0 \qquad f(\bar{x}, \bar{u}_1, \bar{u}_2) \leqslant 0,$$

H_1 and H_2 being again defined by (8.1.19). They are to be compared with the Hamilton-Jacobi conditions (8.1.21) and (8.1.22) which become, on identifying once more $p_i = p_i(x) = \nabla V_i(x) = V_i'(x)$ for $i = 1, 2$,

$$H_1(x, u_1^*(x), u_2^*(x), p_1^*(x)) = \rho V_1(x) \qquad H_2(x, u_1^*(x), u_2^*(x), p_2^*(x)) = \rho V_2(x)$$

$$H_{1u_1}(x, u_1^*(x), u_2^*(x), p_1^*(x)) = 0 \qquad H_{2u_2}(x, u_1^*(x), u_2^*(x), p_2^*(x)) = 0$$

$$p_1(x) \geqslant 0 \qquad p_2(x) \leqslant 0.$$

(8.3.11)

The topmost relations are again the Hamilton-Jacobi equations themselves, while the middle two follow from the optimality conditions (8.1.21), and the last are consequences of the monotonicity of L_1 and L_2 in x. If $u_1^*(x)$ and $u_2^*(x)$ are such that $f(x, u_1^*(x), u_2^*(x))$ vanishes at a point $x = x_\infty$, then all save the first two of the Kuhn-Tucker conditions (8.3.10) must hold at $x = x_\infty$, by virtue of (8.3.11). However, the device of differentiating the Hamilton-Jacobi equations with respect to x now yields only

(8.3.12) $$\frac{\partial H_i}{\partial x} + \frac{\partial H_i}{\partial u_1} \frac{du_1}{dx} + \frac{\partial H_i}{\partial u_2} \frac{du_2}{dx} + \frac{\partial H_i}{\partial p_i} \frac{dp_i}{dx} = \rho p_i(x), \quad i = 1, 2,$$

and (8.3.12) fails to yield the missing Kuhn-Tucker conditions as did (8.3.6) because $\partial H_i / \partial u_j$ typically does not vanish if $j \neq i$.

To appreciate the significance of the foregoing remarks, let us call $(\bar{x}, \bar{u}_1, \bar{u}_2) \in S \times U_1 \times U_2$ an *equilibrium position* if there exists a perfect equilibrium pair $(u_1^*(x), u_2^*(x))$ of strategies such that $\bar{u}_1 = u_1^*(\bar{x})$, $\bar{u}_2 = u_2^*(\bar{x})$, and $f(\bar{x}, \bar{u}_1, \bar{u}_2) = 0$. Then only solutions of the Kuhn-Tucker conditions (8.3.10) can be equilibrium positions if the game (8.3.7) has only one player (as when U_2 consists of a single point) or is zero-sum (so that $L_1 = -L_2$). But an entire continuum of equilibrium positions can occur in nonzero-sum games because certain of the conditions (8.3.10) need not hold at those positions in such games. Σ, for instance, is a surface composed *entirely* of equilibrium positions in the two-player Ad Game. In short, property (A), which is a *consequence* of property (B) in one-player or zero-sum games, is independent of (B) in others and must be assumed separately.

There is more to be said. For the most effective way of solving the Hamilton-Jacobi equation (8.2.12) is called the "method of characteristics" and makes use of the "adjoint equation" (8.3.6). But no such method has ever been found for the system (8.1.22) of simultaneous Hamilton-Jacobi equations which arise from nonzero-sum games. In view of the above remarks, one must doubt that such a method can exist, for if it were possible to write

(8.3.13)
$$\dot{p}_1 = \phi(x, p_1, p_2)$$
$$\dot{p}_2 = \psi(x, p_1, p_2)$$

for some functions ϕ and ψ, one could presumably set $\dot{p}_1 = \dot{p}_2 = 0$ and solve (8.3.13) simultaneously with

(8.3.14) $\quad \dot{x} = 0 = \hat{f}(x, p_1, p_2) = f(x, \hat{u}_1(x, p_1, p_2), \hat{u}_2(x, p_1, p_2))$

to obtain a discrete set of solutions $(\bar{x}, \bar{p}_1, \bar{p}_2)$. And then only the triples $(\bar{x}, \bar{u}_1, \bar{u}_2)$, where $\bar{u}_i = \hat{u}_i(\bar{x}, \bar{p}_1, \bar{p}_2)$ could be equilibrium positions for (8.1.1). So the set of equilibrium positions would be discrete also, which clearly need not be the case.

The lack of a method of characteristics for the system (8.1.22) of Hamilton-Jacobi equations appears, at the present time, to constitute the principal difference between the many-player theory and the more special (and familiar) one-player and two-player zero-sum ones. Its consequences are far-reaching, for the lack of such a method renders the integration of the Hamilton-Jacobi equations in closed form unlikely, save in the simplest cases.

4. ON VALUE FUNCTIONS

If a game like the two-player Ad Game is known to have an entire continuum of equilibria, one wonders if it cannot have more which have not yet been found. Therefore it is of interest to deduce a theorem which implies, among other things, that *all* continuously differentiable equilibrium strategy pairs $(u^*(x), v^*(x))$ defined on $0 \leqslant x \leqslant 1$ are solutions of (8.2.8).

To discover such a theorem, it is easiest to turn one's attention once more to the optimal control problem (8.1.5). Let $\phi(x)$ again be a twice continuously differentiable function defined on a neighborhood of S, such that solutions of (8.1.6) starting in S never escape from S. Then by standard theorems [6] on the dependence of solutions of differential equations on initial data, $\chi(t, \xi) = x_\phi(t; \xi)$ and $\phi(t; \xi) = \phi(x_\phi(t; \xi))$ are twice continuously differentiable functions of both t and ξ. So another standard theorem [1] on differentiation of functions defined by integrals implies that

$$(8.4.1) \qquad J(\xi; \phi) = \int_0^\infty e^{-\rho t} L(\chi(t, \xi), \phi(t, \xi))\, dt$$

is also a twice continuously differentiable function of ξ. So if $\phi^*(\cdot)$ is a twice continuously differentiable *optimal* strategy, then $V(\xi) = J(\xi; \phi^*)$ is twice continuously differentiable too. $V(\cdot)$ is called the *value* function for the one-player game (8.1.5), as it specifies the amount a player can expect to earn starting in the information state ξ, that is, the "value" to the player of being in that information state.

Next we show that $V(\cdot)$ solves a certain partial differential equation. For if the interval $0 \leqslant t < \infty$ be broken up into $0 \leqslant t \leqslant h$ and $h \leqslant t < \infty$, one may write

$$V(\xi) = \int_0^h e^{-\rho t} L(\chi(t; \xi), \phi(t; \xi))\, dt$$

$$+ \int_h^\infty e^{-\rho t} L(\chi(t - h; \chi(h; \xi)), \phi(t - h; \chi(h; \xi)))\, dt$$

$$(8.4.2) \qquad = \int_0^h e^{-\rho t} L(\chi(t; \xi), \phi(t; \xi))\, dt$$

$$+ e^{-\rho h} \int_0^\infty e^{-\rho s} L(\chi(s; \chi(h; \xi)), \phi(s; \chi(h; \xi)))\, dt.$$

Therefore

$$(8.4.3) \quad \frac{1}{h} \int_0^h e^{-\rho t} L(\chi(t; \xi), \phi(t; \xi))\, dt + \frac{e^{-\rho h} V(\chi(h; \xi)) - V(\xi)}{h} = 0,$$

and passing to the limit

$$(8.4.4) \qquad L(\xi, \phi^*(\xi)) + \frac{d}{dt} e^{-\rho t} V(\chi(t; \xi)) \bigg|_{t=0} = 0.$$

So finally

(8.4.5) $L(\xi, \phi^*(\xi)) + \nabla V(\xi) \cdot f(\xi, \phi^*(\xi)) = \rho V(\xi).$

But if some constant control u is employed until $t = h$, before optimal play is begun, the information state at time $t = h$ will be typically $x_u(h) \neq \chi(h; \xi)$. So then

(8.4.6) $V(\xi) \geqslant \displaystyle\int_0^h e^{-\rho t} L(x_u(h), u)\, dt$

$$+ e^{-\rho h} \int_0^\infty e^{-\rho s} L(\chi(s; x_u(h)), \phi(s; x_u(h)))\, ds,$$

so proceeding as before

(8.4.7) $L(\xi, u) + \dfrac{d}{dt}\, [e^{-\rho t} V(x_u(t))] \leqslant 0.$

The content of the equation (8.4.5) and the inequality (8.4.7) are often expressed in the form

(8.4.8) $\max\limits_{u}\ [L(x, u) + \nabla V(x) \cdot f(x, u)] = \rho V(x),$

which the reader will recognize immediately as but another form of the Hamilton-Jacobi equation (8.1.12). So every (twice) continuously differentiable optimal strategy $\phi^*(x)$ is derivable *via* (8.1.14) from a solution $V(\cdot)$ of (8.1.12). And if $\phi_1^*(x), \ldots, \sigma_N^*(x)$ is an equilibrium N-tuple, the ϕ_i^*'s are derivable *via* (8.1.23) from a solution N-tuple $V^1(\cdot), \ldots, V^N(\cdot)$ of (8.1.22). The Hamilton-Jacobi method does not "ignore" any smooth optimal strategies or N-tuples of smooth equilibrium strategies. In fact, it is quite effective in practice for discovering even *discontinuous* optima because, as is apparent from the manner of its derivation, (8.4.8) must hold at every point x in whose vicinity $V(\cdot)$ is (even once) continuously differentiable. For subsequent reference we state the fact as

Theorem B: At any point x in whose vicinity the value function $V(\cdot)$ is continuously differentiable, the Hamilton-Jacobi equation (8.2.12) associated with the control problem (8.1.5) is valid.

As mentioned earlier, results connecting optimization with the Hamilton-Jacobi equation (which had been known earlier from mechanics and optics) were apparently first proven by Carathéodory [3].

To apply the theorem to the two-player Ad Game, let $(u^*(x), v^*(x))$ be a pair of twice continuously differentiable equilibrium strategies therefore, and let $V(x) = J_1(x; u^*, v^*)$ and $W(x) = J_2(x; u^*, v^*)$ be the value functions associated therewith. Then $V(\cdot)$ and $W(\cdot)$ are twice differentiable too and satisfy, respectively, the Hamilton-Jacobi equations

$$\max_{u} [Px - u^2 + V'(x)(1 - x)u - \alpha x v^*(x) V'(x)] = \rho V(x)$$

(8.4.9)

$$\max_{u} [Q(1 - x) - v^2 + W'(x)(1 - x)u^*(x) - \alpha x V'(x)v] = \rho W(x)$$

which they must if $u^*(\cdot)$ is to be optimal against $v^*(\cdot)$ and vice versa. Eliminating u from the first and v from the second by performing the indicated *max* operations yields exactly (8.2.4), to which (8.2.11) were earlier shown to be equivalent. The hypothesis that $u^*(\cdot)$ and $v^*(\cdot)$ is twice differentiable could be weakened to once differentiable if one had available a uniqueness theorem for the integrated form (8.2.8) of (8.2.11).

The possibility remains, of course, that less regular equilibrium pairs remain undiscovered. But we shall not pursue the matter here, as our primary objective is to exhibit strategies for the various players which have properties (A) and (B) in common with robust strategies. The multiplicity of such strategies seems less important than their identification, at least for the present.

5. A DYNAMIC FORMULATION OF COURNOT'S GAME

An interesting version of Cournot's game has recently been suggested by M. Simaan and T. Takayama [12]. Their idea was to introduce a dynamic price law of the form

(8.5.1)
$$\dot{x}(t) = -k[x(t) - (1 - u_1(t) - \cdots - u_N(t))],$$

where $x(t)$ denotes price at time t, and $u_i(t)$ is firm i's current output level. For then the price law $x = 1 - u_1 - \cdots - u_N$ need not hold identically at each instant but tends to be restored during periods wherein output levels remain constant. It may be observed that the first-order model (8.5.1) can never give the *oscillations* about an equilibrium price that one might expect, so that perhaps a second-order model is more appropriate really. But we shall confine our attention to (8.5.1) for simplicity.

If each firm i has a cost-of-production function of the form

(8.5.2)
$$K_i(u_i) = c_i u_i + (a_i/2)u_i^2,$$

one is led to consider the differential game

$$i \text{ maximize}_{u_i \geqslant 0} \qquad J_i = \int_0^{\infty} e^{-\rho t} [(x(t) - c_i)u_i(t) - (a_i/2)u_i^2(t)] \, dt$$

$$\text{subject to} \qquad \dot{x} = 1 - x(t) - u_1(t) - \cdots - u_N(t),$$

(8.5.3)

wherein the relaxation constant k has been normalized to one by choice of an appropriate time unit. The Hamilton-Jacobi method, if successful, may be expected to yield an N-tuple of feedback strategies $u_1^*(x), \ldots, u_N^*(x)$ whereby each player may observe the current price and adjust his output rate accordingly. In practice, a moving average of recent prices would probably be used instead, but we ignore such details here.

The ith player's Hamiltonian function is

(8.5.4) $H_i = (x - c_i)u_i - (a_i/2)u_i^2 + p_i(1 - x - u_1 - \cdots - u_N)$,

and setting $\partial H_i / \partial u_i = 0$ yields

(8.5.5) $x - c_i - a_i u_i - p_i = 0$.

So solving (8.5.5) for $u_i = \hat{u}_i(x, p_i)$ and writing $V_i'(x) = p_i$ permits one to write the Hamilton-Jacobi differential equations for the unknown functions $V_1(x), \ldots, V_N(x)$. However it seems simpler, in the present case, to eliminate p_i from (8.5.4) by use of (8.5.5) and thus to obtain equations for the unknown control laws $u_1^*(x), \ldots, u_N^*(x)$ directly. When that is done, one obtains

$$H_i = \frac{a_i}{2} + a_i u_i \Omega_i - a_i(1 - x)u_i - (x - c_i)\Omega_i + (x - c_i)(1 - x)$$

(8.5.6)

$$= \rho\left(x^2/2 - cx - a_i \int^x u_i(z)\,dz\right) + \theta_i$$

where

(8.5.7) $\Omega_i(x) = \sum_{\substack{j=1 \\ j \neq i}}^{N} u_j(x)$,

unknown constants of integration being again incorporated into the arbitrary θ_i.

In the symmetric case $a_1 = \cdots = a_N = a$ and $c_1 = \cdots = c_N = c$, it makes sense to look for a symmetric solution $u_1^*(x) = \cdots = u_N^*(x) = u(x)$, wherefore $\Omega_i(x) = (N - 1)u(x)$. Then (8.5.6) reduces to

(8.5.8) $\psi(x, u) = u^2(x) - P_1(x)u(x) + Q_1(x)$

$$- \rho\left(R_1(x) - \frac{1}{N - 1/2}\int^x u(z)\,dz\right) - \theta = 0,$$

where

$$P_1(x) = (a(1 - x) + (N - 1)(x - c))/a(N - 1/2)$$

(8.5.9) $Q_1(x) = (x - c)(1 - x)/a(N - 1/2)$

$$R_1(x) = x^2/2 - cx.$$

Equation (8.5.8) plays much the same role here that (8.2.8) did in the two-player Ad Game. Indeed, as is shown in the appendix to this chapter, it possesses only a single solution $u(x; \rho)$ through each point (x_0, u_0) for which $u_0 \neq (1/2)P_1(x_0)$. So it is entirely equivalent to the differential equation obtained by differentiating (8.5.8) with respect to x.

Setting $\rho = 0$, (8.5.8) becomes a secular quadratic equation with solutions

$$(8.5.10) \qquad u(x; 0) = 1/2\, P_1(x) \pm \sqrt{P_1^2(x)/4 - Q_1(x) + \theta}.$$

And by solving (rather finding the Cournot-Nash equilibrium of) the associated static game, one may obtain appropriate initial conditions $x_0 = x^*$, $u_0 = u_1^* = \cdots = u_N^*$ and $V_0 = \pi_1(x^*, u_1^*, \ldots, u_N^*) = \cdots = \pi_N(x^*, u_1^*, \ldots, u_N^*)$. Then choosing θ so that $u(x_0, 0, \theta) = u_0$, one obtains a limit of optimal strategies $u^*(x)$. In the case $N = 2$, $a = 1$, $c = 1/2$, for instance, one finds $P_1 = 1/3$, $Q_1 = -1/3(2x^2 - 3x + 1)$, $x_0 = 3/4$, and $u_0 = 1/8$. So the negative sign must prevail in (8.5.10) if it is to hold when $x = x_0$, and θ must be $1/64 = .015625$. The graph of the resulting function $u^*(x)$ appears in Figure 8.5A; $u^*(x)$ is positive only in the interval $.575 < x < .975$. So the solution of (8.5.8) fails to provide equilibrium strategies outside that interval, for negative production is meaningless.

In fact, another difficulty arises since, as is obvious from the portion of the line $u = 1/2\,(1 - x)$ shown in Figure 8.5A, the quantity $1 - x - 2u^*(x)$ changes sign not once but twice (at $x^* = .75$ and again at $x = .85$) in the interval $0 \leqslant x \leqslant 1$. So the strategies $u_1 = u_2 = u^*(x)$ drive $x(t)$ to x^* only from starting points $x_0 < .85$; $x_0 > .85$ implies $x(t) \rightarrow 1$, which is not the result of any pair of good strategies. In short, our method has not led us to a pair of equilibrium strategies defined on the entire interval $0 \leqslant x \leqslant 1$; $u_1 = u_2 = u^*(x)$ is only in equilibrium on $0 \leqslant x < .85$.

It may be argued, however, that because not all prices $0 \leqslant x \leqslant 1$ need really be anticipated, the information provided by (8.5.8) does permit the construction of good strategies. The fact that the maximal joint profit in the static version of the game is achieved when $u_1 = u_2 = 1/10$, for instance, leads one to expect $u_1 + u_2 \geqslant 1/5$ whenever prevailing prices are high, and in consequence, $x < 4/5$ always. And since $u_1 > 1/6$ and $u_2 > 1/6$ are dominated in the static game, one may expect $u_1 + u_2 \leqslant 1/3$ whenever prevailing prices are low, so that $x > 2/3$ always. In short, it really seems necessary to define good strategies $u_1^*(\cdot)$ and $u_2^*(\cdot)$ only for $2/3 < x < 4/5$. In that interval, the choices $u_1(x) = u_2(x) = u^*(x)$ drive $x(t)$ to $x^* = 3/4$ from any initial position, and have both properties (A) and (B). For values of x outside that interval, it seems adequate to stipulate just that u_i should be large when $x > 4/5$ and small when $x < 2/3$.

Whatever practical purpose is to be served by the analysis of the game at hand has doubtless been served by now, but we shall pursue it longer because it is one of the few we know that is simple enough to permit a solution for $\rho > 0$.

Substituting $u(x) = y(x) + (1/2)P_1(x)$ into (8.5.8) and differentiating once yields

$$(8.5.11) \qquad 2y(x)\,y'(x) = P'(x) - \rho a y(x) = Ax - B - \rho a y(x)$$

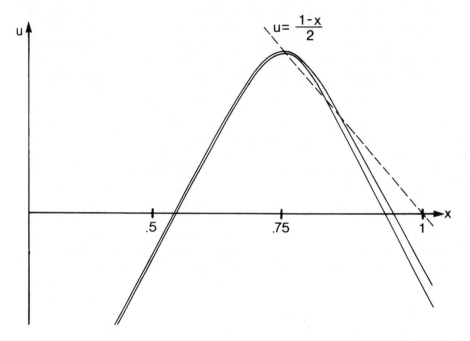

FIGURE 8.5A

where now $\sigma = 1/(N - 1/2)$ and

$$(8.5.12) \qquad P(x) = \rho R_1(x) - Q_1(x) + (1/4)P_1^2(x) - \frac{\rho\sigma}{2} \int_{x_0}^{x} P_1(s)\,ds.$$

So if one defines

$$r_1, r_2 = (-\rho\sigma \pm \sqrt{\rho^2\sigma^2 + 8A})/2$$

$$(8.5.13) \qquad c_1 = (r_2(x_0 - B/A) - 2y_0)/(r_2 - r_1)$$

$$c_2 = (2y_0 - r_1(x_0 - B/A))/(r_2 - r_1)$$

one need only eliminate t between the relations

$$(8.5.14) \qquad x = c_1 e^{r_1 t} + c_2 e^{r_2 t} + B/A$$

$$y = (1/2)c_1 r_1 e^{r_1 t} + (1/2)c_2 r_2 e^{r_2 t}$$

to obtain the solution of (8.5.10) thru (x_0, y_0). For the expressions (8.5.14) for
x and y satisfy

$$(8.5.15) \qquad \dot{x} = 2y \quad \text{and} \quad \dot{y} = Ax - B - \rho\sigma y.$$

The result of such a computation is shown also in Figure 8.5A for the parameter values $N = 2$, $a = 1$, $c = 1/2$, $\rho = 1/10$. It is interesting how little the optimal strategy $u^*(\cdot)$ changes in response to the increase in ρ.

It is of interest too to mention certain computational methods which do *not* work for the present game. The first rests on the fact that (8.5.3) is an instance of the general *linear-quadratic game*, so called because $\dot{x}$ equals a linear form in the $N + 1$ variables $x, u_1, \ldots, u_N$, while the payoff integrands all are quadratic in those variables. And the Hamilton-Jacobi equations of a linear-quadratic game ordinarily have quadratic solutions, which may be found by the method of undetermined coefficients. But if $V_i(x)$ is quadratic in x, then $V_i'(x)$ is linear and so is $u_i(x)$ by (8.5.5). The strategies corresponding to quadratic solutions of the Hamilton-Jacobi equations in the present game, for instance, may be found by substituting $y = mx - b$ in (8.5.11). There are exactly two of them. But the method can never yield the highly nonlinear strategies $u^*(x)$ depicted in Figure 8.5A. Generally speaking, the linear equilibrium strategy pairs will fail to have the property (A) described in Chapter VII.

Another method of solving the problem at hand which immediately suggests itself is simply to expand the solutions of (8.5.11) in their Taylor series about $x = x_0$. By differentiating the equation again and again, one obtains successively

$$2yy'' = A - \rho\sigma y' - 2y'^2,$$

$$2yy''' = -(\rho\sigma y'' + by'y''),$$

(8.5.16)

$$2yy^{iv} = -(\rho\sigma y''' + 8y'y''' + by''^2),$$

$$2yy^v = -(\rho\sigma y^{iv} + 10y'y^{iv} + 20\,y''y'''),$$

and so on. But $y_0 = u_0 - P_1/2 = -1/24$ in the case $N = 2, a = 1, c = 1/2$ and $\rho = 1/10$, so the Taylor series coefficients for the expansion about $x_0 = 3/4$ are $a_0 = y_0 = -.04167$, $a_1 = -.1$, $a_2 = -8.32$, $a_3 = 17.75$, $a_4 = 791.62$, $a_5 = -5317.43$, $a_6 = -142236.11, \ldots$ which do not quickly become small, as they must if the series is to converge rapidly, and it does not. For instance, at $x = .85$ the partial sums are successively .115, .032, .041, .047, .047, .047, and do not converge quickly to the correct value of about .102. In short, little is to be expected of *this sort* of series expansion when more complex problems are undertaken.

More special series expansions, however, seem more promising. For instance, an expansion of the form

(8.5.17) $$y(x) = y_0(x) + \rho y_1(x) + \rho^2 y_2(x) + \cdots$$

in the parameter ρ seems natural, because ρ is so often a small parameter in cases of interest. Trying (8.5.17) in the integrated form

(8.5.18) $$y^2(x) = P_0(x) + \rho Q_0(x) - \rho\sigma \int_{x_0}^{x} y(s)\,ds,$$

of (8.5.11), where now

(8.5.19) $P(x) = P_0(x) + \rho Q_0(x)$

$$= \left(\frac{1}{4} P_1^2(x) - Q_1(x)\right) + \rho\left(R_1(x) - \sigma \int_{x_0}^{x} P_1(s)\, ds\right),$$

yields successively

(8.5.20) $y_0(x) = \pm\sqrt{P_0(x)}, \quad y_1(x) = \frac{-1}{2y_0(x)}\left(Q_0(x) + \sigma \int_{x_0}^{x} y_0(s)\, ds\right),$

and so on, the indeterminate sign being again negative, since $y_0 = y(x_0) = y_0(x_0) < 0$. There can be no doubt that the present method works better than the previous one for this game, since $y_0(x)$ is already a better approximation to $y(x)$ than even the sixth partial sum of its Taylor expansion about $x_0 = 3/4$. And $y_0(x) + \rho y_1(x)$ is an *excellent* approximation for rather larger values of ρ than $1/10$. But additional coefficients $y_2(x)$, $y_3(x)$, ... can be determined only by numerical integration, as the closed form of $y_1(x)$ is not simple.

The method of expansion in series of the form (8.5.17) seems by far the best we know for solving the relatively complex and nonlinear games which are of greatest interest for economic applications. However, the method as presently constituted is very special in that it applies only to problems with a single-state variable. An extension of the method to problems of higher dimension would represent a very important advance indeed for the theory.

6. A LINEARIZED VERSION

In what has gone before, we have largely been concerned with the effects of nonlinearity. Such was invariably the case for the static games considered, and it was the case also for the two differential games discussed because of the quadratic terms which appear in their payoff integrands. When the players' action variables appear only *linearly* in the model, the nature of the games and of their solutions differ markedly. To illustrate, we consider the game (8.5.3) in the case $N = 2$ and $a_1 = a_2 = 0$.

The Hamiltonian functions now become

(8.6.1)
$$H_1 = (x - c_1 - p_1)\, u_1 + p_1(1 - x - u_2)$$
$$H_2 = (x - c_2 - p_2)\, u_2 + p_2(1 - x - u_1),$$

and are maximized by the choices

(8.6.2)
$$\hat{u}_i(x, p_i) = m \quad \text{if} \quad p_i < x - c_i$$
$$= 0 \quad \text{if} \quad p_i > x - c_i,$$
$$\text{indeterminate} \quad \text{if} \quad p_i = x - c_i,$$

m being some upper bound on the rate of production. There is no reason m must be the same for both players, but we assume it so for simplicity. We also assume m very large, so that it will not later prove restrictive. The cases $p_i \neq x - c_i$ seem uninteresting, as they arise only during periods of zero or peak production. Hence we shall investigate first the cases in which $p_i = x - c_i$.

Recalling that $p_i = V_i'(x)$, it is clear that $p_i = x - c_i$ implies

$$(8.6.3) \qquad V_i(x) = \frac{x^2}{2} - c_i x + k_i,$$

where k_i is an undetermined constant of integration and $i = 1, 2$. So in case $p_1 = x - c_1$ and $p_2 = x - c_2$, the Hamilton-Jacobi equations become

$$(8.6.4) \qquad \begin{aligned} H_1(x, \hat{u}_1, \hat{u}_2, p_1) &= (x - c_1)(1 - x - \hat{u}_2) = \rho V_1(x) \\ H_2(x, \hat{u}_1, \hat{u}_2, p_2) &= (x - c_2)(1 - x - \hat{u}_1) = \rho V_2(x), \end{aligned}$$

which may be solved independently and uniquely for

$$(8.6.5) \qquad \begin{aligned} u_1^0(x) &= \hat{u}_1(x, V_1'(x)) = (1 + \rho c_2/2) - (1 + \rho/2) x \\ u_2^0(x) &= \hat{u}_2(x, V_2'(x)) = (1 + \rho c_1/2) - (1 + \rho/2) x. \end{aligned}$$

We note the circle of implications

$$(8.6.6) \qquad \begin{aligned} p_1 = x - c_1 &\Rightarrow u_2 = u_2^0(x) \Rightarrow u_2 \notin \{0, m\} \Rightarrow p_2 = x - c_2 \\ &\Rightarrow u_1 = u_1^0(x) \Rightarrow u_1 \notin \{0, m\} \Rightarrow p_1 = x - c_1, \end{aligned}$$

whereby the intervals on which $u_1 = u_1^0(x)$ and $u_2 = u_2^0(x)$ must coincide if the equations (8.6.4) and the specifications (8.6.2) are to remain valid. Remark too that the strategies $u_1^0(x)$ and $u_2^0(x)$ are well and uniquely defined on the interval $0 \leq x \leq 1$. And $u_i^0(x)$ is nonnegative for $x \leq (2 + \rho c_i)/(2 + \rho)$. Moreover, if the two are played against one another, they cause $x(t)$ to decrease without bound when $x(0) < x^0 = (1 + \rho \bar{c})/(1 + \rho)$, where $\bar{c} = (c_1 + c_2)/2$, to remain constant if $x(0) = x^0$, and to increase if $x(0) > x^0$. So $u_1^0(x)$ and $u_2^0(x)$ cannot be played indefinitely. For they drive $x(t)$ out of the interval $0 \leq x \leq 1$ when $x(0) \neq x^0$, and they keep it at that absurd level when $x(0) = x^0$. It is clear that x^0 is an absurd price level because it is nearly one when ρ is small, whereas only dominated production levels u_1 and u_2 can produce such large prices in the static version of the game. One may therefore conclude that while robust strategies may agree with $u_i^0(x)$ on certain subintervals $a < x < b$ of $0 \leq x \leq 1$, they may not do so for x near 0 or 1.

Accordingly, it seems natural to seek equilibrium pairs $(u_1^*(x), u_2^*(x))$ of strategies which agree with $(u_1^0(x), u_2^0(x))$ in the middle portion of $0 \leq x \leq 1$, while assuming extreme values at the ends of that interval.

In an interval $a < x < b$ wherein u_1 and u_2 are constant, the Hamilton-Jacobi equations take the form

$$(8.6.7) \qquad (x - c_i) u_i + (1 - x - u_1 - u_2) V_i'(x) = \rho V_i(x),$$

$i = 1, 2$. So differentiating once and setting $p_i(x) = V_i'(x)$, one obtains

(8.6.8)
$$\frac{dp_i(x)}{dx} = \frac{(1 + \rho) p_i - u_i}{1 - x - u_1 - u_2}.$$

The derivatives of the value functions $V_1(x)$ and $V_2(x)$ must be solutions of (8.6.8), wherein u_1 and u_2 are either 0 or m *except* on subintervals of the unit interval whereon $p_i(x) = V_i'(x) = x - c_i$ for $i = 1, 2$. Hence the situation is as shown in Figure 8.6A; the graph of $V_i'(x)$ coincides with the line $p_i = x - c_i$ in the middle portion of $0 \leqslant x \leqslant 1$, with a solution of (8.6.8) for which $u_1 = u_2 = m$ to the right of that interval, and with another for which $u_1 = u_2 = 0$ to the left of it. The last mentioned solutions of (8.6.8) do in fact lie below and above the line $p_i = x - c_i$ as shown, provided only that $x^1 \leqslant (1 + (1 + \rho) c_i)/(2 + \rho)$ and $m > 1/2$.

The curve indicated in Figure 8.6A, of course, represents an entire continuum of solution pairs $(V_1(x), V_2(x))$ of the Hamilton-Jacobi equations, because constants of integration are introduced in passing from $V_i'(x)$ to $V_i(x)$ *and* because the "nodes" x^1 and x^2 at which the various local solutions are pieced together into a global one may vary continuously. The additive constants of integration are of little interest here, as the equilibrium strategies $u_i^*(x) = \hat{u}_i(x, V_i'(x))$ are independent of them. But the nodes x^1 and x^2 are of critical import.

To understand the roles of x^1 and x^2, one need only glance at the field of trajectories $x(t)$, $0 \leqslant t < \infty$ generated by the equilibrium strategies defined through (8.6.2) by a pair of solutions $(V_1(x), V_2(x))$ of the Hamilton-Jacobi equations. They are as shown in Figure 8.6B, and assume the value x^1 after a finite time. So x^1, whatever it is and however determined, is the steady-state price which results from the equilibrium strategy pair $u_1^*(x), u_2^*(x)$ generated by

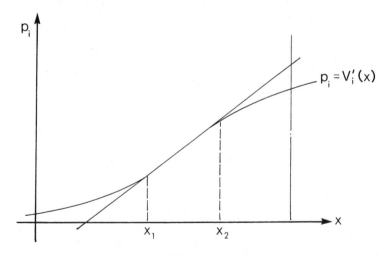

$p_i = V_i'(x)$

FIGURE 8.6A

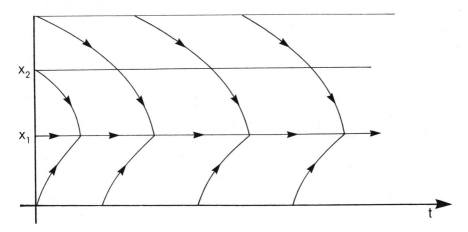

FIGURE 8.6B

a pair of solutions $V_1(x)$, $V_2(x)$ of the Hamilton-Jacobi equations. There can be no doubt, incidentally, that such a pair of strategies *is* in Nash equilibrium, since the graph of $V_i'(x)$ shown in Figure 8.6A is continuous. For then $V_1(x)$ and $V_2(x)$ are continuously differentiable on the entire interval $0 < x < 1$, and theorem A guarantees that each $u_i^*(x)$ is optimal against the other. In short, the strategy pairs $(u_1^*(x), u_2^*(x))$ constructed in the above described manner have property (B). But they do not, typically, have property (A).

To see this, one must find an equilibrium triple $(x, \bar{u}_1, \bar{u}_2)$ for the static game

(8.6.9)
$$\text{1 maximize } (x - c_1)\, u_1 \qquad \text{2 maximize } (x - c_2)\, u_2$$
$$\quad 0 \leqslant u_1 \leqslant m \qquad\qquad 0 \leqslant u_2 \leqslant m$$
$$\text{subject to} \quad x = 1 - u_1 - u_2.$$

The method of Lagrange multipliers yields quickly

(8.6.10)
$$\bar{x} = (1 + c_1 + c_2)/3$$
$$\bar{u}_1 = (1 - 2c_1 + c_2)/3$$
$$\bar{u}_2 = (1 + c_1 - 2c_2)/3.$$

But

$$u_1^0(\bar{x}) = (1 - 2c_1 + c_2)/3 + (1 - \rho/2)(1 - c_1 + 2c_2)/3,$$

which equals $\bar{u}_1$ only if $\rho = 2$. For other values of ρ, and in particular for the important *small* values of ρ, the two are quite different. In the case $c_1 = c_2 = 1/2$, $\rho = 1/10$, for instance, $u_1^0(\bar{x}) = 13/40$ which is almost twice $\bar{u}_1 = 1/6$. So even if

$x^1 = \overline{x}$, players employing the equilibrium strategies

$$u_i^*(x) = m \qquad \text{if} \quad x \geqslant x^2$$

(8.6.12)
$$\qquad\qquad = u_i^0(x) \quad \text{if} \quad x^2 > x > x^1$$

$$\qquad\quad = 0 \qquad \text{if} \quad x^1 > x$$

will not produce at anything like the rates $\overline{u}_1$, $\overline{u}_2$, as $x(t)$ nears its equilibrium position x^1. Rather, they will produce at the much greater rates $u_1^0(x)$ for $x > x^1$, and will not produce at all when $x < x^1$. It is not clear what rates they will produce at when $x = x^1$.

To resolve that question, one observes that the knowledge $u_i^*(x) = u_i^0(x)$ for $x > x^1$ and $u_i^*(x) = 0$ for $x < x^1$ determines $u_1^*(x^1)$ and $u_2^*(x^1)$ in a natural fashion. For if $x(t)$ is imagined to oscillate minutely about the line $x = \overline{x} = x^1$, instead of lying always on it, the players would produce at roughly the rates $u_1^0(\overline{x})$ and $u_2^0(\overline{x})$ while $x(t) > \overline{x}$, and would not produce while $x(t) < \overline{x}$. So the effect achieved would be identical with that of defining $u_1^*(\overline{x})$ and $u_2^*(\overline{x})$ to be the solutions of the simultaneous equations $u_1/u_2 = u_1^0(\overline{x})/u_2^0(\overline{x})$ and $u_1 + u_2 = 1 - \overline{x}$. Then $u_1^*(\overline{x})$ and $u_2^*(\overline{x})$ are substantially smaller than $u_1^0(\overline{x})$ and $u_2^0(\overline{x})$, since $1 - \overline{x} - u_1^0(\overline{x}) - u_2^0(\overline{x})$ is negative, and consequently each $u_i^*(x)$ is *discontinuous* as x approaches $\overline{x} = x^1$ from *either* side.

To appreciate fully the violence that such a conclusion does one's economic intuition, it is instructive to consider a pair of firms introducing a new product into the market. Recent experience (with jet air travel, color TV, and pocket calculators, for instance) suggests that initially the supply will be small and the price dear. Then gradually the supply will increase and the price decline until a steady state is achieved, but that is not at all what would be observed if the game were played according to the strategies (8.6.12). Instead, total production would rise gradually to the level $u_1^0(\overline{x}) + u_2^0(\overline{x})$ as $x(t)$ came near to $\overline{x}$, then drop precipitously to the lower level $u_1^*(\overline{x}) + u_2^*(\overline{x}) = 1 - \overline{x}$. And that drop in production would *not* be followed by any price rise!

Such phenomena are ubiquitous in games wherein the action variables appear only linearly; their solutions are often in terms of "bang-bang" strategies (which take *only* extreme values) and nearly always in terms of discontinuous strategies of the sort described above. While such games are perhaps intriguing, it is not at all clear that their solutions can be expected to convey economic insight. Indeed, the opposite would appear to be the case in the present example.

7. A PARTIAL SUMMARY

It is perhaps appropriate to recap what we have learned thus far concerning nonzero-sum differential games and their solutions. Our principal conclusion seems to be that the analysis of a differential game *supplements* but does not *comprehend* the analysis of a related static game. Though the Nash equilibrium conditions imply a set of Hamilton-Jacobi differential equations from whose solutions one may compute strategies, they do not imply side conditions whereby a particular solution of the Hamilton-Jacobi equations may be chosen. So appeal must be made to a previous static analysis of the same game before a robust strategy can be selected for each player. In the two-player Ad Game, for instance, the equilibrium position $(\bar{x}, \bar{u}, \bar{v})$ was found from the static analysis of Chapter VI. The methods of the present chapter then provided rules $u(x)$ and $v(x)$ for choosing advertising expenditures appropriate to other market shares than $\bar{x}$.

The same procedures can be followed in determining strategies whether action variables enter the model linearly or not. Indeed, the required integrations are typically easier in the linear case. But the solutions in that case can, it would seem, be *bereft* of any practical significance. This is in direct contrast to the nonlinear games examined, for the robust strategies obtained from their analysis are quite as one might have expected and seem well worthy of the attention of anyone endeavoring to play those games.

From all this it would seem that nonlinear differential games are a more worthy object of investigation than their linear counterparts. Such a conclusion is well and good when there is but one *state variable x*, as has been the case heretofore; then Hamilton-Jacobi equations are ordinary differential equations. But when there are more state variables about, the Hamilton-Jacobi equations are partial differential equations, often very difficult to solve. It is not, therefore, to be expected that the techniques of the present chapter will be effective in any but the simplest instances. Rather, special techniques taking advantage of the particular structure of individual games of interest appear at present to hold more immediate promise than the general Hamilton-Jacobi method. The expansion in powers of ρ suggested earlier for the nonlinear Cournot problem was one such method. Another will be presented in the next chapter for the class of "Trading Games."

8. THE THREE-PLAYER AD GAME

To illustrate the difficulties that arise when more than one state variable is present, we consider very briefly the following three-player version of the Ad Game:

$$i \text{ maximize} \qquad J_i = \int_0^\infty e^{-\rho t} \left[P_i x_i(t) - u_i^2(t) \right] dt$$

(8.8.1) \qquad subject to \qquad $\dot{x}_i = \alpha_i u_i - (\alpha_1 u_1 + \alpha_2 u_2 + \alpha_3 u_3) x_i$

and \qquad $u_i \geqslant 0$ \quad for \quad $i = 1, 2, 3.$

Introducing the differential operators $\partial_i = \partial/\partial x_i$ and $\partial_0 = x_1\,\partial/\partial x_1 + x_2\,\partial/\partial x_2 + x_3\,\partial/\partial x_3$, as well as the familiar gradient operator ∇, the Hamiltonian functions for the game are

$$(8.8.2) \qquad H_i(x_1, x_2, x_3, \nabla V^1, \nabla V^2, \nabla V^3) = P_i x_i - u_i^2 + \sum_{j=1}^{3} \alpha_j u_j (\partial_j V^i - \partial_0 V^i)$$

The H-maximal controls are

$$(8.8.3) \qquad \hat{u}_i(x_1, x_2, x_3, \nabla V^i) = (\alpha_i/2)\,(\partial_i V^i - \partial_0 V^i),$$

and the Hamilton-Jacobi equations are

$$P_i x_i + \frac{1}{4} \sum_{j=1}^{3} \alpha_j^2\,(2 - \delta_{ij})\,(\partial_j V^i - \partial_0 V^i)(\partial_j V^i - \partial_0 V^i) = \rho V^i + \theta_i,$$

(8.8.4)

δ_{ij} denoting the standard Kronecker symbol. These constitute a system of three simultaneous nonlinear partial differential equations for the three unknown functions $V^i(\cdot, \cdot, \cdot)$; $i = 1, 2, 3$. Only in rare instances can such systems of equations be solved in closed form. The equations (8.8.4) do not appear to provide one of those instances. So only such general solution techniques as power-series expansion or finite-difference methods are available. Nor is it clear what boundary conditions one ought to impose on the solutions of (8.8.4). The Cauchy-Kowalewski theorem [7], for instance, suggests that initial values for the unknown functions $V^i(\cdot, \cdot, \cdot)$ be prescribed on a curve in the plane $x_1 + x_2 + x_3 = 1$, while property (A) of robust strategies, from which we obtained initial conditions in earlier problems, appears to give initial values only at one point of that plane.

These difficulties can sometimes all be met in problems with special internal structure, as will be shown in Chapter IX, but there are at present no general answers for the questions raised above. Indeed it seems likely that a theory as intimately involved with nonlinear partial differential equations as the theory of many-player differential games quite obviously is will be forced to proceed on a problem-by-problem basis for some time to come. Nonetheless, these are the sorts of problems which must be solved if one seeks rules of action which respond instantaneously to the slightest change in the values of the state variables. It will be shown, too, in Chapter IX that less sensitive rules of action may often be calculated by a substantially simpler procedure.

9. GAMES THAT TERMINATE

The differential games we have considered to date have all been of infinite duration. But some games either can or must end after a finite period of time.

Those games too have a Hamilton-Jacobi theory, the outlines of which we shall now present.

The games we shall consider may all be represented in the form

$$i \text{ maximize} \qquad J_i = K_i(x(T)) + \int_0^T L_i(x(t), u_1(t), \ldots, u_n(t)) \, dt$$

(8.9.1)

$$\text{subject to} \qquad \dot{x} = f(x, u_1, \ldots, u_n)$$

$$\text{and} \qquad u_i(t) \in U_i, \ x(t) \in S, \ \text{and} \ x(T) \in C,$$

where T is the first instant $t \geqslant 0$ such that $x(t) \in C$, and the other constraints are assumed to hold for $0 \leqslant t \leqslant T$. C is called the *terminal set* of the game, which is considered to continue until the moving point $x(t)$ reaches C. Ordinarily, C is a portion of the boundary of the set S of all admissible information states. To play such a game, each player chooses a strategy $\phi_i(x)$, and sets $u_i(t) = \phi_i(x(t))$ at each instant t. Then the progress of the moving point $x(t)$ is determined (assuming the functions $\phi_i(\cdot)$ are sufficiently regular), and so are the time T and position $x(T)$ ot termination. Therefore, each player's *terminal reward* $K_i(x(T))$, *integral reward* $\int_0^T L_i dt$, and *total reward* (the sum of the previous two) are determined also. Of course each player's objective is to choose a strategy $\phi_i(x)$ which is reasonably certain to yield a large reward. As before, we shall first consider games with only one player.

One-player differential games are more commonly known as optimal control problems, and they have an extensive literature [2] under that name. The problem we wish now to examine may be represented in the form

$$\text{maximize} \qquad J = K(x(T)) + \int_0^T L(x(t), \phi(x(t)) \, dt$$

(P)

$$\text{subject to} \qquad \dot{x} = f(x, \phi(x))$$

$$x(0) = x_0, \phi(x) \in U, \ x(T) \in C,$$

$$\text{and} \qquad x(t) \in S \ \forall \, t \in [0, T].$$

We seek first a test, whereby it may be determined whether a given strategy $\phi(\cdot)$ is or is not an optimal strategy.

In certain instances, it is easy to demonstrate that a given strategy is optimal. Suppose, for instance, that

$$\text{(i)} \ \ K(x) = 0 \qquad \forall \, x \in C$$

(8.9.2) $\quad$ (ii) $L(x, \phi(x)) = 0 \qquad \forall \, x \in S$

$$\text{(iii)} \ \ L(x, u) \leqslant 0 \qquad \forall \, x \in S \ \text{ and } \ u \in U,$$

and let S_0 be the set of all $x_0 \in S$ such that the solution of the differential equation

$$(8.9.3) \qquad \dot{x} = f(x, \phi(x))$$

starting at x_0 eventually reaches C. Then $\phi(\cdot)$ is an optimal strategy for all $x_0 \in S_0$ because the use of $\phi(\cdot)$ yields zero reward, and no other strategy can yield more. In other cases, the matter is not so transparent.

Next, suppose that $\psi(x)$ is a several-times differentiable function defined on an open set containing S, and let $\hat{L}(\cdot, \cdot)$ be defined by

$$(8.9.4) \qquad \hat{L}(x, u) = L(x, u) + \nabla \psi(x) \cdot f(x, u),$$

"$\cdot$" denoting the usual inner product of two vectors. Consider the control problem $(\hat{P})$ which differs from (P) only in that the reward junction J is replaced by

$$(8.9.5) \qquad \hat{J} = K(x(T)) - \psi(x(T)) + \int_0^T \hat{L}(x, \phi(x))\, dt.$$

Then if strategy ϕ_1 is better than ϕ_2 in problem $(\hat{P})$, it is better than ϕ_2 in (P) as well. For

$$\hat{J}(x_0, \phi_i) = K(x_{\phi_i}(T_{\phi_i})) - \psi(x_{\phi_i}(T_{\phi_i}))$$

$$(8.9.6) \qquad + \int_0^{T_{\phi_i}} L(x_{\phi_i}(t), \phi_i(x_{\phi_i}(t)))\, dt + \int_0^{T_{\phi_i}} \frac{d}{dt}\, \psi(x_{\phi_i}(t))\, dt$$

$$= J(x_0, \phi_i) - \psi(x_0), i = 1, 2,$$

so that

$$(8.9.7) \qquad \hat{J}(x_0, \phi_1) - \hat{J}(x_0, \phi_2) = J(x_0, \phi_1) - J(x_0, \phi_2).$$

Here the subscript ϕ_i on a trajectory $x(t)$, $a \leqslant t \leqslant b$ or a termination time T indicates the particular trajectory or termination time which results from the use of the strategy ϕ_i. Those quantities, as mentioned earlier, are uniquely defined by the choice of a (sufficiently regular) function ϕ_i. We shall have little occasion in this book to consider ϕ_i which are not regular.

Because of the identity (8.9.7), it is customary to call (P) and $(\hat{P})$ *equivalent* problems of optimal control, for if a given strategy $\phi^*(\cdot)$ is optimal for either of them, it is optimal for both. The value of this observation derives from the fact that it is often possible, for a given problem (P), to discover an equivalent problem $(\hat{P})$ which has the simplifying characteristics (8.9.2). Then, of course, an optimal strategy may be found by inspection.

The method of producing the required equivalent problem $(\hat{P})$, or rather the function ψ which defines it, is already familiar. One begins by writing again the Hamiltonian function (8.1.10), and the $\hat{u}(x, p)$ which maximizes it. Then one constructs a solution $V(x)$ of the Hamilton-Jacobi equation

(8.9.8) $H(x, \hat{u}(x, \nabla V(x)), \nabla V(x)) = 0$

for the problem (P), which satisfies the additional condition

(8.9.9) $V(x) = K(x)$

at every x in C. Then $V(\cdot)$ is the required $\psi(\cdot)$, as substituting V for ψ in the definition (8.8.9) of $\hat{L}$ yields an equivalent $(\hat{P})$ having by construction the simplifying properties (8.9.2). Therefore, the strategy $\phi^*(x)$ defined by (8.1.14) is optimal for $(\hat{P})$ and (P) as well. Indeed, if S_0 be as previously defined, we may state the following:

> *Theorem C:* ϕ^* is an optimal strategy for (P) in the sense that $J(x_0 ; \phi^*) \geqslant J(x_0 ; \phi)$ for every $x_0 \in S_0$ and for every ϕ which transfers x_0 to C *without* leaving S_0.

The assertion of the theorem is illustrated (for clarity) in Figure 8.9A. There the region $S_0 \subset S$ is shown, covered with trajectories generated by the strategy ϕ^* and ending in C. The theorem guarantees that the reward for following Γ^* (which comes from ϕ^*) from x_0 to C is not exceeded by that obtained along any other Γ^0 in S_0. But it does not preclude the possibility that a still greater reward may be gotten along a Γ which *leaves* S_0 on its way to C. It should be remarked that (8.9.8) is (8.1.2) with ρ set equal to zero.

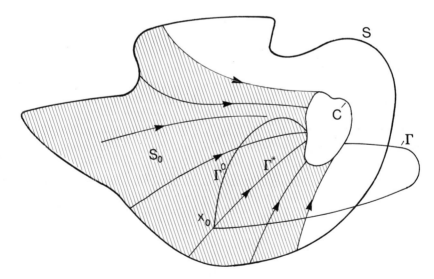

FIGURE 8.9A

The application of the theorem to many-player games will also seem familiar to the reader by now. It begins with the writing of the N Hamiltonian functions (8.1.19) and N equilibrium controls $\hat{u}_1(x, p_1, \ldots, p_N), \ldots, \hat{u}_N(x, p_1, \ldots, p_N)$ which are in (Nash) equilibrium for the game (8.1.20) and therefore satisfy the inequalities (8.1.21). Then one can construct functions $V^1(x), \ldots, V^N(x)$ which satisfy the Hamilton-Jacobi equations (8.1.22) with $\rho = 0$ *and* the side conditions

(8.9.10) $$V^i(x) = K_i(x) \qquad \forall x \in C$$

as well. Then the theorem asserts that the strategies (8.1.23) form an equilibrium N-tuple for the game (8.9.1) because each is, in the sense of Figure 8.9A, optimal against the rest.

The application of the theorem to such games is, as it was for nonterminating games, inhibited by the difficulty of integrating the Hamilton-Jacobi equations for the unknown value functions $V^1(x), \ldots, V^N(x)$. For there is, as mentioned earlier, no general method of integrating systems of simultaneous nonlinear partial differential equations. One must presume that only in very special circumstances will it be possible to solve games of the present sort by the Hamilton-Jacobi method. We remark in passing that theorem C is an analogue for the terminating case of theorem A. An analogue of theorem B also exists. We leave it as an exercise for the interested reader to discover that theorem, either for himself or [4] in the literature.

10. TERMINATING LINEAR-QUADRATIC GAMES

One class of games for which it is always possible to integrate the Hamilton-Jacobi equations is the so-called class of linear-quadratic ones. Since this is possible for information-state vectors of arbitrary dimension, we specify at the outset that lower-case Latin letters denote vectors while upper-case ones denote matrices. E_k is the usual k-dimensional Euclidean space, and the inner product of two vectors v_1 and v_2 will be denoted $\langle v_1, v_2 \rangle$. Also, *in this section only*, the transpose of a matrix A will be denoted by A'. Finally, the resultant of the operator $(\partial/\partial x_1, \ldots, \partial/\partial x_n)$ with a function $F(t, x_1, \ldots, x_n)$ will be written $\nabla_x F$ and that of $\partial/\partial t$ with the same function $\nabla_t F$.

The sets $U_1, \ldots, U_N$ for the games we consider will be the entire spaces $E_{m_1}, \ldots, E_{m_N}$, while S will be the set of $(t, x_1, \ldots, x_N)$ for which $t \leqslant T$ and C will be the entire boundary of S, namely the part of S wherein $t = T$. The kinematic equations will be

(8.10.1)
$$\dot{x}(t) = A(t)x(t) + B_1(t)u_1(t) + \cdots + B_N(t)u_N(t) + f(t)$$
$$\dot{t} = 1,$$

$A(t)$ being of size $n \times n$ and $B_i(t)$ of size $m_i \times n$. The functions

(8.10.2) $$y_1(t) = C_1(t)x(t), \ldots, y_N(t) = C_N(t)x(t)$$

are called the outputs of the system, and we shall assume N "target schedules" $z_1(t), \ldots, z_N(t)$ to be given for the players to imitate as nearly as they can. That is, we assume i wishes to choose his controls so as to keep $y_i(t)$ near $z_i(t)$ without expending undue control effort. That is, we shall assume that each player seeks to minimize an integral of the form

$$(8.10.3) \quad J_i = \int_0^T \{(1/2) \langle (z_i(t) - y_i(t)), Q_i(t) (z_i(t) - y_i(t)) \rangle$$

$$+ (1/2) \langle u_i(t), R_i(t) u_i(t) \rangle \} \, dt,$$

where the matrix $Q_i(t)$ is a positive semidefinite symmetric matrix and is not the zero matrix, while $R_i(t)$ is positive definite. If $Q_i(t)$ were zero, the optimal policy for i would be $u_i \equiv 0$.

We shall solve the game by the use of theorem C. To this end we write down the ith Hamiltonian function

$$H_i(t, x, u_1, \ldots, u_N, p_i)$$

$$(8.10.4) \quad = 1/2 \langle (z_i(t) - C_i(t) x), Q_i(t) (z_i(t) - C_i(t) x) \rangle$$

$$+ 1/2 \langle u_i, R_i(t) u_i \rangle + \langle f(t), p_i \rangle + \langle A(t) x, p_i \rangle + \langle B_1(t) u_1, p_i \rangle$$

$$+ \cdots + \langle B_N(t) u_N, p_i \rangle$$

and observe that the minimizing control $u_i^*(t, x, p)$ will be that u_i for which the sum

$$(8.10.5) \quad 1/2 \langle u_i, R_i(t) u_i \rangle + \langle B_i'(t) p_i, u_i \rangle$$

takes on the least value (since we are trying to minimize J_i, we minimize H_i instead of maximizing it). Since the gradient of (8.10.5) is just

$$(8.10.6) \quad R_i(t) u_i + B_i'(t) p_i$$

and the gradient of (8.10.6) is the positive definite matrix $R_i(t)$, it is clear that $u_i^*(t, x, p)$ renders H_i a minimum if and only if it renders (8.10.6) equal to zero. Hence

$$(8.10.7) \quad u_i^*(t, x, p) = -R_i^{-1}(t) B_i'(t) p_i$$

and the Hamilton-Jacobi equations (8.1.22) may be written

$$\nabla_t V_i + (1/2) \langle (z_i(t) - C_i(t) x), Q_i(t) (z_i(t) - C_i(t) x) \rangle$$

$$+ 1/2 \langle S_i(t) \nabla_x V_i, \nabla_x V_i \rangle + \langle f(t), \nabla_x V_i \rangle$$

$$(8.10.8) \quad + \langle A(t) x, \nabla_x V_i \rangle - \langle S_1(t) \nabla_x V_i, \nabla_x V_i \rangle$$

$$- \cdots - \langle S_N(t) \nabla_x V_N, \nabla_x V_i \rangle = 0,$$

where $S_i(t) = B_i(t) R_i^{-1}(t) B_i'(t)$, $i = 1, \ldots, N$. Motivated by the results of Kalman [9], we shall try to solve the system (8.10.8) by separating variables. That is, we shall substitute the trial solutions

(8.10.9) $V_i(t, x) = 1/2 \langle x, K_i(t) x \rangle - \langle g_i(t), x \rangle + \phi_i(t)$

into (8.10.8) in the hope that the problem will reduce to one of ordinary differential equations. If we assume that the matrices $K_i(t)$ are symmetric and differentiate with respect to x and t, we obtain

$$\nabla_t V_i(t, x) = (1/2) \langle x, \dot{K}_i(t) x \rangle - \langle \dot{g}_i(t), x \rangle + \dot{\phi}_i(t)$$

(8.10.10)

$$\nabla_x V_i(t, x) = K_i(t) x - g_i(t),$$

$i = 1, \ldots, N$; and substitution of these expressions into (8.10.8) yields

$$1/2 \langle x, \dot{K}_i(t) x \rangle - \langle \dot{g}_i(t), x \rangle + \dot{\Phi}_i(t) + (1/2)$$

$$\cdot \langle (z_i(t) - C_i(t) x), Q_i(t) (z_i(t) - C_i(t) x) \rangle$$

$$+ 1/2 \langle S_i(t) (K_i(t) x - g_i(t)), (K_i(t) x - g_i(t)) \rangle$$

(8.10.11)
$$+ \langle A(t) x, (K_i(t) x - g_i(t)) \rangle$$

$$- \langle S_1(t) (K_1(t) x - g_1(t)), (K_i(t) x - g_i(t)) \rangle - \cdots$$

$$- \langle S_N(t) (K_N(t) x - g_N(t)), (K_i(t) x - g_i(t)) \rangle$$

$$+ \langle f(t), (K_i(t) x - g_i(t)) \rangle = 0.$$

After some relatively tedious manipulations, (8.10.11) may be put in the form

$$\langle x, (\dot{K}_i(t) + C_i'(t) Q_i(t) C_i(t) + K_i(t) S_i(t) K_i(t) + 2A'(t) K_i(t)$$

$$- 2K_1(t) S_1(t) K_i(t) - \cdots - 2K_N(t) S_N(t) K_i(t)) x \rangle$$

$$- \langle x, (2g_i(t) + 2C_i'(t) Q_i(t) z_i(t) - K_i(t) S_i(t) g_i(t) 2A'(t) g_i(t)$$

$$- 2K_i(t) S_1(t) g_1(t) - 2K_1(t) S_1(t) g_i(t) - 2K_i(t) S_N(t) g_N(t)$$

(8.10.12)
$$- 2K_N(t) S_N(t) g_i(t) + K_i(t) f(t))) + 2\Phi_i(t)$$

$$+ \langle z_i(t), Q_i(t) z_i(t) \rangle - \langle g_i(t), S_i(t) g_i(t) \rangle$$

$$- 2 \langle S_1(t) g_1(t), g_i(t) \rangle - \cdots - 2 \langle S_N(t) g_N(t), g_i(t) \rangle$$

$$- \langle f(t), g_i(t) \rangle = 0.$$

Now the first term in (8.10.12) is a quadratic form $\langle x, A(t) x \rangle$ and is unchanged if we replace $A(t)$ by its symmetrization $(1/2) (A(t) + A'(t))$. Hence if we demand that the matrices $K_1(t), \ldots, K_N(t)$ satisfy the equations

$$\dot{K}_i(t) = K_1(t) S_1(t) K_i(t) + K_i(t) S_1(t) K_1(t) + \cdots$$

$$+ K_N(t) S_N(t) K_i(t) + K_i(t) S_N(t) K_N(t)$$

(8.10.13)
$$- A'(t) K_i(t) - K_i(t) A(t) - K_i(t) S_i(t) K_i(t)$$

$$- C_i'(t) Q_i(t) C_i(t), \qquad i = 1, \ldots, N,$$

$i = 1, \ldots, N$, the first term in (8.10.12) will vanish identically. Similarly, if we require that

(8.10.14)
$$\dot{g}_i(t) = K_i(t) S_1(t) g_1(t) + K_1(t) S_1(t) g_i(t) + \cdots$$
$$+ K_i(t) S_N(t) g_N(t) + K_N(t) S_N(t) g_i(t)$$
$$- (1/2) K_i(t) S_i(t) g_i(t) - A'(t) g_i(t)$$
$$- C_i'(t) Q_i(t) z_i(t) + K_i(t) f(t)$$

and

(8.10.15)
$$\dot{\Phi}_i(t) = \langle S_1(t) g_1(t), g_i(t) \rangle + \cdots + \langle S_N(t) g_N(t), g_i(t) \rangle$$
$$- 1/2 \langle g_i(t), S_i(t) g_i(t) \rangle - 1/2 \langle z_i(t), Q_i(t) z_i(t) \rangle$$
$$- \langle f(t), g_i(t) \rangle$$

then the last two terms in (8.10.12) will also vanish identically, so that the functions (8.10.9) are indeed solutions of (8.10.8). Moreover, if we demand that $K_1(T), g_1(T), \phi_1(T), \ldots, K_N(T), g_N(T), \phi_N(T)$ all vanish, $V_1(t, x), \ldots, V_N(t, x)$ satisfy the boundary conditions (8.9.9) of theorem C on the terminal set C given by $t = T$. In order to compute the functions $K_i(t)$, we begin by solving the system of $(1/2) Nn(n + 1)$ ordinary differential equations (8.10.13), subject to the initial conditions $K_1(T) = 0 = \cdots = K_N(T)$, on some interval $(a, T]$. When this has been done, the coefficients of the nN linear equations (8.10.14) are known so that these too may be solved in $(a, T]$ subject to $g_1(T) = 0 = \cdots = g_N(T)$. Then the functions $\phi_1(t), \ldots, \phi_N(t)$ in (8.10.15) may be obtained by simple quadrature.

Once this has been accomplished, the value functions (8.10.9) are known in the region $(a, T) \times E_n$ of E_{n+1}. If we define strategies

(8.10.16) $\quad \phi_i^*(t, x) = u_i^*(t, x, \nabla_x V_i(t, x)) = -R_i^{-1} B_i'(t) (K_i(T) x - g_i(t))$,

the conditions of theorem C are satisfied, and $\phi^* = (\phi_1^*, \ldots, \phi_N^*)$ must indeed be an equilibrium point for our game. The equilibrium trajectories $x^*(t)$ are the solutions of

(8.10.17)
$$\dot{x}^*(t) = A(t) x^*(t) - B_1(t) R_1^{-1}(t) B_1'(t) (K_1(t) x^*(t) - g_1(t))$$
$$- B_N(t) R_N^{-1}(t) B_N'(t) (K_N(t) x^*(t) - g_N(t)) + f(t).$$

In short, the solution of the game has been reduced to the solution of the three systems (8.10.13)-(8.10.15) of ordinary differential equations. These systems always have solutions in an interval $(a, T]$, but since (8.10.13) is nonlinear, one cannot be certain that the number a may be chosen to be arbitrarily small. For $N = 1$, this difficulty does not arise (see [9]), but the corresponding result for $N > 1$ is untrue [11].

The fact that these games may be solved in so straightforward a manner has found little application in the several years it has been known. Presumably that is because real games are not well modeled in this fashion. So it would seem that the principle value of the results is as a simple illustration of the Hamilton-Jacobi method.

11. AN EXAMPLE

One problem which does fit readily into the linear-quadratic framework is Cournot's game with quadratic costs. With a prescribed termination time it becomes

(8.11.1)
$$i \text{ maximize} \quad J_i = \int_0^T [(x - c_i) u_i - (a_i/2) u_i^2] \, dt$$
$$u_i \geq 0$$
$$\text{subject to} \quad \dot{x} = 1 - x - u_1 - u_2$$

if $N = 2$. And the Hamilton-Jacobi equations are

(8.11.2)
$$V_t^i + \frac{V_x^i}{2a_i} - \frac{(x - c_i)}{a_j} V_x^i - \frac{(x - c_j)}{a_j} V_x^i + (1 - x) V_x^i + \frac{V_x^i V_x^i}{a_j}$$
$$+ \frac{(x - c_i)^2}{2a_i} = 0$$

when $i \neq j = 1, 2$. Moreover, these have solutions of the form

(8.11.3)
$$V^i(x, t) = (1/2) k_i(t) x^2 - g_i(t) x + \Phi_i(t)$$

which vanish at $t = T$ if $k_i(\cdot)$, $g_i(\cdot)$, and $\Phi_i(\cdot)$ do. And such solutions yield equilibrium strategies of the form

(8.11.4)
$$u_i^*(t, x) = (1/a_i) (x - c_i - k_i(t) x + g_i(t)).$$

Finally, if the functions $k_i(t)$ and $g_i(t)$ tend to limits as $t \to -\infty$, the functions $u_i^*(t, x)$ tend to limits which are functions of x alone, and which may be shown to be equilibrium strategy pairs for the game on the infinite time interval. But they are only the linear ones; they are *not* the nonlinear equilibrium strategies which were found to be of the greatest interest earlier, when the game on the infinite interval was studied in detail.

This is an interesting conclusion, and one which would not change if a quadratic terminal payoff term $K_i(x(T))$ were added to the reward functional J_i. But it *would* change if a $K_i(\cdot)$ of higher degree were added thereto. For the fixed duration games obtained in that way would have value functions of degree higher than two and therefore equilibrium strategies of degree higher than one which could tend in the limit to nonlinear strategies $u_i^*(x)$ for the game on the infinite interval. In short, the attempt to solve games of infinite duration by solving purely linear-quadratic games on the finite interval and passing to a limit as $T \to \infty$ is doomed to almost certain failure; only two among the entire continuum of solutions may be obtained in this way, and the two differ markedly from the most interesting members of the continuum in the single case of which detailed knowledge is available.

Otherwise put, the particular terminal payoff terms $K_i(\cdot)$ postulated in the linear-quadratic model (8.10.1)–(8.10.3) substantially influence the nature of the equilibrium strategy N-tuples, not only toward the end of the game, but throughout the time of play. So that model is only an appropriate formulation of an actual competition if the duration of that competition is known to the players at its outset, and if the conditions which will prevail at its end are adequately represented by a quadratic terminal payoff function. When, as is more often the case, the game may be expected to continue into the dim and distant future, it is *essential* that it be modeled as one of infinite duration.

12. A TERMINATING GAME

We close this chapter with a brief description of a game which does terminate. We do not, however, furnish the solution of the game, as it is long, technical, and already available [5] in the literature.

Let us suppose that all of the coal deposits in a small country, isolated from the rest of the world by a range of high mountains, are owned by two competing firms. Let us further suppose that a tunnel is under construction which, when completed at time $t = T$ in the not-too-distant future, will link the country with the outside world. At that time, the internal price of coal will become equal to the world price of $\$Q_w$ per ton. Until then, because the demand for coal in the country is highly inelastic, it will be possible for the firms to charge more.

We shall also assume that, at time $t = T$, it will become possible to sell an operating coal mine for a price $\$P_w$ to foreign investors who wish to become exporters of coal from our small but coal-rich nation. We shall not admit the possibility of selling mines prior to the completion of the tunnel, as it seems unlikely that either firm would allow a third competitor to enter the domestic market while they can so easily prevent it.

We shall assume further that both firms mine coal in essentially the same way and that by burning one ton of coal as fuel to operate its mining machinery and by spending $\$k$ in labor and other costs, 1 can produce $b - 1$ (net) tons of new coal, while the same expenditure nets c tons for 2. But we suppose that their prospects differ in that 1 has only a few mines in operation at the time $t = t_0$ when the firms begin to compete, but owns large undeveloped coal fields, whereas 2 starts the game with numerous mines in operation, but no undeveloped resources. Thus we should expect 1, at least during the early stages of the competition, to be opening new mines and to be equipping them with the newest and most efficient equipment available. For this reason, we shall assume $b - 1 > c$.

Finally, we assume that, in order to place a single new coal mine in operation, firm 1 must invest A tons of coal and \$$K$ in labor and other costs. Thus, on each day of the period $t_0 \leqslant t \leqslant T$, which we take to be of several years' duration, firm 1 must decide; (1) how much of its present stock of coal to allocate to the production of coal for present market consumption; (2) how much to invest, along with the required amounts of labor and other inputs, in the development of new mines; and (3) how much to stockpile against future market demands.

That is, if $M(t)$ is the number of mines 1 has in operation on day t, and $S(t)$ is the supply of coal it has on hand, and if the directors of 1 elect to allocate $u_1(t)$ tons of that coal to the development of new coal mines and consume $u_2(t)$ tons in the production of new coal on that day, then firm 1 will have

$$(8.12.1) \qquad M(t + 1) = M(t) + u_1(t)/A = M(t) + au_1(t)$$

mines in operation and

$$(8.12.2) \qquad S(t + 1) = S(t) + bu_2(t) - (u_1(t) + u_2(t))$$

tons of coal on hand at the start of day $t + 1$. If we append to the finite difference equations (8.12.1) and (8.12.2) the inequality constraints

$$(8.12.3) \qquad \begin{gathered} u_1(t) \geqslant 0, \qquad\qquad u_2(t) \geqslant 0, \\ u_1(t) + u_2(t) \leqslant S(t), \quad \text{and} \quad u_1(t) \leqslant \alpha M(t), \end{gathered}$$

we obtain a complete description of 1's technological alternatives on day t. Clearly, 1 can not allot a negative amount of coal to either of its productive activities, consume more coal in a day as fuel than it had at the start of that day, or extract more than $b\alpha$ (gross) tons of coal in a day from a single mine, if α is the maximum number of tons of coal which may be burned for fuel in a day in a single mine.

However, since the competition is to extend over a large number of days, we may approximate $S(t + 1) - S(t)$ and $M(t + 1) - M(t)$ by $\dot{S}(t)$ and $\dot{M}(t)$, and so replace the difference equations (8.11.7) by the system

$$(8.12.4) \qquad \begin{gathered} \dot{M}(t) = au_1(t) \\ \dot{S}(t) = bu_2(t) - (u_1(t) + u_2(t)) \end{gathered}$$

of ordinary differential equations. But we emphasize that it is really the discrete time process (8.12.1) and (8.12.2) which we wish better to understand; the introduction of continuous time is merely an analytical device which, in this case, facilitates the solution of the problem.

As to firm 2, its technology is even simpler, for it does not have the option of developing new mines. Indeed, if $I(t)$ is 2's coal inventory at time t, we may write simply

$$(8.12.5) \qquad \begin{gathered} \dot{I}(t) = cv(t), \\ 0 \leqslant v(t) \leqslant I(t), \quad \text{and} \quad v(t) \leqslant \beta, \end{gathered}$$

where $v(t)$ is the quantity of coal consumed on day t as fuel to power 2's machines, and β is the maximum number of tons of coal which can be burned in a day as fuel in 2's mines, which are fixed in number.

Next we assume that the demand for coal in the country in which they operate is totally inelastic, and is equal to $m_0 = m\sqrt{\pi}$ tons of coal per day, regardless of the prices the two firms choose to charge. However, if firm 1's price $p_0(t)$ for a ton of coal on day t is higher than firm 2's price $q_0(t)$, then the demand $\delta(t)$ on firm 2 for coal on day t would exceed $m\sqrt{\pi} - \delta(t) = d(t)$, the demand on firm 1. More precisely, we assume that

(8.12.6)
$$d(t) = m\Phi(q_0(t) - p_0(t))$$
$$\delta(t) = m[\sqrt{\pi} - \Phi(q_0(t) - p_0(t))] = m\Phi(p_0(t) - q_0(t)),$$

where the function Φ is defined for every real number x by the relation

(8.12.7)
$$\Phi(x) = \int_{-\infty}^{x} e^{-u^2}\, du.$$

Thus $0 < \Phi(x) < \sqrt{\pi}$ and $\Phi(0) = \sqrt{\pi}/2$. Also $\Phi(-x) = \sqrt{\pi} - \Phi(x)$, $\Phi'(x) = e^{-x^2}$, and $\Phi''(x) = -2xe^{-x^2} = -2x\Phi'(x)$. We shall assume too that $m_0 = m\sqrt{\pi} < c\beta$, so that firm 2 has sufficient productive capacity to fill the entire market's demand. This would be the case, for instance, if 2 had historically been the only coal producer in the nation and 1 had come into being largely as a speculation, seeking to exploit the opportunity afforded by the new tunnel.

The particular forms (8.12.6) for the demand functions $d(t)$ and $\delta(t)$ will not, of course, be appropriate in all situations. But they would be, for instance, if the two firms were located at opposite "ends" of the country, and each forced their customers to bear all of the transportation costs. Then, as indicated schematically in Figure 8.12A, there could be a point E somewhere between them where the price $p_0(t)$ plus the cost of transporting a ton of coal from 1 to E exactly equals $q_0(t)$ plus the cost of transportation from 2 to E. So the customers to the left of E will buy from 1, while those to the right will buy from 2. The location of E will depend, in simple cases at least, only on the difference $p_0(t) - q_0(t)$, and will move continuously and monotonically from 2 to 1 if that difference is allowed gradually to increase from $-\infty$ to $+\infty$.

Now let $P = P_w - K$, $Q = Q_w - K$, $p(t) = p_0(t) - K$, and $q(t) = q_0(t) - K$. P, Q, $p(t)$, and $q(t)$ are the profits associated with the world and domestic market prices P_w, Q_w, $p_0(t)$, and $q_0(t)$. In terms of them, the firms' profits over the

FIGURE 8.12A

period $t_0 \leqslant t \leqslant T$ may be expressed as

$$J_1 = P(M(t) - M(t_0)) + Q(S(T) - S(t_0))$$

(8.12.8)

$$+ m \int_{t_0}^{T} p(t)\Phi(q(t) - p(t))\, dt$$

and

(8.12.9) $\qquad J_2 = Q(I(T) - I(t_0)) + m \int_{t_0}^{T} q(t)\Phi(p(t) - q(t))\, dt,$

since $p_0(t) - q_0(t) = p(t) - q(t)$. The complete evolution (often called "kinematic") equations for $M(t)$, $S(t)$, and $I(t)$ are obtained by appending the demand terms to the $\dot{S}$ and $\dot{I}$ equations given earlier. This yields

(8.12.10) $\qquad \begin{aligned} \dot{M}(t) &= au_1(t) \qquad \dot{I}(t) = cv(t) - m\Phi(p(t) - q(t)) \\ \dot{S}(t) &= bu_2(t) - (u_1(t) + u_2(t)) - m\Phi(q(t) - p(t)). \end{aligned}$

The problem of maximizing the functionals (8.12.8) and (8.12.9) subject to the differential equation constraints (8.12.10) and the inequality constraints

(8.12.11) $\qquad \begin{aligned} u_1(t) &\geqslant 0 \quad u_2(t) \geqslant 0 \quad v(t) \leqslant \beta \\ u_1(t) + u_2(t) &\leqslant S(t), \ u_2(t) \leqslant \alpha M(t) \quad \text{and} \quad 0 \leqslant v(t) \leqslant I(t) \end{aligned}$

is a differential game which *will* terminate on a definite date and in which the conditions at termination seem entirely predictable. Indeed it is only because those conditions *are* predictable that the newer (speculating) firm came into existence in the first place. So it does seem appropriate to model the situation as a game of finite duration.

13. CONCLUSIONS

We hope to have persuaded the reader, by now, that: (a) a large number of important conflict situations are appropriately cast as many-player differential games; (b) useful strategies can often be identified for those games by means of the Hamilton-Jacobi method provided that computational difficulties do not intervene; and finally (c) such is the complexity of the partial differential equations whose solution the method requires that computational difficulties will scarcely ever fail to intervene. The next chapter represents attempts, of one sort or another, at accommodation to conclusion (c). For of the three enunciated above, it seems quite the most inescapable.

Appendix

It is to be established that, for any positive numbers u_0, v_0 and any x_0 between zero and one, functions $U(x; \rho)$, $V(x; \rho)$ exist which are continuous in ρ, continuously differentiable in x, satisfy the initial conditions

(A1) $U(x_0; \rho) = u_0, \ V(x_0, \rho) = v_0$

and a pair of equations of the form (8.2.8) in a neighborhood of the point $(x_0, 0)$ in $x\rho$-space. Observe that (8.2.8) represents not a single pair of equations but a two-parameter family of such pairs indexed by (c, γ). For the purposes of differential game theory, it suffices to produce solutions $U(\cdot, \cdot)$, $V(\cdot, \cdot)$ of *any* such pair.

For definiteness, we fix (x_0, u_0, v_0) and set $c = \psi_1(x_0, u_0, v_0)$, $\gamma = \psi_1(x_0, u_0, v_0)$. Also, take the lower limit of integration equal to x_0. If $\rho = 0$, the equations (8.2.8) are easy to solve, for the Jacobian determinant

(A2) $\begin{vmatrix} \partial \psi_1/\partial u & \partial \psi_1/\partial v \\ \partial \psi_2/\partial u & \partial \psi_2/\partial v \end{vmatrix}$

does not vanish in the region $u > 0$, $v > 0$, $0 < x < 1$. So the standard implicit function theorem implies the existence of $U(x; 0)$, $V(x; 0)$ in an interval about x_0.

If $\rho \neq 0$, we may consider a subinterval $a < x_0 < b$ of the one referred to above, and the Banach space $B = C'(a, b)$ of continuously differentiable functions $f: [a, b] \to R$. Because the particular function $f(x) \equiv x$ belongs to B, ψ_1 and ψ_2 may be thought of as continuous functions mapping $R \times B \times B \to B$, their arguments being $(\rho, U(\cdot), V(\cdot))$. And (8.2.8) may be solved in Banach space.

To that end, consider the Banach spaces $E_1 = R$ and $E = B \times B$. Denote by σ a typical element of E, and by σ_0 the pair of solutions $(U(x; 0), V(x; 0))$ of (8.2.8) obtained above for $\rho = 0$. Then the function $\psi: E_1 \times E \to E$ defined by

(A3) $\psi(\rho, U(\cdot), V(\cdot)) = (\psi_1(\rho, U(\cdot), V(\cdot)), \psi_2(\rho, U(\cdot), V(\cdot)))$

is continuous in a neighborhood of $(0, \sigma_0)$ in $E_1 \times E$, and has the property $\psi(0, \sigma_0) = 0$. If it can be shown that $\psi(\rho, \sigma)$ has also a continuous derivative $\psi_\sigma(\rho, \sigma)$ in a neighborhood of $(0, \sigma_0)$, and that $[\psi_\sigma(0, \sigma_0)]^{-1}$ exists, then it will follow [13], that a continuous function $f: R \to E$ exists in a neighborhood of $\rho = 0$ such that $f(0) = \sigma_0$ and the only solutions of $\psi(\rho, \sigma) = 0$ near $(0, \sigma_0)$ are given by $\sigma = f(\rho)$. Plainly, the components of $f(\rho)$ in the product space $E = B \times B$ will be the desired functions $U(x; \rho)$ and $V(x; \rho)$. It remains only to show that $\psi_\sigma(\rho, \sigma)$ exists and has the requisite properties.

The differential

(A4) $\psi_\sigma(\rho, \sigma_0; \delta) = \lim\limits_{\epsilon \to 0} \dfrac{\psi(\rho, \sigma_0 + \epsilon\delta) - \psi(\rho, \sigma_0)}{\epsilon}$

is said to exist if the indicated limit does. For fixed (ρ, σ) it is typically a linear operator on the last argument $\delta = (h(\cdot), k(\cdot)) \in E$. Its components are

(A5)
$$\left. \frac{d}{d\epsilon} \psi_i(\rho, \sigma; \delta) \right|_{\epsilon=0},$$

$i = 1, 2$. So from calculus

(A6)
$$\begin{bmatrix} \psi_{1u}(\rho, U(x), V(x)) & \psi_{1v}(\rho, U(x), V(x)) \\ \\ \psi_{2u}(\rho, U(x), V(x)) & \psi_{2v}(\rho, U(x), V(x)) \end{bmatrix} \begin{bmatrix} h(x) \\ \\ k(x) \end{bmatrix} + \begin{bmatrix} \rho \int^x \dfrac{h(z)\,dz}{1-z} \\ \\ \rho \int^x \dfrac{k(z)\,dz}{z} \end{bmatrix}$$

is the desired differential $\psi_\sigma(\rho, 0; \delta)$, where $\sigma = (U(\cdot), V(\cdot))$. Clearly it acts continuously on δ. The derivative $\psi_\sigma(0, \sigma_0)$ is the linear operator from E to itself obtained by setting $\rho = 0$, $U(x) = U(x; 0)$, and $V(x) = V(x; 0)$ in (A6). It obviously exists and is invertible because the Jacobian determinant (A2) does not vanish. In short, the local existence, uniqueness, and differentiality of the desired functions

(A7) $\sigma = f(\rho) = (u(\cdot; \rho), v(\cdot; \rho))$

are consequences of the implicit function theorem [13] for Banach spaces.

A similar analysis is possible for equation (8.5.8), which is not really an equation at all, but a one-parameter family of them indexed by θ. For definiteness, fix (x_0, u_0) and choose $\theta = \psi(x_0, u_0)$. Assume too that $u_0 \neq (1/2)P_1(x_0)$; nothing is asserted for the opposite case. Now setting $\rho = 0$ yields a scalar quadratic equation in u whose only solutions are (8.5.10). Moreover, the negative sign must prevail therein if the result is to have physical meaning. So there is only one relevant solution of (8.5.8) for $\rho = 0$; call it $\sigma_0 = u(\cdot) \in B$.

For $\rho \neq 0$, regard ψ as a function of ρ and $u(\cdot)$ mapping $R \times B \to B$. Then we have already $\psi(0, \sigma_0) = 0$ and $\psi(\rho, \sigma)$ is continuous on a neighborhood of $(0, \sigma_0)$ in $R \times B$. So if $\psi_\sigma(\rho, \sigma)$ exists and is continuous on a neighborhood of $(0, \sigma_0)$ and if $\psi_\sigma(0, \sigma_0)$ is invertible, the desired continuous solution $u(\cdot; \rho) = f(\rho)$ will exist, be unique, and have a derivative in x. But

(A8) $\psi_\sigma(\rho, \sigma; h) = (2u(\cdot) - P_1(\cdot))h(\cdot) - \dfrac{\rho}{N - 1/2} \displaystyle\int^x h(z)\,dz$

is the desired differential, which obviously exists and acts continuously on $h(\cdot)$. Moreover, the derivative $\psi_\sigma(0, \sigma_0)$ exists and is invertible, provided only that the underlying $a \leqslant x \leqslant b$ be chosen to include no zeros of $2\sigma_0(x) - P_1(x)$.

Problems

(8-1) *Exercise* Solve the N-player differential game

$$i \max_{u_i} J_i = \int_0^\infty e^{-\rho t} [\lambda u_1(t) x(t)] \, dt$$

(DG)

s.t. $\dot{x}(t) = kx(t)[\theta - x(t)]/\theta - \lambda[u_1(t) + \cdots + u_N(t)] x(t)$

obtained from the one-dimensional fisherman's game of §2.4 by the transliterations $N(t) \to x(t)$ and $x_i(t) \to u_i(t)$ introduced for conformity with this chapter's notation.

(8-2) *Question* The equations (2.4.12) describe the dynamics of a three-state variable version of the fisherman's game. The Hamilton-Jacobi equations for it are simple enough so that condition (B) of Chapter VII is easily met, but it is no longer clear what boundary conditions to impose in lieu of condition (A).

(8-3) *Question* If $\dot{x}(t)$ is replaced by $\epsilon \dot{x}(t)$ in all the kinematic equations of this chapter, each DG will be embedded in a continuum of such, $\epsilon = 0$ representing a static problem and $\epsilon = 1$ the given one. Does such a full-blown "singular perturbations approach" yield new results for the examples presented here?

REFERENCES

1. Apostol, T. M., *Mathematical Analysis* (Reading, Mass.: Addison-Wesley, 1957).
2. Athans, M. and P. L. Falb, *Optimal Control* (New York: McGraw-Hill, 1966).
3. C. Carathéodory, *Variationsrechnung und Partielle Differentialgleichungen*, Erste Ordnung, (Berlin: B. G. Teubner, 1935).
4. Case, J., "Towards a Theory of Many-Player Differential Games," *SIAM J. Control*, 7 (1967), 1-19.
5. Case, J., "A Differential Game in Economics," *Management Science Theory*, 17 (1971), 394-410.
6. Coddington, E. A. and N. Levinson, *Theory of Ordinary Differential Equations* (New York: McGraw-Hill, 1955).
7. Garabedian, P. R. *Partial Differential Equations* (New York: John Wiley, 1964).
8. Hestenes, M. R., *Calculus of Variations and Optimal Control Theory* (New York: John Wiley, 1966).

9. Kalman, R. E., "Contributions to the Theory of Optimal Control," *Bol. Soc. Mat. Mexicana*, 5 (1960), pp. 102–119.

10. Kaplan, W., *Ordinary Differential Equations* (Reading, Mass.: Addison-Wesley, 1958).

11. Lukes, D. L., "Equilibrium Feedback Control in Linear Games with Quadratic Costs," *J. SIAM Control*, vol. 9, no. 2 (1971), pp. 234–252.

12. Simaan, M. and T. Takayama, "Dynamic Duopoly Game: Differential Game Theoretic Approach," *Proceedings of the Sixth Triennial World Congress, International Federation for Automatic Control*, Boston/Cambridge, Mass., August 1975.

13. V. J. Sobolev and L. A. Lusternik, *Elements of Functional Analysis* Hindustan Publ. Corp. Delhi (1961).

Chapter 9

Tractable Classes of Differential Games

The class of linear-quadratic differential games introduced in the previous chapter is notable chiefly for the ease with which its Hamilton-Jacobi equations may be integrated. In this chapter, certain other classes of games will be introduced whose Nash equilibria can likewise be found without first integrating some complicated system of partial differential equations. As always, we stress that such equilibria are not automatically to be regarded as solutions of the games in question, but only as likely candidates.

1. GAMES IN WHICH ONLY THE CLOCK IS OBSERVABLE

Varaiya [26] has considered the class of games

$$i \text{ maximize} \quad J_i = K_i(x(T)) + \int_0^T L_i(t, x(t)) \, dt + \int_0^T \Lambda_i(t, u_i(t)) \, dt$$

(9.1.1)

$$\text{subject to} \quad \dot{x} = A(t) x + B_1(t) u_1 + \cdots + B_N(t) u_N$$

$$\text{and} \quad \int_0^T |u_i(t)|^2 \, dt \leq M \leq \infty,$$

wherein strategies are simply functions of time alone. And subject to the conditions

(i) $K_i(x), L_i(t, x), \Lambda_i(t, x)$ are continuous in all variables, bounded from below, and for each fixed t, they are convex in the remaining variables; and
(ii) $K_i(x), L_i(t, x), \Lambda_i(t, x)$ are twice continuously differentiable and there exist positive numbers ϵ_1, ϵ_2 such that, for all t, x, u_i, the matrices

$$\nabla_x^2 L_i(b, x) - \epsilon_2 I, \quad \nabla_{u_i}^2 \Lambda_i(t, u_i) - \epsilon_1 I, \quad \nabla_x^2 K_i(x) - \epsilon_2 I$$

are positive definite,

253

he has proved that there exists at least one equilibrium N-tuple $(u_1^*(t), \ldots, u_N^*(t))$ for (9.1.1) unless T is too large. And in the special case $M < \infty$ and $L_1 = \cdots = L_N \equiv 0$, such an N-tuple exists for every T. Variaya's result is an unexpected one, because so many games do *not* have equilibria in strategies depending on time alone.

To see this, consider the game of pursuit and evasion wherein the pursuer's position at time t, namely $(x(t), y(t))$, and the evader's position $(\xi(t), \eta(t))$ at that instant, are governed by the kinematic equations

(9.1.2)
$$\dot{x} = 2 \cos \phi \qquad \dot{\xi} = \cos \psi$$
$$\dot{y} = 2 \sin \phi \qquad \dot{\eta} = \sin \psi.$$

Thus, each moves with constant speed in the plane, but the pursuer goes twice as fast. Both choose, at each instant t, a direction $\phi(t)$ (resp. $\psi(t)$) of motion independent of the other's current choice and of all past choices. The pursuer seeks to capture the evader as quickly as possible, while the evader endeavors to postpone that event. And an equilibrium pair (ϕ^*, ψ^*) for the game satisfies the inequalities

(9.1.3) $T(\phi^*, \psi) \leqslant T(\phi^*, \psi^*) \leqslant T(\phi, \psi^*),$

for each $\phi \neq \phi^*$ and $\psi \neq \psi^*$, where $T(\phi, \psi)$ denotes the time required for capture when the pursuer adopts strategy ϕ and the evader ψ. It is clear that if the pursuer knows of such a pair (ϕ^*, ψ^*), he can announce his choice of the strategy ϕ^* with impunity. For he will then capture in time $T(\phi^*, \psi^*)$ if the evader chooses ψ^* and more quickly if not. From this it follows that no pair $(\phi^*(t), \psi^*(t))$ of functions of time alone can satisfy the inequalities (9.1.3).

To see why, observe that the substitution of such functions for ϕ and ψ in (9.1.2) determines a pair of paths $(x^*(t), y^*(t))$ and $(\xi^*(t), \eta^*(t))$ in the plane, emanating from the players' initial positions P and E, respectively. If, however, the pursuer were to announce the choice of $\phi^*(t)$, the evader could elect a $\psi(t)$ for which $(\xi(t), \eta(t)) \neq (x^*(t), y^*(t))$ for every t. Then $T(\phi^*, \psi^*) \geqslant T(\phi^*, \psi) = \infty$, which is absurd.

On the other hand, the game certainly does [12] have an equilibrium $(\phi^*(\xi - x, \eta - y), \psi^*(\xi - x, \eta - y))$ in strategies depending on (relative) position, namely that the pursuer should always steer directly toward the evader and the latter should run directly away from the former. Moreover, as Isaacs [12] and others have shown, a considerable variety of pursuit and evasion games work in essentially this way; they are solvable in position dependent strategies but not in time dependent ones. So it comes as something of a surprise that any class of games at all has equilibria in strategies which are functions of time alone.

Such strategies are known, for historical reasons, as "open-loop" strategies, as opposed those which depend on additional information and are called "closed-loop." A number of discussions of the relative merits of the two sorts of strategy have appeared in the literature. We mention [11] in particular, but do not attempt to summarize the dialogue that has taken place to date. Suffice it to say that the relationship between the two sorts of strategy is more complex by far in games among many players than it is for optimal control problems, wherein the two are virtually equivalent. New aspects of that relationship will doubtless come to light in the future.

Open-loop equilibria, when they exist, are significantly easier to compute than closed-loop ones because theorems of the following sort have [26] been proven:

Maximum Principle: Let $M = \infty$ and let $u_1^*(t), \ldots, u_N^*(t)$ be an equilibrium N-tuple for the game (9.1.1) in bounded and measurable functions of t alone. Then there exist absolutely continuous vector-valued functions $p_1(t), \ldots, p_N(t)$ having as many components as x, such that

(M_1) $\Lambda_i(t, u_i^*(t)) + p_i(t) \cdot B_i(t) u_i^*(t) = \max_{u_i} [\Lambda_i(t, u_i) + p_i \cdot B(t) u_i]$

(M_2) $\dot{p}_i(t) = -\nabla_x L_i(t, x^*(t)) - A^T p_i(t),$

(M_3) $p_i(T) = \nabla_x K_i(x^*(T)),$

$x^*(t)$ being the state-space trajectory corresponding to the strategy N-tuple $u_1^*(t), \ldots, u_N^*(t)$.

The present maximum principle is an immediate corollary of Pontryagin's well-known one [22] for optimal control problems and can be used in much the same way to discover $u_1^*, \ldots, u_N^*$, and x^*. We shall not pause here to illustrate the process, but we shall point out that the games (9.1.1.) include the linear-quadratic games discussed in the previous chapter. So linear-quadratic games have *both* kinds of equilibrium N-tuples; they have the N-tuples $(u_1^*(t), \ldots, u_N^*(t))$ whose existence is guaranteed by Varaiya's theorem *and* the N-tuples $u_1^*(t, x), \ldots, u_N^*(t, x)$ calculated earlier by integrating the Hamilton-Jacobi equations. Moreover, the two are quite different! This was discovered by D. Lukes [16] when he recomputed $u_1^*(t, x), \ldots, u_N^*(t, x)$ by an abstract Hilbert-space approach, having previously (with D. Russell) obtained [17] $u_1^*(t), \ldots, u_N^*(t)$ in a related manner. For the latter (computed for a specific starting point x_0) yield a *different trajectory* through that starting point than do the former.

The same discovery was made earlier for discrete games by Ho and Starr [11], who noted that often all players receive greater rewards by choosing $u_1^*(t), \ldots, u_N^*(t)$ than by using $u_1^*(t, x), \ldots, u_N^*(t, x)$. That is, they are better off to agree in advance to forget what they know of the state variable x and behave as though they knew only the time. But of course, if one player begins to make use of his knowledge of x, the rest must typically do so too to protect themselves.

The phenomenon was noticed again by Simaan and Takayama [25] when they examined the linear price law Cournot game on the finite time interval. Thus, there is often a definite incentive for the players to cooperate, at least to the extent of ignoring what they know of the state variable x; there is usually an incentive to cooperate still further, as the equilibria $u_1^*(t), \ldots, u_N^*(t)$ typically are not Pareto optimal. But if, in a particular negotiation among players about to participate in a differential game, agreement cannot be reached on any Pareto optimal N-tuple, a so-called open-loop equilibrium $u_1^*(t), \ldots,$ $u_N^*(t)$ may be a sensible intermediate goal to explore before allowing negotiations to break off entirely. If that happens, everyone may be expected to use all the information at his disposal and thereby to depress the general level of reward in the game still further.

Indeed, open-loop equilibria have a property which seems entirely desirable in a negotiated solution; no single party to the agreement to play $u_1^*(t), \ldots, u_N^*(t)$ until $t = T$ has any incentive to renege first. And for that reason L. F. Pau [19] has calculated an open-loop equilibrium solution for a rather formidable model of the Danish economy. His results appear to be at least potentially useful because, *and only because*, the actions with which he is concerned are chosen after extended negotiations among representatives of the most important special-interest groups (or "sectors") comprising that economy. When agreement has been reached on a "five-year plan," of the sort to which Pau's open-loop analysis leads, it is reasonable to expect the signatories to adhere to that plan in desregard of subsequent revelations of information. But in the absence of such an agreement, it is *not* to be expected that useful information will be ignored.

2. PAU'S MODEL OF THE DANISH ECONOMY

Space limitations preclude a systematic presentation of Pau's work here, but its importance demands at least a brief synopsis. The details appear in Pau's own publications [19]-[21]. His model is adapted from one proposed by D. Kendrick and L. Taylor [13], while his data and input-output matrix were obtained from publications of the Danish government.

The game Pau constructs includes, as players, six sectors of the Danish economy: the public sector; the industrial sector; a so-called tertiary sector; and sectors of agriculture, housing, and transportation.

The public sector seeks to maximize the money accumulated by financial means for the support of public projects and the like, while housing seeks to maximize the total value of the dwellings built. The other sectors maximize accumulated cash flow.

There are only two state variables in the model, namely foreign debt and budget deficit, but twenty-one control variables belonging to the various players. These are: (i) primary investment by sector; (ii) production by sector; (iii) amortization and internal financing by sector; (iv) income and/or profits tax by sector; and (v) importation of finished products. When kinematic equations linking state and control variables are specified along with the inequality con-

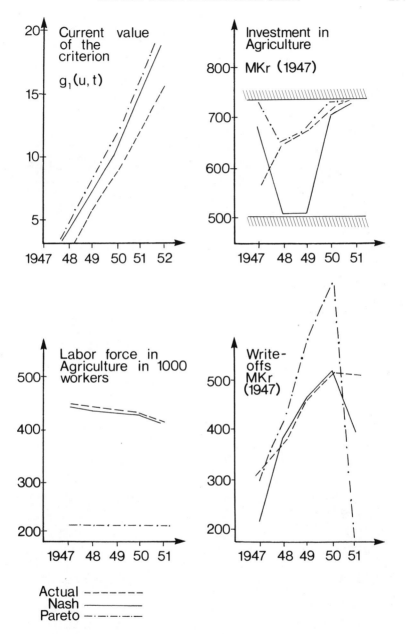

FIGURE 9.2A

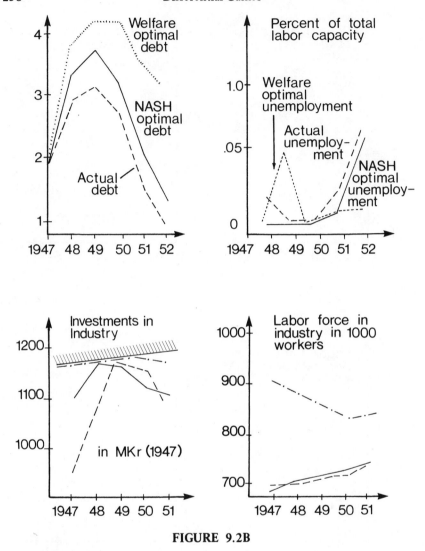

FIGURE 9.2B

straints required to circumscribe the players' allowable actions, the model is complete.

The conclusions to be drawn from the model are perhaps best displayed graphically. We reproduce here just a few of Pau's drawings, showing the way various economic indicators actually did vary during the years 1947-51, as opposed to the way they would have varied if Nash equilibrium controls had been employed. The third curve shown in each case shows the variation that would have been observed had the players acted in concert to maximize a certain measure of total welfare.

An interesting phenomenon is apparent in each instance, as Pau points out; namely, the actions historically taken resemble the Nash equilibrium ones much more closely than they do the welfare-optimal (in particular Pareto-optimal) actions shown. This adds weight to our earlier suggestion that when agreement cannot be reached on any Pareto-optimal five-year plan, it may be worthwhile to seek agreement on an open-loop Nash equilibrium plan. Such plans may (as in the present instance) seem less strange to the negotiators and (as in the examples of Ho and Starr or Simaan and Takayama mentioned above) leave all of them better off than the closed-loop behavior likely to prevail if no agreement at all is reached. It seems likely, therefore, that the theory of open-loop Nash equilibria may find significant application in the field of economic planning, wherein bargained solutions are sought. Pau has made admirable progress in that direction.

3. A CLASS OF TRILINEAR GAMES

In games in which the clock is but one of several observables, the open-loop strategies are included among the closed-loop ones. For a function of the state variable t alone is a function of the state vector $(t, x_1, \ldots, x_n)$ as well. It is sometimes the case that the Nash equilibrium closed-loop strategies for such a game are independent of all other state variables than t. S. Clemhout and H. Y. Wan [9] have isolated a class of games, their *trilinear games*, which behave in this manner. They have also examined [10] a differential game model of oligopoly which lies in that class. As remarked earlier, open-loop equilibria are easier to find than those which depend on additional variables, because of the availability of maximum principles like that stated in §1.

The class of games introduced by Clemhout and Wan are all of the form

$$i \max \quad J_i = \int_0^T \left\{ \left(\sum_{j=1}^N c_{ij}^0(u_j)\, d^j + e_i^0(t) \right) \cdot x(t) + b_i^0(t) \right\} dt$$

(9.3.1) subject to $\quad u_i \in U^i, \quad x \in S,$

$$\text{and} \quad \dot{x} = \left(\sum_{j=1}^N (c_j(u_j) \otimes d^j) + E(t) \right) \cdot x + b(t),$$

where x is a variable n-vector, each d^j is a constant one for $j = 1, 2, \ldots, N, E(t)$ is an $n \times n$ time-varying matrix, $e_1^0(t), \ldots, e_N^0(t)$ and $b(t)$ are time-varying n-vector valued functions, and $b_1^0(t), \ldots, b_N^0(t)$ are scalar functions of t. Each c_j is an n-vector valued function defined on a neighborhood of the compact convex set U^j, and each c_{ij}^0 is a scalar valued function* defined on the same set.

---

*Little generality is lost if one assumes that all the given functions are several times differentiable in each of their arguments.

Finally,

$$(9.3.2) \qquad\qquad S = \{(x,t) : 0 \leqslant t \leqslant T \ \ \& \ \ Dx > 0\},$$

where D is the matrix whose rows are $d^1, \ldots, d^N$, and $c_j \otimes d^j$ denotes the matrix obtained when the n-dimensional column vector c_j is *post multiplied* by the n-dimensional row vector d^j.

The games are called trilinear because their Hamiltonian functions are all of the form

$$(9.3.3) \qquad H^i = L_i + p_i \cdot f = (1 \vdots p_i) \begin{pmatrix} b_i & \vdots & \sum\limits_{j=1}^{N} c_{ij}^0 d^j + e_i^0 \\ \text{-----} & \text{+} & \text{----------} \\ b & \vdots & \sum\limits_{j=1}^{N} c_j \, d^j + E \end{pmatrix} \begin{pmatrix} 1 \\ \text{--} \\ x \end{pmatrix},$$

and are therefore linear in p_i, x, and (c_{ij}^0, c_j). One may compute open-loop Nash equilibria by finding functions $\hat{u}_i(p_i)$ which maximize the quantities

$$(9.3.4) \qquad\qquad c_{ii}^0(u_i) + p_i \cdot c_i(u_i),$$

then integrating the ordinary differential equations

$$(9.3.5) \quad \dot{p}_i = -\left\{ \sum_{j=1}^{N} c_{ij}^0(\hat{u}_j(p_j)) \, d^j + e_i^0 + p_i \left(\sum_{j=1}^{N} c_j(\hat{u}_j(p_j)) \, d^j + E \right) \right\}$$

subject to the conditions that p_i vanish when $t = T$, and writing

$$(9.3.6) \qquad\qquad u_i^*(t) = \hat{u}_i(p_i(t)).$$

The proof that the above procedure does in fact yield an equilibrium N-tuple $u_1^*(t), \ldots, u_N^*(t)$ makes use of a sufficiency criterion due to Leitmann and Stalford [15] and appears in [9]. Though it is short, that proof will not be reproduced here.

The results described above apply to an digopoly model examined [10] by Clemhout, Leitmann, and Wan. The principle ingredient of that model is a very strong form of brand loyalty, which is influenced only by advertising, and so allows each oligopolist to control his sales through the manipulation of his own price without alienating old customers with price hikes or attracting new ones by the reverse.

Specifically each firm i has a "market capacity"

$$(9.3.7) \qquad\qquad \gamma_i = a - bQ + C_i$$

which depends linearly on the number C_i of customers currently loyal to brand i, and on the number Q of units of output (or "articles") currently in use among the entire pool of customers. Then if q_i be i's current sales rate, it is assumed that Q varies as

$$(9.3.8) \qquad\qquad \dot{Q} = (q_1 + \cdots + q_N) - rQ,$$

$-rQ$ being a depreciation term. It is also assumed that each C_i, $i = 1, \ldots, N$ varies as

$$(9.3.9) \qquad \dot{C}_i = A_i - \frac{1}{N-1}\left(\sum_{j \neq i} A_j\right),$$

so that one's current endowment of loyal customers varies at a rate depending on all current advertising budgets $A_1, A_2, \ldots, A_N$.

It is convenient to take, as i's control variables, the quantities

$$(9.3.10) \qquad u_{i1} = q_i/\gamma_i \quad \text{and} \quad u_{i2} = A_i/\gamma_i,$$

so that the equations (9.3.8) and (9.3.9) together constitute an $(N + 1)$-dimensional system of the form postulated in (9.3.1), x being the transpose of the row-vector $(Q, C_1, \ldots, C_N)$. Finally, if it is assumed that each oligopolist i seeks to maximize the functional

$$(9.3.11) \qquad J_i = \int_0^T \left\{ \gamma_i u_{i1} + \frac{\omega}{N-1} \sum_{j \neq i} \gamma_j u_{j1} \right\} dt,$$

it becomes clear that J_i is also of the form postulated in (9.3.1). So the game in which i seeks to maximize (9.3.11) subject to the equality constraints (9.3.8)–(9.3.9) and the inequalities

$$(9.3.12) \qquad u_{i1} \geqslant 0 \qquad u_{i2} > 0 \qquad \gamma_i f(u_{i1}) = G_i \geqslant A_i \geqslant 0$$

whereby the sets $U^1, \ldots, U^N$ are defined, is of the form (9.3.1), and may be solved by the method outlined above. The last written of the inequalities (9.3.12) expresses the authors' assumption that oligopolists never borrow money in order to advertise at a rate greater than their current gross earning rate.

As mentioned earlier, certain assumptions in the model are exceedingly dubious, namely (i) the assumption that brand loyalty is so strong that customers remain loyal in the face of (possibly large) price differentials and (ii) the fact that each firm's market capacity (9.3.7) is unaffected by a redistribution of the articles currently held by the public. Thus, if all articles were taken away from the customers currently loyal to i and distributed among his competitors' customers, γ_i would (since Q is unchanged by such a redistribution) remain constant. In spite of such obvious drawbacks, the model is an interesting one and deserves further attention. One wonders, in particular, what happens if it is formulated on the infinite time interval.

4. THREATS AND MEMORY-DEPENDENT STRATEGIES

So far, we have considered strategies depending only on currently observable quantities; but all players are endowed with memories and are capable of recalling (at least some of) their past observations. One wonders what profit, if any, they can realize by so doing.

Tamer Basar [1] was among the first to confront this question. He considered a very simple two-stage problem wherein player 1 may act once at time $t = 0$ and again at time $t = 1$, while 2 acts only at $t = 0$. There is a single (scalar) state variable x, which "evolves" according to the law

(9.4.1)
$$x_1 = x_0 + u_0 + v_0$$
$$x_2 = x_1 + u_1,$$

x_0 being the given initial state, u_0 being 1's action at $t = 0$, v_0 being 2's (simultaneous) action, and u_1 being 1's action at $t = 1$. It is assumed that 1 and 2 seek to minimize J_1 and J_2, respectively, where

(9.4.2)
$$J_1 = x_2^2 + u_1^2 + u_0^2$$
$$J_2 = x_2^2 + v_0^2.$$

Player 1's strategy is a pair

(9.4.3) $$(u_0, u_1) = (s_0(x_0), s_1(x_0, x_1))$$

of functions depending on the history of the state variable up to the moment of decision and 2's is simply a function

(9.4.4) $$v_0 = \sigma(x_0)$$

of the information at his disposal when he must act. A triple $(s_0^*(\cdot), s_1^*(\cdot, \cdot), \sigma^*(\cdot))$ constitutes a Nash equilibrium for this game if it satisfies the inequalities

(9.4.5)
$$J_1(s_0^*, s_1^*, \sigma^*) \leq J_1(s_0, s_1, \sigma^*)$$
$$J_2(s_0^*, s_1^*, \sigma^*) \leq J_2(s_0^*, s_1^*, \sigma)$$

for all s_0, s_1, and σ.

It is not difficult to verify that the strategies

(9.4.6) $u_0 = s_0(x_0) = -2x_0/7$ $u_1 = s_1(x_1) = -x_1/2$ $v_0 = \sigma(x_0) = -x_0/7$

constitute a Nash equilibrium pair in linear functions of the state variables. This may be demonstrated in a manner similar to that used for finding linear equilibria in the continuous time linear-quadratic games of finite duration discussed in the previous chapter. But though it is the only *linear* equilibrium pair, it is hardly the only equilibrium. For Basar has shown that the strategies

(9.4.7)
$$u_0 = s_0^*(x_0) = \mu/12p - (\mu^2 + 36px_0)^{1/2}$$
$$u_1 = s_1^*(x_0, x_1) = px_1^2 - x_1/2 - p\,[x_0 + 3\mu/p - 2(\mu^2 + 36px_0)^{1/2}]$$
$$v_0 = \sigma^*(x_0) = -x_0 - \mu/4p - (\mu^2 + 36px_0)^{1/2},$$

where $\mu = 21/4$ and p is a nonzero real parameter such that $\mu^2 + 36px_0 \geqslant 0$, constitute an equilibrium pair. There are many others as well.

The reason for the plethora of history-dependent equilibria is really quite transparent; because he has the last move, 1 can threaten 2. That is, 1 can instruct 2 to transfer x_0 to $x = 0$ by taking the action $v_0^0(x_0) = -x_0$, on penalty of having x_0 transferred to $2x_0$ should he (2) fail to comply. 1 can accomplish this by adopting for himself the strategy

(9.4.8)
$$u_0^0(x_0) \equiv 0 \quad \text{and} \quad u_1^0(x_0, x_1) = 0 \qquad \text{if} \quad x_1 = 0$$
$$= 2x_0 - x_1 \quad \text{if} \quad x_1 \neq 0.$$

It is clear that (u_0^0, u_1^0) is optimal against v_0^0, since it renders $J_1 = 0$ when v_0^0 is played. Likewise v_0^0 is optimal against (u_0^0, u_1^0), since it gives $J_2 = x_0^2$, while any other choice yields $J_2 \geqslant 4x_0^2$. So $((u_0^0, u_1^0), v_0^0)$ is an equilibrium in history-dependent strategies, whereby 1 threatens 2. Basar has found a way to accomplish the same thing with smoothly defined strategies. Actually, Shapley [24] appears to have been the first to point out the presence in almost every differential game (with either discrete or continuous time) of threat equilibria. Of course, the existence of threats and their credibility are not to be confused.

Three quite different questions have arisen here: that of the existence of nonlinear equilibria for linear-quadratic games; that of equilibria in history-dependent strategies; and a third concerning threat equilibria. The first, of course, is of interest only for linear-quadratic games. We already knew linear-quadratic games (on the infinite time interval) can have equilibria in nonlinear strategies, since we found several of them for Cournot's dynamic game. Basar's result and its generalizations [2] demonstrate that this is not an isolated phenomenon. The questions concerning threat equilibria and equilibria in history-dependent strategies may be asked about any differential game. The theory, at its present stage of development at least, provides no general answers. Rather, the questions must be treated on an individual basis, regarding each separate game as a case apart.

In fact, the questions have been little discussed in this book because they did not seem important for the games considered. The players do so well in most of them (i.e., have such robust strategies) using only current information, or none at all as was the case in the static versions of the various games, that there seems little incentive to introduce strategies depending on history as well. The obvious threats, at least, seem quite incredible. Perhaps it is best to illustrate these claims with an example; the two-player Ad Game seems a natural choice.

For the instance $P = Q = 8$ and $\alpha = 1$ of that game, the strategy $u^*(x)$ was shown in Chapter VII to be better than 90 percent efficient against all (constant) values of v wherewith player 2 can hope to earn a positive profit. So 2's threats to employ such large v that 1 suffers dire consequences are not usually* credible because they cost so much to carry out that 2 cannot long sustain them. And so highly efficient is $u^*(x)$ that (see table 7.2C) it scarcely seems worthwhile to try to improve upon it with the aid of history-dependent strategies!

Nothing is asserted now about any other game than this one. The questions must be asked anew for each game individually, but there seems little reason to suppose that in other differential games constructed on the static ones discussed in earlier chapters (the variations and possible combinations of which seem quite endless), either threats or memories should play substantially more important roles than they do in this one. So it does not seem premature to suggest to a decision maker looking for a *good way* to play such a game that he consider a closed-loop Nash equilibrium strategy. In this case, at least, one of them works very well!

5. SIMPLE TRADING GAMES

For some classes of games, the task of integrating the Hamilton-Jacobi partial differential equations may be greatly simplified. Such was the case for the terminating linear-quadratic games discussed in the last chapter and for the trilinear ones introduced in this. Shortly we shall present another class, the class of *differential trading games*, for which the procedure may likewise be simplified. But first we must ponder the static versions of those games which have not heretofore engaged our attention. Certain notational conventions will prove convenient.

All scalars discussed in this section are real, and all vectors are elements of the real N-dimensional Euclidean space E_N. The symbol 0 denotes either the null vector of that space or the number zero, as context demands. We say that the vector $V = (V_1, \ldots, V_N)$ is greater than $v = (v_1, \ldots, v_N)$ if $V_i > v_i$ for each $i = 1, \ldots, N$, and we write $V > v$ in this case. Or if $V_i \geqslant v_i$ for each i, we write $V \geqslant v$. Also we define $E_N^+ = \{V : V \geqslant 0\}$. The inner product of the vectors V and v is written $\langle V, v \rangle$. Finally, if K is any subset of E_N, and if $\langle V, v^* \rangle \geqslant \langle V, v \rangle$ for every $v \in K$, we write

$$(9.5.1) \qquad\qquad v^* = \operatorname*{argmax}_{v \in K} \langle V, v \rangle.$$

Of course argmax $\langle V, \cdot \rangle$ will be a set-valued function in many cases. When the value of the argmax function is in fact a set, our statements concerning that value will hold for each vector contained in it.

Consider now two islands, 1 and 2, which trade only with one another. A native of 1 owns a boat and sails it to 2 each month. There he meets the local

---

*Of course if 2 is really *very much* richer than 1, the threat of being driven out of business is *entirely* credible. But the advertiser caught in such a bind needs something no theory can give him, so we shall not concern ourselves with his plight here.

chief, with whom he conducts his business. Both islands use the same currency, which is measured in dollars ($).

N goods are produced in the two-island economy; we call them $x_1, \ldots, x_N$. Let $P_1 = (P_{11}, \ldots, P_{1N})$ and $P_2 = (P_{21}, \ldots, P_{2N})$ be the prevailing market prices on 1 and 2, respectively. Then the trader can either buy or sell a unit of X_r for $\$P_{1r}$ on 1, and the chief can either buy or sell a unit of X_r for $\$P_{2r}$ on 2.

Next let Δ_1 be the set of commodity bundles 1's boat can transport from 2 to 1, and let Δ_2 be the set of bundles he can carry from 1 to 2. Thus, 1 can deliver any bundle $d_2 \in \Delta_2$ to 2 and return with any $d_1 \in \Delta_1$. We shall assume that (i) Δ_i is a compact convex subset of E_N^+, and (ii) that if Δ_i contains a vector v, it contains the entire (vector) interval $0 \leqslant d \leqslant v$ as well.

There will ordinarily be certain handling charges which must be paid if goods are to be moved between islands. Let c_{ir} be the cost of moving one unit of X_r from j to i. We write $c_i = (c_{i1}, \ldots, c_{iN})$.

On each round trip, the trader can transport a bundle $d_2 \in \Delta_2$ of goods from 1 to 2 to be sold there at a profit $\langle P_2 - c_2 - P_1, d_2 \rangle$, and a bundle $d_1 \in \Delta_1$ from 2 to 1 for $\langle P_1 - c_1 - P_2, d_1 \rangle$ dollars profit. So if we write $P_1' = P_1 - c_1$ and $P_2' = P_2 - c_2$, the trader's books will show earnings of not more than

$$(9.5.2) \qquad H_2^* = \max_{d_2 \in \Delta_2} \langle P_2' - P_1, d_2 \rangle$$

on the trip from 1 to 2 and not more than

$$(9.5.3) \qquad H_2^* = \max_{d_1 \in \Delta_1} \langle P_1' - P_2, d_1 \rangle$$

on the return. And in theory the players are free to divide their total income $H_1^* + H_2^*$ in any way they choose.

We wish to determine whether or not the trader and the chief may realistically be expected to obtain this maximum possible profit $H_1^* + H_2^*$ and, if so, how they may be expected to share it. To that end we observe that if $P_{2r}' > P_{1r}$, the chief will be willing to pay more than $\$P_{1r}$ for a unit of X_r. Similarly the chief feels no obligation to offer his goods to the trader for the same price he paid for them. So let $p_1 = (p_{11}, \ldots, p_{1N})$ be the vector of prices at which 1 offers his goods to 2, and let $p_2 = (p_{21}, \ldots, p_{2N})$ be the price at which 2 offers his goods to 1.

We assume that, in the interest of efficiency, orders are placed each trip for delivery the next. Thus, at each meeting 1 presents 2 with his price list p_1 and asks which bundle $d_2 \in \Delta_2$ the latter wants delivered next time. Simultaneously, 2 presents p_2 to 1, who requests that a certain $d_1 \in \Delta_1$ await him on his return. The profits on the next trip will then be

$$(9.5.4) \qquad H_1 = \langle p_1 - P_1, d_2 \rangle + \langle P_1' - p_2, d_1 \rangle$$

for 1, and

$$(9.5.5) \qquad H_2 = \langle p_2 - P_2, d_1 \rangle + \langle P_2' - p_1, d_2 \rangle$$

for 2, assuming that the buyer pays all handling charges. The functions H_1 and H_2 are the payoff functions in a game between the players 1 and 2; player i's object in that game is to choose his price p_i and his demand d_i so as to maximize his profit H_i. It is emphasized that the players' decisions are made in two stages: first they announce what prices they have decided to charge; later, which bundles they wish to purchase.

Thus, a strategy for player i consists of two parts: a price vector p_i and a demand function $\delta_i : E_N - \Delta_i$ which specifies, for each price vector p_j which j might announce, the bundle $d_i = \delta_i(p_j)$ which i wishes to purchase.

Once p_j is announced, i must choose d_i to maximize $\langle P_i' - p_j, d_i \rangle$. So

$$(9.5.6) \qquad d_i = \delta_i^*(p_j) = \operatorname*{argmax}_{d_i \in \Delta_i} \langle P_i' - p_j, d_i \rangle.$$

Clearly, since $d_{ir} = 0$ if $p_{jr} \geqslant P_{ir}'$, j can never hope to earn more than

$$(9.5.7) \qquad \max_{d_i \in \Delta_i} \langle P_i' - P_j, d_i \rangle = H_i^*$$

from the sale of any bundle $d_i \in \Delta_i$ to i. This is the reason for the assumption (ii) made earlier; if there were a good x_r of which i had to buy at least one unit, then j could earn an arbitrarily large profit just by inflating p_{jr} sufficiently.

Now let $p_j = p_j(\epsilon) = \epsilon P_j + (1 - \epsilon) P_i'$. Then

$$(9.5.8) \qquad \delta_i^*(p_j) = \operatorname*{argmax}_{d_i \in \Delta_i} \epsilon \langle P_i' - P_j, d_i \rangle,$$

so that from (3.5.8),

$$(9.5.9) \qquad \begin{aligned} &\lim_{\epsilon \to 0} \langle p_j(\epsilon) - P_j, \delta_i^*(p_j(\epsilon)) \rangle \\[2mm] &= \lim_{\epsilon \to 0} (1 - \epsilon) \langle P_i' - P_j, \delta_i^*(p_j(\epsilon)) \rangle \\[2mm] &= \max_{d_i \in \Delta_i} \langle P_i' - P_j, d_i \rangle = H_i^*. \end{aligned}$$

Therefore the strategy

$$(9.5.10) \qquad p_j^*(\epsilon) = \epsilon P_j + (1 - \epsilon) P_i'$$

is ϵ-optimal for j; using it with ϵ sufficiently small, j can drive the "export" term $\langle p_j - P_j, d_i \rangle$ of his payoff H_j as near as he likes to its upper bound (9.5.7). Observe that in so doing, he drives i's import earnings $\langle P_i' - p_j, d_i \rangle$ to zero. Simultaneously, of course, i will be driving his own export earnings toward their upper bound and j's import earnings to zero. Thus, when they play the strategy pairs.

$$(9.5.11) \qquad (p_1^*(\epsilon), \delta_1^*(p_2)), \quad (p_2^*(\epsilon), \delta_2^*(p_1))$$

defined by (9.5.6) and (9.5.10), the players earn nearly the joint profit $H_1^* + H_2^*$ shown earlier to be maximal, i's share being essentially H_j^*. The above results may be restated in the form of the following

Theorem: The strategy pairs (9.5.11) are simultaneously in Nash equilibrium, since each is ε-optimal against the other, and Pareto optimal since the sum of the quantities (9.5.5) is $H_1^* + H_2^*$.

In short, here is a class games in which the Nash equilibria are also Pareto optima. Objections were raised in Chapter I to the notion of Pareto optimality *as an assumption*, since it seemed so often to lead to the wrong conclusions, but here Pareto optimality emerges as a consequence of more primitive assumptions.

We remark in passing that there is no need that the sets Δ_1 and Δ_2 lie in spaces of finite dimension. If they are subsets of Banach spaces B_1 and B_2, we need only reinterpret prices as elements of the adjoint spaces B_1^* and B_2^*. This is helpful if we wish to consider a good X which varies continuously in quality from $q = 0$ (very bad) to $q = 1$ (very good). Then the demand for X is represented by a function $d(q)$ defined on the interval $0 \leqslant q \leqslant 1$, and the price of the bundle $d = d(q)$ is the value $\langle P, d \rangle$ of a continuous linear functional $\langle P, \cdot \rangle$ on the space of all such bundles. Alternatively, the sets Δ_1 and Δ_2 might contain only a finite number of points. In that case, the game will have the same solution as the augmented one in which Δ_1 and Δ_2 are replaced by their convex hulls.

One thing strikes most readers as strange about these results (which first appeared in [6]), namely that each player earns everything through exports and nothing through imports. But the result is correct, and the reason for it is immediately apparent. We have taken all domestic price vectors P_1, P_1', P_2, and P_2' to be known constants, while in reality they are random variables which are (most likely) lognormally distributed about an unknown mean. Therefore, the purchase each player makes from the other is actually the outcome of a single-buyer auction, and it was seen in Chapter III that, as uncertainty becomes negligible in such auctions, the likely sale prices all tend to the value of the property at auction while simultaneously the probability of no sale goes to zero. The theorem stated above pertains, therefore, to the limiting case in which uncertainty vanishes of the more realistic game wherefor domestic prices all are random variables. It is a useful approximation for problems in which those prices have small variance.

6. AN EXTENSION

The model of the previous section has been extended by K. T. Lee [14] to allow domestic prices to vary in a natural fashion instead of remaining fixed and immutable. To be precise, he assumed that a demand law of the form (2.19) prevails on each island. Also, he assumed that the population of island i has a fixed weekly budget $\$B_i$ to spend.

Then if good X_j arrives in the market on island i at the rate r_{ij} and is sold at the price P_{ij} there, we must have

(9.6.1) $$P_{i1}r_{i1} + \cdots + P_{in}r_{in} = B_i$$

for the budget to be spent, and

(9.6.2) $$\frac{r_{ik}}{r_{i1} + \cdots + r_{in}} = D_{ik}(P_{i1}, \ldots, P_{in})$$

for X_k's share of the market to obey (2.19). Observe that the various goods $X_1, \ldots, X_n$ must be measured in a common unit, since the fractions $D_{ik}(P_{i1}, \ldots, P_{in})$ are dimensionless. There is no difficulty if the goods are competing brands of toothpaste or varieties of meat, but if they are more diverse in nature an abstract unit like the nebulous "utile" must be introduced.

Next, dividing the jth of equations (9.6.2) by the kth, one obtains

(9.6.3) $$\frac{r_{ij}}{r_{ik}} = \left(\frac{m_{ik}P_{ik}}{m_{ij}P_{ij}}\right)^{\alpha_i},$$

wherefrom it may be established that

(9.6.4) $$P_{ik} = B_i\left[(m_{ik}/m_{i1})\, r_{ik}^{\beta_i} r_{i1}^{1-\beta_i} + \cdots + (m_{ik}/m_{in})\, r_{ik}^{\beta_i} r_{in}^{1-\beta_i}\right]^{-1}$$

is the price at which X_k must be sold on island i if the market is to clear. Here $\beta_i = 1/\alpha_i$. For simplicity, we restrict attention to the case of only two goods. The index i will always be either 1 or 2, as will $j \neq i$.

We assume that island i has a source of good X_k which produces A_{ik} units thereof per week, and we write

(9.6.5)
$$q_{1k}(d_1, d_2) = P_{1k}(A_{11} + d_1, A_{12} - d_2)$$
$$q_{2k}(d_1, d_2) = P_{2k}(A_{21} - d_1, A_{22} + d_2),$$

so that $q_{ik}(d_1, d_2)$ is the price of X_k on island i if 1 buys d_1 units of X_1 on 2 and sells d_2 units of X_2 there. If it is assumed that

(9.6.6) $$q_{21}(0,0) < q_{11}(0,0) \quad \text{and} \quad q_{12}(0,0) < q_{22}(0,0),$$

so that X_1 is cheaper on island 2 and X_2 is cheaper on 1 when there is no trade, that is the pattern of trade to be expected. For then i can offer X_j to j at a price $p_i > P_{ij}$. The profit to player i when there is trade d_1, d_2 is then

(9.6.7)
$$H_i((p_1, \delta_1(p_2)), (p_2, \delta_2(p_1)))$$
$$= (p_i - q_{ij}(d_1, d_2))d_j + (q_{ii}(d_1, d_2) - c_i - p_j)d_i,$$

c_i being a transportation cost, as before. We seek an equilibrium pair for the game, subject to the constraints $0 \leqslant d_i \leqslant D_i$, D_i being some given constant smaller than A_{ji}.

Lee proceeds by considering first the game that must be played after both players have named their prices. He calls that game $G(p_1, p_2)$, and he proves

Theorem 1: For any (p_1, p_2), the subgame $G(p_1, p_2)$ has a unique equilibrium pair $(d_1^*(p_1, p_2), d_2^*(p_1, p_2))$ of demands.

We shall not rehearse the proof here, except to remark that it makes use of Rosen's uniqueness criterion [23].

Next Lee considers a game $\bar{G}$ in the (p_1, p_2)-plane wherefor the payoff functions are

$$(9.6.8) \qquad \bar{H}_i(p_1, p_2) = H_i(p_1, d_1^*(p_1, p_2), p_2, d_2^*(p_1, p_2)).$$

Concerning it, he finds intervals $I_i = [a_i, b_i]$ such that the strategy $p_i = a_i$ strictly dominates any strategy $p_i < a_i$ and $p_i = b_i$ is at least as good as any $p_i > b_i$, $i = 1, 2$. And then defining

$$(9.6.9) \qquad \begin{aligned} K_1(p_2) &= \{p_1 : \bar{H}_1(p_1, p_2) = \max_{x \in I_1} \bar{H}_1(x, p_2)\} \\ K_2(p_1) &= \{p_2 : \bar{H}_1(p_1, p_2) = \max_{x \in I_2} \bar{H}_2(p_1, x)\}, \end{aligned}$$

he proves

Theorem 2: If there exist continuous functions $k_1(\cdot), k_2(\cdot)$ such that $k_i(p_j) \in K_i(p_j)$ for all p_j in I_j, $i = 1, 2$, then there exists an equilibrium pair for $\bar{G}$.

The main body of the proof consists of a series of lemmas whereby the sets $K_i(p_j)$ are characterized in terms of a certain constrained maximization problem. These established, the theorem becomes an immediate consequence of Brouwer's fixed-point theorem. Finally he proves

Theorem 3: Let $(\bar{p}_1, \bar{p}_2)$ be an equilibrium pair for $\bar{G}$. Then an equilibrium pair $(p_1^*, \delta_1^*), (p_2^*, \delta_2^*)$ for G is given by the relations

$$(9.6.10) \qquad \begin{aligned} p_1^* &= \bar{p}_1, \quad p_2^* = \bar{p}_2 \\ \delta_1^*(p_2) &= \delta_1^*(\bar{p}_1, p_2) \\ \delta_2^*(p_1) &= d_2^*(p_1, \bar{p}_2). \end{aligned}$$

The three theorems provide relatively mild and easily verified conditions sufficient for the existence of an equilibrium, but that, of course, is no guarantee of robustness or approximate solvability. Those things can be checked only for particular values of the parameters.

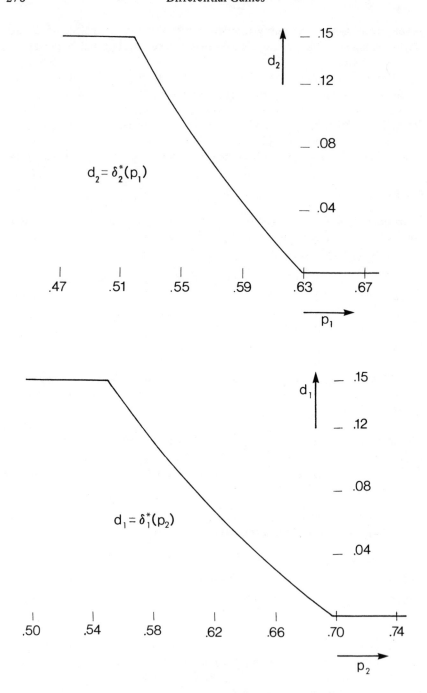

FIGURE 9.6A

For the case $A_{11} = .512$, $A_{12} = 1.331$, $A_{21} = 1$, $A_{22} = .729$, $B_1 = B_2 = 1$, $\beta_1 = \beta_2 = 1/3$, $m_{11} = m_{12} = m_{21} = m_{22} = 1$, $c_1 = c_2 = 0$, and $D_1 = D_2 = .15$, the unique equilibrium prices are $p_1^* = .5665$ and $p_2^* = .6281$ while the equilibrium demand functions $\delta_1^*(p_2)$, $\delta_2^*(p_1)$ (tabulated in Tables 9.6B and 9.6C have the shapes shown in Figure 9.6A. It should be pointed out that such a result is possible only because D_1 and D_2 are not large; when $D_1 = .9$ and $D_2 = 1.1$, the subgame $G(.59, .55)$ has equilibrium points at $(.1337, .0868)$ and $(.8851, 1.011)$.

To show that $(p_1^*, \delta_1^*(\cdot))$ is a robust strategy, we proceed in two steps. Table 9.6D gives the ratios $\overline{H}_1(.5665, p_2)/\overline{H}_1(p_1^*(p_2), p_2)$ for several values of p_2. So player 1 is little hurt if 2 chooses his demands by the law $d_2 = \delta_2^*(p_1)$, but behaves erratically in his choice of p_2. Next one must ask if 2 can hurt 1 by choosing both p_2 and d_2 in an unexpected fashion. A partial answer may be found in Tables 9.6E and 9.6F.

In Table 9.6E, $p_2 = .6218$ and d_2 takes a number of values between 0 and .15. Since $\delta_1^*(.6218) = .065$, the ratios $H_1(.065, d_2)/H_1(d_1^*(d_2), d_2)$ are shown there too. They are, except when d_2 is nearly zero, close to one. So island 1 suffers little if 2 chooses $p_2 = .6218$ and $d_2 \in [0, .15]$. It is shown in Table 9.6F that 1 likewise is not much hurt if 2 chooses $p_2 = .5928$ and $d_2 \in [0, .15]$. A complete demonstration would, of course, demand that a large number of possible p_2's be considered, and therefore require a long list of additional tables. But it

TABLE 9.6B

P_2	$d_1 - \delta^*(p_2)$	$\overline{H}_2(p_1^*, p_2)$
>.6975	0	
.6975	0	.001104
.6845	.01	.002603
.6720	.02	.003795
.6601	.03	.004695
.6486	.04	.005316
.6375	.05	.005670
.6281 ($= p_2^*$)	.05887	.005768
.6269	.06	.005766
.6167	.07	.005617
.6069	.08	.005230
.5974	.09	.004614
.5883	.10	.003777
.5796	.11	.002727
.5711	.12	.001470
.5629	.13	.000013
.5551	.14	-.001640
.5475	.15	-.003482
<.5475	.15	

TABLE 9.6C

P_1	$d_2 - \delta^*(p_1)$	$\bar{H}_1(p_1, p_2^*)$
$>.6298$	0	
$.6298$	0	.000795
$.6205$	.01	.002210
$.6115$	.02	.003403
$.6027$	.03	.004380
$.5943$	.04	.005149
$.5860$	.05	.005717
$.5781$	.06	.006090
$.5703$	.07	.006274
$.5665$ $(= p_1^*)$	.07503	.006297
$.5628$	.08	.006275
$.5555$	.09	.006097
$.5484$	.10	.005746
$.5415$	.11	.005226
$.5348$	.12	.004542
$.5283$	.13	.003698
$.5219$	.14	.002699
$.5158$	.15	.001547
$<.5158$	.15	

is clear from the above that $(p_1^*, \delta_1^*(\cdot))$ is a good strategy for 1 even if 2 does not choose *exactly* $(p_2^*, \delta_2^*(\cdot))$, for the former performs well even in the face of *some* rather wide deviations on 2's part from the latter. A similar argument shows that $(p_2^*, \delta_2^*(\cdot))$ also possesses a certain robustness.

The equilibrium here is not Pareto optimal. Indeed, it yields only about

TABLE 9.6D

P_2	$\bar{H}_1(.5665, p_2)/\bar{H}_1(K_1(p_2), p_2)$
$\leq .5100$	$\geq .9834$
$.5400$	.9795
$.5796$	.9978
$.5928$	.9988
$.6069$	.9995
$.6218$	.9999
$.6281$ $(= p_2^*)$	1.0000
$.6375$	.9999
$.6543$	.9991
$.6720$	.9974
$\geq .6981$	.9995

TABLE 9.6E

x_2	$H_1(.065, x_2)/H_1(h_1^{.6218}(x_2), x_2)$
0	.5955
.01	.8341
.02	.9155
.03	.9547
.04	.9764
.05	.9889
.06	.9960
.07	.9993
.08	.9999
.09	.9986
.10	.9954
.11	.9907
.12	.9845
.13	.9768
.14	.9677
.15	.9570

The Subgame $G(.5665, .6218)$

TABLE 9.6F

x_2	$H_1(.095, x_2)/H_1(h_1^{.5928}(x_2), x)$
0	.7650
.01	.8646
.02	.9169
.03	.9481
.04	.9681
.05	.9813
.06	.9899
.07	.9955
.08	.9987
.09	.9999
.10	.9996
.11	.9979
.12	.9950
.13	.9909
.14	.9857
.15	.9794

The Subgame $G(.5665, .5928)$

.75($H_1^* + H_2^*$). So there is room for cooperation in the case of variable domestic prices, as there was not in the fixed-price case. We shall not explore the matter further here nor shall we attempt to extend Lee's results to more than two commodities, for technical difficulties impede the extension of his theorems to higher dimensions, and increased dimensionality also renders the verification of robustness exceedingly tedious. These difficulties do not in any way detract from the elegance of Lee's results for the case he considered.

7. DYNAMIC TRADING GAMES

We begin with an example. In the seventeenth century, England was unable to produce sufficient naval stores (tar, pitch, masts, spars, etc.) domestically to maintain her large navy and merchant marine. Hence, she was forced to buy them abroad, primarily in the Scandinavian countries. She would have preferred, however, to influence her New England colonies to produce the necessary items. In return, the English were willing to sell the colonists the rope and sails and iron implements which they were unable to make for themselves.

To formalize the above as a differential game, we let $x(t)$ and $y(t)$ denote the stocks of iron tools and of "rope and sails" (one good) present in the colonies at time t, and represent by $z(t)$ the quantity of naval stores then in England. Next we assume that because the rope and sails are used to equip a fishing fleet, the colonists consume fish at a rate $c_1(t) = k_1 y(t)$. Other goods are consumed as they are produced, at the rate $c_2(t) = k_2 x(t)$. Similarly, we assume England consumes foreign goods at a rate $\gamma(t)$ proportional to the size of her merchant fleet, which in turn is proportional to the quantity of naval stores available, and write $\gamma(t) = kz(t)$. Also, we denote the colonial stock of currency (silver) by $s(t)$ and assume that England and her colonies seek to maximize the functionals

$$J_1 = \bar{s} - s(0) + m \int_0^\infty e^{-\rho t} c_1(t) \cdot c_2(t)\, dt$$

(9.7.1)

$$J_2 = s(0) - \bar{s} + \int_0^\infty e^{-\rho t} \gamma(t)\, dt,$$

$\bar{s}$ being the average return equivalent to the utility stream $s(t)$, namely

(9.7.2)
$$\bar{s} = \int_0^\infty \rho e^{-\rho t} s(t)\, dt.$$

This maximization is to be performed subject to the differential constraints

$$\dot{x}(t) = d_1 - r_1 x(t) \qquad \dot{z}(t) = \delta(t) - rz(t)$$

(9.7.3)

$$\dot{y}(t) = d_2 - r_2 y(t) \qquad \dot{s}(t) = p(t) - \pi_1(t) d_1(t) - \pi_2(t) d_2(t)$$

and the inequalities

(9.7.4)
$$d_1(t) \geqslant 0, \quad d_2(t) \geqslant 0, \qquad 0 \leqslant s(t) \leqslant S$$
$$a_1 d_1(t) + a_2 d_2(t) \leqslant D, \qquad 0 \leqslant \delta(t) \leqslant D.$$

Here S is the (fixed) quantity of silver (measured in pounds sterling) available for use as a medium of exchange, and $\gamma(t)$ is measured in pounds sterling (£) per day. Likewise $c_1(t) \cdot c_2(t)$ is measured in colonial dollars per day, so that m is an exchange rate in £/\$. Also r_1, r_2, and r are depreciation rates for goods X, Y, and Z; $d_1(t)$, $d_2(t)$, and $\delta(t)$ are the corresponding demand rates; and $\pi_1(t)$, $\pi_2(t)$, and $p(t)$ are their prices. Finally, D is the maximum rate at which it is possible to transport Z across the Atlantic, measured in tons per day, and a_1 and a_2 are the ratios of the densities of X to Z and Y to Z, respectively. The colonies choose $d_1(t)$, $d_2(t)$, and $p(t)$ at each instant t, while England chooses $\pi_1(t)$, $\pi_2(t)$, and $\delta(t)$ in its efforts to maximize the functionals (9.7.1) subject to the constraints (9.7.3) and (9.7.4). Observe that if the constraint $0 \leqslant s(t) \leqslant S$ may be ignored, the functionals (9.7.1) may be replaced by

$$J_1 = m \int_0^\infty e^{-\rho t} \{p\delta - \pi_1 d_1 - \pi_2 d_2 + mk_1 k_2 xy\}\, dt$$
$$J_2 = \int_0^\infty e^{-\rho t} \{\pi_1 d_1 + \pi_2 d_2 - p\delta + kz\}\, dt,$$

since

(9.7.6) $$\int_0^\infty e^{-\rho t} \dot{s}(t)\, dt = \int_0^\infty \rho e^{-\rho t} s(t)\, dt + \int_0^\infty \frac{d}{dt} e^{-\rho t} s(t)\, dt = \bar{s} - s(0).$$

So if a solution of (9.7.3)–(9.7.5) does not violate $0 \leqslant s(t) \leqslant S$, it will be a solution of (9.7.1), (9.7.3), and (9.7.4) as well.

We shall return to this game, indeed solve it, presently, but first we wish to describe a large class of games which contains this one and to discuss the matter of threats and history-dependent strategies for games of that class.

Consider again an economy involving N entrepreneurs (players) called $1, 2, \ldots, N$, and n goods $X_1, \ldots, X_n$. We denote by $x_i^j(t)$ the quantity of good X_j possessed by player i at time t, and we call the vector

$$x_i(t) = (x_i^1(t), \ldots, x_i^n(t))$$

the "commodity bundle" belonging to player i at time t. For simplicity, we assume there is a fixed stock of silver S in circulation for use as a medium of exchange, and we denote player i's stock of it at time t by $s_i(t)$. As before, silver will be measured in pounds sterling (£).

We assume that each player i has a production vector $A_i(x_i)$ over which he exercises no control. He also has a price vector $p_i(t) = (p_i^1(t), \ldots, p_i^n(t))$ and N demand vectors $d_{i1}(t) = (d_{i1}^1(t), \ldots, d_{i1}^n(t)), \ldots, d_{iN}(t) = (d_{iN}^1(t), \ldots, d_{iN}^n(t))$. The component $d_{ij}^k(t)$ is given in units of X_k per month and represents the rate at which i demands (buys) good X_k from j at time t. Similarly $p_i^k(t)$ is given in £ per unit X_k and represents the price which i charges for Good X_k at time t.

The commodity bundles $x_i(t)$ must therefore satisfy

$$(9.7.7) \qquad \dot{x}_i(t) = A_i(x_i(t)) + \sum_{j=1}^{N} (d_{ij}(t) - d_{ji}(t))$$

for each $i = 1, \ldots, N$ while the corresponding silver flows follow

$$(9.7.8) \qquad \dot{s}_i(t) = \sum_{j=1}^{N} \langle p_i(t), d_{ji}(t) \rangle - \langle p_j(t), d_{ij}(t) \rangle.$$

All vectors must remain nonnegative at all times and may have to obey other inequality constraints as well. Finally, we shall assume that the game is to continue indefinitely and that each player has a utility functional of the form

$$(9.7.9) \qquad J_i = \bar{s}_i - s_i(0) + \int_0^\infty e^{-\rho t} L_i(x_i(t))\, dt,$$

which he wishes to maximize. The problem of maximizing (9.7.9) subject to the differential constraints (9.7.7) and (9.7.8), along with whatever inequality constraints may be present, is a differential game and may be attacked in the usual fashion. It is a reasonable model for international trade if the goods $X_1, \ldots, X_n$ are "capital goods" which need not be consumed (as ropes and sails, iron tools, and naval stores need not) in order to yield their benefits. If "consumption goods" (like food and drink) are to be included, their rates of consumption must be included as control variables which appear both in the stock equations (9.7.7) and under the integrals (9.7.9). This has been done in a special case [7] but appears to complicate general analyses unduly.

The threats available to the various players and groups of players in such a game are of two kinds: they can elevate their prices and/or depress their demands. When these actions are carried to their logical extremes, the effect is to cut off trade entirely. Such things happen. The state of California, for instance, has in essence driven the price of abalone to infinity by prohibiting its export across the state line. In that case, the threat was entirely credible. However, in most instances, more limited threats are more likely to be believed than such extreme ones.

The colonies, for instance, might seek to "punish" the English when the latter's demand for naval stores fell below some prescribed level δ_0. This could be done by regarding the quantity

$$(9.7.10) \qquad I(t) = \int_0^t (z'(u) - rz(u) - \delta_0)\, e^{\alpha u}\, du$$

as a measure of the past deviations of England's demand from the fixed rate δ_0 and by refusing to buy English goods whenever $I(t) < 0$.

The new "economic indicator" $I(t)$ may be incorporated as a state variable into the earlier formulation of the game. To do this, consider a fictitious good W. Then if $w(t)$ is the quantity of W present in England at time t, if $w(0) = 0$, and if $w(t)$ obeys the equation

$$(9.7.11) \qquad \dot{w}(t) = \delta(t) - \delta_0 - \alpha w(t),$$

we immediately have $I(t) = e^{\alpha t}w(t)$. A great deal of the history of a general trading game can be incorporated into its formulation by the device of fictitious goods. Indeed, the entire history may be so incorporated if one is willing to contemplate an infinite number of such goods. Hence little or no generality is lost by admitting only strategies which depend on state variables alone. For the state variables in such a game are the current inventories of both real and fictitious goods held by all players. So a wide variety of threats and history-dependent strategies are present among the state-dependent ones to be considered in our treatment of differential trading games.

Demand strategies, we shall assume, depend on state variables $(s(t), x(t))$ and on prices as well, for no one, in our experience, ever agrees to any major purchase without knowing the price in advance. Hence at time t, player i will be charging $p_i(t) = P_i(s(t), x(t))$ for the goods he has, and buying at the rates $d_i(t) = D_i(s(t), x(t), p_1(t), \ldots, p_N(t))$. So a strategy for player i is a pair $\sigma_i = (P_i, D_i)$ consisting of one price strategy and one demand strategy. It is assumed that the vector $x(t)$ has been augmented to include current inventories of both real and fictitious goods.

We return to the colonial example, which we cast in the form

$$1 \text{ max} \qquad J_1 = \int_0^\infty e^{-\rho t} \{p_1 \delta + p_2 \delta - \pi_1 d_1 + \pi_2 d_2 + mxy\} \, dt$$

$$2 \text{ max} \qquad J_2 = \int_0^\infty e^{-\rho t} \{\pi_1 d_1 + \pi_2 d_2 - p_1 \delta - p_2 \delta + z\} \, dt$$

$$(9.7.12)$$

$$\text{subject to} \qquad \dot{x} = d_1 - rx \qquad \dot{z} = \delta - rz$$

$$\dot{y} = dz - ry \qquad \dot{w} = \delta - \delta_0 - \alpha w$$

$$\text{and} \qquad d_1 \geqslant 0 \qquad ad_1 + a_2 d_2 \leqslant D$$

$$d_2 \geqslant 0 \qquad 0 \leqslant \delta \leqslant D.$$

Here we have specialized the model in an inconsequential manner by assuming $k = 1 = k_1 k_2$ and $r_1 = r_2 = r$. We have also included the fictitious good W in our formulation so that we may later demonstrate its irrelevance. The game thus posed fits into the general trading game framework if one defines

$$(9.7.13) \quad \begin{aligned} \Delta_1 &= \{(d_1, d_2): d_1 \geqslant 0, d_2 \geqslant 0, a_1 d_1 + a_2 d_2 \leqslant 0\} \\ \Delta_2 &= \{(\delta_1, \delta_2): \delta_1 = \delta_2 = \delta, 0 \leqslant \delta \leqslant D\} \end{aligned}$$

Incidentally, p_2 is the price 1 charges 2 for W, and it too will be shown to be irrelevant.

To begin the solution process, we write the Hamiltonian functions which, in this case, may be put in the form

$$(9.7.14) \quad \begin{aligned} H_i &= \langle (p_1, p_2) + (v_z, v_w), (\delta, \delta) \rangle + \langle (v_x, v_y) - (\pi_1, \pi_2), (d_1, d_2) \rangle \\ &\quad + mxy - rxV_x - ryV_y - rzV_z - \alpha w V_w - \delta_0 V_w \\ H_2 &= \langle (\pi_1, \pi_2) + (W_x, W_y), (d_1, d_2) \rangle + \langle (W_z, W_w) - (p_1, p_2), (\delta, \delta) \rangle \\ &\quad + z - rxW_x - ryW_y - rzW_z - \alpha w W_w - \delta_0 W_w, \end{aligned}$$

$V = V(x, y, z, w)$, $W = W(x, y, z, w)$ being the unknown value functions for players 1, 2, respectively, and $V_x, V_y, \ldots, W_w$ being their first partial derivatives. So if one ignores the parts of H_1 and H_2 which are independent of the control variables $(p_1, p_2, \pi_1, \pi_2, d_1, d_2, \delta)$ and makes the identifications

$$(9.7.15) \quad \begin{aligned} \vec{p}_1 &\rightarrow (p_1, p_2) & \vec{p}_2 &\rightarrow (\pi_1, \pi_2) \\ \vec{P}_1 &\rightarrow (-V_z, -V_w) & \vec{P}_2 &\rightarrow (-W_x, -W_y) \\ \vec{P}_1' &\rightarrow (V_x, V_y) & \vec{P}_2' &\rightarrow (W_z, W_w) \\ \vec{d}_1 &\rightarrow (d_1, d_2) & \vec{d}_2 &\rightarrow (\delta, \delta) \end{aligned}$$

between the quantities appearing in (9.7.14) and those of (9.5.4)-(9.5.5), the present functions H_1, H_2 are seen to have exactly the form of those in §9.5. The quantities appearing in (9.5.4)-(9.5.5), all being vectors, appear beneath the "$\rightarrow$" notation in (9.7.15). It is apparent, when the identifications (9.7.15) are made, that the players in this dynamic trading game must play a new *static* one at each instant, the domestic prices for the latter being furnished by the partial derivatives of the value functions V and W. Therefore, when 1 and 2 choose $(p_1^0, p_2^0, d_1^0, d_2^0)$ and $(\pi_1^0, \pi_2^0, \delta^0)$, respectively, in such a way that

$$(9.7.16) \quad \begin{aligned} H_1(p_1^0, p_2^0, d_1^0, d_2^0, \pi_1^0, \pi_2^0, \delta^0) &\geqslant H_1(p_1, p_2, d_1, d_2; \pi_1^0, \pi_2^0, \delta^0) \\ H_2(p_1^0, p_2^0, d_1^0, d_2^0, \pi_1^0, \pi_2^0, \delta^0) &\geqslant H_2(p_1^0, p_2^0, d_1^0, d_2^0, \pi_1, \pi_2, \delta^0), \end{aligned}$$

it will happen that

$$(9.7.17) \quad \begin{aligned} &H_1(p_1^0, p_2^0, d_1^0, d_2^0, \pi_1^0, \pi_2^0, \delta^0) \\ &= \max_{(d_1, d_2) \in \Delta_1} [(V_x + W_x) d_1 + (V_y + W_y) d_2] \\ &\quad + mxy - rxV_x - ryV_y - rzV_z - \alpha w V_w - \delta_0 V_w \end{aligned}$$

$$H_2(p_0, p_2, d_1, d_2, \pi_1, \pi_2, \delta)$$

$$= \max_{(\delta, \delta) \in \Delta_2} (V_z + V_w + W_z + W_w)\, \delta$$

$$+ z - rxW_x - ryW_y - rzW_z - \alpha wW_w - \delta_0 W_w.$$

And V, W must be solutions of the Hamilton-Jacobi partial differential equations

(9.7.18)

$$\max_{(d_1, d_2) \in \Delta_1} [(V_x + W_x)\, d_1 + (V_y + W_y)\, dz] + mxy$$

$$- rxV_x - ryV_y - rzV_z - \alpha wV_w - \delta_0 V_w = \rho V$$

$$\max_{0 \leqslant \delta \leqslant D} [(V_z + V_w + W_z + W_w)\, \delta + z]$$

$$- rxW_x - ryW_y - rzW_z - \alpha wW_w - \delta_0 W_w = \rho W.$$

So the sum $U = V + W$ must be a solution of

(9.7.19)

$$\max_{(d_1, d_2) \in \Delta_1} (U_x d_1 + U_y d_2) + \max_{0 \leqslant \delta \leqslant D} (U_z + U_w)\, \delta$$

$$+ mxy + z - rxU_x - ryU_y - rzU_z - \alpha wU_w - \delta_0 U_w = \rho U.$$

And if U^1 and U^2 are solutions of

(9.7.20)

$$\max_{(d_1, d_2) \in \Delta_1} (U_x^1 d_1 + U_y^1 d_2) + mxy - rxU_x^1 - ryU_y^1 = \rho U^1$$

$$\max_{0 \leqslant \delta \leqslant D} (U_z^2 + U_w^2)\, \delta + z - rzU_z^2 - \alpha wU_w^2 - \delta_0 U_w^2 = \rho U^2,$$

then $U = U^1 + U^2$ is a solution of (9.7.19). But (9.7.19) and (9.7.20) are themselves Hamilton-Jacobi equations, the latter two arising from the optimal control problems

$$\text{maximum} \quad \int_0^\infty me^{-\rho t}\, xy\, dt$$

(CP_1) subject to $\dot{x} = d_1 - rx \qquad \dot{y} = d_2 - ry$

$$d_1 \geqslant 0, d_2 \geqslant 0, \qquad a_1 d_1 + a_2 d_2 \leqslant D$$

and

$$\text{maximum} \quad \int_0^\infty e^{-\rho t}\, z\, dt$$

(CP_2) subject to $\dot{z} = \delta - rz \qquad \dot{w} = \delta - \delta_0 - \alpha w$

$$0 \leqslant \delta \leqslant D,$$

while (9.7.19) arises from the direct sum $CP_1 \oplus CP_2$ of the two.

The problems CP_1 and CP_2 have the unique optimal strategies

$$
\begin{aligned}
&= (0, D) && \text{if } a_1 x > a_2 y \\
(9.7.21) \quad (d_1^*(x, y), d_2^*(x, y)) &= (D, 0) && \text{if } a_1 x < a_2 y \\
&= (D/2)(1/a, 1/a_2) && \text{if } a_1 x = a_2 y
\end{aligned}
$$

and

$$(9.7.22) \qquad\qquad \delta^*(z, w) \equiv D,$$

as one may deduce from the standard results [22] of optimal control. And clearly (9.7.21) and (9.7.22) must be optimal for $CP_1 \oplus CP_2$ as well.

But (9.7.19) asserts that when the players play their Nash equilibrium strategies, starting with initial stocks (x_0, y_0, z_0, w_0), the sum of their payoffs is as large as $U^1(x_0, y_0) + U^2(z_0, w_0)$, which total is attainable only with the demand strategies (9.7.21) and (9.7.22). So when Nash equilibrium strategies are played by both players, the real goods X, Y, Z must change hands at the rates dictated by (9.7.21) and (9.7.22). But we know nothing, as yet, of the rate at which silver changes hands.

To find out, we must solve the equations (9.7.18) for the unknown functions V and W. For the prices which yield (9.7.17) are

$$(9.7.23) \qquad
\begin{aligned}
(p_1, p_2) &= \vec{P_2} = (W_z, W_w) \\
(\pi_1, \pi_2) &= \vec{P_1} = (V_x, V_y).
\end{aligned}
$$

Let us try first to find solutions of the form $V = V(x, y)$ and $W = W(z, w)$. Clearly such solutions, if they exist at all, will be solutions of (9.7.20) as well.

Observe first, that under the influence of the demand strategies (9.7.21)–(9.7.27), the values of x, y, z, and w will tend rapidly to

$$(9.7.24) \qquad \frac{D}{2ra_1}, \frac{D}{2ra_2}, \frac{D}{r}, \quad \text{and} \quad \frac{D - \delta_0}{\alpha}.$$

And simultaneously, $V_x = U_x^1$, $V_y = U_y^1$, $W_z = U_z^2$, and $W_w = U_w^2$ must tend, since they are solutions of

$$(9.7.25) \qquad
\begin{aligned}
\dot{V}_x &= (r + \rho)\, V_x - my, & \dot{V}_y &= (r + \rho)\, V_y - mx, \\
\dot{W}_z &= (r + \rho)\, W_z - 1, & \text{and} \quad \dot{W}_w &= (\alpha + \rho)\, W_w,
\end{aligned}
$$

to the values

$$(9.7.26) \qquad \frac{mD}{2r(r + \rho)\, a_2}, \quad \frac{mD}{2r(r + \rho)\, a_1}, \quad \frac{1}{r + \rho}, \quad \text{and} \quad 0.$$

Therefore $\dot{s}(t)$ goes rapidly to the constant value

$$(9.7.27) \qquad \dot{s}(\infty) = \frac{mD^2}{2r(r + \rho)\, a_1 a_2} - \frac{D}{r + \rho},$$

which vanishes only if

$$(9.7.28) \qquad\qquad m = \frac{2ra_1 a_2}{D}.$$

In short, the exchange rate in £/$ must have the value (9.7.28). if neither the English nor their colonies are to exhaust their supplies of currency. It seems at least plausible that the players would discover the right "exchange rate" (9.7.28) by some adaptive process even if they did not know how to compute it.

To see that the equilibrium so discovered is essentially unique, observe that the long-term inventories and demand rates are already determined by the fact that they must be optimal for $PC_1 \oplus PC_2$, and therefore for PC_1 and PC_2 individually. So the "real parts" mxy and z of the payoff integrands are already determined. Also the steady-state net flow of silver must vanish in order to avoid bankrupting one or another of the players. So the relative prices cannot change either.

Of course, the absolute prices could all be doubled without altering the equilibrium state we have discovered in an essential way. But that is all one *could* change without destroying the Nash equilibrium conditions. In short, though there may be other equilibria depending on W or other fictitious goods, there are none which yield real benefits to either player in the sense of increasing the mxy term or the z term in their individual payoff integrands. There is no advantage, then, in considering history-dependent strategies or the sorts of threats which depend on past behavior.

Similar conclusions are possible concerning any two-person differential trading game. The Pareto optimality of the Nash equilibria allows one to compute the demand strategies from the solution of a related optimal control problem, which simplifies this class of games both conceptually and computationally. No similar result for game between three or more players is known at this time.

8. IMPULSIVE CONTROLS

A different sort of decision faces a player who must act once, or only occasionally, then live with the consequences of his act over a protracted period. For simplicity we begin with an example involving only one player.

Consider the owner of a roadside inn who has but a few regular customers. The bulk of his business must come from strangers, of whom many pass by on the road each day. The ability to attract new customers into the inn depends heavily on the appearance thereof, which we assume to be indexed by a number x between zero and one.

The index x of the inn's appearance is clearly a function of time t, since paint does get old and needs to be renewed. Thus we shall assume that $x(t)$ decays according to the law

(9.8.1) $\dot{x} = -kx$

during time intervals $a < t < b$ between paint jobs. Here k is a positive constant. Also we shall assume that the inkeeper's total profit in the planning period $0 \leqslant t \leqslant T$ is

(9.8.2) $$J(T) = A \int_0^T x(t)\, dt - CN(t),$$

$N(T)$ being the number of times he has the inn repainted during the period, C the cost (in \$) of each paint job, and A another positive constant.

The state of such a game is a vector (τ, x), where x is as above, and $\tau = T - t$ is the time remaining. The options in any such state are just two: to repaint, in which case the state jumps immediately to $(\tau, 1)$ or not to, in which case x continues to decay according to (9.8.1). The latter, incidentally, may be rewritten

(9.8.1′) $\dfrac{dx}{d\tau} = kx.$

The set of all possible information states is then the semi-infinite strip $0 \leqslant x \leqslant 1$, $\tau \geqslant 0$, and the *desideratum* an optimal repainting policy.

Clearly no infinite number of repaintings could ever be optimal in a finite period $0 \leqslant t \leqslant T$, for such would render (9.8.2) negative and infinite. Therefore, there must be a last paint job. We seek first the states at which that might occur.

Suppose that (τ, x) is such a state. Then the payoff to be had by following the upper path Γ_1 in Figure 9.8.1 is no less than that from Γ_0. That is

(9.8.3) $Ax(1 - e^{-k\tau})/k \leqslant A(1 - e^{-k\tau})/k - C,$

or equivalently

(9.8.4) $x \leqslant 1 - \dfrac{Ck}{A(1 - e^{-k\tau})}.$

Above the curve Γ whereon (9.8.4) holds with equality, repainting immediately is not worth the expense. But below Γ, it is.

Next, consider the set of states (τ, x) such that the solution of (9.8.1′) through (τ, x) does not meet Γ. That set is bounded below by a single solution curve Γ_P of (9.8.1′) which meets Γ at just one point P. Both P and Γ_P are indicated in Figure 9.8.1. Finally let Γ_* be the curve consisting of the part of Γ below P and the part of Γ_P above it. It is optimal never to repaint if the game begins in a state above Γ_*, for then no state below Γ_* can subsequently be reached.

If, however, the game begins in a state (τ, x) which lies vertically under Γ_*, it is optimal to repaint once before the end. For the payoff achieved by repainting

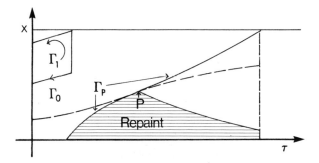

FIGURE 9.8.1

at an intermediate instant $0 < \sigma < \tau$ is

$$(9.8.5) \qquad A(1 - e^{-k\sigma})/k - C + A \int_0^\tau x(s)\, ds,$$

which is maximized by $\sigma = \tau$ if $x \leqslant e^{-k\tau}$, and by some $\sigma < \tau$ if not. Thus, if (τ_*, x_*) are the coordinates of the intersection of Γ_* with the line $x = 1$, the optimal repainting policy for the rectangle $0 \leqslant x \leqslant 1, 0 \leqslant \tau \leqslant \tau_*$ is that shown in Figure 9.8.1.

If larger values than τ_* are to be considered, the segment $0 \leqslant x \leqslant 1, \tau = \tau_*$ may be considered a new "terminal set" and the process repeated. Indeed, it may be repeated many times if necessary, though the computations quickly become tedious in practice.

The above game can also be called a problem of "impulsive optimal control." Such problems have been discussed from time to time in the literature, and A. Bensoussan and J. L. Lions [3]-[5] have formulated a rather complete theory for an extensive class of such problems, wherein stochastic disturbances enter the equation governing the evolution of the state. A rather more modest [8] approach has been suggested for problems in which that evolution is deterministic. As yet, both approaches are new and have had but little impact.*

An interesting variant of the innkeeper's problem presents itself if the planning period be extended to infinity and the payoff functional (9.8.2) replaced by

$$(9.8.6) \qquad J = A \int_0^\infty e^{-\rho t} x(t)\, dt - C \sum_{i=1}^\infty e^{-\rho t_i},$$

*A. Blaquière has lately proved elegant theorems about optimal control problems and zero-sum differential games of this general type. His methods solve the inn-keeper's problem for arbitrarily large τ, and are quite noteworthy. See his "Differential Games with Piece-Wise Continuous Trajectories" *in* Differential Games and Applications (P. Hagedorn, H. W. Knobloch and G. J. Olsder Ed.), Lecture notes in Control and Information Sciences Vol. 3, Springer-Verlag, Berlin (1977).

where $t_1, t_2, \ldots$ are the times at which repainting is done. Since "time remaining" is then always infinite, it cannot be a determinant of policy. So the optimal decision must depend on x alone. Moreover, if it is optimal to repaint when $x = x_1$, then it must be optimal to repaint when $x < x_1$ too. Likewise if repainting when $x = x_2$ is inadvisable, it must be even more so when $x > x_2$. So the nature of an optimal strategy can only be to repaint when $x < s$ and not to when $x > s$. So it remains but to determine the optimal value of s.

Let $V(x; s)$ be the value of (9.8.6) if the game starts with the inn in condition x and the strategy s is used indefinitely. Then for any fixed x, $V(x; s)$ must have a constant value on the interval $0 \leqslant x \leqslant s$ and increase in $s \leqslant x \leqslant 1$. For the better the inn looks initially, the more its keeper may expect to prosper. So one need only calculate $V(x; s)$ for $x \geqslant s$.

Next observe that if x exceeds s initially, it will continue to do so for some short period $0 \leqslant t \leqslant h$ of time. Therefore one may write

$$(9.8.7) \qquad V(x; s) = \int_0^h e^{-\rho t} \cdot A x e^{-kt} \, dt + e^{-\rho h} V(x e^{-kh}; s),$$

the first term on the right representing benefits earned during the initial period of duration h, and the second representing those earned thereafter. Rearranging somewhat gives

$$(9.8.8) \qquad \frac{1}{h} \int_0^h e^{-\rho t} \cdot A x e^{-kt} \, dt + \frac{e^{-\rho h} V(x e^{-kh}; s) - V(x; s)}{h} = 0,$$

and passing to the limit yields finally

$$(9.8.9) \qquad A x - k x V'(x; s) = \rho V(x; s).$$

So, integrating the ordinary differential equation (9.8.9), one concludes that $V(x; s)$ must have the form

$$(9.8.10) \qquad V(x; s) = \frac{A x}{k + \rho} - B x^{-\rho/k}$$

in the interval $s \leqslant x \leqslant 1$ whereon it is not constant. Also the obvious fact that $V(s; s) = V(1; s) - C$ implies

$$(9.8.11) \qquad B = B(s) = \frac{s^{\rho/k}}{s^{\rho/k} - 1} \left(\frac{A(1 - s)}{\rho + k} - C \right).$$

So to maximize $V(x; s)$ for any fixed value of x, one must minimize $B(s)$. And that is easily done if $A/(\rho + k) \geqslant C$, for then $B(0) = 0 = B(1 - C(k + \rho)/A)$, and $B(s)$ is convex in the interval $0 \leqslant s \leqslant 1 - C(k + \rho)/A$. But it cannot be done if the opposite inequality holds, because the repainting cost is then too large. One should never repaint in such instances.

It should be observed that the Hamilton-Jacobi method (so called because (9.8.9) is in fact a sort of Hamilton-Jacobi equation) does not yield an optimal strategy in this instance. Rather, it yields the expressions (9.8.10)–(9.8.11) for $V(x; s)$. The latter has then to be minimized with respect to the parameter s by ad hoc methods. This fact comes as a surprise to one who approaches the problem from the point of view of Bensoussan and Lions [3].

The innkeeper's problem could be turned into a real game if one were to consider a pair of inns located on opposite sides of the road, but we shall not. Rather, we shall consider Oskar Morgenstern's favorite "gadfly" question [18], namely "shall we build the Edsel," from the point of view of impulsively controlled differential games.

We assume that Edsel, and its principal competitor Pontiac, will sell their cars in a market governed by Cournot's linear price law; that is, the price at which they are able to sell their cars is

$$(9.8.12) \qquad p = 1 - x - y,$$

where x is the instantaneous rate of Pontiac production and y is the rate of Edsel production. Then if both producers continue to produce at the fixed rates x and y indefinitely, Pontiac will earn

$$(9.8.13) \qquad J_P = \int_0^\infty e^{-\rho t}(x - x^2 - xy)\, dt = \frac{x - x^2 - xy}{\rho}$$

in total, while Edsel earns

$$(9.8.14) \qquad J_E = \frac{y - xy - y^2}{\rho}.$$

Of course Edsel's initial production rate was zero.

Next assume that the cost to either firm of building enough new production facilities to produce an additional h cars is

$$(9.8.15) \qquad C(h) = a + bh.$$

Then Pontiac can earn as much as

$$(9.8.16) \qquad
\begin{aligned}
&\max_{h \geqslant 0} \frac{(x + h)(1 - x - h - y)}{\rho} - a - bh \\
&= \frac{1 + y^2 - 2y - \rho^2 b^2}{4\rho} - a - 1/2\, b(1 - y - \rho b) + bx
\end{aligned}$$

total dollars by constructing new facilities. Moreover, the quantity (9.8.15) exceeds (9.8.13) whenever

$$(9.8.17) \qquad 2x + y \leqslant 1 - \rho b - 2\sqrt{a\rho},$$

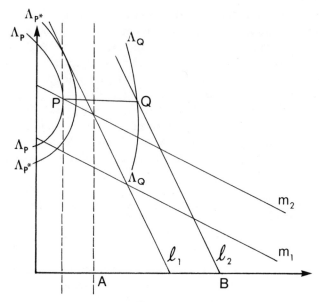

FIGURE 9.8.2

and similar remarks hold for Edsel. Thus the players' optimal decisions are as
indicated in Figure 9.8.2. At points below l_1 it pays Pontiac to build enough
new factories so that the new production rates $(x + h, y)$ lie on the line l_2, for
there the maximum (9.8.16) is attained. And similarly, at points below m_1,
it pays Edsel to build enough new facilities so that $(x, y + h)$ lies on m_2.

Now recall that Edsel begins with output $y = 0$. So if $A < x < B$, the point
$(x, 0)$ lies below m_1, and Edsel should produce enough cars that $P(x, h)$ lies on
m_2. Then (x, h) will lie above l_1, and neither firm can benefit from further
expansion. But if $0 < x < A$, then expanding enough so that (x, h) lies on
m_2 is not optimal for Edsel. For (x, h) is then below l_1, so eventually Pontiac
could expand until the yet newer production point $(x + h', h)$ lies on l_2. Examination of the level curves of Edsel's payoff function (Λ_P, Λ_Q, and Λ_{P*} in Figure
9.8.2) shows that Ford does better to expand to (x, h^*) on or just above l_1. For
then Pontiac cannot benefit from an answering production increase. If $x > B$,
Edsel cannot even hope to earn back its initial investment, and so should not
enter the market at all.

In practice, of course, the position of the lines l_1, l_2, m_1, and m_2 is neither
fixed nor precisely known, so occasional mistakes in their apprehension will be
made. Indeed in a growing market, all four lines move upward and to the right,
but no one knows how far or fast, and vast sums often change hands due to speculation on those matters.

9. FUTURE PROSPECTS

By now it must be apparent to even the most casual reader that the subject of games in which information and its disposition play a role is a complex one, fraught with difficulties both conceptual and computational. But it must also be apparent that such games are played every day for stakes that are often vast indeed. So a theory of them is a matter of pressing intellectual import.

What has been presented here represents only a beginning. While it does not pretend to completeness, an effort at least has been made to exhibit the most important steps yet taken toward the construction of such a theory. If the reader forms the impression that the subject consists of little more than a series of worked examples, he cannot be blamed. Attempts to unify the subject have been largely excluded from the presentation here because they seem more to obscure than to illuminate the specific properties of *certain games* which make those games comprehensible. For it is the major premise of this book, and we have striven mightily to establish it, that certain games of common occurence and significant interest *are* comprehensible! But we know of no theory which makes all nonzero-sum games, or even any large class of them, seem that to us.

REFERENCES

1. Basar, T. "A Counterexample in Linear-Quadratic Games: Existence of Non-linear Nash Solutions," *J. Optimization Theory Appl.*, vol. 14, no. 4 (1974), pp. 425-430.
2. Basar, T. "A New Class of Nash Strategies for *M*-Person Differential Games with Mixed Information Structures," *Proceedings of the Sixth Triennial World Congress, International Federation for Automatic Control*, Boston/Cambridge, Mass., August 1975.
3. Bensoussan, A., and J. L. Lions, "Nouvelle Formulation de Controle Impulsionnel et Applications," *CRAS* (1973).
4. Bensoussan, A., and J. L. Lions, "Controle Impulsionnel et Inequations Quasi-Varietionnelles Stationnaires," *CRAS* (1973).
5. Bensoussan, A., and J. L. Lions, "Controle Impulsionnel et Inequations Quasi-Varietionnelles d'Evolution," *CRAS* (1973).
6. Case, J., "A Class of Games with Pareto Optimal Nash Equilibria," *J. Optimization Theory and Appl.* 13 (1974), pp. 379-385.
7. Case, J., "On Ricardo's Problem," *Journal of Econ. Th.*, 3 (1971) pp. 134-145.
8. Case, J., "Impulsively Controlled Differential Games," *The Theory and Application of Differential Games*, J. D. Grote, ed. (Holland, Dardrecht; Boston, Mass: D. Reidel Pub. Co., 1975), pp. 179-187.

9. Clemhout, S., and H. Wan, "A Class of Trilinear Differential Games," *J. Optimization Theory Appl.*, vol. 14, no. 4 (1974), pp. 419–424.
10. Clemhout, S., G. Leitmaan, and H. Wan, "A Differential Game of Oligopoly," *Cybernetics*, vol. 3, no. 1 (1973).
11. Starr, A. W., and Y. C. Ho, "Nonzero-sum Differential Games," *J. Optimization Th. Appl.*, 3 (1969), pp. 184–206.
12. Isaacs, R., *Differential Games* (New York: John Wiley, 1965).
13. Kendrick, D., and L. Taylor, "Numerical Solution of Nonlinear Planning Models," *Econometrica*, vol. 38, no. 3 (1970), pp. 433–467.
14. Lee, K. T., "A Non-cooperative Trading Game," Johns Hopkins thesis in the mathematical sciences, 1975.
15. Leitmann, G., and H. Stalford, "Sufficiency for Optimal Strategies in Nash Equilibrium Games," *Techniques of Optimization*, A. V. Balakrishnan, ed. (New York: Academic Press, 1972).
16. Lukes, D. L., "Equilibrium Feedback Control in Linear Games with Quadratic Costs," *SIAM J. Control*, vol. 9, no. 2 (1971), pp. 234–252.
17. Lukes, D. L., and D. R. Russell, "A Global Theory for Linear-Quadratic Differential Games," *J. Math. Analysis Appl.*, 33 (1971), pp. 96–123.
18. Morgenstern, O., "Thirteen Critical Points in Contemporary Economic Theory: An Interpretation," *Journal of Econ. Literature*, vol. X, no. 4 (1972).
19. Pav, L. F., *Differential Games Among Sectors in a Macroeconomy*, IFAC/IFORS Int. Conf. on dynamic modeling and control of national economies, Univ. of Warwick, July 9–12, 1973, Conf. Publ., No. 101, Inst. of Electrical Engineers, London, 1973.
20. Pau, L. F., "Differential Games and a Nash Equilibrium Searching Algorithm," *SIAM J. Control*, vol. 13, no. 3 (1975).
21. Pau, L. F., and P. T. Valstorp-Fredericksen, "Planification Financiere par la commande optimale," Congrès AFCET, 1974, "Aide a la decision."
22. Pontryagin, L. S., V. Boltyanskii, R. Gamkrelidze, and E. Mischenko, *The Mathematical Theory of Optimal Processes* (New York: Interscience, 1962).
23. Rosen, J. B., "Existence and Uniqueness of Equilibrium Points for Concave N-person Games," *Econometrica*, vol. 33, no. 3 (1965), pp. 520–534.
24. Shapley, L. S., "Mathematical Concepts of Game Theory—Some Noncooperative examples," an unpublished lecture delivered at the International Summer School on Mathematical Models of Action and Reaction, held in Varenna, Italy, June 15–27, 1970.
25. Simaan and Takayama, "Dynamic Duopoly Game: Differential Game Theoretic Approach," *Proceedings of the Sixth Triennial World Congress, Int'l Federation for Automatic Control*, Boston/Cambridge, Mass., Aug, 1975.
26. Varaiya, P. P., "N-person Nonzero-sum Differential Games with Linear Dynamics," *J. SIAM Control*, vol. 8, no. 4 (1970), pp. 441–449.

Chapter 10

Epilogue

With the discussion of differential ones, this account of game theory ends. It represents an attempt to place the entire subject in perspective, from primitive assumptions to intended purposes. Perhaps a few closing remarks concerning the latter may yet be in order.

During the early years of this century, the notion of the "free market" enjoyed, with other free institutions, a generally high repute. But the intervening years have seen an ever increasing tendency to rely on rules and regulations instead of "market forces" to achieve the public purpose. Confidence in Adam Smith's "unseen hand" has been gradually transferred to the more readily observable influence of direct intervention; public favor has shifted from one oversimplification to another.

The problem is largely an intellectual one, for public opinion tends to mimic informed opinion rather closely in matters economic. If the public underestimates the force of the unseen hand, it is because science does not adequately explain the matter. Generalities abound, but specific explanations of the activities of actual oligopolists have been sadly few, seldom convincing, and frequently in conflict with one another.

This book proposes explanations for the activities of numerous familiar oligopolists, among them oil companies, automobile dealers, and advertising executives. The explanations offered are all quite similar; the players behave as they do because they need to show a profit and cannot confidently expect to do it without the use of robust strategies. Thus does the unseen hand guide them. It is easy to believe *that* they are so guided once it is explained *how* they are. Without such explanation, however, belief is difficult.

In games wherein the workings of the hand are understood, it is possible to distinguish goals it can accomplish from others it cannot. Of the latter there are many. Rarely, for instance, has the unseen hand prevented the use or abuse of child labor. So child labor laws have long ago been written. Nor has the hand proven effective in disuading the suppliers of food and drugs from diluting their products; now we have pure food and drug acts. When market forces do not lend themselves to the public purpose, regulation is often both appropriate and effective. But only if the forces themselves are understood can one reliably distinguish such situations from those more common, wherein free market remedies like tax credits and the mandatory disclosure of key information are at once less costly and more effective. In today's world the markets and market forces most relevant to the public purpose are nearly all of the oligopolistic kind. Such markets are the *raison d'être* of the theory presented here.

Finally, it is to be emphasized that people make up the rules of the games they play, and people are free to change them. As baseball and football are made more attractive to their fans by periodic rules changes, so the games of commerce can be better suited to the public purpose by the actions of the regulatory agencies charged with their oversight. But the games themselves must be well understood if the actions taken are to have the desired consequences and be relatively free of unforseen ones. I hope that game theory may soon become an important source of such understanding.

Index